D1191188

Approaches to the Study

of Party Organization

Approaches
to the Study of
Party Organization

edited by
William J. Crotty
Northwestern University

Allyn and Bacon, Inc.
Boston

Library of Congress Catalog Card Number: 67–14687

Printed in the United States of America

Preface

This volume results from the mutual belief that studies on political parties are on the threshold of capitalizing on theoretical and methodological advances, some already successful in other disciplines or other subfields of political science, that should introduce a new era of intellectual productivity into political parties' research. The eventual result of the efforts should be a more truly scientific enterprise prepared to treat in a more adequate fashion the traditional problems of concern to the field. By scientific, it is meant a systematic, theoretical, and empirically cumulative enterprise which meets the conventional criteria of veriability and replicability and, in the present case, which should encourage cross-cultural comparisons.

Another belief of the contributors to this volume is that by conceptualizing and empirically investigating the party organization — how it is structured, what it does, how effective its activities are in achieving its objectives, and how it relates to the total social system of which it is a part — the researcher will have a perspective that will enable him to interrelate the diverse concerns of the field in some meaningful pattern.

Each of the selections to follow deals in some manner with the party organization. Individual works are designed to theoretically relate the political party to broader social concerns, or provide a meaningful focus for interrelationships and activities within the organization, or empirically investigate problem areas in a manner intended to suggest means of handling these topics in comparative analysis. Each of the essays adds something informative to the limited quantity of reliable data or imaginative theorizing available on party organizations.

The difficulties encountered in such analysis should not be underestimated. The party organization has few of the attributes of a conventional bureaucratic organization. Still, by incorporating developments from other subject-matter areas or through experimentation each of the original works contained in this volume attempts to indicate the manner in which some of the more pressing problems can be resolved as well as the prospective rewards to be gained from such an analytic orientation.

The general approach itself is not new. Moesi Ostrogorski, Robert Michels, and more recently Samuel Eldersveld, among others, have pioneered in developing such a research perspective. Nonetheless, the number of broader research efforts developed in this vein are few. The extent to which other scholars can be encouraged to undertake such analysis within complementary organizational frameworks will provide some measure of the success of the undertakings presented within.

Bernard Hennessy (Pennsylvania State University) introduces the volume with a lively analysis of the evolution of works on party organization. He pinpoints the problem areas deserving attention and he develops the potential contributions of previous studies as well as recent methodological techniques for researchers undertaking explorations of the topics discussed. The bibliography following Chapter I can serve as an introduction to the literature in the field.

In the second essay, Fred W. Riggs (Indiana University) develops an imaginative theoretical superstructure in which to locate the political party. Professor Riggs attempts to control for cultural dissimilarities by categorizing polities and the parties, the latter a dependent variable within the conceptual schema, in relation to structural characteristics and the functional relevance of the institution for the society as a whole. In the process, he contrasts organizational forms and goals and attempts to clarify the distinction between structural and functional characteristics in his typologies. His work is in the broad tradition of Maurice Duverger (*Political Parties*, 1951) and represents an attempt to introduce some of the imaginative theorizing in cross-cultural comparative analysis to a phenomenon of universal concern, political parties, that could profit from an infusion of new ideas. Through such works as that by Riggs and the one that follows by Samuel H. Barnes (University of Michigan) a fresh perspective possibly can be encouraged in parties' research.

Professor Barnes employs a theoretical orientation in his essay developed by Mancur Olson that emphasizes collective action. The utility of the theory is illustrated through an application to Italian political parties, in particular the Italian Socialist Federation.

A comparative emphasis also predominates in the chapters by Austin Ranney (University of Wisconsin) and Kenneth Janda (Northwestern University). Professor Ranney investigates one of the classic concerns of the American parties' scholar, the relative cohesion of political parties in Britain and the United States; a problem that has invited the attention of social scientists since, as he notes, the time of Woodrow Wilson and A. Lawrence Lowell. Ranney has chosen to explore the process of candidate selection in British parties. This then serves as a base from which to draw comparisons as to party recruitment and organizational coherence in the two countries. Attention is also centered on the pressures inherent in the linkages between the parliamentary party and its members and the local constituency organizations and their needs.

Professor Janda's objectives are quite different. He has undertaken the enormous task of gathering and systematizing the data available in the period 1950–1962 on political parties throughout the world. The background of the study, the information retrieval techniques he has developed, and the categorizations employed in the ordering of the data are to be found in his report.

Environmental factors as reflected in socio-economic variables and as they relate to party competition and more indirectly party organization provide the focus for Douglas S. Gatlin's work. Professor Gatlin (Florida Atlantic University) has abstracted a series of hypotheses from contentions found in the literature on parties and electoral competition. The hypotheses presented are interrelated and operationalized in a manner conducive to empirically testing the relationships between party competition and environmental variables. Gatlin's intention is to theoretically relate variations in socio-economic factors to two-party competition and to suggest the influence of the party organization as an intervening variable in the process.

William J. Crotty (Northwestern University), Thomas M. Watts (University of Pennsylvania), and Dwaine Marvick (University of California, Los Angeles) are more concerned with the various methodological and theoretical problems that can be examined by using data collected on the state and local party organizations and their activists within the United States. Professor Crotty empirically analyzes the extent of party organization and the scope of the party activities engaged in within a one-party system in the process of undergoing change. The differences between the two major parties in organization and how these relate to, in turn, candidate recruitment, campaigning and financing, are all examined.

Professor Watts employs techniques of leadership identification associated with community power structure studies to isolate and analyze the relative influence of the formal and informal leadership at the local levels of the party organization in selecting candidates for public office. The findings of the study concerning communication and decision-making processes as they affect party recruitment are contrasted with comparative data drawn from other localities.

Professor Marvick begins by examining the role of the party cadre at the intermediate levels of the party structure as linkages or "middlemen" serving to connect the mass electorate with the political elite. Then drawing upon empirical data from several studies in which he has been involved, Marvick sketches a composite picture of these middlemen — their backgrounds and their ambitions.

Finally, Professor Lee Anderson (Northwestern University) appraises the literature on organizational theory and indicates the concepts and approaches that could prove to be of the greatest promise in exploring political organizations.

As editor, I have a number of obligations to acknowledge. Primarily, I am indebted to James W. Prothro and Donald R. Matthews of the University of North Carolina and George Goodwin, Jr., of the University of Massachusetts, Boston Center, for their encouragement of my own interest in the general area of political parties.

The National Center for Education in Politics, now extinct, and its former Director, Bernard Hennessy, appropriately represented among the contributors to this volume, have done yeoman service in promoting a more realistic understanding of political parties. This book was conceived as a result of a conference organized by Professors Hennessy and Charles O. Jones of the University of Arizona and sponsored by the National Center for Education in Politics. The diversity of topics treated in the conference presentations and the disparity of perspectives and approaches to party phenomena helped to stimulate some serious thought over the ensuing years as to the most profitable means of investigating parties in order to maximize the long-run rewards to come from the research. If this book were to be dedicated, it would have to be to the National Center for Education in Politics.

I am indebted to the Political Science Editor of Allyn and Bacon for his continuing and expert assistance. To Mrs. Joanne Hayes and Mrs. Carol Nichols I owe my thanks for their most able help at various stages in compiling and typing the manuscript.

William J. Crotty
Northwestern University

Contents

ix

ONE

On the Study of Party Organization

Bernard Hennessy
Pennsylvania State University

IT IS ONE of the inconveniences of political science, and telling evidence of the essentially non-scientific nature of our discipline, that there are no neatly edged definitions for our most common terms, such as "political party." Political parties, let us say for a starter, are social organizations that attempt to influence (1) the selection and tenure of the personnel of government by putting forward candidates for elective office, (2) the policies of government according to some general principles or proclivities upon which most of their members agree and, (3) in the case of the totalitarian party, the attempt is to create a comprehensive system of beliefs, a guide to attitude formation and maintenance, and (ideally) a total commitment to a way of life.

Totalitarian political parties are very different from those typified by Anglo-American parties and centralist parties of western Europe, and it may be, as Barnes suggests in this volume, that "the word 'party' covers several essentially different phenomena" and that different theories and analyses may be required for two-party systems, multi-party systems, and the several kinds of one-party systems. In any case, most of the scholarship by political scientists (as distinguished from political sociologists) has been done on non-totalitarian parties—for better or worse—and in this essay the totalitarian parties will be mainly disregarded.

"The chief thing is the selection of candidates." With this

sentence Bryce begins his famous description of American
political parties at the turn of the century. (Bryce 1910, I, 54.)
He suggests that the parties had earlier been animated by principle, and his denigration of issues-less parties,[1] as well as his
unfavorable comparison with British parties on that score, did
much to oversimplify all subsequent discussion of parties and
principles. The American parties are not so unprincipled, nor
the British parties so principled, as he imagined.

But on the whole, he was right. The chief thing *is* the selection of candidates, and, for the selection *and election* of their
candidates, American political parties take both their organizational forms and policy stands. Certainly there must be exceptions to the generalization that the policy positions of the American parties depend on their electoral prospects. But the genuine
case of a major party choosing principle over victory is very
rare; it is not at all sure that the Goldwater strategists did so
in 1964, for their *avowed* expectation was that principle would
bring victory (for these claims and the demonstration of their
enormous miscalculations, see Converse, Clausen and Miller
1965). This is clearly not so true in developed nations with
multi-party systems, or in underdeveloped nations with transitional and rapidly changing political forms. Under such conditions voter education, or preparation for revolution, or control
of key voting blocs in the representative assemblies, or any
combination of these objectives, may be more important to the
party than the mere selection and promotion of winnable candidates.

The Interest in Party Organization

We are interested in party organization for two reasons.[2]
First, description. Political parties are significant social organizations in every modern state, and in all those communities
that are in transition from traditional to modern forms. Signifi-

---

[1] "When life leaves an organic body it becomes useless, fetid, pestif-
erous: it is fit to be cast out or buried from sight. What life is to
an organism, principles are to a party. When they which are its soul
have vanished, its body ought to dissolve, . . ." (Bryce 1910, I. 23).
[2] An organization can be defined as "a social system that has an
unequivocal collective identity, an exact roster of members, a program of activity, and procedures for replacing members." (Theodore

cant social organizations need to be described, and all the more when, as is the case with parties, their characteristics are so irregular, amorphous, and ill defined. We need thorough, even minute, descriptions of political parties. To understand any polity we have to know something about its party system. To understand how (and sometimes why) a state makes, enforces, and amends its laws we need to know what its parties are and do. Description of the parties may be important for an understanding of constitutional and policy outcomes in any analysis focusing on a single governmental jurisdiction.

Beyond the explanatory value of description in single cases, we need a large accumulation of information (descriptive statements) to suggest relationships and lead us to hypotheses. Description is the raw material of taxonomy and generalization.

And this is precisely the second reason we are interested in party organization: because we want to be able to go beyond description. Not to give up description—we imagine there will always be new data to be recorded—but simultaneously to achieve analysis at a level that transcends the single case. If we believe that political parties, their organization and processes are related to substantive ends such as democracy, the representation of interests, governmental efficiency, or the distribution of indulgences and deprivations, then we want to investigate those relationships to the extent necessary for understanding, prediction, or manipulation. On the basis of what we already know, a powerful argument can be made that the organization of the political parties of a modern or transitional state is, in fact, systematically related to the policies of that state. Whether there are certain invariant and/or causal relationships between party organizations and policy outcomes is a question that is, at the moment, as unclear as it is fascinating.

Despite the importance of parties in the U.S. throughout the 19th century there is no comprehensive treatment of them until 1893. In that year, Bryce published his monumental work *The American Commonwealth*, which included 247 pages on "the party system" plus three case studies of urban party organizations (another 70 pages). He remarks in this first edition, with some surprise, "though the books and articles dealing with

---

Caplow, *Principles of Organization*, New York: Harcourt, Brace and World, 1964, p. 1. Italics omitted.) Political parties have problems in satisfying even these general qualifications. For present purposes, a party organization is an organization that is distinguished by the definitional requirements for political parties stated above.

the public life of the United States may be counted by hundreds, I know of no author who has set himself to describe impartially the actual daily working of that part of the vast and intricate political machine which lies outside the Constitution. . . ." (Bryce 1893, p. 637.)

In 1902, nine years after Bryce's first edition and eight years before his second, Moisei Ostrogorski published *Democracy and the Organization of Political Parties*. Here was the painstaking description that Bryce had called for. Ostrogorski spent many years observing and writing about British and U.S. political parties. His descriptions of party structure, processes, critical events, and actors is rich in scholarship and on-the-spot freshness.

In his excellent introduction to the Anchor edition of *Democracy and the Organization of Political Parties*, Seymour Martin Lipset argues that Ostrogorski was more than describer. Lipset is right: Ostrogorski was an insightful participant-observer and social historian. He had a concern for comparison beyond simply recounting events, for generalizations and theory-building checked always against reality. He wanted to study political "forces" and declared that "to really understand the character of social action, its modes of procedure must be studied in the light of the character of those who apply them, and of the social and political conditions in which their wills are formed and manifested. . . . It is a study . . . conceived in this spirit, a study of social and political psychology, based on observation, that I have tried to undertake. . . ." (Author's Preface, Vol. I, xxviii.) Lipset is dismayed to see "how many of Ostrogorski's fruitful hypotheses concerning opinion and electoral behavior have been almost completely ignored by students of the subject." He points out that none of the major American studies, from *The People's Choice* through *Voting, The Voter Decides, The American Voter*, and the book of commentaries on these studies, *American Voting Behavior*, even refers to his analysis." (Introduction, Vol. I, xliii.)

I suggest the reason for the neglect of Ostrogorski is that he wrote in an older idiom—that of the traveling intellectual and moral reformer. Ostrogorski did not *display* his quantification; he has, therefore, no neat tables of figures, with standard deviations, and tests of significance to commend his work to modern political behaviorists. That his generalizations were based upon judgments on the nature and patterning of events and forces is beyond doubt, but Ostrogorski's knowledge—indeed his "science"—was "personal knowledge" in the sense described by Polanyi (1958, 1960) and not yet sufficiently recognized by our most zealous behaviorists. His other liability in the eyes of present scholars is that he was a reformer—worse, a condescending reformer with more or less open disdain for both the venal politicians and their unthinking followers. Like Bryce, Ostrogorski was a cultivated 19th century liberal whose animadversions on the killing (and killers) of the liberal dream had a powerful influence on the progressive movement at the turn of the century, but are much less noted by the sophisticated pluralists who comprise the American social science establishment of the nineteen-sixties.

Important as Bryce and Ostrogorski were, to Michels (1915) goes the honor of considering first the question whether the organizational forms of political parties were related in any significant way to the other characteristics of the party system or the polity in general. We will not tarry for comment on the validity or usefulness of his so-called "iron law of oligarchy"— except to say that he seems to have wanted democracy in the simplest sense of government by *all* the people and his capacity to look candidly at the organizational behavior of his socialist friends convinced him that democracy in that sense was a vain hope.

Michels' methodology is of more interest here. He was the first student of parties to use data from several parties and national party systems to test his hypotheses about the relation of organizational needs (both those of individual members and of the organization in competition with other organizations) and the actual distribution of influence in decision-making. He dared to think of "the study and analysis of political parties . . . [as] a branch of applied sociology." (vii.)[3]

Since Michels there has been increasing (but sporadic rather than steady) interest in political party organization. The work of the 1920s and 1930s fell mainly into two groups: field investigations, often with an exposé flavor, of local machines and bosses (among the best are Gosnell 1924; McKean 1940;

[3] In an unorthodox treatment of Michels' thought—one I find quite persuasive—May (1965) argues that Michels was not a pessimistic democrat, but a "pessimistic Romantic Revolutionist and a pessimistic Scientific Paternalist" (his capitalization). "While maintaining that Organization is incompatible with pure democracy . . . he also suggested . . . that Organization can and frequently does accompany and facilitate a multitude of changes which constitute or facilitate democratization." (p. 429).

Zink 1930), or text-like treatment of party organization within a broader framework of political institutions and processes (Holcombe 1924; Ray 1922; Sait 1927). Since World War II the empirical investigation of parties has been greatly expanded, concomitantly with the widespread use of survey research and quantification techniques. Theory building has also been an interest of some, with organizations theory, systems theory, and functionalism being brought to play in the analysis of party organization and processes.

The Present State of Knowledge About Party Organization

Description is well along, but much more needs to be undertaken. Comparative analysis has been demonstrated to be possible and fruitful, but only a beginning has been made. The development of theory and "laws" of party organization is hardly beyond the talking stage; a theory of party organization at this level, when or if it comes, may be only a rather trivial case of general organizations theory. However that may be, our present state is one of increasingly detailed and accurate description of party organizations at every level and every part of the world, of increasingly sophisticated comparative analysis, and of some middle-range theory with attendant hypotheses and propositions.

Parties in English-Speaking Countries

Much work continues on American and British parties, and some on their Canadian, Australian, and New Zealand counterparts. While organization is the exclusive focus of only a very few book-length or monographic studies, all investigations of parties treat it as important and closely related to activities such as nominations and campaigning, personnel questions, and decision-making processes. In the most recent general treatments of American political parties, there seems to be little emphasis on the legal-structural aspects of organization (Greenstein 1963; Sorauf 1964), and even in recent editions of the more comprehensive parties-and-politics texts (e.g., Bone 1965).

By contrast, the older standard works were heavy with descriptions of caucuses, committees, conventions, and campaign structure (e.g., Sait 1939).

More recent writings on party structure are confined principally to description and commentary on new organizational forms (Carney 1958; Sorauf 1954; Wilson 1962), case-making for suggested change (Bailey 1959; APSA Committee 1952), comparative descriptions (Scarrow 1964), or analyses of change (Lowi 1963).

Parties in the Developing Areas

The study of American parties has proceeded rapidly since World War II. But until quite recently, American scholarship has concentrated largely on American parties—and on British parties to a lesser extent (Epstein 1956; Hennessy 1955; Ranney 1965). There is currently an encouraging growth of American interest in political parties of the developing areas of the world. Early work by Kantor (1953) in Peru, Pye (1962) in Burma, and Weiner (1957) in India, was rapidly followed by field research in Africa. At first, as one would expect, the study of African parties was only part of whole-nation surveys (Apter 1955 and 1963; Ashford 1961; Coleman 1958; Wallerstein 1959). But monographic treatments of African parties or national party systems soon followed (Moore 1962; Zolberg 1964). Several general analyses of African parties are available (Hodgkin 1961; Carter 1962; Schachter 1958 and 1961).

One important consequence of the vastly increased recent interest in the parties of developing countries was the impetus given to generalization and systems building. The student of parties in developing areas is faced with a bewildering variety of protopolitical behavior, always imperfectly distinguished from what western social scientists would regard as religious, or social class, or caste behavior. Moreover, he has no ready made framework for analysis such as western scholars have in the established legal forms or political institutions. He may then either adopt an anthropological perspective such as Muir's (1962) or Gluckman's (1963)—a response more common among British than American scholars—or find a more directly political conceptual system for his analysis. The perspectives and vocabulary of functionalism have been found useful by many students of politics in developing areas (Schachter 1961; Wallerstein 1960; Holt 1965a and 1965b; Almond and Coleman 1960; Weiner 1964)[4]; others emphasize a psychological, sometimes an avowedly psychoanalytic approach (Pye 1961 and 1962).

Finally, the students of politics in the developing areas have pushed forward the techniques of opinion and attitude surveys, in field work related to what Rokkan (1962) calls "'micropolitics'—the analysis of the individual citizens' reactions to the political events and alternatives in their communities." Here the work of Lerner (1958) and Almond and Verba (1963) are especially valuable for their systematic and transnational approaches, and for pointing the way to "the exploration of general propositions about factors in political behavior" (Rokkan 1962, p. 49).

Political Parties: Generalizations Beyond Time and Place

So far, despite the growing interest in political parties, there is only one bold attempt to treat parties comprehensively, comparatively, and in relation to other features of the political systems. That is, of course, Maurice Duverger's *Political Parties: Their Organization and Activity in the Modern State*, a French edition published in 1951, followed in 1954 by a somewhat revised English edition. Duverger's book crossed the divide between advanced history and kindergarten science. "We find ourselves," says Duverger, "in a vicious circle":

[4] In addition to the works cited, the following are useful for an introduction to functionalism and for discussions of its relative value to political inquiry: Talcott Parsons, *The Social System* (New York: The Free Press, 1951); Parsons and Edward A. Shils, eds., *Toward a General Theory of Action* (Cambridge: Harvard University Press, 1951); Parsons, "'Voting' and the Equilibrium of the American Political System," in Eugene Burdick and Arthur J. Brodbeck, eds., *American Voting Behavior* (New York: The Free Press, 1959), pp. 80–120; William C. Mitchell, *The American Polity* (New York: The Free Press, 1962); Mitchell, *Sociological Analysis and Politics: The Theories of Talcott Parsons* (Englewood Cliffs, N.J.: Prentice-Hall, 1967); H. V. Wiseman, *Political Systems* (New York: Frederick A. Praeger, 1966); and Holt, 1965.

A general theory of parties will eventually be constructed only upon the preliminary work of many profound studies; but these studies cannot be truly profound so long as there exists no general theory of parties. For Nature answers only when questioned and we do not yet know what questions this subject demands. (Duverger, 1954, p. xiii.)

Yet Duverger did what a beginning science demanded. He did what he hoped to do: "To break out of the circle and to sketch a preliminary general theory of parties, vague, conjectural, and of necessity approximate, which may yet serve as a basis and guide for detailed studies." Duverger's theory-building is based on evidence from European multi-party experience and British two-party experience, with only the barest (and in some ways inadequate) familiarity with American parties.[5]

All of this, however, to some extent is prolegomenous. It is meant only to suggest that one future development in the study of political parties is almost certain to be a linking up of the recent scholarship on the politics of the developing areas (necessarily daring in its concepts and methodologies) with the more traditional studies of the Anglo-American party systems. One expects these links to appear primarily in further elaboration of cross-national opinion and attitude studies, and in refinements of developmental constructs relating economic and social change with changes in political institutions. The psychological and social-psychological bases of political loyalties and the dynamics of opinion change are not likely yet to provide productive research foci for cross-cultural study, although our understanding of political parties (and other social institutions) will remain disappointingly incomplete until the varieties and ranges of basic psychological needs are more certainly known (Davies 1963; Hennessy 1962; Pye 1961; McClelland 1961).

Pending these advances, the major study of party organization is that of the parties of the developed areas of the world,

---

[5] It is therefore not surprising that Duverger has not received, even yet, the recognition he deserves from American scholars. He was outside the two main currents of American behavioralism, namely, the empirico-quantification school of Merriam-to-Eulau and the psychoanalytic-taxonomic school of Lasswell-to-Lane. Duverger, of that older school of historico-inductive theorists, cites Merriam only once, and Lasswell not at all.

with heavy emphasis on the English-speaking countries. This essay is directed mainly to some commentary on the literature, and on the principal types of studies, and suggestions of near and future possibilities both substantive and methodological. I borrow from Greer and Orleans (1964, p. 810) the statement, more in disappointment than apology, that I "cannot hope to be definitive, for the more immature a branch of inquiry the more discursive and unsummarized its conclusions."

Party Organization and the Law

Political parties are organized as they are in part because of the laws of the governmental jurisdiction in which they operate. The hornbook treatment of the legal aspects of parties has it that (a) parties were historically extra-legal, and much of their activities remains so today, (b) American parties are subject to only the mildest federal regulation, but (c) many of the states regulate political parties quite closely.

To what extent has the common law doctrine that political parties are private associations, protected by freedom of assembly and speech, and immune from all except basic conspiracy and sedition regulation, generally given way to the view that they have quasi-official status for the performance of some public (even governmental) functions? Have the state legislatures generally (since it is unthinkable that extensive *federal* regulation of parties will soon come about) accepted the doctrine of *Rice v. Elmore?*[6] My impression is that they have not. And there is reason to believe that if state legislatures attempted to restrict the party organizational forms too closely, extra-legal groups and structures would be created for the nomination and election functions. Sorauf (1954) describes what happened in Wisconsin after the progressives, about the turn of the century,

[6] The U.S. Second District Circuit Court said in 1947: ". . . with the passage of years, political parties have become state institutions, governmental agencies through which sovereign power is exercised by the people." (*Rice v. Elmore,* 165 F. 2nd 387.)

In some states, the parties are still required to supervise, administer and pay the full costs of their primaries. This is said by one observer (McCloskey 1963, p. 49) to reflect "the tenacity of the old view that political parties are private rather than public or quasipublic organizations."

wove a legal net around the existing parties. At the other extreme, the minimal regulation of party organization and activity is found in some of the one-party states of the South (South Carolina, Virginia, Georgia, and Arkansas, according to Key 1949) and the strong party states of New England (for the legal self-protection of the parties in strong-party states see Title 17 of the Rhode Island Revised Statutes or Chapters 12 and 15 of Duane Lockard, *Connecticut's Challenge Primary: A Study in Legislative Politics*, Eagleton Institute Cases in Practical Politics, New York: McGraw Hill, 1959). One might hypothesize that parties will be only minimally regulated by law in states where (a) one mass party enjoying unified leadership is electorally strong and commands party loyalty in the legislature; (b) two mass parties are both electorally strong and agree in the legislature to leave themselves as free as possible from legal restrictions. The general proposition is that the organizations that perform the vital functions of selecting candidates and running campaigns will be subject to few legal restrictions: for example, the statutory party organizations in Rhode Island, Connecticut, and Virginia have, in recent years, controlled the selection of party candidates (through conventions or primaries) and in those states the statutory party organization is relatively unregulated. In Florida the other pattern prevails; there the statutory party organization is carefully regulated, but personal and *ad hoc* campaign organizations are used for the critical nominating and electing functions. In most other southern states, too, the statutory parties are weak, and their organizational forms closely prescribed by law, but they are usually only a minor device for maintaining the power of incumbent Democratic office holders and hardly ever important for obtaining the Democratic nomination. The rule is, in short, both in the north and south, that those organizational forms found in practice to be important for controlling nominations and campaigns tend to be least regulated by law—in most instances, probably, completely free of legal regulation.[7]

If, as the foregoing discussion assumes, the laws regulating political parties are determined by the anticipated consequences

[7] British experience confirms the rule, the regular party organizations being almost essential to election and practically unregulated by law (Ranney 1965). It must be said, of course, that the simplicity of the parliamentary system, as contrasted with the complexity of federalism *cum* separation-of-powers, reduces the worth of the confirmation.

for the political leaders who make them, then we would expect that a growing minority party would be disadvantaged by those laws. In the middle 1960s, we would expect the Democratic legislatures and governors in the south to change old statutes or make new ones to restrict the developing Republican party. In fact, we find this in Mississippi where, in 1964, the majority Democrats proposed a series of bills that would have weighed heavily and unfairly on the GOP—among other things, requiring the Republicans to hold primaries, even if there were no contests, at the estimated cost to the party of $150,000 every two years. These efforts were blocked by the minority faction of Democratic legislators who found the growing Republican party in the state to be a useful foil in their maneuvers against Governor Paul Johnson. Currently, however, the Democrats in South Carolina are considering non-partisan local and state elections in a move to protect the Democratic incumbents. In New York State, the Republican controlled legislature has for many years varied the date of the closed primary for its advantage and the Democrats' discomfit, moving it from spring to early or even late summer as its partisan interests dictated. I suspect other evidence could be found for the generalization suggested.

Party Organization: Structures

So far Duverger's is the only systematic attempt to link party organization (defined as the structure of the units *and* their articulation within the party) with party systems, and both with governmental systems. He suggests that party organization tends to assume structure and articulation paralleling that of the governmental system: thus federalism encourages decentralization and weak vertical articulation.[8] (This notion

---

[8] Articulation is the manner in which the primary units of the party are linked together. Vertical articulation refers to the joining of two units, one of which is subordinate to the other. In contrast, horizontal articulation is the linkage among party units at the same level. These dimensions are in addition to the power distribution, or relative centralization, of a given party organization. In Duverger's words: "Vertical links and horizontal links define ways of co-ordinating the basic elements of which the party is made up; centralization and decentralization define the way in which power is distributed amongst the different levels of leadership." (p. 52.)

itself is hardly new to American political scientists.) He suggests further that the electoral system also influences a party's structure and articulation:

> The single-member constituency where a simple majority suffices to elect obviously encourages decentralization by giving priority to narrow local opinions and to the personality of candidates who with their party caucuses may make themselves independent of the centre. But list-voting does not directly encourage centralization: it simply extends the field of decentralization. (Duverger 1954, p. 59.)

Duverger's view that the electoral system determines the party system has been challenged by several scholars; Leys (1959) ably summarizes both the logical and existential arguments against Duverger's "law," and advances a model to explain parliamentary two-partyism in Britain.

The American federal system provides almost unlimited opportunity to investigate a variety of governmental and electoral systems, and their relation to party organization. Though our predominant electoral unit may be the single member constituency, Klain (1955) has shown that many multi-member constituencies exist. Duverger's propositions, and more detailed hypotheses, could be tested in a variety of field situations, relating size and membership of constituency, interparty competition, party discipline (in nominations and record votes, for instance), stability and turnover in party leadership, and other relevant or thought-to-be-relevant variables. The changes and dislocations currently resulting from the reapportionment of state legislatures make the present a propitious moment for the study of the relationships between the electoral system and party organization. But little has been done except Silva's (1964a and 1964b) two useful articles on the effects of single- or multi-member districts on tenure, gerrymandering, interparty competition, and two-party or multi-party systems.

Schlesinger (1965) in a very provocative and useful essay, develops one format for the functional analysis of American party organizations. He makes a number of assumptions about American parties, the most important of which are that they are election-contesting associations, dominated by their public office holders (or candidates for public office), operating in the context of a two-party mold. The party nucleus, in Schlesinger's scheme, consists of three elements: a candidate, a label, and an election to be fought. This becomes the micro-unit upon which the analysis centers, and macro-analysis then involves multinuclear relationships. His single unit is thus what is sometimes referred to as a candidate organization, and the multinuclear pattern is party organization.

Within this analytical framework, Schlesinger proceeds in terms of the functional contributions that may be made by individuals and groups toward the objectives of the party; namely, winning elections. There are, in his scheme, minimal and connective contributions: candidacy and votes are minimal contributions, and connective (indirect and supporting) contributions are discussed under the headings of leadership, recruitment and nomination, issue formation, memory, intelligence and communications, technical services, and money.

The Schlesinger framework would appear to be a useful device for the comparative analysis of election-winning party organizations. In U.S. state and local politics we have a nearly limitless opportunity to study party nuclei (candidate organizations) and multinuclear patterns (party organizations), and it is hoped that cooperative research could be initiated. In fact, the independent and intervening variables employed by Schlesinger (leadership, recruitment, nomination, etc.) might even serve as elements in the comparative study of ideological parties. The point is that these analytical concepts need not be applied only to election-winning party groups, since organizational analysis in terms of functional contributions made by constituent members has a respectable (if not long) tradition in sociology and social anthropology. But we need not press its applicability beyond that claimed by its author to recognize that the Schlesinger framework might be very advantageously applied now by students of American political parties.

What consequences for party organization are to be expected from further development of general socio-economic trends in America? High levels of affluence and education, combined with greater leisure in ever-more-dense conurbations, might be expected to accelerate the development of amateur, issues-oriented, social-hour party groups of the kind described by Carney (1958) and Wilson (1962). Lane (1965) has recently suggested that affluence has taken some of the acrimony out of partisanship as party identifiers—although their interest in politics remains high—"increasingly believe that the opposition is not so dangerous after all." At the same time, the

"Negro revolution" in America, encouraged by doctrines such as the Office of Economic Opportunity's "maximum feasible participation of target groups," might be expected to produce new forms of political organizations, including party groups with narrow racial bases (but concentrated geographical control) reminiscent of earlier urban machines. Students of party organization would be advised to study closely the conflicts over control of antipoverty funds in New York, Newark, and Chicago, for example. Much work remains to be done on urban machines and suburban (or high rise apartment) reformers, and the conflicts and convergences of their political cultures (Litt 1966).

Little has been done in the U.S. (at least by comparison with Britain) on the party structures within legislative bodies. Accounts of Congressional struggles over rules changes, house speaker selection, and committee assignments, give us indirect information on party organization in the House and Senate. Ripley's (1964) study of the House party whip organization and Jones' (1965) volume on the Republican Policy Committee in the House describe in some detail the structure and workings of these party organs. Earlier descriptions of Senate party groups may be found in articles by Bone (1956) and Jewell (1959).

Three other useful essays, focusing on party leadership behavior rather than organization, are Matthews (1960) description of Senate styles and influence-patterns, Huitt's (1961) account of Lyndon Johnson's way as Senate majority leader, and Froman and Ripley's (1965) attempt to identify some general rules of leadership from the experiences of the House Democrats 1961 to 1963. The approach of Matthews, Huitt, and Froman and Ripley is probably, at this point, more productive for understanding the party-in-Congress than are structural or organizational studies.

I am not aware of any comparative treatment of party organization in state legislatures. Wahlke, Eulau, Buchanan and Ferguson (1962) is perhaps the closest work we have, but party organization was not the main focus of that excellent volume. There are fugitive and *ad hoc* descriptions of the powers and uses of leaders, caucuses, and rudimentary whip systems in a few legislatures, but little attention has been paid to these matters. Perhaps it is because the legislative parties are generally so factious, shifting, and personalized in form and operation that organizational analysis would provide, at best, only a low order of understanding. Some exploratory investigations might be urged, however.[9]

Party competition at the state level, as distinguished from *party organization,* has been subject to some analysis. The current reapportionment changes in most state legislatures—changes that are certain to be important and long lasting—may strongly influence party competition and organization. For a recent survey of these changes, with selected references, see Mitau (1966) and, for continuing developments, the National Municipal League's periodical *State Legislatures Reporter.*

Voters, Members, Activists

In the U.S. party members are people who say they are party members. Saying so may not even be necessary; in some states, where there is no registration or where registration is not by party, a Republican is a person who *thinks* of himself as a Republican.

In other nations, party membership has a different meaning and may depend on an act of joining, and/or the periodic payment of dues. One of Duverger's basic differentiations of political parties is based on the concept of membership. U.S. parties are what he calls *cadre* parties, without any regularized concept of membership (i.e., application, initiation, dues, etc.). *Mass* parties have regularized procedures and expectations for their "card-carrying" (often literally) members who are "the very substance of the party, the stuff of its activity" (p. 63). Membership patterns are linked to organizational structure in Duverger's analysis:

[9] The paucity of *scholarly* work on U.S. congressional party organization (as distinguished from journalistic and biographical treatments) is confirmed by a recent bibliography—Charles O. Jones and Randall B. Ripley, *The Role of Political Parties in Congress: A Bibliography and Research Guide* (Tucson, Arizona: Institute of Government Research, University of Arizona, 1966). See also, for scattered articles on party organization in state legislatures, James Herndon, Charles Press, and Oliver P. Williams, *A Selected Bibliography of Materials in State Government and Politics* (Lexington, Kentucky: Bureau of Government Research, University of Kentucky, 1963); and for an incisive article on legislative party leadership in Connecticut, Barber (1966).

This distinction between cadre parties and mass parties coincides with differences arising out of the various kinds of party organization. Cadre parties correspond to the caucus parties, decentralized and weakly knit; mass parties to parties based on branches, more centralized and more firmly knit. (p. 67.)

The cadre parties of the U.S. may be thought of as having four classes of adherents:

(1) *Visible leaders,* who are candidates for public office, officials of regular party groups or campaign organizations, and, in general, persons who are widely known to be in the high councils of the party and are so identified in the mass media.

(2) *Party activists,* who identify with the party, its cause, and its candidates to the extent that they devote their time and energy to its advancement. They may be regular or sporadic workers. They may be paid or unpaid. They may be professional staffers or the most amateur enthusiasts. They are distinguished from the visible leaders by their general anonymity and their exclusion from the highest policy and strategy decisions. They are distinguished from party members by their contributions of time and money, and other behavioral show of commitment to the party and its standard bearers.

(3) *Party supporters,* who are the traditional voters for the party, and identifiers with the party. Their identification is not strong enough to move them to work for the party and its candidates, but they are the persons who readily tell the pollsters they are Republicans or Democrats. They vote the regular party line, except when strongly pulled to *candidates* of another party.

(4) *Party voters* are simply those who voted for the party's candidate(s) in the last election. This is a categorical group, plain and simple, with no normative or motivational implications. But it is not, therefore, a sterile classification fit only for statistical tables and without analytical significance; for the concept has meaning both for the nature of "mandates" arising from specific elections, and for party organization and strategy.

Milbrath (1965) has carefully reviewed the literature on political participation generally, and has identified its major dimensions (pp. 9–16) and the characteristic degrees of involvement in specific political acts (most of which, fortunately for our interests here, relate to parties and campaigning, pp.

22–29). His "conceptual diagram of political behavior variables" is an imaginative summary of the personal meanings and
processes of political participation. Milbrath speaks of political
"gladiators," "spectators," and "apathetics"—a useful classification, the first two of which include the four types described
(in purely partisan terms) above.

Translating Lane's (1959) conclusion into the categories
above, it appears that less than one tenth of one per cent of
Americans are visible leaders, from 5 to 11 per cent are party
activists, and from 60 to 70 per cent are party members (of
whom perhaps one-fourth to one-third will be moved sufficiently
to "talk politics" with their friends during campaigns).

There is at present much welcome concern with understanding who the party leaders, activists, and followers are,
what their needs and drives may be, how they relate to each
other within and outside the party contexts, and how these
relationships are or may be articulated for purposes of party
strategy or wider social engineering. The chapters by Marvick,
Watts, and Barnes in this volume bear heavily on these questions. Research techniques and methodologies from the behavioral sciences are being employed—and have been since
Lasswell (1930)—but even the most benign of these, such as
survey research, are open to criticism for their being, so it is
said, apolitically applied (Key 1961). The reflections or con-
fessions of insiders are not generally focused on party organization as such, but there are some helpful works such as Michelson's (1944) and Redding's (1958). Much diligent field work
is now underway, some of it employing advanced psychometric
and sociometric techniques, but comparative cooperative research by several scholars using common designs and selected
participant observation has not yet been possible in the study
of party leaders, activists, and members. This has been due in
part to the scarcity of politically trained sociologists and psy-
chologically trained political scientists, but it is also a reflection
on the conceptual and methodological inadequacies of psychology and sociology. While Lasswell's (1963) plea for a continuous "basic data survey," that would include, among other
items, information about party participants and their perceptions, is at this point utopian, more modest enterprises include
the Roper Center's (Hastings 1964) and Survey Research Center's materials, the latter now more widely available through
the Inter-University Consortium, and the Indiana University
Bureau of Governmental Research's data bank of biographical

and attitudinal information on Indiana state legislators, local officials, and party leaders (Janda and Francis 1963).

With the data already at hand, and that which can be obtained by selective interviewing and observational techniques, it should be possible now to increase our understanding of the differences and similarities among visible leaders, activists, supporters, and voters. Duverger has advanced as a "working hypothesis" that "there is a disparity [of opinions, attitudes and general political behavior] between the two groups: party electors and party members." This "law of disparity," Duverger says, may mean

> . . . that the essential differences in behavior of the two groups in no way permit one of them to claim that it reflects and represents the other. Measurement of the disparity between electors and members is thus equivalent to measuring the degree of oligarchy which impregnates the systems that we term democratic. (p. 101.)

Leaving aside for the moment Duverger's oversimple and inadequate (as I see it) conception of what is democratic and what is not, the examination of disparities of view between party activists and party voters may be a fruitful device for the understanding of governmental systems and process broadly, and in the narrower sense for understanding intraparty organization and procedures. For example, McCloskey *et al.* (1960) discovered that in 1957 and 1958 "the differences between leaders and followers—among the Republicans at least—are beyond anything we had expected. Indeed, the conclusion is inescapable that the views of the Republican rank and file are, on the whole, much closer to those of the Democratic leaders than to those of the Republican leaders" (p. 422). Had social scientists followed this clue in the winter of 1957–58 they might have noted the increasing importance of the GOP conservative wing; they might have been more closely aware of the rift between Republican leaders and activists on the one side, and supporters and voters on the other, that made possible the nomination of a man as electorally unacceptable as Senator Goldwater.

Supporters are to be regarded as fellow travelers *of* the party, but we know very little about their attitudes *toward* the party. All the survey evidence is that the traditional party identifier who is not among the small activist or leader groups generally holds his party faith lightly—but that mild loyalties persist because politics are not very important to him anyway. For several years the Survey Research Center at the University of Michigan has been distinguishing party orientations from candidate orientations, and both from issue orientations (Campbell, Converse, Miller and Stokes 1960). Recently the dynamic interactions among party, candidate, and issue influences have come under scrutiny by the Survey Research Center scholars. Stokes and Miller (1962) have investigated the consequences of persisting party loyalties and low interest in issues for the theory of party government as it relates to party discipline in Congress. Converse (1962) has suggested that the increasing media exposure by American voters since World War I has had the effect of reducing the relative importance of issue orientations with an attendant decrease in the importance of party loyalty and a greater "amplitude of the oscillations in voting" at the national level. Stokes (1963) and Converse (1966) have developed what they refer to as "spatial models" of voters' attitudes toward parties to give contextual meaning to what the parties "stand for" in the minds of voters and how parties are perceived as being like or different from other parties. These recent efforts to conceptualize the attitudinal field of forces in politics and party loyalties seem to have been triggered by Downs' earlier (1957) work relating economic theory to voting behavior. I suggest that the borrowings by Stokes and Converse from Lewinian psychology and Rokeach's (1960) brilliant investigations of the dynamics of attitude formation and maintenance would have been more useful. They, and others who are courageous enough to enter this bewildering area, may find conceptual aid and experimental comfort from the work being done by Sherif and associates (1965) in extension of earlier investigations in the psychology of ego-involvement.

Investigations of party leaders and activists are ordinarily not directed to organizational questions. Recently some interest has been shown in examining the duties and functions of party officers, as seen by themselves or others. Cotter and Hennessy (1964) describe the responsibilities (or opportunities) of national party chairmen, relating them to the president, congressional leaders, and state party leaders. The gaps in the descriptive literature on American political parties are nowhere more obviously exposed than in the fact that no general treatment of the state party chairman has ever been attempted despite the admitted importance of the office. About the members, duties, procedures, and importance of state party executive committees we know even less.

Earlier efforts such as those by Marvick and Eldersveld (1961) and the contributors to the volume *Inside Politics: The National Conventions, 1960* (Tillett 1962), have provided us with a beginning knowledge of *national* party convention delegates—who they are, how selected, their typical party histories, other offices held, and their role perceptions as delegates. Munger and Blackhurst (1965) relate convention delegates' voting patterns over a 24 year period to enduring factionalism in the national party coalitions. So far, however, we know next to nothing about *state* party convention delegates, despite the fact that conventions in many states either select candidates to go directly on the general election ballot or endorse them for the primaries.

We are beginning to get some data about county chairmen and other *local* party leaders beyond scattered political biographies of the most notorious bosses. Crotty's chapter in this volume, and his earlier (1963) article, provide data on background and perspectives of North Carolina county chairmen. The data gathered by Epstein (1958), Frost (1961), Patterson (1963) and Pomper (1965) on the socio-economic backgrounds of party county chairmen in Kansas, New Jersey, Oklahoma, and Wisconsin provide a comparative basis for additional and replicative studies. Patterson's conclusion teems with potential propositions and hypotheses to be tested:

> When the majority party is dominant in a political sub-system, high socio-economic status elements of the population are likely to be inordinately represented among party leaders of the dominant party whether it be labeled Democratic or Republican. But county party leadership is not essentially a part of the recruitment pipeline for public office in the sense that few county leaders have held public office [Pomper finds this not true in New Jersey], and aspiration for elective public office is not particularly high among county leaders although minority party leaders have a higher aspiration for office.[10] Finally, party leaders

[10] Hanson (1965) finds the same to be true in Oklahoma, where county commissioners show little interest in being party county chairmen.

at the county level are differently oriented in the conceptions of their political leadership role, proportionately tending to be more organization-oriented where their party is
dominant and more campaign-oriented where the other
party is dominant.[11]

Flinn and Wirt (1965) found that Ohio county level leaders tended to agree on issues with other leaders of their own
party and to disagree with leaders of the other party—thus
replicating McClosky's findings from a national sample of party
leaders. Going beyond McClosky, Flinn and Wirt controlled for
socio-economic factors and concluded that "leaders of the two
parties do not differ in attitudes toward public policy issues
because of differences in background, [but] it appears that the
contrasting attitudes and attitude structures which divide Republicans from Democrats relate to party itself and not to some
other factor lurking behind or operating through party."

Marvick's contribution to this volume is based in part on
data he and Nixon (1961) used in earlier analyses of campaign
workers and local party activists. He has sought in this volume
to go beyond recruitment patterns to an examination of the
attitudes toward campaigning and the policy positions held by
the parties' middle management people. The reputational
method he uses for distinguishing "core cadre" from "fringe
cadre," leading to an investigation of characteristically different
attitudes, recommends itself as one strategy in the search for
functionally equivalent roles in other party systems.[12]

In his chapter in this book, Watts uses essentially the same
reputational procedure for identifying the "top influentials" and
"key influentials" in the selection of candidates for party and
public office in Indiana. Again, one would expect equivalent
influentials to be discoverable in other party systems—but from
the research so far on political recruitment we would predict
that the institutional features of the process must vary greatly
from Oregon (Seligman 1961), to England (Ranney 1965, and
in this volume), to Israel (Seligman 1964).

Of the personnel of American political parties we know

[11] However, Bowman and Boynton (1966) found *local* party officials
in North Carolina to be campaign-oriented where their party was
dominant and organization-oriented where the other party was in
control.

[12] The assumptions and techniques associated with reputational
methods are discussed in the Marvick and Watts chapters in this
volume and the references cited therein.

least of all, probably, about the professional staff member. It is the nature of cadre parties to discourage the professionalization of party staffers. Whereas the branch and cell parties of Europe have maintained paid party bureaucrats for many years—in fact, the growth of power of the socialist party bureaucrats weighed heavily in Michel's formulation of the "iron law of oligarchy"—American parties have only recently and hesitantly moved toward professional staffing. Cotter and Hennessy (1964) describe the anomaly of long tenure for some staff members and the complete absence of job security for others at the two national party committees. Almost no research has been done on professional staffing of state and local party committees, although there is good reason to believe that state party committees are employing more permanent staff.

Cotter and I surveyed state committee headquarters in mid-summer 1961—deliberately chosen as a non-campaign period to identify hard-core staff only—and found that of the 47 Republican units responding (46 states plus the District of Columbia), 40 had one or more paid staff workers. The total number of GOP state committees' full time staff members in the summer of 1961 was 181, of whom 108 were classed by the chairmen as clerical and 73 professional. In addition there were 22 part-time clerical employees and 14 part-time professional staff members. Of the 34 Democratic units for which we obtained data (33 states and the District of Columbia), 27 had paid staffs: the Democratic total personnel reported was 117 full-time (74 clerical and 43 professional) plus 2 clerical and one professional part-time. A rough index of state party staffing can be constructed from these data:

STATE PARTY COMMITTEE STAFFING, SUMMER 1961, FULL-TIME STAFF ONLY*

	Clerical	Professional	All	Range
Republican (N=47)	2.30	1.55	3.85	28–1
Democratic (N=34)	2.18	1.27	3.44	16–1

* Figures in the first three columns are average number of staff members per state committee. Averaging aids interparty comparability, in view of the underreporting of Democratic Committees (34 to 47 Republican committees); but averaging seriously distorts the intraparty distribution of staffing, ranging from 28 full-time people in New York State's GOP Committee to one person in many of the smaller states' committees.

Schutz's (1964) study of party bureaucrats in Michigan (described as "a preliminary excursion") raises many possibilities for comparative research among our 50 American party systems. He suggests that the development of professional staffing is retarded by: (1) a "deeply egalitarian" ethic among party activists and supporters, (2) the jealous autonomy of local (county and city) party units, (3) an inherent anti-professionalism in personality-based party organizations (linked obviously to fear that "entrenched party bureaucrats" might control nominations), and (4) interest groups' preference for party organizations that must rely heavily on the groups' own staffs. Hanna (1965) argues that there may be personality differences between party bureaucrats and public leaders "because the latter seek roles which offer the security of external esteem, whereas administrative roles offer the security of routine" (78).

The contrast between state and local party staffing in the U.S. and constituency party agentry in Britain seems sharp, at least superficially and on the basis of the limited research in both countries. McKenzie (1955) quoting the Labour party rules and manuals, says the "agent is encouraged to think of himself as 'the managing director of the party'. . . . With this encouragement a headstrong or self-centered individual sometimes finds himself tempted to convert his party into a one-man organization." One infers from McKenzie that the Conservative party agents are expected to act more as a personal assistant to the Member of Parliament or prospective candidate for the constituency—a difference that, if true, reflects the somewhat greater parliamentary party emphasis of the Conservatives.

Party Organization and Interest Groups

The conception of political interest groups is one that has been developed in the context of the study of pluralistic democratic societies. In that context the relation of party organization and interest groups has been the subject of considerable research in the Bently-Truman-Latham tradition. Calkin's (1952) little book on the CIO and the Democratic Party may be taken as a representative piece. Greenstone (1966) has recently turned around the perspective of pressurer and pressured and concluded that the political party is impelled to put pressure on the interest group, rather than the other way, when the issue is the party's choice of candidates (that being, in Greenstone's words, "the party's narrow constituency"). Masters (1957) had earlier concluded that the simpler notions of interest groups controlling parties, even in a case like that of the Auto Workers and the Michigan Democracy, were inadequate for description and understanding.

Interest groups should be distinguished from broader and fuzzier concepts, such as "power elite" or "establishment," in the analysis of party processes. Studies of nonpartisanship, and community studies generally, often fail to distinguish interest groups from more pervasive and less well defined influences— an inadequacy that Polsby (1963), among others, has noted. These more general influences might better be regarded as aspects of the political culture in Litt's (1965) sense.

Both political cultures and pressure groups relate to forces that create or alter party systems. In some analyses, however, the pressure groups might be regarded as part of the regime; this seems to be the case with the trade unions, for example, in what Riggs (following Tucker) has called "movement regimes."[13]

When do interest groups put forth candidates for party or public office and what conditions facilitate their acceptance by the party? Financially, what part does the interest group seek in funding the party's operations? What in turn does it gain from dollars invested—access? preferential treatment? elective office-holding advocates? Owens and White's study (1960) of lobbies and parties in Michigan is a descriptive beginning in an area that requires substantial exploration. Finally, to what extent and under what conditions does any one lobby or combination of interest groups come to represent the intra-structural nuclear unit in Schlesinger's (1965) typology or one of the stratarchical sublevels in Eldersveld's (1964) model of party organization?

Interparty Competition as a Variable for Analysis

The notion of interparty competition has been a useful, and in some ways unifying, concept for recent American stu-

[13] The expression "movement regimes" is perhaps too ambiguous to be useful. See Peter Wiles, "Comment on Tucker's 'Movement Regimes'," *American Political Science Review*, 55 (June, 1961), pp. 290–293.

dents of political parties. Measurements and analyses of inter-party competition are obviously more easily made in a two-party system than in a multi-party system. The interest in party competition is—again, obviously—linked with party discipline, especially in the legislative party, and thus gets tied into the consideration of party responsibility.

I shall not say much here on the usual arguments and counter-arguments about party responsibility. Since the publication of Woodrow Wilson's *Congressional Government* in 1885 much of American scholarship and polemics about parties has centered on the notion of party government. The debate goes on—mainly because it is an important matter. How the parties funnel and control political power through nominations, elections, and policymaking is (or might be, given responsible parties) the most critical question political analysts could concern themselves with. What can be said for and against party government is well known to American scholars, or can be found easily. Moreover, I think a brief review of interparty competition will get at some of the aspects of party responsibility without arousing the old suspicions and biases.

The study of interparty competition has to do with the identification, measurement, and analysis of conflict between the parties for support (voters and activists) at the electoral level, and for control of offices and policymaking in the government.

There are two kinds of interparty competition: (1) competition between the parties in a single constituency, measured by percentages of votes cast in one or several elections, highly competitive constituencies usually being called "marginal districts"; (2) competition between the parties for control of legislative bodies and/or the state political institutions as a whole. Interparty competition in the second sense has been measured through roll-call votes by many observers (Jewel 1955, Keefe 1956, Patterson 1962), but the relationship between competition, so measured, and organization (Lockard 1954), or constituency pressures (Froman 1963), is not at all clear.

Jones (1964) links the two aspects of interparty competition in a review of turnover in U.S. House seats and concludes that "the House is weighted toward stability in its practical resolution of the competition-stability dilemma. . . . Competition at the constituency level (i.e., between candidates) is low, and the trend is toward less rather than more competition."

Our interest in interparty competition of both kinds might

be considered in brief comments on several hypotheses that are explicit or implied in recent scholarship on the subject.

    1. *The greater the interparty competition at the constituency level, the greater will be citizen participation.*

Turnout figures comparing low and high interparty competition rates from different electoral units at the same time, as well as data from time series in areas with increasing competition, indicate that party competition and citizen participation *in general elections* are positively associated. Whether interparty competition is positively associated with *primary election* turnout is uncertain (Ranney 1965A). Whether greater competition "causes" greater turnout, or vice versa, is also an uncertain (and perhaps not very significant) question; changes in either are probably consequences of more fundamental changes in sociology and loyalties.

    2. *The greater the interparty competition at the constituency level, the greater the sense of political confidence and efficacy in the electorate.*

Sense of political efficacy is a psychological construct developed by Campbell, Gurin and Miller (1954) as a measure of the extent to which individuals think they (and others) can influence public events and policies. It is similar to Gosnell's (1948) sense of representativeness, and may be akin to political alienation although the latter phrase has more deeper psychological implications (Levin 1960 and 1962, Schick 1963). This hypothesis is implicit in some commentary (e.g., Litt 1963), but I have not seen any direct examination of it.

    3. *The greater the interparty competition at the constituency level, the more issue- and party-oriented (as distinguished from candidate-oriented) will be the campaign (Campbell, Gurin and Miller 1954).*

Here again, I think we have no empirical evidence as yet.

    4. *The greater the interparty competition at the aggregate level (i.e., in the legislature, or the political unit as a whole), the greater will be the internal discipline in both the mass parties and the governmental parties.*

With regard to the mass parties, Ranney (1965A) has commented on the proposition that state party organization is more centralized where interparty competition is greatest. But, he says, "the tendency is slight at best," and "*decentralization* is likely to continue to be as characteristic of American state parties as national" (pp. 71 and 73, italics in original). In the state legislatures, however, party "cohesion" (which may not be the same as "discipline") "is generally very low in the one-party and modified one-party states, and tends to be higher in the two-party states" (p. 88). In a recent review of party cohesion in the state legislatures, and factors associated with it, Dye (1965) concludes that "party cohesion is found in the competitive states rather than in the non-competitive states" (p. 187), but not all competitive states have a high degree of party cohesion in legislative votes. Dye suggests that party voting is not so much a product of disciplined organization as of constituency pressures; "the weight of evidence," he says, "seems to support the hypothesis that party influence is only effective where the parties represent separate and distinct socio-economic coalitions" (p. 188).

The general hypothesis that party discipline is positively related to interparty competition is mildly supported by the evidence we have to this date. But it also seems true, as Dye concludes, and as Sorauf (1963) finds in Pennsylvania, that constituency pressures are more influential than the principle of party discipline. This is as one would expect: in a political party system where candidate winnability is the prime desideratum, the party has to be seen as the instrument for victory if it expects first allegiance from its candidates. Where party organization wins elections, there party discipline is high—a conclusion that seems inordinately simple-minded unless one reflects on the absurdities that are committed when it is ignored.

   5. *The greater the interparty competition at the aggregate level, the more responsive to socio-economic needs will be governmental policy.*

Unfortunately, the relation between party competition and legislative outcomes has been investigated very little. In one careful recent attempt to relate party competitiveness to states' welfare policies, Dawson and Robinson (1965) conclude that "political variables [including interparty competition] make a difference for policies about well-being, but socio-economic factors make a greater difference."

The concept of party competition is sometimes used to link party-in-the-government with aspects of voter support for the mass party. Socio-economic variables are thought to be related closely (and causally) to party competition. Little need be said here of these speculations, since Gatlin's chapter in this volume refers to a number of the standard discussions of the subject.

The Gatlin report commendably abstracts testable operational hypotheses from political science literature many of which have potential transnational and transcultural validity (i.e., as socio-economic diversity increases party competition increases). The use of regression analysis for demonstrating correlations between political and non-political phenomena represents a useful employment of a potentially powerful research technique.[14]

Research strategies that require the funding of large amounts of trend data raise questions as to long-run objectives within the field that political scientists would do well to consider now.[15] The historical value of acquiring and interpreting such data is great. Even more important the isolation of general relationships over time and the experimental modification of these under precisely controlled conditions would be possible. But the cost is high. Retrieving the information involves extensive labor. The time lag between the occurrence, the accumulation of relevant data, its analysis, and its dissemination blunts the explanatory power of the scholar interested in understanding and intelligently ordering contemporary events.

We need information about continuing political phenomena. We want measurements of party competition and socio-economic data, for example, immediately applicable to present occurrences—and, most desirably, I might add for North Africa in addition to North Dakota. By a prodigious massing of resources we could, no doubt, maintain sliding current averages of trend data, as Lasswell (1963) proposes, and such as the U.S. Department of Agriculture keeps for parity calculations. But in a social science world of serious and enduring

[14] A cautionary note should be introduced. The powers and limitations of statistical techniques in general for interpreting social science data are not yet clear. The statistical measurement of a relationship (or of several relationships treated together statistically) can not be said to cause, or explain, the phenomena under discussion; a point that textual explanatory statements should make clear (as well as the conditions and limitations under which the statistical relationships are valid). For a commendable instance of the application of statistical techniques in political research in this regard, see Grumm's (1963) use of factor analysis for identifying statistically significant elements in multivariate analysis.

[15] See Karl W. Deutsch, "Recent Trends in Research Methods in Political Science," in James C. Charlesworth, ed., *A Design for Political Science: Scope, Objectives, and Methods* (Philadelphia: The American Academy of Political and Social Science, December, 1966), pp. 152–159.

shortage of human talent, and less serious but continuing financial shortages, can we give the necessary priority to these kinds
of study? I am tempted to answer the questions with a qualified
"yes"—but I raise it at this point not for answering, but only for
pondering.

Political Executives and Party Organization

There is a classic and useful view that political parties
developed, at least in Britain and the United States, as a device
for coordinating the activities of legislatures and political executives. Once the idea of separation of powers took on practical
meaning, and as soon as it became institutionalized in defin-
able groups of men—some to make policy, and others to put
policy into daily governmental activity—some mediating, con-
necting, and even transcending social arrangements were
necessary. The classical explanation is that the British political
parties sprang mainly from the need to coordinate the parliament with the government.

In the American presidential system, where the chief
executive is chosen by a method different from that of Congress
(and from an aggregated constituency different from, and
greater than, the aggregated constituencies of the separate national legislators), the need was all the more clear for party-as-
glue-between-legislature-and-executive. Similarly—but without
suggesting any federal analogy—the states' political systems
were served, right from the beginning, by political parties that
helped to cut across the institutional rivalries between governors and legislatures.

And it is another of the ironic deficiencies of American
political science that so little is known about the party relationships of governors and state legislatures. It would seem,
superficially at least, that the governors as party leaders must
be a less complex matter than the president as party leader.
Moreover, the volume of empirical data that could be gathered
on governors and state parties (much of it comparable and
fundable across the 50 states) is surely many times that obtain-
able on presidents as party leaders. If we were as interested as
we say we are in understanding the *regularities* of politics,
rather than the dramatics or policy content of politics, we would
long since have gathered comparable behavioral data on gover-

nors as party leaders. Kallenbach's (1966) recent tome illustrates how non-empirical and non-quantitative is the folklore that passes for knowledge about American governors and political parties. He says, for example, that lately "governors have established themselves more openly and firmly as the recognized heads of their party organizations in the states" (p. 306), but offers as evidence only the fact that one governor was a delegate to presidential nominating conventions in 1860 and that 35 out of 48 were members of their delegations in 1956. Elsewhere (p. 301) he says that governors may or may not have the power to determine their parties' other state candidates. The point is not to criticize Kallenbach, but merely to underscore the fact that we have hardly begun to gather the evidence that would provide some solid knowledge about these matters. Nor do I suggest that the task of accumulating pertinent comparative data will be easy. It will require many well trained and coordinated researchers. But no other research strategy will do.

Though we know very little *for sure,* some comments might be offered about what we might look for, and where we might look for it, if we want better knowledge of executives and party organization.

First, we might explore the relationship of institutions and organization. We suppose the parliamentary system requires greater control of both legislative and mass parties by the cabinet (prime minister) and shadow cabinet (opposition leader) than the presidential system does of the legislative and mass parties by president (or titular out-party leader) or governor. The combination of such elements as separation of powers, fixed and/or staggered terms, the long ballot, bicameralism, and federalism must be important, severally and together, for the comparative lack of control by American political executives of the party organizations. Some of these institutional elements have been combined by Schlesinger (1965B) into "a general index of the governors' formal powers," and one ready-to-hand test of these elements in their relation to party organization could be done by comparing the Schlesinger ranking with the states ranked by governors' control over party organization. This is not, of course, as simple as the statement implies, because we do not have enough facts about party organization to construct a ranking index of governors' control over party organization.

Such an index could be constructed. Among its components might be the governors' success in: (1) placing their
agents in top party leadership posts such as state chairmen
and party fund raisers; (2) influencing the nominations of
party candidates (a component that might have several quanti-
fied sub-parts such as control of convention delegates, intervention in primaries, etc.); (3) maintaining the loyalty of important local party officers (county and/or city chairmen in most
states); and (4) being able to influence his party's legislative
leaders. Other elements might be considered for the governors-
party organization index, but once the basic data were gathered
and stored for quick retrieval they could be recombined and
updated almost at will by researchers.[16]

My hunch is, if we had a reliable index of governors' power
in party organization, we would find very little correlation with
the formal gubernatorial powers that Schlesinger deals with.
Governors' powers in party organization, I suspect, are more
closely associated with (a) patronage, (b) ideology, and (c)
presumed voter appeal. In many states patronage is still an
important source of the governor's influence on party; the received wisdom of the political science profession is that patronage, overall, is a declining factor in American politics, but, like
most of the received wisdom, this supposed fact has not been
demonstrated. It may be that given the expanding number of
state and local employees, and the increasing politicization of
the health and welfare sectors of our economy, the trend is
toward more rather than fewer patronage jobs.[17] More research
is needed.

At least as important as patronage are two other factors
that relate political executives to party organization: ideology,
and probable success at the polls. We have already considered
in a general way what ideology may mean for activists in cadre
parties (that they *do* care, and that even in our supposedly
non-ideological party system Democratic and Republican enthusiasts are quite sharply distinguishable), and we have noted

[16] The possibilities for university-based, specialized, inter-connecting
data banks on American (and comparative) politics are only now
being seriously considered despite the long time exhortations of
Harold Lasswell and the early work of V. O. Key and his students.
Our eyes (aspirations) are not yet big enough, in my opinion, because our stomachs (capacities) have grown enormously.

[17] Janda's *Cumulative Index to the American Political Science Review* lists only two articles on patronage in that journal from 1906
through 1963. Since 1963 there have been two more.

that "issues-oriented" and ideologically-motivated amateurs seem to be increasing among party workers. Here we need only add that the liberal-conservative divisions, with variations, may be more important for a governor in his relations with his party than the more easily measured numbers and kinds of jobs he has to distribute among the faithful.

Likewise, a governor's reputation as a winner (or loser)— perhaps more accurately as a prospective winner or loser, since the decisive consideration in politics is almost always the next, rather than the last, election—will be a major element in his power-position in his party. Very seldom will a governor lose so much influence in his party that he will be denied re-nomination, but the doubtful prospects of victory may at times be persuasive enough to accomplish even that display of political ingratitude, as with Massachusetts' Governor Peabody in 1964 and Minnesota's Governor Rolvaag in 1966.

Bibliography

Alexander, Herbert E. (Ed.), *Studies in Money in Politics.* Princeton, N.J.: Citizens' Research Foundation, 1965.

Almond, Gabriel A. and James S. Coleman (Eds.), *The Politics of the Developing Areas.* Princeton, N.J.: Princeton University Press, 1960.

————, and Sidney Verba, *The Civic Culture: Political Attitudes and Democracy in Five Nations.* Princeton, N.J.: Princeton University Press, 1963.

Apter, David, *Ghana in Transition.* New York: Atheneum, 1963.

————, *The Politics of Modernization.* Chicago: The University of Chicago Press, 1965.

Ashford, Douglas E., *Political Change in Morocco.* Princeton, N.J.: Princeton University Press, 1961.

————, *The Elusiveness of Power: The African Single Party State.* Ithaca, N.Y.: Cornell University Center for International Studies, 1965.

Bailey, Stephen K., *The Condition of Our National Political Parties,* Occasional Paper, Fund for the Republic, 1959.

Barber, James D., "Leadership Strategies for Legislative Party Cohesion." *Journal of Politics,* XXVIII (May 1966), 347–367.

Beer, Samuel, *British Politics in the Collectivist Age.* New York: Alfred A. Knopf, 1965.

Bone, Hugh A., "An Introduction to the Senate Policy Committees." *American Political Science Review,* L (June 1956), 339–359.

Bowman, Lewis and G. R. Boynton, "Activities and Role Definitions of Grassroots Party Officials." *Journal of Politics,* XXVIII (February 1966), 121–143.

Brown, Bernard E., "Interest Groups and Parties in Comparative Analysis," in Crotty, William J., Donald M. Freeman, and Douglas S. Gatlin (Eds.), *Political Parties and Political Behavior* (Boston: Allyn and Bacon, 1966), 546–560.

Burns, James M., *The Deadlock of Democracy.* Englewood Cliffs, N.J.: Prentice-Hall, Inc., 1963.

Calkins, Fay, *The CIO and the Democratic Party.* Chicago: The University of Chicago Press, 1952.

Campbell, Angus, Philip E. Converse, Warren E. Miller, and Donald E. Stokes, *The American Voter.* New York: John Wiley & Sons, 1960.

———, *Elections and the Political Order.* New York: John Wiley & Sons, 1960.

———, Gurin, Gerald, and Warren E. Miller, *The Voter Decides.* Evanston, Ill.: Row Peterson & Co., 1954.

Carney, Francis, *The Rise of the Democratic Clubs in California.* Eagleton Institute Case Studies in Politics, New York: McGraw-Hill, 1958.

Carter, Gwendolen M. (Ed.), *African One-Party Systems.* Ithaca: Cornell University Press, 1962.

Chalmers, Douglas A., *The Social Democratic Party of Germany: From Working Class Movement to Modern Political Party.* New Haven: Yale University Press, 1964.

Clark, Peter and James Q. Wilson, "Incentive Systems: A Theory of Organizations," *Administrative Science Quarterly,* VI (June 1961), 129–166.

Clausen, Aaage R. and Warren E. Miller, "Electoral Myth and Reality: The 1964 Election," *American Political Science Review,* LIX (June, 1965), 321–336.

Coleman, James S., *Nigeria: Background to Nationalism.* Berkeley: University of California Press, 1958.

———, and Carl G. Rosberg (Eds.), *Political Parties and National Integration in Tropical Africa.* Berkeley: University of California Press.

Converse, Philip E., "Information Flow and the Stability of Partisan Attitudes," *Public Opinion Quarterly,* XXVI (Winter 1962), 578–599.

———, "The Problem of Party Distances in Models of Voting Change," in Jennings, M. Kent, and L. Harmon Zeigler

(Eds.), *The Electoral Process*. (Englewood Cliffs, N.J.: Prentice-Hall, Inc., 1966), 175–207.

Cotter, Cornelius P., and Bernard C. Hennessy, *Politics Without Power: The National Party Committees*. New York: Atherton Press, 1964.

Crotty, William J., "Attributes of Party Organization." Mimeo.: Prepared for the National Center in Education's Teachers' Seminar, 1963.

————, "The Social Attributes of Party Organizational Activists in a Transitional Political System," *Western Political Quarterly*, XX (September, 1967).

————, "The Utilization of Mail Questionnaires and the Problem of a Representative Return Rate," *Western Political Quarterly*, XIX (March 1966), 44–53.

Cutright, Phillips, "Activities of Precinct Committeemen in Partisan and Nonpartisan Communities," *Western Political Quarterly*, XVII (March 1964), 93–108.

————, "Nonpartisan Electoral Systems in American Cities," *Comparative Studies in Society and History*, V (January 1963), 212–226.

————, "Measuring the Impact of Local Party Activity on the General Election Vote," *Public Opinion Quarterly*, XXVII (Fall 1963), 372–386.

Davies, James C., *Human Nature in Politics: The Dynamics of Political Behavior*. New York: John Wiley and Sons, Inc., 1963.

Dawson, Richard E., and James A. Robinson, "The Politics of Welfare," in Jacob, Herbert, and Kenneth N. Vines, *Politics in the American States*. (Boston: Little, Brown & Co., 1965), 371–410.

Downs, Anthony, *An Economic Theory of Democracy*. New York: Harper and Brothers, 1957.

Dye, Thomas R., "State Legislative Politics," in Jacob, Herbert, and Kenneth N. Vines, *Politics in the American States*. (Boston: Little, Brown & Co., 1965), 151–206.

Eldersveld, Samuel J., *Political Parties: A Behavioral Analysis*. Chicago: Rand McNally & Co., 1964.

Englemann, Frederick, "A Critique of Recent Writings on Political Parties," in Eckstein, Harry, and David Apter (Eds.), *Comparative Politics*. (New York: The Free Press of Glencoe, 1963).

Epstein, Leon D., "A Comparative Study of Canadian Parties," *American Political Science Review*, LVII (March 1964), 46–59.

————, "British Mass Parties in Comparison with American Parties," *Political Science Quarterly*, LXXI (March 1956), 97–125.

————, "Cohesion of British Parliamentary Parties," *American Political Science Review*, L (June 1956), 360–377.

————, *Politics in Wisconsin*. Madison, Wisconsin: University of Wisconsin Press, 1958.

Flinn, Thomas A., and Frederick W. Wirt, "Local Party Leaders: Groups of Like Minded Men," *Midwest Journal of Political Science*, IX (February 1965), 77–98.

Froman, Lewis A., Jr., "Inter-Party Constituency Differences and Congressional Voting Behavior," *American Political Science Review*, LVII (March 1954), 166–173.

————, and Randall B. Ripley, "Conditions for Party Leadership: The Case of the House Democrats," *American Political Science Review*, LIX (March 1965), 52–63.

Frost, Richard T., "Stability and Change in Local Politics," *Public Opinion Quarterly*, XXV (Summer 1961), 221–235.

Gluckman, Max, *Order and Rebellion in Tribal Africa*. New York: The Free Press of Glencoe, 1963.

Golembiewski, Robert, "A Taxonomic Approach to State Political Party Strength," *Western Political Quarterly*, XI (September 1958), 494–513.

Gosnell, Harold F., *Boss Platt and His New York Machine*. Chicago: University of Chicago Press, 1924.

————, *Democracy: The Threshold of Freedom*. New York: The Ronald Press Co., 1948.

————, *Machine Politics: Chicago Model*. Chicago: University of Chicago Press, 1937.

Greenstone, J. David, "Party Pressure on Organized Labor in Three Cities," in Jennings, M. Kent, and L. Harmon Zeigler (Eds.), *The Electoral Process*. (Englewood Cliffs, N.J.: Prentice-Hall, Inc., 1966), 55–80.

Greer, Scott, and Peter Orleans, "Political Sociology," in Robert E. L. Faris (Ed.), *Handbook of Modern Sociology*. (Chicago: Rand McNally & Co., 1964), 808–851.

Grumm, John G., "A Factor Analysis of Legislative Behavior," *Midwest Journal of Political Science*, VII (November 1963), 336–356.

Hanna, William John, "Poltical Recruitment and Participation: Some Suggested Areas for Research," *Psychoanalytic Review*, LII (Winter 1965–66), 67–80.

Hanson, Bertil L., "County Commissioners in Oklahoma," *Midwest Journal of Political Science*, IX (November 1965), 388–400.

Hastings, Philip K., "International Survey Library Association of the Roper Public Opinion Research Center," *Public Opinion Quarterly*, XXVIII (Summer 1964), 331–333.

Heard, Alexander, *The Costs of Politics*. Chapel Hill: University of North Carolina Press, 1960.

Hennessy, Bernard C., "Psycho-Cultural Studies of National Character: Relevances for International Relations," *Background: Journal of the International Studies Association*, VI (Fall 1962), 27–49.

————, "Trade Unions and the British Labour Party," *American Political Science Review*, XLIX (December 1955), 1050–1066.

Hodgkin, Thomas, *African Political Parties: An Introductory Guide*. London: Penguin Books, Ltd., 1961.

Holcombe, Arthur N., *The Political Parties of Today*. New York: Harper and Brothers, 1925.

Holt, Robert T., "A Proposed Structural-Functional Framework for Political Science," in Martindale, Don (Ed.), *Functionalism in the Social Sciences*, American Academy of Political and Social Science Monograph 5, Philadelphia, February 1965.

Huitt, Ralph K., "Democratic Party Leadership in the Senate," *American Political Science Review*, LV (June 1961), 333–344.

Janda, Kenneth, and Wayne Francis, *Indiana University Data Library on State Politics: Descriptive Materials*. Bloomington, Indiana: Bureau of Government Research, Indiana University, mimeographed, 1963.

Jewell, Malcolm E., "Party Voting in American State Legislatures," *American Political Science Review*, XLIX (September 1955), 773–791.

————, "The Senate Republican Policy Committee and Foreign Policy," *Western Political Quarterly*, XII (December 1959), 417–441.

Jones, Charles O., "Inter-Party Competition for Congressional Seats," *Western Political Quarterly*, XVII (September 1964), 461–476.

————, *Party and Policy-Making: The House Republican Policy Committee.* New Brunswick, N.J.: Rutgers University Press, 1965.

Kantor, Harry, *The Ideology and Program of the Peruvian Aprista Movement.* Berkeley, Calif.: The University of California Press, 1953.

Karpat, Kemal H., *Turkey's Politics: The Transition to a Multi-Party System.* Princeton: Princeton University Press, 1959.

Katz, Daniel, and Samuel J. Eldersveld, "The Impact of Local Party Activity upon the Electorate," *Public Opinion Quarterly,* XXV (Spring 1961), 1–24.

Keefe, William J., "A Comparative Study of the Role of Political Parties in State Legislatures," *Western Political Quarterly,* IX (September 1956), 726–742.

Key, V. O., Jr., "The Politically Relevant in Surveys," *Public Opinion Quarterly,* XXIV (Spring 1960), 54–61.

Kilson, Martin L., "Authoritarian and Single-Party Tendencies in African Politics," *World Politics,* XV (January 1963), 262–294.

Klain, Maurice, "A New Look at the Constituencies: The Need for a Recount and a Reappraisal," *American Political Science Review,* XLIX (December 1955), 1105–1119.

Landau, Jacob M., *Parliaments and Parties in Egypt.* New York: Praeger, 1954.

Lane, Robert E., *Political Life: Why People Get Involved in Politics.* New York: The Free Press of Glencoe, 1959.

————, "The Politics of Consensus in an Age of Affluence," *American Political Science Review,* LIX (December 1965), 874–895.

La Palombara, Joseph, and Myron Weiner (Eds.), *Political Parties and Political Development.* Princeton: Princeton University Press, 1966.

Lasswell, Harold A., *Psychopathology and Politics.* Chicago: University of Chicago Press, 1930.

————, *The Future of Political Science.* New York: Atherton Press, 1963.

Lerner, Daniel, *The Passing of Traditional Society.* New York: The Free Press of Glencoe, 1958.

Levin, Murray B., *The Alienated Voter: Politics in Boston.* New York: Holt, Rinehart and Winston, Inc., 1960.

————, *The Compleat Politician: Political Strategy in Massachusetts.* Indianapolis: Bobbs-Merrill, 1962.

Lipset, Seymour Martin, Martin Trow, and James Coleman, *Union Democracy*. Glencoe: The Free Press, 1956.

Litt, Edgar, "Political Cynicism and Political Futility," *Journal of Politics*, XXV (May 1963), 312–323.

――――, *The Political Cultures of Massachusetts*. Cambridge: M.I.T. Press, 1965.

――――, "The Politics of a Cultural Minority," in Jennings, M. Kent, and L. Harmon Zeigler (Eds.), *The Electoral Process*. (Englewood Cliffs, N.J.: Prentice-Hall, Inc., 1966), 105–121.

Lockard, W. Duane, "Legislative Politics in Connecticut," *American Political Science Review*, XLVIII (March 1954), 166–173.

Lowi, Theodore, "Toward Functionalism in Political Science: The Case of Innovation in Party Systems," *American Political Science Review*, LVII (September 1963), 570–583.

Macy, Jesse, *Party Organization and Machinery*. New York: The Century Co., 1904.

Mair, Lucy, *New Nations*. Chicago: University of Chicago Press, 1963.

Martz, John D., "Political Parties in Colombia and Venezuela: Contrasts in Substance and Style," *The Western Political Quarterly*, XVIII (June 1965), 318–333.

――――, "The Place of Latin America in the Study of Comparative Politics," *Journal of Politics*, XXVIII (February 1966), 57–80.

Marvick, Dwaine, and Samuel J. Eldersveld, "National Convention Leadership: 1952 and 1956," *The Western Political Quarterly*, XIV (March 1961), 176–194.

――――, and Charles Nixon, "Recruitment Contrasts in Rival Campaign Groups," in Marvick, Dwaine (Ed.), *Political Decision-Makers*. (New York: The Free Press of Glencoe, 1961), 193–217.

Masters, Nicholas A., "The Politics of Union Endorsement of Candidates in the Detroit Area," *Midwest Journal of Political Science*, I (August 1957), 136–150.

Matthews, Donald R., *U.S. Senators and Their World*. Chapel Hill: University of North Carolina Press, 1960.

――――, and James W. Prothro, "Political Factors and Negro Voter Registration in the South," *American Political Science Review*, LVII (June 1963), 355–367.

――――, "Social and Economic Factors and Negro Voter Registration in the South," *Ibid.*, LVII (March 1963), 24–44.

May, John D., "Democracy, Organization, Michels," *American Political Science Review*, LIX (June 1965), 417–429.

McClelland, David C., *The Achieving Society*. Princeton, N.J.: D. Van Nostrand Co., 1961.

McKean, Dayton D., *The Boss: The Hague Machine in Action*. Boston: Houghton Mifflin Co., 1940.

Michelson, Charles, *The Ghost Talks*. New York: G. P. Putnam's Sons, 1944.

Milbrath, Lester W., *Political Participation: How and Why Do People Get Involved in Politics*. Chicago: Rand McNally & Co., 1965.

Mitau, G. Theodore, *State and Local Government: Politics and Processes*. New York: Charles Scribner's Sons, 1966.

Moore, Clement Henry, "The Neo-Destour Party: A Structure for Democracy?", *World Politics*, XIV (April 1962), 461–482.

Moynihan, Daniel Patrick, and James Q. Wilson, "Patronage in New York State, 1955–1959," *American Political Science Review*, LVIII (June, 1964).

Munger, Frank, and James Blackhurst, "Factionalism in the National Conventions, 1940–1964: An Analysis of Ideological Consistency in State Delegation Voting," *The Journal of Politics*, XXVII (May 1965), 375–394.

Patterson, Samuel C., "Characteristics of Party Leaders," *The Western Political Quarterly*, XVI (June 1963), 332–352.

————, "Dimensions of Voting Behavior in a One-Party State Legislature," *Public Opinion Quarterly*, XXVI (Summer 1962), 185–201.

————, and Althoff, Phillip, "Political Activism in a Rural County," *Midwest Journal of Political Science*, X (February 1966), 39–51.

Polsby, Nelson W., *Community Power and Political Theory*. New Haven: Yale University Press, 1963.

Pomper, Gerald, "New Jersey County Chairmen," *The Western Political Quarterly*, XVIII (March 1965), 186–197.

Pye, Lucian W., *Aspects of Political Development*. Boston: Little, Brown & Co., 1965.

————, "Personal Identity and Political Ideology," in Marvick, Dwaine (Ed.), *Political Decision-Makers*. New York: The Free Press of Glencoe, 1961, 290–313.

————, *Politics, Personality and Nation Building: Burma's Search for Identity.* New Haven: Yale University Press, 1962.

Ranney, Austin, *The Doctrine of Responsible Party Government.* Urbana: The University of Illinois Press, 1962.

————, "Parties in State Politics," in Jacob, Herbert, and Kenneth N. Vines (Eds.), *Politics in the American States.* (Boston: Little, Brown & Co., 1965), 61–99.

————, *Pathways to Parliament: Candidate Selection in Britain.* Madison, Wisconsin: The University of Wisconsin Press, 1965.

Ray, P. Orman, *An Introduction to Political Parties and Practical Politics.* New York: C. Scribner's Sons, 1922.

Redding, Jack, *Inside the Democratic Party.* Indianapolis: Bobbs-Merrill Co., Inc., 1958.

Ripley, Randall B., "The Party Whip Organizations in the United States House of Representatives," *American Political Science Review,* LVIII (September 1964), 561–576.

Rokeach, Milton, *The Open and Closed Mind.* New York: Basic Books, Inc., 1960.

Rokkan, Stein, "The Comparative Study of Political Participation: Notes Toward a Perspective on Current Research," in Ranney, Austin (Ed.), *Essays on the Behavioral Study of Politics.* Urbana, Illinois: University of Illinois Press, 1962.

Rossi, Peter H., and Phillips Cutright, "Grass Roots Politicians and the Vote," *American Sociological Review,* XXIII (April 1958), 171–179.

————, "The Impact of Party Organization in an Industrial Setting," in Morris Janowitz (Ed.), *Community Political Systems* (Glencoe: The Free Press, 1961), 81–116.

————, "Party Organization in Primary Elections," *American Journal of Sociology,* LXIV (November 1958), 262–269.

Rourke, Francis R., "Urbanism and the National Party Organizations," *The Western Political Quarterly,* XVIII (March 1965), 149–163.

Sait, Edward McChesney, *American Parties and Elections.* New York: The Century Co., 1927.

————, *American Parties and Elections.* Revised Edition: New York: D. Appleton-Century Co., 1939.

Scarrow, Howard A., "Distinguishing Between Political Parties —The Case of Canada," *Midwest Journal of Political Science,* IX (February 1965), 61–76.

————, "Nomination and Local Party Organization in Canada: A Case Study," *The Western Political Quarterly*, XVIII (March 1964), 55–62.

Schachter, Ruth, "Political Parties in French West Africa." Unpub. Ph.D. Diss., Oxford University, 1958.

————, "Single Party Systems in West Africa," *American Political Science Review*, LV (June 1961), 294–307.

Schick, Allen, "Massachusetts Politics: Political Reform and 'Alienation'," in Robert R. Robbins (Ed.), *State Government and Public Responsibility 1963*, (Medford, Mass.: Lincoln Filene Center for Citizenship and Public Affairs, Tufts University, 1963), 92–127.

Schlesinger, Joseph A., "Political Party Organization," in James G. March (Ed.), *Handbook of Organizations*. Chicago: Rand McNally & Co., 1965, pp. 764–801.

————, "The Politics of the Executive," in Jacobs, Herbert, and Kenneth N. Vines (Eds.), *Politics in the American States*. Boston: Little, Brown & Co., 1965, pp. 207–237.

Schutz, Charles E., "Bureaucratic Party Organization Through Professional Political Staffing," *Midwest Journal of Political Science*, VIII (May 1964), 127–142.

Seligman, Lester G., *Leadership in a New Nation: Political Development in Israel*. New York: Atherton Press, 1964.

————, "Political Recruitment and Party Structure: A Case Study," *American Political Science Review*, LV (March 1961), 77–86.

Sherif, Carolyn W., Muzafer Sherif, and Roger E. Nebergall, *Attitude and Attitude Change: The Social Judgment-Involvement Approach*. Philadelphia: W. B. Saunders Co., 1965.

Silva, Ruth C., "Compared Values of the Single and the Multi-Member Legislative District," *Western Political Quarterly*, XVII (September 1964), 504–516.

————, "Relation of Representation and the Party System to the Number of Seats Apportioned to a Legislative District," *Western Political Quarterly*, XVII (December 1964), 742–769.

Sorauf, Frank J., "Extra-Legal Political Parties in Wisconsin," *American Political Science Review*, XLVIII (September 1954), 692–704.

————, *Party and Representation: Legislative Politics in Pennsylvania*. New York: Atherton Press, 1963.

————, "Patronage and Party," *Midwest Journal of Political Science,* III (May 1959), 115–126.

————, "State Patronage in a Rural County," *American Political Science Review,* L (December 1956), 1046–1056.

Stokes, Donald E., "Spatial Models of Party Competition," *American Political Science Review,* LVII (June 1963), 368–377.

————, and Warren E. Miller, "Party Government and the Saliency of Congress," *Public Opinion Quarterly,* XXVI (Winter 1962), 531–546.

Tillett, Paul (Ed.), *Inside Politics: The National Conventions, 1960.* Dobbs Ferry, N.Y.: Oceana Publications, Inc., 1962.

Valen, Henry and Daniel Katz, *Political Parties in Norway.* Oslo: Universitetsforlaget, 1964.

Von Vorys, Karl, *Political Development in Pakistan.* Princeton: Princeton University Press, 1965.

Wahlke, John C., Heinz Eulau, William Buchanan, and Leroy C. Ferguson, *The Legislative System.* New York: John Wiley and Sons, 1962.

Wallerstein, Immanuel, "Ethnicity and National Integration in West Africa," *Cahiers d' Etudes Africaines,* I (October 1960), 129–139. Reprinted in Pierre L. Van Den Berghe (Ed.), *Africa: Social Problems of Change and Conflict.* San Francisco: Chandler Publishing Co., 1965.

————, "The Emergence of Two West African Nations." Unpub. Ph.D. Diss., Columbia University, 1959.

Weiner, Myron, *Party Politics in India: The Development of a Multi-Party System.* Princeton, N.J.: Princeton University Press, 1957.

————, "Traditional Role Performance and the Development of Modern Political Parties: The Indian Case," *Journal of Politics,* XXVI (November 1964), 830–849.

White, John P. and John R. Owens, *Parties, Group Interests and Campaign Finance: Michigan '56.* Princeton, N.J.: Citizens' Research Foundation, 1965.

Wilson, James Q., *The Amateur Democrat: Club Politics in Three Cities.* Chicago: The University of Chicago Press, 1962.

————, "The Economy of Patronage," *Journal of Political Economy,* LXIX (August 1961), 369–380.

Zink, Harold, *City Bosses in the United States.* Durham, N.C.: Duke University Press, 1930.

Zolberb, Aristide R., *One Party Government in the Ivory Coast.* Princeton: Princeton University Press, 1964.

TWO

Comparative Politics and the Study of Political Parties: A Structural Approach

Fred W. Riggs

Indiana University

THE DIFFICULTIES which confront students of comparative politics in their attempt to classify and theorize about political parties are nicely illustrated by the following quotation from Coleman and Rosberg's discussion of African political parties:

> Parties that might cluster together on the basis of shared organizational features are found poles apart in terms of their ideology or of their relationship to traditionalism. Others that might fall into a common category in terms of the total monopoly they have established over nonparty associations may be widely separated on such important counts as the degree of mass participation or of involvement in the political process. As in all efforts to classify complex phenomena, one confronts the dilemma that the units to be classified either are ultimately *sui generis* or are not consistently and meaningfully distinguishable for analytical purposes.[1]

In a way, the purpose of this essay is to come to grips with the difficulties stated by Coleman and Rosberg. I shall attempt to formulate a mode of classifying and comparing political

[1] James S. Coleman and Carl G. Rosberg, Jr., eds., *Political Parties and National Integration in Tropical Africa* (Berkeley: University of California Press, 1966), pp. 4–5.

parties. The purpose of the proposed scheme, however, is not merely to establish a taxonomy. Rather, the value of this, as of any typology, can be tested by its usefulness in formulating and testing hypotheses. These would concern relationships between parties and their changing characteristics, and correlations, or cause-effect relationships, between parties and other variables. Many such variables would be dealt with in a comprehensive treatment, but here I propose to deal only with the relation between parties and the various types of governmental and political party systems in which they are found.

Types of Political Parties

In accordance with this prescription, let us first ask how can we most usefully classify political parties? Various schemes have been proposed. Sigmund Neumann, for example, suggests the value of distinctions between in-group and out-group parties, between those which stress patronage and expediency and those which insist upon fundamental principles, between parties dominated by personalities and those which are more programmatic. More comprehensively, he distinguishes between parties of "individual representation" and those of "social integration." The latter are subdivided into parties of "democratic integration" and those of "total integration."[2]

But Neumann himself admits the many problems implicit in these criteria, e.g., the difficulty of drawing sharp lines, a tendency for particular parties to shift their orientation over time. He seems to be more impressed with the distinction between one-, two-, and multiparty systems. But this is not a classification of parties as such. Rather, it seeks to distinguish between several major contexts of political parties, and then hypothesizes correspondences, for example, between parties of total integration and multiparty systems, and between parties of individual representation and two-party systems. However crudely, such correspondences suggest a type of hypothesis relating party types to system types for which we should be searching.

[2] Sigmund Neumann, ed., *Modern Political Parties: Approaches to Comparative Politics*. (Chicago: University of Chicago Press, 1956), pp. 400–405.

Neumann's approach stresses the goals sought or the social posture of political parties as a basic criterion for classification. By contrast, Duverger, in discriminating between cadre and mass parties and direct and indirect parties, points to the basis of membership as a distinguishing factor.[3] Essentially, his mass parties have enrolled membership rosters and his cadre parties do not. Mass parties, by Duverger's definition, always have direct membership. Indirect parties, consisting of electoral committees chosen by constituent organizations, resemble cadre parties formally, yet may have the popular base of mass parties.

Duverger also pays considerable attention to distinctions in the character of the basic elements of political parties. These he identifies as caucus, branch, cell, and militia. The caucus consists of ad hoc electoral committees of notables, the branch of local membership chapters, the cell of occupationally oriented membership groups, and the militia of armed units of party activists.[4] Duverger points to correspondences in the sense that the caucus is most characteristic of cadre parties, and the other components, of mass parties. He does not attempt to classify parties by their basic elements, although he does distinguish among them in terms of their strength of "articulation," i.e., the degree to which the components are firmly linked through a formal organization and party bureaucracy. And, he classifies parties by the exclusiveness of "vertical links" among components as contrasted with permissiveness for "horizontal links" at the same hierarchic level. He further relates these distinctions to differences in the relative centralization and decentralization of party organization.

Kenneth Janda draws on this typology in the code which he presents in his chapter of this book. It is significant, however, that he transforms Duverger's dichotomies into a set of scales. For example, the cadre-mass distinction becomes a five-point scale for the basis of party affiliation as follows:

1. No formal membership: merely interest and support
2. Formal membership: register as member or sign membership card *only*

[3] Maurice Duverger, *Political Parties: Their Organization and Activity in the Modern State* (London: Methuen & Co., 1954), pp. 5–16, 63–71.

[4] *Ibid.*, pp. 17–40.

3. Formal membership: pay dues but *not* sign membership form

4. Formal membership: sign membership form *and* pay dues

5. Formal membership: sign membership form, pay dues, *and* go through a probationary period or have application reviewed by party officials before membership is granted.[5]

Duverger's categories appear to be more operational, especially if elaborated in a manner similar to Janda's, than those of Neumann. Moreover, certain relationships suggest themselves. Neumann's parties of personal representation overlap Duverger's cadre parties. Neumann's parties of democratic integration are most likely mass parties with branch organization, and his parties of total integration are also mass parties, but with cells and militia units as components. Working along these lines, can we discover a more rigorous basis for classifying and comparing parties?

PROBLEMS OF DEFINITION AND CLASSIFICATION   Arthur Kalleberg makes some useful methodological suggestions in this connection. He warns that we must distinguish sharply between criteria appropriate for classification and those useful in comparison. "Classification," he writes, "is a matter of 'either/or'; comparison is a matter of 'more or less.' "[6] If two items are to be compared, Kalleberg argues that they must be shown to belong to the same class; they must have some common characteristics. Items which belong to the same class may then be contrasted relative to their variation or rank on common dimensions.

Duverger's categories appear useful both for establishing classes of political parties and for comparing individual parties within these classes. Before a meaningful classification of parties can be developed, it is first necessary to establish the criteria by which we can determine whether a given entity is a "political party." In the opening remarks of his essay in this volume, Hennessy observes that political parties have not been clearly

---

[5] Janda, Appendix A. Data on Parties, Column 21. Column 22 gives a similar five-point analysis of Duverger's direct-indirect dichotomy.

[6] Arthur L. Kalleberg, "The Logic of Comparison: A Methodological Note on the Comparative Study of Political Systems," *World Politics*, 19 (October, 1966), p. 81.

defined. He distinguishes them as organizations that put forward candidates for elective office, a function of their concern with the selection and tenure of the personnel of government; that advocate government policies; and that even, in the case of totalitarian parties, advance a "comprehensive belief system . . . a total commitment to a way of life."

Hennessy, no doubt, is not arguing that any political party must meet all these criteria. Certainly American parties do not satisfy the last set. If a definition could include both American and Russian parties as members of a single class, then we might specify a variable, such as degree of commitment to a total world view, on which the Republican and Communist parties might be compared, perhaps as examples of polar extremes. Do the first items in Hennessy's statement meet this condition? Can we assert with confidence that the major American parties seek to influence the policies of government "according to some general principles . . . upon which most of their members agree"? If not, then can this be an element which must be present in every party, by definition?

Hennessy quotes Bryce with approval to the effect that "the chief thing *is* the selection of candidates. . . ." Is there any political party for which this statement would not be true? Is there any non-party organization which also selects candidates for election?

Judging by the following, Coleman and Rosberg would answer "yes" to these questions:

> Political parties are associations formally organized with the explicit and declared purpose of acquiring and/or maintaining legal control, either singly or in coalition or electoral competition with other similar associations, over the personnel and the policy of the government of an actual or prospective sovereign state.[7]

Coleman and Rosberg go on to comment that "the definition of a party in terms of electoral competition, and the notion of a 'one-party system,' create a host of conceptual problems." Since the word party suggests, "by definition" a "part," they find it difficult to accept the "one-party system" concept. They prefer to define a party by its goals rather than its relation to

[7] Coleman and Rosberg, *op. cit.*, p. 2.

an electoral procedure. Yet they go on to point out that, with few exceptions, "African political parties initially emerged through electoral competition."[8]

Perhaps the difficulty with Hennessy's statement is the specification that candidate selection is "the chief thing." Close examination of the various criteria offered in most definitions of political parties shows that they contain functional elements: they refer to consequences of party activity for the political system, and they impute purposes to party organizations. By contrast, the criterion "nominating candidates" is structural, not functional. It specifies a pattern of activity engaged in by a party without suggesting motives or consequences. Nominated candidates may or may not be elected. If elected, they may or may not shape policies in accordance with party principles. Also, a variety of reasons may lead parties to nominate candidates.

In other words, we have discovered one structural criterion among the mass of functional criteria often found in descriptions of political parties. Let me now add to Kalleberg's statement by saying that criteria should be structural, not functional. Progress has been made in the natural sciences by making *structural criteria the basis for classification, and then by using functional variables in hypotheses*. Chemical elements are defined by atomic structure, biological species by anatomical structure, linguistic forms by morphological and syntactic structure. Social structures, similarly, ought to be defined in terms of concrete structures of action, not in terms of functions.

The contemporary development of comparative politics has served a great purpose by making us more explicitly aware of the importance and variety of political functions. Still, it has rendered a great disservice by confusing the basis of classification through the use of functional criteria. The result has been a proliferation of tautologies. An item is defined by its functions and then used in propositions which assert functional correspondence. Only when items are defined by their concrete structures can hypotheses be confidently made about their functions. Conversely, meaningful statements about how functions are performed in any social system require that the units of action be structurally defined.

Any of a wide variety of structural characteristics could

[8] *Ibid.*, p. 3.

be used to distinguish parties. There is a problem of inclusiveness here. If one desired to consider only competitive parties in developed polities, the definition would exclude the Communist party in the Soviet Union and the "Democratic Party" of Thailand. For my part, I would like to include those organizations, but omit interest groups, categoric groups, parliamentary cliques and revolutionary movements that do not nominate candidates for election. The category, *"any organization which nominates candidates for election to a legislature,"* meets these needs. I find it coextensive with what I have in mind when I talk about political parties. It strikes me as a good definition, and it is the one I propose to use in this paper.

Undoubtedly this definition does not specify many things which are generally true of parties. But I prefer to deal with these characteristics as variables by which to compare them, not as defining criteria. Parties differ in the emphasis they put on electing their nominees. Some are more interested in other objectives. Some parties offer candidates for positions other than seats in legislatures, and some do not. All parties, however, must nominate candidates for legislative seats, by my definition, or they are not parties. This definition may not identify the most important characteristic of parties—it does not pretend to do so. It only specifies a way of deciding what to include and what to exclude from the category under consideration. In this case, I believe that virtually all the organizations most people think of when they speak of political parties are covered by this definition, and virtually all organizations they would think of as not being parties are excluded.

For particular purposes, one may wish to deal only with some sub-class of political parties. Those who are not interested in totalitarian parties, for example, can specify that they will deal with parties only if the candidates they 'nominate for election to legislatures have to meet competition from other parties. Kenneth Janda explicitly states that he will deal only with political parties whose elected representatives constitute at least five per cent of national legislatures. This reduces the number to manageable proportions, but it represents a sub-class of parties, not the whole. Nor, it should be pointed out, can this sub-class be regarded as a "sample" of the universe of parties. When Coleman and Rosberg write about political parties in Tropical Africa, they also select a sub-class to examine. Many political scientists deal only with American parties, a small subclass of the general category. I have no objection to such selections. But if one generalizes about all "political parties" in terms of the characteristics of any sub-class, it is misleading, both in terms of my definition and in terms of the conceptions most people have about this category of social organizations.

DIFFICULTIES IN FAMILIAR SCHEMES   How should we classify political parties into a variety of subtypes? Such terms as African, American, or European merely specify where parties are to be found, not their structural characteristics. It may be, of course, that all African parties or all European parties will be found, on examination, to have the same structural features. This has to be demonstrated, it cannot be taken for granted. There may be historical or cultural reasons why one is interested in the parties found in one continent or country but this has nothing to do, intrinsically, with party structure.[9] A particular type of party, or party system, may be found in a particular area, but the analytic problem is to identify the characteristics of the systems, not to assume that they possess common characteristics because of their geographic location.

Nor should parties be classified by the types of party system in which they are found. The correlation between party and system types is probably much greater though than the correlation between party types and their geographical habitat. Party systems as a framework for describing political parties are illustrated in a sophisticated essay by LaPalombara and Weiner.[10] They classify political parties under three system headings: nonparty, competitive, and noncompetitive. For the one-, two- and multiparty systems of Neumann, they substitute the 0, 1 and 1-plus party systems. There is irony in this. It would seem that an 0-party system has no parties and therefore adds little to our survey. Some new and some older states, many under military rule, suppress parties, forcing many to go "under-

---

[9] As an example, an extremely perceptive essay by Giovanni Sartori is entitled "European Political Parties: The Case of Polarized Pluralism." It is no criticism of the article to say that a more accurate title would have been "Polarized Pluralism in Competitive Parliamentary Polities to Be Found in Europe." In Joseph LaPalombara and Myron Weiner, eds., *Political Parties and Political Development* (Princeton, N.J.: Princeton University Press, 1966), pp. 137–176.

[10] Joseph LaPalombara and Myron Weiner, "The Origin and Development of Political Parties," in LaPalombara and Weiner, eds., *ibid.*, pp. 3–42.

ground." Or, such states tolerate parties as a means for mobilizing popular support for a dictator. Insofar as these organizations do in fact nominate candidates for a legislature, they would meet my criterion of political parties. Paradoxically, then, parties may exist in nonparty systems. The nonparty setting, however, reveals no more about the structure of these parties than the label "European" or "American" does about those parties.

Under the heading of noncompetitive systems, LaPalombara and Weiner list three types of political parties: one-party authoritarian, one-party pluralistic, and one-party totalitarian. The characteristics ascribed to these dominant parties (under the adjectives, authoritarian, pluralistic, and totalitarian) refer to functional relationships between the parties and their political systems. They do not specifically identify any concrete structural characteristics by which these parties could be distinguished from each other, nor from parties in competitive systems. For example, authoritarian parties are described as monolithic and ideologically oriented, pluralistic parties as pragmatic and absorptive rather than destructive of other groups, and totalitarian parties as monolithic. Pluralistic parties tolerate other groups. Totalitarian and authoritarian parties are more inclusive in their demands. Essentially, these criteria indicate what these parties seek to accomplish in their polities, but they do not provide structural criteria for distinguishing among the parties. Structural differences may be present, but they are not identified.

LaPalombara and Weiner's more complex treatment of competitive systems is also designed to reduce the variety of systems implicit in the traditional two-party and multiparty system categories. Two dimensions of variation are postulated: *turnover-hegemonic* and *ideological-pragmatic*. The first variable refers to the relative dominance of one party in a polity, and the latter the emphasis it puts on formulating and promoting ideological goals. By combining these variables in a four-cell matrix, LaPalombara and Weiner give us the following categories: hegemonic-ideological, hegemonic-pragmatic, turnover-ideological, and turnover-pragmatic.[11] Again, these cate-

---

[11] The classification advanced by LaPalombara and Weiner is, in their words, ". . . based in part on internal characteristics of the parties and in part on the way political power is held." A hegemonic system is defined as "one in which over an extended period of time

gories tell us something about the political systems in which
parties are found, and their functions (or would-be functions)
in these systems, but they do not tell us what structural differentiations to observe in studying parties.

A comparable four-type classification is offered by Apter.[12]
He suggests that political groups—a category which includes
parties—should be classified in terms of their staffing as *bureaucratic* or *personal,* and in terms of duration as *durable* and
fragile. The cross-classification of these dimensions creates four
categories for analysis: bureaucratic-durable, bureaucratic-
fragile, personal-durable, and personal-fragile. To an extent,
the concepts of durable match that of hegemonic and fragile
that of turnover. Similarly, bureaucratic parties tend to be
ideological and personal parties pragmatic. Thus Apter's classification roughly matches the more recent LaPalombara-Weiner
scheme. However, Apter's suggestion has the merit of including
a structural criterion, namely whether or not a political party
employs career officials. The duration of parties, however, would
seem to be a measure of relative success in winning elections
over a period of time rather than a structural trait. The Apter
criteria only slightly advance structural classification.

Strangely enough, Apter himself appears to abandon even
this modest approach toward a structural criterion for party
classification. In his later book, *The Politics of Modernization,*
the criteria are not mentioned. They are replaced by a broad
distinction between parties of representation and solidarity.[13]
The former is pragmatic in approach and permissive of competition. The latter is more ideological and repressive of opposition. Admittedly, this classification is designed for use in Africa
and other "developing" areas, but the underlying categories are
more universal in scope. Apter finds that these party types are

---

the same party, or coalitions dominated by the same party, hold
governmental power." In contrast, a turnover system is one in which,
although there may be hegemonic cycles, the prevailing pattern is a
"relatively frequent change in the party that governs or in the party
that dominates a coalition."

A fuller explanation of these terms and their cross-classifications,
as well as examples of their use, can be found in *ibid.,* pp. 35–37.

[12] David Apter, "A Comparative Method for the Study of Politics,"
The American Journal of Sociology, 64 (November, 1958), pp. 227–
228.

[13] David Apter, *The Politics of Modernization* (Chicago: University
of Chicago Press, 1965), pp. 206–212.

characteristic of two corresponding forms of political system, reconciliation and mobilization. All polities can be ranged on developmental scales by employing these dimensions. Modernizing autocracies, military oligarchies and neomercantilist societies form an intermediate residual category. Interestingly, the residual category corresponds to LaPalombara-Weiner's non-party system, the reconciliation and mobilization systems to their competitive and noncompetitive party systems.

Apter offers some interesting hypotheses about structural characteristics to be found in parties of representation and solidarity. These do not represent defining characteristics however. In other words, after having created his categories by classifying political systems functionally, he then looks for distinctive structural characteristics of each of the two major party types. A more fruitful approach would be to identify the salient structural features of political parties and then relate these to the political system.

An essentially structural approach to party classification is found in the coding categories presented by Kenneth Janda in his essay in this volume. Undoubtedly, many of the categories used are structural. Possibly through factor analysis of the variables one could discover patterns of correlation in the empirical data. I suspect a logical difficulty in this procedure however. First, the usefulness of classification criteria is not dependent on the statistical frequency of occurrence. Even one case of a particular pattern is enough to establish it. The table of elements in chemistry illustrates the point. On a statistical basis one might neglect the rare elements, building a classification on the basis of those most common to all. The logical sequence of atomic structures, however, suggested the presence of hitherto unsuspected elements. A useful classification of party structures could indicate patterns, previously unrecognized, that could be profitably explored. Indeed, while the criteria used in Janda's scheme are based on familiar distinctions, a final category, "other," is frequently left to catch the unknowns. Data bearing on key distinctions among parties conceivably could be submerged in this catch-all final category. It would appear more worthwhile to start by reflecting on the logical distinctions in party structure, suggested by previous observations, and from these to generate new, and potentially more useful, categories.

PARTIES DEFINED STRUCTURALLY   I suggest we begin to identify promising criteria for a concrete structural classification of political parties with the definition of parties as organizations that nominate candidates for election to legislatures. Key structural variables can be inferred from the main terms in this definition. For example, if candidates are nominated, then we may infer that some procedures are regularly followed to make the nominations, and that some individuals take part in these procedures. Who nominates? By what means? Variations in these processes and in the identity of the nominators can be used to establish a typology. Again, if parties are organizations, then this suggests a pattern of membership. Who participates in party activities? In what ways? Parties clearly also require money. How are their funds obtained? The answers to these questions shed light on the patterns of activity, i.e., the structures of political parties.

Other questions suggested by the definition lead to related structures. For example, since parties, by definition, nominate candidates for election, it follows that they exist within an electoral system. An electoral system can be defined as a procedure for casting votes to legitimize the selection of candidates for some office. Such procedures involve patterns such as ballots of varying length, districts from which one or more persons may be elected to a legislature, and numerous procedures for counting votes to determine who is elected. The structure of elections has a bearing on the structure of parties. Electoral structures are separate from, although related to, the structure of the parties themselves. Similarly, the definition of political parties implies the existence of legislatures. We could therefore raise questions about the various types of legislatures and how they, in turn, are related to party structures.

Further questions about political parties arise when we consider what the definition does not specify. It indicates only one thing all parties do. We can therefore ask what else parties may do. Do they, for example, nominate candidates for election to other offices than seats in legislatures? No doubt some do. This represents another way of classifying parties. Do parties engage in other activities besides nominating candidates for office? Some parties run schools, operate hospitals, promote insurance schemes, and conduct businesses, others do not. Do the parties provide public offices for members by means other than election, e.g., through a patronage or "spoils" system? Do the parties maintain close relationships with such nongovernmental organizations as labor unions, churches, farmers associations, secret societies, tribes and caste associations? Do the parties employ a career staff to conduct their activities? Do they rely on voluntary workers? Many questions come to mind, but these are sufficient to indicate the wide range of possible structural variations in political parties. It is useless to specify in a definition the list of things which parties may do. Indeed, if all such variables are included, then no organization could meet the terms of the definition. Rather, a minimal definition is required. The definition should specify variables common to every organization we want to classify as a party: Those variables, when taken together, should distinguish parties from other types of organizations.

Many criteria found in discussions of political parties relate to the consequences of party activity for the political system. Their success in electing candidates, in finding public offices for their members by other means, in shaping government policies, or in transforming their societies are examples. Questions concerning the pragmatic or ideological orientation of parties present difficulties in analysis. Such questions imply at least three levels of analysis, none of which necessarily correlate. Functionally speaking, the comprehensiveness of the party's impact on the state could serve as a guide. If the scope of its impact is narrow, then the party may be classified as "pragmatic," if broad, "ideological." The impact of the Republican party on American governmental policies, and of the Communist party on Russian policies, can be taken as examples of these polar extremes.

Statements about party orientation often imply judgments about the "goals" or "objectives" of parties. The party is pragmatic if it seeks only the election of its candidates, ideological if it wants sweeping governmental and social transformations. Such statements tend to be reifications since they impute motivations to collectivities. It is safer to attribute motives only to individuals. These are difficult enough to uncover. More operationally, statements about party orientations may be revealed through the kinds of pronouncements issued, e.g., platforms, manifestos, campaign speeches, declarations of party committees, etc. A content analysis of these could be made. The documents could be coded for ideological and pragmatic themes, as well as internal consistency, persistence over time, degree of affect or violence, and other such variables. Many question the significance of such statements. These can be poor indicators of a party's intentions. Also, their relationship to party victories can be indirect at best. Consequently, I propose to employ the

distinction between pragmatic and ideological orientations only
in the functional sense, that is, in terms of the consequences for
a political system of the exercise of power by a political party.
This variable will not be used in a structural classification. It
may be quite relevant in hypotheses about the functions performed by parties, a topic we return to later in this chapter.

PARTIES CLASSIFIED BY INPUT STRUCTURES   Two sets of criteria, inputs and nominations, will be used in constructing a
provisional classification of parties based on structural criteria.
No doubt additional variables could be incorporated, but these
yield a scheme which may prove more complex than needed. In
devising this scheme, and as required by Kalleberg's criteria for
classification, a set of binary categories of the either/or type
will be used. Hypothetical cells are created which may or may
not be filled by actual parties. The categories are not based on
an effort to characterize this or that particular political party.
There are no basic assumptions that the American, British,
German, French, Indian or Thai parties illustrate a variety of
types. Nonetheless, the value of the typology is tested by our
ability to classify particular parties according to the resultant
scheme. Moreover, the scheme will seem unsatisfactory if
parties which we think of as very dissimilar appear in the same
cell. Surprises may occur. Systems which are thought to be
quite different may turn out, on further analysis, to have important similarities.

   Taking inputs—membership and revenues—as the key ingredients, let us consider the following possibilities.

   1. *A party may or may not be membership oriented.* This
is the familiar distinction which Duverger makes between cadre
and mass parties. But how shall we operationalize the distinction? Various membership tests are used, such as having a
card, signing a declaration form, paying dues, and being admitted by some ceremony or test. We need a single criterion to
meet the Kalleberg test. Let us take dues payment. A party
could have a small coterie of dues-paying members, hardly
enough for us to argue that it was membership oriented. To add
a quantitative dimension to the test, therefore, let us calculate
the value of all dues paid in relation to the total party income
from nongovernmental sources. Any party which collects more
revenue from membership dues than it does from other nongovernmental sources can be classified as "membership
oriented."

2. *A party may or may not be privately financed.* Just as it needs members or supporters, so it needs money. Political parties are normally thought of as "private organizations" which seek to mobilize political support for candidates and positions. In some countries, however, political parties are officially sponsored by the government, their revenues derived from the public purse. Whether or not party income is obtained from the government therefore is a critical variable. Parties can be classified according to whether or not most of their income, let us say 80 per cent, comes from nongovernmental sources.

3. *A party may or may not be dues oriented.* If more than half of a party's income is derived from dues paid by regular and affiliated members, then a party is dues oriented. A party is not membership oriented if a large part of the income from dues is paid by affiliated rather than regular members. Individuals who belong to some other organization, such as a trade union, political club, or farmers' association, and part of whose dues to these organizations is paid to a political party, may be classified as affiliated members. This variable enables us to establish a systematic criterion for Duverger's "indirect parties."

4. *Parties which are membership oriented may or may not be affiliation oriented.* If anyone who wishes to affiliate may become a member by declaration of loyalty and payment of dues, then a party can be considered affiliation oriented. If other tests or hurdles are placed in the way of the prospective member, then the party is not affiliation oriented. This test enables us to distinguish between ruling parties which seek to keep their membership selective and competitive parties which desire to maximize their rolls.

5. *Membership oriented parties may or may not be victory dependent.* If a party which is affiliation oriented seeks to attract and hold party workers or activists primarily because of their interest in the candidates and platforms of the party, including the prospect of holding office, rather than because of broad ideologcal concerns and/or social and financial perquisites of party membership, then the party is *victory dependent*.

These five criteria may be combined to produce six different party types. If every possible combination of variables were developed, a five-dimensional matrix with 2^5, or 32, cells would result. Such a complex scheme would be difficult to manage. Fortunately, it is possible to simplify the typology by eliminating many of the cells. If for one of the alternatives on a given criterion, only one alternative on a second criterion is possible, then the hypothetical cell for the other choice on the second criterion can be eliminated. For example, if we represent the first alternative as 1a and 1b, and the second as 2a and 2b, but show that if 1a exists, then 2b is not possible, we then arrive at three instead of four possibilities, i.e., 1a–2a, 1b–2a, and 1b–2b, dropping 1a–2b. This procedure produces the following results with reference to the party input criteria.

A party which is government financed does not need income from dues, so it will not be dues oriented. If a party is privately financed but does not depend on dues, then it will not be membership oriented as defined above. If a party is dues oriented, but does not depend on membership dues (because it receives most of its income from affiliated members), then it will not be affiilation oriented, since it does not require more members to provide its income. A party which is membership oriented but not affiliation oriented will not be victory dependent, since it must have enough members to satisfy its needs. If it were victory dependent, it would have an insatiable impulse toward adding members. I shall not add further arguments for the proposition that a party which is not dues oriented is also not membership or affiliation oriented or victory dependent; a party which is not membership oriented is also not affiliation oriented or victory dependent. Such a party may desire victory, but it does not need members to secure this end.

The statements made in the previous paragraph can be summarized as shown in Table 1. Although this looks like a Guttman scale, it is not. No scaling or rank ordering is imputed. This form conveniently records for easy reference the six combinations which result when the vacant cells, specified in the previous paragraph, are taken into account.

These categories are hypothetical and might not have counterparts in real life. Moreover, there are no natural names for the types of political party designated by the letters A to F in Table 1. However, adjectives have been placed under each of the letters to suggest possible characteristics of such parties. The words refer to the combination of characteristics, not to what the dictionary says. For example, in this usage a party of type A, which will be called a *strategic party*, would be so called if it were privately financed, dues and membership oriented, affiliation oriented, and victory dependent. A possible example might be the Conservative party in England.

TABLE 1

POLITICAL PARTIES CLASSIFIED BY INPUT CRITERIA

CRITERIA	A Stra-tegic	B Norma-tive	C En-trenched	D In-direct	E Tacti-cal	F Offi-cial
Privately financed	+	+	+	+	+	−
Dues oriented	+	+	+	+	−	−
Membership oriented	+	+	+	−	−	−
Affiliation oriented	+	+	−	−	−	−
Victory dependent	+	−	−	−	−	−

Similarly a type B, or *normative party,* is one which is privately financed, dues, membership and affiliation oriented, but not victory dependent. A possible example might be a European Socialist or Christian Socialist party. A Communist party in opposition to the government might also fit these criteria. However, a Communist party in control of a government might well meet the criteria for a type C, or *entrenched party,* namely being privately financed, and dues and membership oriented, but not affiliation oriented and victory dependent. If the party's income satisfies the criteria for type F, *official parties,* then a ruling Communist party would be classified under this heading.

The British Labour party is perhaps the most obvious example of an *indirect,* or type D, *party.* It is privately financed and dues oriented, but since most of its income comes from payments made by associated members, it is not membership oriented. It does not, therefore, rely extensively on increasing the number of its direct members, a qualification for affiliation orientation. It is not victory dependent since its activists are motivated by their roles in associated organizations rather than party success at the polls.

The two major parties in America may well satisfy the criteria set forth for a *tactical party,* type E. Since they rely on voluntary contributions rather than membership fees, they are privately financed, but not dues oriented. Therefore also, they are not membership or affiliation oriented. Since they do not depend on dues-paying members, they are not victory dependent. Of course, they require victories to sustain party morale and integrity, but not for memberships in the formal sense. Activists work for the party chiefly during campaign periods. Others are associated with local clubs which work for the party, again during campaigns, but they are not party members in the sense defined for types A to C.

PARTIES CLASSIFIED BY NOMINATOR STRUCTURES   The party typology that results from the structural criteria specified is arbitrary in the sense that only one type of criteria is used. A different kind of criteria would result in a different typology. Let us examine a second set of criteria and compare the results with those secured by the input (membership and financing) criteria. We shall use the procedure employed in nominating candidates for election to the national legislature, again breaking it into a range of five dichotomies, as follows:

1. *A party may or may not be leader oriented.* If the nomination of candidates is determined by its leaders alone, without formal consultation with other party members and supporters, then it will be considered leader oriented. It is not possible here to provide a more operational definition of "leaders." In this volume, Hennessy speaks of the "visible leaders" in American parties. This statement is vague: it includes "persons who are widely known to be in the high councils of the party. . . ." Thomas Watts in his chapter explores in more depth the use of the reputational method for determining the "top influentials" and the "key influentials" at the county level in American party organizations. For Duverger, party leaders are clearly the office holders. He states that "Officially the party leaders are almost always elected by the members . . . ," although, as he observes, in Fascist parties the "subordinate leaders are chosen by the supreme chief of the party."[14] Three criteria appear to be involved: those who hold key official positions in a party, those who work for the party professionally on a salaried basis, and those who are reputed to be party

14 Duverger, *op. cit.,* p. 135.

leaders. No doubt substantial overlapping of those who meet these criteria would occur in any party. It is sufficient for present purposes to leave the conception vague. If we could determine who a party's leaders were, we could then decide whether or not they acted alone in nominating its candidates. Parties which met this criterion are unlikely to meet Duverger's definition of a "cadre party." They would include his "mass parties" in which leadership domination prevailed. Fascist parties meet this criterion and perhaps Communist parties also.

2. *A party may or may not be activist oriented.* Party activists may be fully drawn into the processes of candidate nomination, in addition, of course, to party leaders. Nominating conventions are typically employed as a means of giving activists such a voice. Duverger's "cadre party" is usually activist oriented. The definition of activists is even more elusive than that of leaders. Hennessy discusses the concept as applied to American parties. Duverger uses the term "militant" for a similar concept which can be recognized most easily as the nucleus of party cells and branches in his mass parties. He suggests that the caucus in a cadre party is typically composed of party militants.

3. *A party may or may not be member oriented.* If all members are taken into consideration in nominating candidates, then it is member oriented. (The term "member" is used here instead of "membership" which has already been employed above.) In a mass party having a definite membership roster, it is possible to poll members in the selection of candidates, although there are few parties which do this. A functional equivalent can be identified in limited membership cadre parties that employ the "closed primary," a party referenda in which only regular supporters can vote.

4. *A party may or may not be voter oriented.* If it seeks to consider the views of all potential voters in making its nominations, it is voter oriented. This can be accomplished by the use of "open primaries" in which every voter who wishes to may take part in candidate selection, regular party supporter or not. It could be argued that no mass and few cadre parties are voter oriented in this sense.

5. *A party may or may not be officially oriented.* The foregoing criteria have all assumed that nominations are made by parties without reference to outside organizations and interests. This, of course, is unlikely. To some degree, persons whose primary identifications lie outside the party play a part in mak-

ing nominations. Watts' chapter explicitly inquires into the relation between those whose participation in making nominations stems from their formal roles in the party and those whose participation is informal, an outgrowth of some extra-party role. Since party and nonparty roles are normally held concurrently, it is difficult to evaluate the relative influence of each in the nomination process. There is one kind of informal party role, however, which is critically important in a number of parties; official positions in government. There are *some parties in which nominations are made by public office holders* who may concurrently hold party leadership positions. When this occurs, the party is *officially oriented.* The normal dynamics of nomination and election to public office are inverted in these cases. Instead of the party recruiting candidates who acquire office through election, officials nominate candidates through a party mechanism. These leaders safeguard their control over government while enhancing their legitimacy through voter demonstrations of popular support for hand-picked candidates.

An officially oriented party seems to contradict the common sense conception of a political party, normally thought of in functional as well as structural terms. This can serve to illustrate the confusions which arise from mixing structural and functional criteria in a definition. If the party is seen functionally as a means to achieve power, or as an instrument of "interest aggregation," then although an organization may consider itself a party, it will be omitted from the analysis if it does not perform these functions. Such an organization would be classified as a party in a structural definition based on the criterion of nomination of candidates. Provision should be made for those cases in which the party does not perform the functions usually associated with it.

Consideration should also be given to parties in which nominations are chiefly influenced by persons who are neither formal party leaders nor government officials. Examples might be parties which serve the purposes of other nongovernmental organizations, such as trade unions, churches, trade or industrial organizations, agricultural associations, and tribal or ethnic groups. In these cases, individuals whose chief interest and power rest in these extra-party entities may actually make the nominations, using formal party leaders as puppets. A party which met this criterion would be nonleader oriented and also unofficially oriented. The criterion, "unofficially oriented," is a key variable. Most parties are unofficially oriented. Those which are unofficially, but not leader, oriented may be thought of as puppet or front parties.

A typology can now be constructed using the procedure given above to reduce the number of combinations by eliminating hypothetical possibilities. For example, an officially oriented party can scarcely be oriented toward leaders, activists, members or voters. A front party, which is not leader oriented, cannot be activist, member or voter oriented. The various categories of party leaders, activists, members and supporters, may be thought of as a set of concentric circles, the leaders being in the center, the activists in the next circle, etc. The decision about whom to include in the nominating process involves a decision about where to draw the circle. Wherever the line is drawn, it includes those who are nearer the center and excludes those who are farther from the center. A party which is voter oriented and provides for open primaries allows for leader, activist and member participation in making nominations; they can all vote in the primaries. Similarly, a member oriented party, using a closed primary, would provide for leaders and activists to vote also. If activists are involved in nominations, then so are leaders. The combinations which result from these considerations are depicted in Table 2.

As in the earlier instance, the party typology generated by this scheme can be assigned code letters, e.g., M,N,P,Q,R,S. Alternatively, descriptive words can be used. The first three are relatively easy: *open primary, closed primary,* and *conference,*

TABLE 2

POLITICAL PARTIES CLASSIFIED BY NOMINATORS

NOMINATORS	M Open P.	N Closed P.	P Confer-ence	Q Elite	R Front	S Coopted
Unofficials	+	+	+	+	+	−
Leaders	+	+	+	+	−	−
Activists	+	+	+	−	−	−
Members	+	+	−	−	−	−
Voters	+	−	−	−	−	−

each indicating the means used to secure the participation of voters, members, or activists, respectively. It is more problematical to name the remaining three. *Elite party* can be employed to designate one in which only leaders, who are not officials, make nominating decisions; *front party* for one in which nominations are made by those whose formal party offices, if any, are not the roles on which they base their influence as nominators, and provided that they are also not official roles. If they are official roles, however, then a *coopted party* will be found.

American parties at various times, and in different states, meet the criteria for all three of the first categories. Parenthetically, this raises a point which should be mentioned in passing. The definition of political party which has been used would cover a state party organization in a federal system as well as a national party. However, there are important differences between national and local party systems even in as loosely articulated a political framework as the American. The national system sets boundaries for the behavior of its state and local components. Consequently, in a federalized governmental structure, a one-party state system nested within a national two-party system is different from a one-party system in an independent state. Although, for some purposes, American political parties can be treated as a set of fifty state party systems, it should be realized that this is an analogy with party systems in national states, not a precise equivalent.

A Fascist or Communist party, not in power, might illustrate the pattern of an elite party. Once in power, the pattern could shift to that of a coopted party. If the distinction between party and official roles is maintained, then we may ask whether, for example, leaders in a Communist state hold government office because of their party position, or play a part in the party because of their official posts. If the former is true, then the party would be an elite rather than a coopted party. Of course, the status of the party might change over time. The Communist party in the Soviet Union may have shifted from an elite to a coopted status under Stalin and returned again to an elite status under Khrushchev.

Examples of front parties may occur in countries where a church-dominated religious party, a trade-union-dominated labor party, or an industrialist-dominated conservative party are found.

A SUGGESTED TAXONOMY   Let us now consider the relations that may exist between the two typologies of parties, one defined by input and the other by nominator criteria. In principle, all possible combinations could be developed. For example, strategic parties which were also open or closed primary, elite, front, or coopted parties might occur. More abstractly, combined forms of type A and M, symbolized as AM, type A and N, symbolized as AN, and others (e.g., AP, AQ, AR, and AS) might be found. Similarly, type B parties might appear in combinations BM, BN, BP, BQ, BR, and BS. In practice, however, these types are unlikely, and some can be ruled out by logical considerations.

For example, an official party must be a coopted party. If the government is paying the bills, officials will also choose the candidates. A tactical party might be of type M, N, or P, but probably not Q or R, and definitely not S. If it is assumed that a tactical party is interested in victory, then its electoral prospects are enhanced through increased popular participation in candidate nomination. A tactical party which was also an elite or front party would fare so poorly in elections that its financial supporters would lose interest. Private interests would not pay the costs of a coopted party—unless forced to through official extortion. This situation is marginal. Funds extorted by officials, although they do not enter the public treasury, ought to be regarded as non-private financing. The party concerned then would be an official rather than a tactical party.

In the case of an indirect party, the use of primaries is unlikely. Also, such parties would not be coopted. Most indirect parties would be conference, or possibly elite and front parties. Entrenched parties are probably elite in most instances. They could be coopted, but if officials are making the nominations, private financing, primarily through membership dues, would be unusual. The rulers of an autocracy might compel subjects to join a government party and pay dues, but this would constitute a form of taxation, similar to a poll tax, and therefore could not be regarded as private financing.

Conference and elite patterns of nomination would be most common in strategic and normative parties. Strategic parties would probably be of the conference type, normative parties the elite. The matrix presented in Table 3 visualizes these hypotheses.

Such hypotheses can be tested empirically by data of the sort that Janda proposed to collect in his essay. However,

Fred W. Riggs

TABLE 3

POLITICAL PARTIES BY INPUT CRITERIA AND NOMINATORS

Input:	Stra-tegic	Norma-tive	En-trenched	In-direct	Tacti-cal	Offi-cial
Nominators:						
Open Primary					X	
Closed Primary					X	
Conference	X	X		X	X	
Elite	X	X	X	X		
Front				X		
Coopted						X

modifications in his coding categories would be required to make such a test. He would have to code parties in terms of the criteria set forth for the types stipulated above. Only a part of the information required for such an analysis would be secured by his present code. This illustrates, I think, the relationship between theory and data. A conceptual framework of the sort presented above directs attention to the needed data. To base theorizing on available data is to limit oneself to the conceptual and theoretical premises which guided the original data collection. This is not an argument intended to favor the categories presented. Other criteria might also be employed. For example, Duverger's notions about strong and weak articulation, about centralized and decentralized structure, about vertical and horizontal patterns of organization, possibly could be reduced to structural terms and made the criteria of classification. The character of party bureaucratization, as determined by the extent and distribution of professional staff, might serve as a criterion. One might classify parties in terms of the characteristics of nominees: for example, whether there are residential or ascriptive limitations on eligibility. However, enough has been said to illustrate the approach recommended and further elaboration at this point would be redundant. Let us turn, now, to some problems of theory formation in which this party typology can be used.

Types of Polities

Many kinds of propositions can be formulated in which one variable, whether dependent or independent, would be a type of political party and the other variable(s) conditions thought to influence or be influenced by the party form. Such hypotheses would often relate to functions. Conditions could be specified under which a particular type of party contributes to a political system's interest aggregation, stability or change, economic growth or alterations in the distribution of power, nation building or fragmentation. Present space limitations make it impossible to develop such hypotheses, but they constitute a fascinating possibility for future research.

Here a more restricted, but crucial, type of hypothesis will be explored. There are a set of possible relationships between the characteristics of political parties and characteristics of the political systems in which they are found. These relationships may run either way, party characteristics may influence the system, or the system may shape the parties in it. Normally, they run both ways, in patterns of circular causation. Consequently, I shall hypothesize in terms of mutual association, not in terms of causation.

The concept "political system" has been as much confused as the concept "political party" by the failure to distinguish carefully between structural and functional criteria. For the most part, functional concepts have been used of recent years in the literature on comparative politics. For reasons explained above, a clear set of structural categories is needed to distinguish the various types of political systems, in terms of which hypotheses can then be stated concerning the manner in which they function.

There are many serious analytic problems in discussions concerning political systems. For example, in the references cited above such concepts as one-party, two-party, and multi-party systems are treated as virtually equivalent to the political system. Surely, there are other ingredients in the structure of a political system in addition to parties. Political party systems can be analyzed as components of governmental systems. Other elements would include bureaucracies, executives, courts, armed forces, monarchs, legislatures, and interest groups. These can best be represented in a structural typology of governmental systems. Functionally or analytically speaking, such systems will be considered as having political and administrative aspects. But the rest of this essay shall avoid the confusing phrase "political system." And the word "polity" will be substituted as a synonym for "governmental system." Polities will be thought of as composed of elements, including "political party systems." Among the components of party systems are one or more political parties. In this sense, the party system is an intervening variable between the party and the polity.

SOME FAMILIAR APPROACHES   Let us start by considering the problem of classifying polities. Gabriel Almond, in his latest writings, has set forth a classification consisting of three major categories: primitive, traditional, and modern. The first two, which lack political party systems, can be skipped and our attention directed to the third which, Almond says, is marked by a differentiated political infrastructure. The fundamental criteria applied in this classification are degree of structural differentiation and cultural secularization.[15]

The modern system is subdivided into three sub-types; secularized city-states, mobilized modern systems and premobilized modern systems. The city-states which are not contemporary (Athens is given as an example) and which lacked party systems can be disregarded. Party systems are found in the other two modern types. Almond and Powell subdivide the category of mobilized modern into democratic and authoritarian systems, the main variable being the relative autonomy of political subsystems. The premobilized modern systems, characterized by limited subsystem differentiation, are again subdivided into democratic and authoritarian, judged by the autonomy of their partially differentiated infrastructures.

This framework of analysis is superior to an earlier typology which Almond based on a mixture of geographic, functional, and economic criteria. Resulting divisions were the Anglo-American, Continental European, partially industrialized,

[15] Gabriel A. Almond and G. Bingham Powell, Jr., *Comparative Politics: A Developmental Approach* (Boston: Little, Brown & Co., 1966), p. 217.

and totalitarian systems.[16] The classification is inherently functional in character. Structural differentiation—the first of the two major criteria which Almond and Powell employ—is not a characterization of structures as such. Rather, it is based on the degree of functional specificity of the structures in the polity. The second dimension of variation, the autonomy of subsystems, is essentially a question of the distribution of power within polities, a matter concerning the relation between the components and the whole. The first variable involves the scope of power exercised by the same components. The classification, thus, is based on functional variables, although the units being classified, "political systems," give the impression that the categories are structural. The authors write that their first major type of system is characterized by "intermittent political structures," their second by "differentiated governmental-political structures," and their third by "differentiated political infrastructures" such as political parties, interest groups, and mass communication media.[17] But if the concrete patterns of activity of these "infrastructures" are not specified, then the criteria remain functional—they tell what the components do for the system, not what the characteristics of the components are. As this illustrates, the term "political system" has been adopted for a concept which appears to be a concrete structure, but is in fact handled as an "analytic structure," or an aspect of concrete structure.

A structural approach toward the classification of polities is presented by Banks and Textor, and utilized in Janda's country code (see Appendix A, column 17, of his chapter in this book). This scheme is developed from six component structures: president, republic, parliament, royalty, monarchy, and Communist party. Table 4 illustrates the manner in which they are combined.

Examination of this table reveals many difficulties in the interpretation of the scheme. It is assumed that, where not specified in the title, the other components are not present. Is a non-presidential system monarchic? Yet four systems are neither presidential nor monarchic. Is parliamentary the opposite of republican? Clearly not, for systems which are neither parliamentary nor republican are present, and both are combined in a parliamentary-republican system. If the polity is

---

[16] Gabriel A. Almond, "Comparative Political Systems," *Journal of Politics*, 18 (August, 1956), pp. 391–409. Kalleberg's essay, cited above, contains a careful critique of this classification scheme.

[17] Almond and Powell, *op. cit.*, pp. 215–216.

TABLE 4

STRUCTURES OF POLITIES (BANKS AND TEXTOR, FROM JANDA)

	Pres.	Repub.	Parl.	Royal.	Monarch	C.P.
1. Presidential	+	−	−	−	−	−
2. Presidential- Republican	+	+	−	−	−	−
3. Parliamentary- Republican	−	+	+	−	−	−
4. Pure Parliamentary	−	−	+	−	−	−
5. Parliamentary- Royalist	−	−	+	+	−	−
6. Monarchical- Parliamentary	−	−	+	−	+	−
7. Monarchical	−	−	−	−	+	−
8. Communist	−	−	−	−	−	+
9. Other—explain						

Communist, it presumably has none of the other components. It is scarcely necessary to explore further the curious array of anomalies in this scheme for it surely fails to meet Kalleberg's criteria of classification.

A STRUCTURAL TYPOLOGY—UNBALANCED AND BALANCED POLITIES   Let me present an alternative scheme which is described in more detail elsewhere.[18] Only a brief summary will be given here. Four key components are utilized in this scheme, seemingly the minimum number required for the design of a useful typology. The elements are: executive, bureaucracy, legislature, and party system. Each of these elements may be present or absent in a polity. An *executive* is defined as the chief of a

[18] "The Comparison of Whole Political Systems," (Bloomington, Ind.: CAG Occasional Paper, 1966). This manuscript is to appear in a book on comparative methodology in research design edited by Robert Holt and John Turner and published by the Center for Comparative Political Analysis, University of Minnesota.

polity. Some primitive societies, described by anthropologists as segmental or stateless, lack executives, most polities have them. Whether they are called kings, presidents, prime ministers, leaders, or supremos is not important here. These terms refer to variations in the characteristics of executives which can be independently analyzed, just as the various types of parties and party systems can be dealt with separately.

A *bureaucracy* is defined as a hierarchy of offices responsible to an executive. A *legislature* is defined as an elected national assembly. An assembly is any collegial body which makes decisions by voting. It can reach decisions by other means also, but it is only an assembly if it sometimes votes.* Provisionally, a *party system* includes one or more parties, an electoral system, legislative seats, and a means of voting for the executive. Each of these components may be treated on an either/or basis. A maximum of sixteen possible cells can be created in a matrix that includes all possible combinations. Some of these cells can be eliminated, following the procedure utilized above. For example, every polity with a political party must have a legislature, by definition. Is it possible to have a legislature without a bureaucracy? It is logically possible, but empirically unlikely. At any rate, this case can be disregarded for practical purposes. Table 5 then gives us the following five-fold classification:

All of these types can be found historically. E can be

TABLE 5

A CLASSIFICATION OF POLITIES BY BASIC STRUCTURES

COMPONENTS:	A	B	C	D	E
Executive	+	+	+	+	−
Bureaucracy	+	+	+	−	−
Legislature	+	+	−	−	−
Party System	+	−	−	−	−

* The word, "legislature," unfortunately implies a functional criterion, namely legislating or rule-making. However, I have been unable to find a strictly structural term without using a cumbersome phrase, like "elected national assembly," or coining a new word, such as "ENA," using the acronym of the phrase. To minimize neologisms, let us keep the unsatisfactory word, "legislature," so long as no confusion arises.

illustrated by primitive foodgathering tribes; D by classical city states in virtually all the Aristotelian forms, democratic, oligarchic, and monarchic; C by the governments of traditional civilizations, both feudalistic and bureaucratic in character; and B by pre-modern European states in the early nineteenth century. Virtually all contemporary states have the structural form indicated by type A. Moreover, since it is only in this form that party systems are found, types B, C, D, and E can be eliminated. However, in a comprehensive approach to comparative politics, these would have to be included. If this typology is useful, it will show that what are often spoken of as "traditional," "pre-modern" or "non-Western" political systems include a variety of polities which have a wide range of variation in their structures.

This table also suggests what I believe to be true, namely that party systems are a distinctive and ubiquitous feature of contemporary polities. *Contemporary polities, in a word, are polities with party systems*, a most significant fact for the study of comparative politics. Political behavior in polities which lack party systems can be analyzed only by relying on historical data. The so-called "non-party political systems" discussed by La-Palombara and Weiner are actually contemporary polities of type A. Their distinctive feature is the fact that the executive in these polities is not selected by the party system. They lack powerful parties, but not parties. Non-contemporary polities, which did not have any political parties, might better be called "non-party polities." The LaPalombara-Weiner category might be thought of as weak party polities.

This distinction paves the way for an analysis of structural differences within category A. These include the following:

1. *Polities having political parties may or may not be party oriented*. A party oriented polity is one in which the chief executive is elected by the party system. Weak party polities are type A states which are not party oriented. Their executives are selected by one of the other components, either the bureaucracy or the legislature. I think it is safe to say that the legislature never plays a decisive role in the selection of an executive in any type A polity which is not party oriented. It may play such a role in type B polities. The executive is chosen through the bureaucracy, which means that he is an official, normally, a military officer.

2. *Polities having bureaucracies may or may not be merit oriented*. By merit orientation, it is meant the use of achievement tests rather than ascriptive criteria, e.g., personal identity

or mere party activity, as a means of recruitment to bureaucratic offices. I say "mere party activity" because a polity with a dominant party may insist that officials be members of that party and still have a merit system. It can also impose tests of competence as a condition of appointment. Since incumbents who perform competently are likely to be better qualified than others, we can include as a corollary to achievement oriented recruitment the safeguarding of career tenure in public bureaucracies.

All positions in a merit-oriented bureaucracy need not be under the merit system. To direct the bureaucracy, a party in power may need to appoint a variable number of persons to positions at the top two layers. Merit orientation can be defined more precisely if the cabinet level of departmental or ministry secretaries can be thought of as the first, undersecretaries as the second, and the chiefs of bureaus as the third level of positions. A bureaucracy is merit oriented if most positions on the third level are filled on an achievement and career basis.

These two criteria permit a simple classification of type A polities. A polity which is both party and merit oriented may be called a *balanced polity;* one which is party oriented but not merit oriented a *partisan polity;* and one which is merit oriented but not partisan oriented a *bureaucratic polity.* The fourth possibility, a polity which is neither merit nor party oriented, is not common among type A states. Perhaps such a system could be found in a few of the remaining autocracies ruled by hereditary monarchies. Both partisan and bureaucratic polities will be called unbalanced polities.

Additional criteria help sub-classify each of these forms. Modern states, or what Almond and Powell refer to as "mobilized modern systems," are primarily balanced polities by the definitions given above. This amounts to saying that polities which, structurally speaking, have party systems, executives, and a bureaucracy which are both party oriented and merit oriented, are, functionally speaking, highly differentiated. They may also be found in societies whose political culture, in terms of the Almond-Powell criteria, are secularized. This relationship, however, is a matter of hypothesis not definition. One could examine empirical data to discover whether there are polities meeting the structural specifications which do not fulfill the functional characteristics, and vice versa.

FORMS OF BALANCED POLITIES   A structural classification of balanced polities does not coincide as closely to the democratic-

authoritarian dichotomy. Still, hypotheses can be formulated
to relate structural and functional criteria. Let us first distinguish among balanced polities by the following tests:

    3. *A balanced polity may or may not be parliamentary.* It
is parliamentary if the selection of the executive is legitimized
by action of the legislature. For a polity to be considered parliamentary, its legislature must take a formal vote on every new
executive. Such a legislature may be called a parliament. Any
legislature which is not expected to vote on the selection of a
new executive may be called a congress. This distinction divides
all balanced polities into two sub-categories, parliamentary and
congressional.

    4. *A balanced polity which is parliamentary may or may
not have a majority of its members belonging to a single party.*
If no party commands a majority in the parliament, then an
executive can only be elected by two or more parties voting together. Whenever a parliament requires the support of two or
more parties to choose an executive, a *coalition* is needed. Parliamentary balanced polities may therefore be divided into two
types, the coalitional and non-coalitional.

    5. *The number of seats held by a dominant party in a non-
coalitional parliament clearly can vary from 51 to 100 per cent.*
We would not expect to find a normal bell-shaped curve for the
distribution of frequencies however. Rather, a bi-modal curve
would be expected, with a concentration at one extreme of
parties having, let us say, from 50 to 60 per cent of the seats,
and at the other, extreme cases in which the ruling party has
from 90 to 100 per cent of the seats. For classification purposes,
however, it is probably safe to draw a line at a mid-point, e.g.,
80 per cent. A non-coalition parliamentary polity is a *ruling
party system* if the majority party has more than four-fifths of
the legislative seats. If a non-coalition parliament does not have
a ruling party, it has a *governing party*.

    Table 6 summarizes this classification scheme.
As in earlier cases, the number of types can be reduced by
eliminating empty cells. Any ruling party system is non-coalitional and parliamentary since the legislature votes on the
executive. However, since there is no question of opposition in
the legislature, the legislature itself loses influence and comes
to be regarded as a purely formalistic structure. In practice, a
distinction arises between the president and the party head,
who becomes the effective executive, behind a façade presented
by the elected formal executive. Thus, a ruling party polity is
characterized by the weakness of its parliament and a lack

TABLE 6

A CLASSIFICATION OF BALANCED POLITIES

CRITERIA:	A1 Ruling Party Polity	A2 Governing Party Polity	A3 Coalition Party Polity	A4 Congressional Polity
Parliamentary	+	+	+	−
Non-coalitional	+	+	−	−
Ruling Party	+	−	−	−

of opposition in the party system. In the Almond-Powell classification, there are four sub-types of authoritarian systems: radical totalitarian, conservative totalitarian, conservative authoritarian, and modernizing authoritarian. The Soviet Union, Nazi Germany, Spain and Brazil are examples, respectively, of each category. Only the first case, the radical totalitarian, appears to have the structure of a balanced polity with a ruling party. The governmental structure in the other three authoritarian systems mentioned are probably unbalanced polities by my definition. Perhaps, because of the propensity to assume a correlation between geographic area (Europe) and economic growth levels with political systems, polities have been classified together which, by structural criteria, belong in different categories.[19]

[19] For convenience of reference, I have proposed elsewhere a set of special terms which would simplify discussions of governmental systems and make hypotheses less ambiguous. Since the focus of this essay is on political parties, it does not seem necessary to use these terms here, and I have resorted therefore to the more cumbersome and conventional expedient of using descriptive phrases. However, for any readers· who might be interested, let me merely offer these terms as a footnote:

Tonic—any balanced polity

Anatonic—a balanced polity with a ruling party

Monotonic—a balanced polity, parliamentary, but not with a ruling party (may be subdivided into coalitional and non-coalitional monotonic)

Isotonic—a balanced polity, non-parliamentary, i.e., congressional

Syntonic—a partisan polity

Hypertonic—a bureaucratic polity

For further details, see "The Comparison of Whole Political Systems," *Ibid.,* pp. 44–49.

POLITICAL PARTIES RELATED TO POLITIES   Most of the literature on political parties deals only with parties in balanced
polities. American writers who treat only parties in the United
States are restricted to writing in the context of a congressional
system. Most European writers are primarily concerned with
parties in parliamentary systems, especially those without a
ruling party. Writers on Soviet politics and totalitarian regimes
are mainly occupied with parties in unbalanced polities, usually
without noting the structural differences between these two
categories of governmental system.[20]

Hypotheses can be offered regarding the type of political
party typically found in different kinds of balanced polity. For
example, a ruling party polity will have a party which is classified as entrenched by input and elitist by nomination criteria.
A non-parliamentary (congressional) balanced polity tends to
have tactical parties whose nominating criteria range from
elitist to open primary. A parliamentary governing party polity
is likely to have strategic and indirect parties, a parliamentary
coalitional system normative parties. The conference and elite
modes of nomination probably prevail in parliamentary regimes
that do not have ruling parties. The statement of such propositions does not preclude exceptions. These are thought to be
testable statistical correlations with probable exceptions.

Let us turn now to an examination of the structure of unbalanced polities. If the premises for this chapter turn out to
be valid, then the criteria applied to parties in unbalanced
polities will differ in character from those that prevail in balanced polities. Indeed, much of the confusion in the literature
stems from the failure to make such a distinction. The result
is that concepts like one-party and multiparty system have one
meaning in the context of balanced polities and another in
unbalanced polities.

Consider first the question of a partisan polity. By definition, the executive is selected by the party system and a merit
orientation does not prevail in the bureaucracy. If a merit
orientation is not prevalent, then the administrative capabilities

[20] To illustrate how technical terms can simplify statements, let me
translate the foregoing paragraph as follows: American writers on
political parties are concerned primarily with isotonic polities;
Europeans with monotonic, except for those interested in authori-
tarianism, who deal with both anatonic and syntonic polities. This
sentence is hard to follow because the terms are unfamiliar, but once
the terms have been learned, it is much simpler and perhaps even
clearer than the same ideas expressed in familiar words.

of the bureaucracy are relatively limited. Laws tend to be poorly enforced and a high degree of formalism prevails. Votes taken in the legislature have restricted meaning—their enforcement is not assured. Power is to a large extent exercised outside the formal structures of authority; it gravitates into the hands of a ruling party. The norms which safeguard the ability of opposition parties to function are undermined, or never initially develop. These systems are marked by weak-to-impotent legislatures and a single ruling party. Whether the polity is formally congressional or parliamentary makes little difference in the actual organization of government.

The ruling party may permit opposition parties to organize and present candidates for election. In these cases, it relies on its ability to defeat opponents at the polls, to prorogue unfriendly legislatures, or to coopt elected opposition candidates into the ruling party. Ruling parties in partisan polities can also refuse to permit opposition candidates to run for office in the legislature. The ruling party declares its own monopoly of the right to nominate candidates.

This distinction has been made by others. Partisan polity which denies other parties the right of nominating candidates will be called a "movement regime," employing Robert Tucker's term, but giving it a different definition.[21] By contrast, a partisan polity which permits other parties to nominate candidates will be called a "conciliation regime." LaPalombara-Weiner characterize one-party systems as authoritarian, pluralistic, or totalitarian. To translate in the terminology offered here, one-party authoritarian regimes are movement regimes in partisan polities and one-party pluralistic regimes are conciliation regimes in partisan polities. (One-party totalitarian, of course, is probably the same as a ruling party system of balanced polities.) A similar comparison can be made with Apter's typology. The former type of polity is similar to his "mobilization system," the latter to his "reconciliation system." Coleman and Rosberg, in their analysis of African political parties, call attention also to two tendencies associated with one-party dominance. These they refer to as "revolutionary-centralizing" and "pragmatic-pluralistic," corresponding to our movement and conciliation regimes.

[21] Robert C. Tucker, "Toward a Comparative Politics of Movement Regimes," *American Political Science Review*, 55 (June, 1961), pp. 281–289.

All these terms, however, are rarely defined structurally.
The Coleman-Rosberg treatment is an example. Having presented the terms, they offer a table listing a variety of characteristics relating to ideology, popular participation and organization in these two systems. Under organizational aspects,
they include differences in hierarchism and centralism within
the ruling party, degree of assimilation between party and government, and degree of associational monopoly exercised by
the party in relation to other groups. Many hypotheses, including functional variables, are implicit in such a table. The term
"revolutionary-centralizing," therefore, cannot be taken simply
as a synonym for "movement regime." Rather, a movement
regime, defined as one in which a ruling party denies other
parties the right to nominate candidates, is also characterized,
by hypothesis, by a range of additional structural and functional
traits such as those listed in the Coleman-Rosberg table.[22]

The type of party found in partisan polities is likely to be
entrenched, as classified in terms of input criteria, and the
pattern of nomination elite. Exceptions will be found, but this
should be the dominant correlation. Further distinctions can be
made between different kinds of entrenched-elite parties that
correspond to the two sub-types of partisan polity. Ruth Morgenthau finds that two basic membership types prevail in French
West African parties which she refers to as "mass" and "patron."
The category of patron party is substantially the same as
Duverger's "cadre" party. The chief difference is membership.
Before independence, the patron parties were probably tactical
or indirect parties, after independence they have some of the
characteristics of indirect or entrenched parties. In general, they
associate congeries of political groups having an ethnic orientation with tribal social structures. By contrast, the mass parties
form local branches and cells which rely on categoric groups
that cut across ethnic identifications. A comparable distinction
is made by Apter in his "parties of representation" and "parties
of solidarity." If we adopt these terms, the entrenched-elite
parties characteristic of partisan polities can be subdivided into
two types, depending on whether their local organizations are
oriented toward ascriptive-ethnic or categoric groups. By hypothesis, "parties of representation" are associated with conciliation regimes, "parties of solidarity" with movement regimes.[23]

[22] See Coleman and Rosberg, *op. cit.*, p. 5.
[23] Apter, *Politics of Modernization, op. cit.*, pp. 206–212.

We turn, finally, to the situation in bureaucratic polities. These are the systems which LaPalombara-Weiner refer to as "non-party." As indicated, these systems do have political parties, although, by definition, the executive is not selected by the party system. The government response to parties varies. Usually parties are permitted, even encouraged; intermittently, however, they may be suppressed. Parties serve different functions in these polities from those in balanced, or even partisan, polities. In general, there are two kinds of parties: those which are officially sponsored by the rulers, and those which seek to overthrow the existing system of government. Exceptions do occur. Parties can run candidates for election to legislatures and play an influential role in government. The former American administration in the Philippines and the British rule in a number of dependent territories are examples. Our concern at present, however, is more with typical situations. In new states, and some older states under monarchic rule, official counter-elite, or revolutionary, parties and officially sponsored parties are found. The former have normative-elite or tactical-elite party characteristics, depending on whether they are of the mass or patron type in Morgenthau's classification. The latter are official-coopted parties.

Types of (Constitutive) Party System

Many propositions can be stated directly relating variations of polities and parties. The picture is clearer, however, if the "party system" is introduced as an intervening variable between polity and political party. First, the meaning of "party system" needs clarification. Some scholars contend that there must be two or more parties before one can properly speak of a "party system." There are perhaps two assumptions underlying this unnecessary precondition.

The first is a commitment to democratic values and the conception that political development involves, and possibly is equivalent to, democratization. Polities then which have weak parties, or only one party, must be nondemocratic and underdeveloped, and hence need not be included in an analysis of party systems. No doubt, any scholar has the right to select whatever subject he wants to study. If he is interested only in democratic parties, European parties, African parties, or American parties, that is his privilege. But the right to concentrate on a segment does not convey the right to treat it as a whole. Moreover, a decision to study a phenomenon does not imply approval of it. Our objectives are scholarly, not normative.

A second objection grows out of the definition of "system." It is argued that since a system must have two or more parts, a party system must have two or more parties. However, this is to confuse a system with a category. No doubt there can be no category of items if there is only one item in it. But a system is not a category. Its parts interact and any part of a system may be unique within the system. To illustrate, the circulatory system is a part of the human body and it contains only one heart. The circulatory system may also be regarded as an intervening variable between the body and the heart, exactly as the "party system" intervenes between polity and party.

This analogy suggests a different reason why the objection seems cogent. It is as though anatomists called the circulatory system the "heart system," naming it after its most salient organ. The "party system," as conceived here, includes not only one or more political parties, but also a means of conducting elections, legislative seats, and an executive office. A type of polity which includes an executive, bureaucracy, legislature, and "party system" has been identified. How are these fundamental structures related to each other? The sub-system now under investigation involves voting for an executive. Executives may be chosen in many ways. One possibility would involve one or more political parties, a legislature, a body of constituents, and a mode of voting. A political party is a necessary component in such a system. In short, the "party system" under consideration might be defined as *any system for legitimizing the choice of an executive by voting which includes constituents, a party or parties, and a legislature.* Just as it would be misleading to call a "circulatory system" a "heart system," confusion is bound to occur when this type of political system is called a "party system," even though parties play decisive roles within it. Consequently, I propose to call it a *constitutive system.* "Constitutive system" is a synonym for "party system," allowing us to avoid the latter term wherever ambiguity threatens. A constitutive system, then, includes not only one or more political parties as key elements, but also constituents, voting, legislatures and an executive.

The executive role in constitutive systems may be subdivided into two aspects, formal and effective. Sometimes both roles are combined in a single office, and sometimes they are separated. Executives may also be elected or chosen by other means, notably by inheritance of office. A simple paradigm clarifies the difference between these types of executive role, and shows also the poverty of common sense terminology.

EXECUTIVE ROLES

	SEPARATED		NOT SEPARATED
	FORMAL	EFFECTIVE	
ELECTED	President (presidiary)	Premier	President (presidial)
NOT ELECTED	King	Tyrant	Ruler

The terms defined by this paradigm will be employed in the rest of this chapter. A non-elective executive will be called a ruler if he combines the effective and formal roles, but a king if he exercises only the formal role of head of state, and a tyrant if he commands only the effective role of head of government. This usage corresponds only roughly, but perhaps as well as any other, with the ordinary meaning of these terms.

An elected head of government is unequivocally called a premier, an elected head of state a president. The latter term encompasses both elected heads of state who exercise the role of head of government and those who do not. The word president shall appear, therefore, only when the context indicates which of these meanings is intended. Otherwise the word *presidial* shall be employed in an artificial sense to indicate a president who is also head of government, and *presidiary* in an equally artificial sense to indicate a president who is not the head of government.

A constitutive system is defined in terms of the manner of voting for the office of head of government, either the premier or president. The mode of selecting the head of state affects the structure of a constitutive system, but is not its basic structural characteristic.

A STRUCTURAL TYPOLOGY   Let us now try to classify types of constitutive systems using structural criteria of an either/or character. The number of parties in a constitutive system will be an important variable. Other criteria would include the manner in which executives are selected, a decisive variable in this classification. The number of parties, as well as various functional variables, are basically affected by electoral structural considerations. When Duverger stressed the importance of single-member districts as against multi-member constituencies, he was emphasizing a significant relationship which had long been noticed. The mistake which has frequently been made in this connection, however, is to extend the relevance of the distinction beyond the category of party (or constitutive) systems to which it properly applies.

To demonstrate the other types of constitutive systems, therefore, let us now examine a number of classification criteria.

1. *Constitutive systems may or may not be elective.* A constitutive system is considered elective if the effective executive is elected. The formal executive, of course, may or may not be elected, and may or may not be the same office as the effective executive.

All voting procedures do not result in elections. If the effective executive does in fact gain power through the constitutive system, whether by vote of the constituents, choice of the party, or approval of the legislature, then the system is elective; the procedure of selecting the executive is an "election." Since a constitutive system has been defined in terms of voting for an effective executive, it should be clear that a non-elective constitutive system is one in which voting for the executive involves the ratification of a decision already made, rather than a choice among competitors. Alternative candidates may be considered only by the ruling party's elite, or by the constituents or the legislators.

Functionally speaking, therefore, the effective choice of executives in a non-elective constitutive system can be hypothesized to rest elsewhere, e.g., the inheritance of office by a monarch, the seizure of power by a military dictator, or the appointment of a governor by a colonial regime. Such non-elective executives may be rulers or tyrants. Bureaucratic polities, of course, do not need a constitutive system. They have means of installing rulers without one. For a variety of reasons, rulers may decide to establish a constitutive system, to permit one or more parties, a legislature, and elections. They may then manipulate the procedures for nominating and electing candidates so that the voters are given no effective choice; the ruler merely secures a ratification of his incumbency. This may take the form of voting for a rubber stamp legislature or a pliable "prime minister" who is not an effective executive, a "premier." A ruler may even arrange to be nominated himself as a so-called president and his incumbency of this post ratified.

When a non-elective constitutive system is established, it will contain one or more political parties. These parties may include a party sponsored by the ruler. They may also include oppositional or revolutionary parties.

There is a relationship between what LaPalombara and Weiner call a "non-party system" and the concept of a non-elective constitutive system. A system of this type will have one or more political parties, but functionally speaking, they are not operative. The structural reason for their non-operational characteristics, it is hypothesized, is the non-elective character of the voting processes established in their constitutive system.

Historically, there have been a variety of polities which do not have political parties. Collectively, these polities could properly be called "non-party" systems, a more accurate designation than "traditional" or "feudal." For this reason, it is confusing to refer to contemporary states which have non-elective constitutive (party) systems as "non-party systems."

There are three arenas in which the choice of an executive may occur in elective systems: a constituency, a legislature, and a ruling party. In the latter case, those who vote are the party nominators. The number of party nominators may be a small elite in proportion to the total population, as are legislators. Moreover, just as the legislators are elected by constituents, so party nominators may be elected by a much larger body of party members. To consider the choice of an executive by a ruling party a form of election simplifies the description of constitutive systems and makes it more operational. Consideration of elective constitutive systems in which party nominators elect the executive suggests the second classification criterion.

2. *An elective constitutive system may or may not be competitive.* A constitutive system is considered competitive if the election of the executive occurs outside a ruling party. As a corollary of this definition, voting must be either by constituents or legislators. If only one party makes such nominations, then voting by constituents or legislators would not constitute an election, but a ratification. By definition, the executive would not be elected outside the ruling party. The system might still be elective, however, if the party nominators who elect the

executive are presented with a real choice among competitors. A non-competitive and elective constitutive system, in other words, is a one-party system.

The above definitions stipulate that a competitive system must be elective. They do not require that a competitive system be a two-or-more-party system. It is possible for a competitive system to be one-party, two-party, or more-than-two-party. It will constitute a one-party system if the executive is always the candidate of the same party, although other parties are permitted nominations for the office.

Before examining the varieties of competitive constitutive systems, the kinds of parties that will be found in non-competitive systems and the types of polities that will contain non-competitive systems should be discussed.

In terms of the input and nominator criteria proposed above for classifying political parties, it can be hypothesized that entrenched-elite parties will be found in non-competitive systems. This is not true by definition; it should be tested empirically.

In terms of the criteria for polity types, it can be hypothesized that non-competitive systems can be found in both unbalanced and balanced polities. Among balanced polities, non-competitive constitutive systems will be found in ruling party polities, and among unbalanced polities, non-competitive systems will be found in movement regimes. Two sets of criteria serve to distinguish between balanced and unbalanced polities: the election of the effective executive by a party system and the maintenance of a merit system. If the constitutive system is elective, the first of these criteria is met. Non-competitive elective systems, therefore, satisfy the first of these criteria. But the second criterion is determined by characteristics of the bureaucratic system which lie outside the constitutive system. Consequently, the difference between a non-competitive system in a movement regime and a non-competitive system in a ruling party regime is determined by the functional relationships between the constitutive system and the polity, not by the structure of the constitutive system itself.

It could be argued that a ruling party system could not enforce the merit principle in its bureaucracy because of its insistence on party membership as a criterion of recruitment and promotion. However, if a substantial majority of all potential candidates for appointment are party members, then achievement criteria can still be applied in personnel administration.

Functionally similar criteria of "patriotism" or "loyalty" are often employed in competitive party systems where partisanship is considered an improper criterion for merit system recruitment.[24] There are cases, nevertheless, where the merit principle is not enforced in a polity with a ncn-competitive constitutive system. This leads to the classification of such a polity as unbalanced and to identification of the polity type as that of a movement regime.

Finding non-competitive constitutive systems in two types of polities is not to argue that, structurally, these represent two types of constitutive system. In this regard, LaPalombara-Weiner distinguish between "one-party totalitarian" and "one-party authoritarian" systems. To be more precise, only one type of constitutive (party) system is involved here, but it may be found in two types of polities, i.e., a ruling party and a movement regime. Apter's concept of a "mobilization system" appears to include both the ruling party and movement regime, with emphasis on the latter. His concept of a "party of solidarity" is equivalent to the entrenched-elite type of party which I hypothesize to be the characteristic form of party organization in any non-competitive constitutive system.

Let us now return to a consideration of the varieties of competitive constitutive systems.

3. *Competitive constitutive systems may or may not be reciprocative.* A constitutive system is reciprocative if the executive is not always a member of the same party. This idea is similar to the concept of "turnover" formulated by LaPalombara-Weiner. Their concept of "hegemonic" might be compared also to the idea of a non-reciprocative system. The examples they give, however, i.e., the United States during the New Deal and Fair Deal periods, postwar Japan, and Norway until recently, should, in my judgment, be classified as reciprocative. The critical difference is the time span involved. Ten or even twenty years is too short a period to establish the characteristics of the system definitively. A "generation," perhaps thirty years, presents firmer proof that a competitive elective system is non-reciprocative. If a regime has been operating for less than thirty years, only an informed guess is possible. For example, although it is too early to be definite, it would now appear that only mem-

[24] This leads to the need for a redefinition of the concept of "partisanship" to mean considerations of party membership as a criterion of appointment and action in a bureaucracy.

bers of the Congress party will be elected as executives in India, and hence the system is non-reciprocative. Certainly there have been enough reciprocations in the party label of executives in the United States to classify this as a reciprocative system. In other words, all the turnover and some of the hegemonic systems in the LaPalombara-Weiner classification would be reciprocative systems in my typology. All of the non-reciprocative systems in my classification would be hegemonic in theirs.

Why should any competitive elective system be non-reciprocative? The answer to this question is found in the characteristics of the bureaucratic system, especially the lack of a merit orientation. If a merit system is not institutionalized in the bureaucracy, it is difficult for the government to enforce its laws effectively. Neither the legal rights of opposition parties nor voters will be protected. Abuses in public administration hamper opposition parties in their efforts to organize, nominate, and campaign. Pressure can be exercised at the polls to intimidate voters, miscount ballots, and falsify returns, all designed to block the election of opposition party candidates.

Another possibility should be considered. An excessive or premature establishment of the merit system can also hinder the development of opposition parties. If all positions in the bureaucracy are on a merit basis, with little or no opportunity to name party leaders to key bureaucratic posts at the higher levels or place party activists in less critical routine positions on a "spoils" basis, then the practical incentives for individuals to work with opposition parties are greatly reduced. Only highly motivated persons may be interested in party work, and these individuals may be so extreme in their ideological orientations and so doctrinaire and uncompromising in their attitudes as to block effective coalitions between competing opposition groups. Under these conditions, it can be hypothesized that opposition groups will not coalesce into one or more political parties capable of effectively challenging the dominant party.

If non-reciprocative competitive systems exist because of the lack of a responsible merit system in the state bureaucracy, then, by definition, the politics involved would be unbalanced. I advance the hypothesis, therefore, that non-reciprocative competitive constitutive systems are to be found in unbalanced polities of the conciliation partisan regime type. It will be recalled that a conciliation partisan regime was defined in terms of one-party rule combined with permission for opposition parties to nominate candidates at elections. Such regimes are referred to by Apter as "reconciliation" and by LaPalombara-Weiner as "one-party pluralistic" systems.

The dominant party in such a system is probably, by my input and nominator criteria, an entrenched-elite party. It might also be the indirect-front type. The more the party's basic units are composed of non-ethnic branches and categoric cells, the more likely it is to be an entrenched elite party. The more ethnic they are in character, the more likely it is to be an indirect-front party. Both Morgenthau's mass and patron parties are probably found in such systems as well as Apter's "parties of representation."

The opposition parties in a non-reciprocative system are likely to be normative-elite, depending on membership contributions, services volunteered by party leaders and activists unrelated to tangible rewards, intensity of orientation towards religious or secular ideologies, and determination to overthrow the system of government.

No further sub-categories of non-reciprocative competitive systems need be mentioned. However, note that since such systems have a single dominant party, they may be classified as "one-party." Also, one-party systems include both non-competitive and competitive constitutive systems.

The foregoing discussion is summarized in Table 7.

TABLE 7

BASIC TYPES OF PARTY SYSTEM

	A	B	C	D
	Recipro-cative	Non-Recipro-cative	Non-Competi-tive	Non-Elec-tive
Elective	+	+	+	−
Competitive	+	+	−	−
Reciprocative	+	−	−	−

The analysis has shown why non-elective systems must be non-competitive and non-reciprocative (type D) and why an elective system which is non-competitive must also be non-reciprocative (type C). Also, it has demonstrated why a reciprocative system must be both competitive and elective (type A) and how a non-reciprocative system can be both competitive and elective (type B).

The similarities and differences between the structural classification of constitutive systems proposed here and the types of party systems defined by LaPalombara-Weiner are summarized in Table 8.

TABLE 8

COMPARISON OF TWO TYPOLOGIES FOR PARTY SYSTEMS

Riggs:	Re-ciproca-tive	Non-Re-ciproca-tive	Non-Competi-tive	Non-Elec-tive
LaPalombara-Weiner:				
Non-Party				X
One-Party Totalitarian			X	
One-Party Authoritarian			X	
One-Party Pluralistic		X		
Competitive-Hegemonic	X	X		
Competitive-Turnover	X			

An X, in each instance, indicates an overlapping of categories. Thus a non-party system is non-elective, a competitive-turnover system is reciprocative, and a one-party pluralistic system is non-reciprocative. Competitive-hegemonic systems may be reciprocative or non-reciprocative, reciprocative systems may be hegemonic or turnover, non-reciprocative systems may be one-party pluralistic or hegemonic, and non-competitive systems may be totalitarian or authoritarian.

In general, students of "Western" and "democratic" political systems have been interested only in polities with reciprocative constitutive systems. They are sometimes inclined not to recognize non-reciprocal and non-elective constitutive systems—which occur only in unbalanced polities—as authentic party systems. These students face difficult definitional problems. Non-competitive systems, notably as found in the Soviet Union and Eastern Europe, come within the geographic domain of their interests. Non-reciprocative systems have competing parties and electoral contests, thereby qualifying them also for consideration as "democratic" polities. The more complete typology of constitutive (party) systems clarifies the relationships between these political systems and provides a more comprehensive framework for the study of political parties.

FORMS OF RECIPROCATIVE CONSTITUTIVE SYSTEMS   As Table 8 shows, reciprocative systems include some of LaPalombara-Weiner's hegemonic and all of their turnover party systems. It would include also their ideological and pragmatic types of competitive systems. As indicated above, the latter criteria are functional rather than structural and the former involve a definition of reciprocative which sets too short a time span. There are more useful structural criteria for classifying reciprocative systems. Let us examine several of these.

4. *Reciprocative constitutive systems may or may not be parliamentary.* A constitutive system is parliamentary if the executive is elected by a legislature. Since a reciprocative system is, by definition, competitive, the election of the executive must occur outside a party. In other words, the election must be by constituents or legislators. If a parliamentary system is one in which the legislators elect the executive, then a non-parliamentary system is one in which the constituents elect the executive. Whenever an executive is elected by constituents, the role of formal and effective executive is combined. The term "president" has been designated to identify an elected head of state who may or may not also be the head of government. It is ambiguous, therefore, to call a non-parliamentary reciprocative system "presidential." Perhaps in rough, common sense usage, referring to such a system as "presidential" would not create misunderstanding, but our objective is precision. A qualifying

adjective could be employed such as "paramount presidential," or a new term could be introduced, "presidial." Although this word has another meaning, it is not likely to be confused with the idea of a non-parliamentary constitutive system.

The American party system is perhaps the leading example of a reciprocative non-parliamentary (presidial) party system. It is found, typically, in a congressional polity. Parties in a "presidial" system are, by hypothesis, tactical. When classified by nominators, they may vary from the conference to the open primary.

Since a presidial president is elected directly by constituents, clearly minority parties cannot hope to win. The whole electorate, in other words, becomes a single district. Any party which wishes its nominee to succeed must strive for a national electoral majority.[25] It must be a pragmatic, essentially non-ideological party of compromise. It cannot afford to be very specific on programs and it must support the existing constitutional system. Parties in a non-parliamentary (presidial) system become oriented primarily toward the office of president. Congressional seats are of secondary importance. Many European evaluations of the American party system are based on comparisons with political behavior in parliamentary systems, i.e., systems where the election of parliamentarians is the primary consideration. But party organization criteria relevant to parliamentary systems differ significantly from those germane to presidential systems.

Let us now consider variations in parliamentary constitutive systems.

5. *Parliamentary systems may or may not be proportional.* A party system is proportional if it provides for minority representation from electoral districts. Such representation can be guaranteed through a variety of voting techniques. These include what is formally called proportional representation, list systems and a wide variety of electoral methods catalogued by Janda in his chapter in this book.[26] A proportional distinction is relevant primarily in parliamentary systems. Under such an arrangement a minority could secure representation in an assembly, although in a non-parliamentary system it could not

[25] See Leon D. Epstein, "A Comparative Study of Canadian Parties," *American Political Science Review*, 58 (March, 1964), p. 57.

[26] Consult columns 37–38 in the country data section of Appendix A in Janda's chapter.

elect a president. Indeed, so powerful are the pressures in a parliamentary system to make minority representation possible, it may be hypothesized that, other things being equal, any parliamentary system will utilize a proportional voting system.

This hypothesis illustrates an important methodological point. Whether or not a hypothesis by itself "explains" all cases is not a good test of its value. It is often useful to state hypotheses in a universal form, knowing full well that there are exceptions by which they can be proven false. In the process of falsification, one can search for additional variables that explain the exception. An illustration from natural science is helpful. Galileo's hypothesis about the velocity of falling bodies does not apply empirically to all falling bodies. Falling leaves or parachutes immediately suggest some of the many exceptions. Still, the hypothesis remains a valid basic premise. It can be qualified by supplementary statements indicating how variables other than gravitation modify the behavior of falling objects.

Similarly in dealing with reciprocative constitutive systems, to state that non-parliamentary systems have two parties and district voting and parliamentary systems are proportional and have more than two parties is a good starting hypothesis. However, it can immediately be falsified by the case of Great Britain and the English-settled Dominions. This forces a search for a qualifying variable. British history may provide it. Let us assume that the English method of voting was institutionalized before the dynamics of parliamentary systems came into effect. This appears to be the case. The House of Commons emerged as a legislature while the king was still ruler. A non-elective constitutive system emerged at that time. Factions appeared in the House of Commons either in support of or in opposition to the monarch and his government. Thus, a dualistic tendency within the legislature arose which provided the institutional framework for the subsequent emergence of a two-party system. Moreover, the available technology of voting at that time included only a system of majority voting in electoral districts, even though more than one member might be chosen from a district. A historical pattern was established. The emergence of a viable two-party system and district structure preceded the formation of a parliamentary system. By the time of the transfer of effective power from the monarch to the premier symbolizing the establishment of the parliamentary system, the district and two-party system was well accepted. Whatever dissatisfaction there was with the system, if it existed, was not strong enough to force its subsequent revision. The institution, moreover, was concurrently exported abroad to areas of English settlement, including the American colonies. When the United States Constitution was framed, an elected president was substituted for the king, leading to the creation of a non-parliamentary reciprocative system. The monarch in England combined the functions of formal and effective executive. These roles were also united in the American presidency. Indeed, the possibility of separating them, discovered only after parliamentary structures emerged, did not occur to the American founding fathers. This, I submit, reinforces the argument for the pre-parliamentary origins of the electoral system in England.

Is the same pattern of development evident in the history of parliamentarism on the European continent? Party organizations were not well institutionalized in these countries during the latter part of the nineteenth century when the parliamentary principle was established. The development of run-off elections as a primitive modification of the district system is interesting in this connection. Run-offs provide opportunities for minority groups to make a showing in the first election, and then to bargain for a place in the run-offs. The inherent tendency of run-off elections is towards a multi-party system. Because of the cost and difficulty of running two elections, various schemes for proportional voting were then devised, permitting the direct representation of minorities in parliament.

If these historical speculations are valid, the hypothesis can be reformulated to state that parliamentary reciprocative systems will be characterized by more than two parties and multi-member districts, except where a two-party system with single member districts had been well institutionalized prior to the adoption of a parliamentary system.

It is this exceptional historical circumstance which brought into being an important category of party systems which are both parliamentary and non-proportional. These are found in some Commonwealth countries, including the United Kingdom.[27] A strong correlation is now hypothesized between

---

[27] Epstein argues, *op. cit.*, pp. 57–58, that the system of voting is non-decisive. Perhaps so, but it may reinforce or counteract otherwise weighty tendencies. Thus, one might argue for a tendency toward a multi-party system in Canada, as a parliamentary system, but this tendency is counteracted, to some extent, by the single member voting system. The regional character of third parties in Canada seems to confirm this argument. In the absence of the need for a national

nonproportional parliamentary systems and their political parties, which will tend to be the strategic-conference type. However, indirect-conference type parties will also be found in nonproportional parliamentary systems. These hypotheses are, I believe, non-tautological and subject to falsification by inductive methods.

Comparing this typology with others in common use, both the non-proportional parliamentary system and the non-parliamentary reciprocative systems can be seen as two-party systems. Just as the familiar category of one-party systems overlaps both competitive and non-competitive systems in my classification, so the familiar two-party category covers two sub-types of reciprocative systems, namely the non-proportional parliamentary and non-parliamentary.

It may be argued that this is hair splitting. If some parliamentary and the non-parliamentary systems have two parties, why not consider the number of parties to be the basic characteristic and the use or non-use of parliament to be a basis for sub-classification? The answer lies in the basic proposition about the inherent tendency of parliamentary systems to be multi-party systems. Thus, the two-party (non-proportional) parliamentary system is, as a system, exceptional, and the manner of classification draws attention to the need for a historical explanation.

Perhaps the ultimate test of the validity of this classification scheme is its ability to facilitate predictions. Copernican or non-Copernican astronomies can be employed to describe the behaviors of celestial bodies. The Copernican schema is simpler. So I believe the classification proposed here will provide a simpler description of social realities than the more conventional established pattern.

PRESIDIARY SYSTEMS AND POLARITY   Giovanni Sartori has argued that "multipolar" and "bipolar" represents the most important dividing line between European party systems. The bipolar systems, in his view, include both two-party and multi-party systems. Bipolar systems, whether they have two, three, or four parties, have no "center." Multipolar systems have several pivots and are characterized by a "center." The former type of system

---

majority to secure the election of a president, regional majorities can nevertheless secure effective parliamentary representation. However, regional minorities cannot obtain representation in parliament as they would in a parliamentary proportional system of voting.

has low "polarity"; the latter high "polarity." The distinction is based on the degree of political distance or irreconcilability between opposed tendencies in the system.[28]

Sartori finds the number of parties in a political system is the key variable: moderate pluralism occurs with from two to four parties, extreme pluralism with more than five parties. As shown, the number of parties in constitutive systems does not correspond exactly to a typology based on structural principles. Even more risky is the attempt to distinguish among polarized party systems on the basis of the number of parties they contain. Polarization is a functional, not a structural, criterion. It is a distinction of significance, since it contributes to an explanation of the relative stability and vigor of the less polarized systems and the greater instability, or "immobilisme," of the more polarized systems. I propose that we consider the following as a relevant structural variable.

6. *Proportional parliamentary systems may or may not be presidiary.* A constitutive system can be said to be "presidential" if it elects its formal executive. An elected formal executive has already been categorized as a president. It is necessary, however, to distinguish between presidents who are also effective, and those who are only formal executives. It was suggested above that a system in which the president exercises effective power be called a "presidial" system. A system in which the president exercises only formal power should be called a *presidiary* system. The normal adjective, "presidential," is ambiguous. This adjective will be avoided except where the context indicates whether the reference is to a presidial or presidiary system.

A non-elected formal executive has been defined as a "king." Any non-presidiary parliamentary system can be defined as *regal*. Normally, a regal system will have a constitutional monarch or a king as its formal executive, but the concept of a regal system is defined so as to include not only kings but any other non-elective head of state in a parliamentary system.

Let us now consider the hypothesis that the more polarized parliamentary systems are presidiary and the less polarized systems are regal. The smaller democracies of northern and western Europe—Belgium, the Netherlands, Norway, Denmark, and

[28] Giovanni Sartori, "European Political Parties: The Case of Polarized Pluralism," in LaPalombara and Weiner, *op. cit.*, pp. 137–140.

Sweden—are regal and not polarized by Sartori's definition. England is also regal, but a non-proportional parliamentary system. Switzerland is not polarized and non-regal, but it is unlikely that it would meet the criteria for a parliamentary system. Iceland and Finland are exceptional systems which test the hypothesis. These should be examined for additional variables. Greece might also be considered as "regal," although power may be distributed between the king and prime minister in such a way that it does not meet the criteria of a parliamentary system.

Let us consider presidiary parliamentary systems. Contemporary Italy, France under the Fourth Republic, Germany under the Weimar Republic and the Spanish Republic from 1931 to 1936, are leading examples of highly polarized presidiary systems. Exceptions may include contemporary West Germany. Again, if the general correlation appears to be significant, one could look for additional variables to explain the deviations. Qualifications added to the general proposition might then categorize the atypical cases.

What plausible arguments explain why regal polities are less polarized than presidiary polities? Perhaps a king who contented himself with ceremonial duties except for cabinet crises could mediate party conflict more readily than a president elected by parliament and therefore more identified with one political party. No doubt, elected presidents in Italy and France were able to create roles for themselves beyond partisanship. This point is worth more intensive investigation.

Historical variables could be important. Perhaps countries in which constitutional monarchies survive are characterized by more local autonomy and less pervasive state bureaucracies. A monarch under these conditions might have been willing to accept constitutional reform, to surrender effective power and assume the modest role of head of state. At a minimum, a history of this sort would mean polarization in the political culture regarding the monarch. Political parties might find more opportunities to exercise political power, especially at the local and urban levels, and a greater access to patronage appointments. In turn, this would attract more pragmatic men to roles of party leadership.

By contrast, it may be that those monarchs who were most firmly attached to their power as effective executives were backed by a far-reaching bureaucracy. Countervailing centers of pluralistic power did not become well institutionalized. If a constitutive system was established under such monarchs, it probably remained non-elective and purely formalistic. Revolutionary movements were then directed not only at the creation of representative institutions but also at the destruction of monarchic institutions. In such countries, notably Spain, Italy, France, and Germany, republicanism flourished at the expense of monarchism and presidiary parliamentary systems were established at various times. Are such relationships more than coincidental?

I have argued elsewhere that an excessive development of the merit orientation in bureaucracies retards political development because it starves party activists and leaders of practical incentives.[29] Although this argument was designed primarily for the case of bureaucratic polities, as mentioned, it might also be a factor impeding the formation of opposition party coalitions in conciliation regimes in partisan polities. In addition, it might apply to some of the European countries with extremely polarized political systems. The prevalence of a far-reaching merit-based bureaucracy in these countries would be associated with the doctrinaire, ideological orientation of opposition parties; an opposition characterized by an inability to form stable coalitions and larger, more effective party organizations. This, in turn, might be a major cause of extreme polarization.

Empirical studies may lead to a substantial revision of these preliminary speculations. Meanwhile, the evidence appears strong enough to justify inclusion of the structural criterion of presidiary and non-presidiary (regal) sub-types of proportional parliamentary systems.

The taxonomy of reciprocative constitutive systems, type A in Table 7, generated by the three criteria, parliamentary, proportional, and presidiary, is summarized in Table 9.

The reasons a non-parliamentary system must also be non-proportional have been examined. It must also be non-presidiary. A non-proportional parliamentary system might, in principle, be presidiary, but in practice they are non-presidiary. Governors appointed by a king are as non-elective as kings themselves, so they meet the criterion of non-presidiary systems. It is conceivable that if a two-party parliamentary system tried

[29] "Bureaucrats and Political Development: A Paradoxical View," in Joseph LaPalombara, ed., *Bureaucracy and Political Development*. (Princeton, N.J.: Princeton University Press, 1963), pp. 120–167. For an interpretation bearing on this point, see the Barnes' chapter in this volume.

to elect a president to replace a king, the two-party system would itself be destroyed. As for the types represented in columns A1 and A2, systems which are both parliamentary and proportional, these, as seen, may be either presidiary or non-presidiary, i.e., regal.

TABLE 9

TYPES OF RECIPROCATIVE PARTY SYSTEMS

	A1 Presidiary	A2 Regal	A3 Non-Proportional	A4 Presidial
Parliamentary	+	+	+	−
Proportional	+	+	−	−
Presidiary	+	−	−	−

Let us compare this taxonomy with those developed by others. My category of competitive systems is broader than La-Palombara-Weiner's because it includes non-reciprocative (one-party pluralistic) systems. My category of reciprocative systems is the same as their category of competitive systems. The familiar category of two-party systems includes both the presidial and non-proportional parliamentary systems. The category of multi-party system coincides with my category of proportional parliamentary systems, including both the presidiary and regal sub-types. These sub-types are significant. They provide a structural sub-category which correlates with the functional distinction between polarized and non-polarized party systems made by Sartori.

The hypothesized relationships between polity type, party type, and constitutive systems can now be summarized. These relationships are presented in Table 10.

Table 10 involves hypothetical relationships, not definitions. When exceptions are found, new variables should be sought to explain the deviation from normal patterns. Meanwhile, we may hypothesize as follows:

TABLE 10

POLITY, POLITICAL PARTY, AND CONSTITUTIVE SYSTEM

PARTY: \ POLITY:	Coalition	Governing	Congress	Ruling P.	Partisan	Bureaucratic
Strategic	Regal	Non-propor. Parliament				
Normative	Presidiary				Non-Recip.	Non-Elective
Entrenched				Non-Comp.	Non-Recip.	
Indirect		Non-propor.				
Tactical			Presidial			
Official				Non-Comp.	Non-Compet.	Non-Elective

In coalition polities, regal constitutive systems will tend to be associated with strategic type parties and presidiary systems with normative parties. Both regal and presidiary systems, of course, are proportional parliamentary systems. (Only the input criteria for party classification are employed here, the nominator categories are omitted.)

In governing party polities, non-proportional parliamentary systems will be found: the parties will be predominantly strategic, less frequently indirect.

In a congressional polity, presidial constitutive systems will be found, predominantly with tactical parties.

In ruling party regimes, non-competitive systems with an entrenched party will be found.

In partisan polities, non-competitive constitutive systems will be found, sometimes containing official and sometimes normative parties.

Conclusion

If space permitted, this chapter might serve as an introduction to the main body of a substantive treatise on functional characteristics of political parties and party systems. Such questions as party stability and instability, their programmatic and ideological orientation, the extent to which they control or monitor governmental administration, and other related issues could then be considered. Under each functional heading, patterns of correlation, and if possible of causation, could be explored linking particular types of party systems with particular functional manifestations.

Let me illustrate by a brief discussion of the question of ideology. In general, there are three dimensions to party ideology: intensity, right-left variation, and pro-anti-system variation. The *intensity* of ideology is reflected in the familiar distinction between a pragmatic and ideological orientation. A look at the constitutive system taxonomy suggests that ideological intensity (non-pragmatism) tends to be lowest in presidial systems, highest in presidiary systems. Regal and non-proportional parliamentary systems are somewhere in between. Non-competitive systems will propagate an elaborate formal ideology with considerable intensity, especially during the early years of the regime, but will slacken as the regime grows older. More than

likely, the ideological intensity of the parties in non-reciprocative competitive systems and non-elective systems will vary
considerably.

The distinction between *right and left* is essentially a difference of opinion about how decisions should be made. Parties on
the left demand more polyarchy in decision-making, that is, an
increase in the number of actors in the political arena, e.g.,
expanding the number of constituents or changing the system
to make possible a broader distribution of power. By contrast,
parties of the right demand a reduction in the number of actors
in the political arena. The distinction between right and left
is peculiarly applicable to proportional parliamentary systems.
It becomes exacerbated in presidiary as compared with regal
systems. In presidial systems, there may be a tendency to associate the two parties with rightist and leftist tendencies, but
the relationship is likely to be diffused. Non-proportional parliamentary systems will be intermediate on this scale. The entrenched party in a non-competitive system is likely to give
lip-service to pronounced rightist or leftist views, but a disparity
between announced goals and actual practice is likely. In a
non-reciprocative competitive system, the party in power is
likely to take a more rightist orientation and the opposition
parties leftist. In a non-competitive system in a partisan polity,
the official party may adopt rightist or leftist views without regard to actual practice. The situation in a non-elective system
is also likely to involve the adoption of rightist goals by the
official party and leftist programs by the opposition parties.

The third dimension involves the question of whether
parties sustain the established constitutional system of government. Parties can be classified as *"pro-system"* or *"anti-
system,"* the terminology proposed by Sartori.[30] Most writers on political parties, including Sartori, seem to think the
pro-anti-system orientations are either extreme right or extreme
left. To me, the distinction involves essentially a third dimension different from both intensity of feeling and right-left variation. The extent and manifestations of pro-anti sentiment vary
with the type of constitutive system. Perhaps its extreme form
in the electoral arena is the presidiary systems. Sartori characterizes these polities as highly polarized. His "center" might
be defined as the pro-system parties and their deputies in parliament. In these terms, a highly polarized system is one in which

[30] Sartori, *op. cit.*, pp. 148–150.

the size of the center has dwindled to the point where the members of the center parties in parliament number scarcely more than half. This probably occurs most frequently in presidiary constitutive systems.

By contrast, in non-proportional parliamentary and non-parliamentary (presidial) systems, the overwhelming majority of the members of parliament or congress tend to be pro-system in orientation.[31] It can be hypothesized that in regal systems the number of seats held by pro-system members in parliament falls between the characteristic poles of presidiary and presidial systems. It is the narrowness of the majority available to form government coalitions in a highly polarized parliamentary system that creates instability in these systems. By contrast, of course, the large center in bipolar systems may lead to institutional conservatism, or rigidity, and to a lack of concern with broad issues of political reform or revolutionary change.

The distinction between pro- and anti-system parties takes different forms in non-reciprocative systems. In general, the ruling party in a non-competitive system would be solidly pro-system to the extent that no members of the legislature (council) would oppose it. The same proposition applies to the official party in a non-competitive system in a partisan (movement) regime. However, the permitted opposition parties in a non-reciprocative but competitive system will tend to be strongly anti-system, whereas the official party will be pro-system with an overwhelming legislative majority. This distinction will apply to the parties in a non-elective system in bureaucratic polities.

Any sustained examination of such hypotheses involves analysis of empirical data and the formulation of new hypotheses to cover exceptional cases. Further discussions could focus on relationships between the various types of political parties, party systems, and polities, and the political functions identified by Gabriel Almond's input-output model. Or, following Lipset, Coleman, or Organski, the relationships between levels of economic development and the various governmental, constitutive, and party structures might be examined. Also, such questions as the relation between social values and class systems, cultural orientations, language and religion, communica-

---

[31] It might be useful to employ a different word, such as "middle," for those who take an intermediate position on the right-left dimension. If we did, the MP's in the systems noted would belong to the center by my definition, although a few might belong to the "middle," i.e., the "center" by Sartori's definition.

tions, and a host of related issues could be investigated. These could be studied both as cause and consequence, as conditions leading to the emergence of particular systems and as consequences of the establishment of these systems. We would want to investigate the relation between stability and change, or development, and types of party system.

It has been frequently argued that the lack of consensus and cultural heterogeneity of countries like France and Italy are responsible for the extreme polarization and immobilisme found in their party systems. It is equally plausible that the presidiary structure of their party systems, accompanied by extreme polarization and intensity, led to continuous indoctrination of the population by the highly charged and contradictory dogmas of emotional politicians. The party system, therefore, produced heterogeneity and dissensus, reinforcing and exaggerating natural differences among the subcultures.

Party and constitutive system could also be related to Duverger's variables of centralization and articulation. Geographic locations of various types of parties and constitutive systems could be reviewed and hypotheses, based on historical or other reasons, formulated to account for the distribution patterns.

It is impossible to go into such questions here. Perhaps it is enough to conclude this essay by reminding the reader that our purpose was to take the problem of classification of political parties seriously, to employ structural criteria of an either/or type, and to indicate hypotheses relating party to polity, with constitutive systems as an intervening variable. The resulting taxonomies are of intrinsic interest. More importantly, they generate empirically testable hypotheses that could lead to exciting discoveries concerning parties within a comparative context.

THREE

Party Democracy and the Logic of Collective Action

Samuel H. Barnes

University of Michigan

IT IS EVIDENT that *the* theory of the party or indeed of any political institution or process does not now and will never exist. There are numerous theories of the party that may be more or less useful, powerful, and reasonable; but there is no theory for all seasons. Political reality is multifaceted. One's perception of it, as in the case of the blind men and the elephant, depends upon which part one takes hold of; and the usefulness of a particular theory, of course, varies according to the uses to which it is put. While I do not suggest that one theory is as good as another, it is evident that no single theory of the party is likely to be adequate for all purposes.

The treatment that party democracy has received from students of politics reflects the diversity of the subject and the multiplicity and inadequacy of theories of the party. Although the problem of party democracy is an ancient one, its modern formulation can be credited to Robert Michels. In *Political Parties*, he formulated the "Iron Law" that oligarchy is the "pre-ordained form of the common life of great social aggregates."[1]

[1] Robert Michels, *Political Parties* (New York: Dover Publications, 1959), p. 408. For recent evaluations of the iron law of oligarchy, see Robert A. Dahl, "A Critique of the Ruling Elite Model," *American Political Science Review*, 52 (June, 1958), pp. 463–469; C. W. Cassinelli, "The Law of Oligarchy," *American Political Science Review*, 48 (September, 1953), pp. 773–784; John D. May, "Democracy, Organizations, Michels," *American Political Science Review*, 58 (June, 1965), pp. 417–429; Giovanni Sartori, "Democrazia, buro-

The so-called oligarchical nature of political parties and other large organizations has often been demonstrated, refuted, pointed to with pride, and viewed with alarm. Party democracy is viewed as a key contemporary problem because the political party is a crucial institution of our time. If the iron law of oligarchy applies to the party, the polity must likewise be affected.

My immediate interest in party democracy stems from a study of the internal politics of the Italian Socialist Federation (PSI).[2] That study, described in greater detail below, utilized a communications model to relate democracy in the party to democracy in the polity and to isolate and examine factors conducive to oligarchy and democracy. Not itself a theory, the communications approach makes it possible to merge several theoretical trends and juxtapose theory with data gathered from several sources; archives, observation, and interviews. Given my interest in examining the factors conducive to oligarchy and democracy, rather than merely testing one theory or another, I found the communications approach useful, powerful, and reasonable. But it is obvious that other important theoretical questions can be posed: data answer only questions that are asked.

One of these questions concerns the relationship between various theories of the party and general theories of organizations. One can, for example, maintain that the word party covers several essentially different phenomena and that a single generalization cannot be applied to all. There may be a need for one body of theory for two-party systems, another for multi-party systems, and still another—or several others—for various types of one-party systems. And the party, as an organization, may be *sui generis* and hence impossible to merge with other organizational types for analysis. But a useful, powerful, and reasonable proposition that could reconcile several theories of the party and tie parties into a general theory of organizations is highly desirable, if elusive. Although I do not claim to

---

crazia e oligarchia nei partiti," *Rassegna italiana di sociologia,* 1 (Luglio–Settembre 1960), pp. 119–136; and Juan Linz, "Leadership, democrazia e oligarchia: In margine alla 'Sociologia del partito politico' di R. Michels," *Rassegna italiana di sociologia,* 6 (Luglio–Settembre 1965), pp. 361–386.

[2] *Party Democracy: Politics in an Italian Socialist Federation* (New Haven: Yale University Press, forthcoming).

have found such a theory, I will present and evaluate a promising contender.

The Logic of Collective Action

To place the logic of collective action in perspective, let us examine three representative approaches to empirical theory. I recognize that they are not mutually exclusive, but theories, like reality, are often less orderly than one would prefer. Even descriptive theories have normative implications, for example, and the line between normative and non-normative statements often must be drawn *ad hoc*, depending upon the purpose at hand. The following distinctions are useful, if only for heuristic purposes.

One approach is essentially normative even though it is often presented as empirical. Thus some theorists have labeled the party the primary instrument for aggregating interests. Empirically, it may or may not fulfill these functions; yet many are prepared to argue that it should. Numerous propositions concerning party responsibility, democracy, and oligarchy are likewise disguised normative statements.

A second approach to theory is inductive. It seeks to formulate empirical propositions, free of normative elements, that encompass as much data as possible. Generalizing from specific cases one can, for example, arrive at the inclusive proposition that the goal of the party is public office. This is seemingly a widely applied empirical generalization; I will return to it below.

The third approach I will call formal theory. Deriving primarily from economic notions of rational man and recent developments in game and decision theory, this approach differs in several ways from the previous two. It assumes that man seeks rationally to maximize the returns on his investments. These returns, or utilities, are usually, although not necessarily, conceived in material terms. Further, formal theory is largely concerned with the systemic level; as long as its propositions facilitate prediction, it is irrelevant whether or not they are realistic descriptions of the behavior and attitudes of individuals. Its validity can scarcely be challenged by empirically unrealistic evidence. Rational models of the economy have not been rejected simply because assumptions concerning "economic man" have been demonstrated to rest on shaky empirical foundations.

The formal approach to the study of politics can be illustrated by reference to spatial models of party competition.[3] Downs uses analogies from economic models developed to facilitate the optimum location of retail outlets in relation to markets, competition, and sources of supply. He argues that parties compete for voters in an ideological space by searching for the position on some hypothetical ideological continuum that will maximize their support.[4] Stokes has demonstrated that a unidimensional spatial model does not fit the perceptions of voters in the United States[5] or Great Britain.[6] Nevertheless, his findings do not require the immediate abandonment of spatial models of party competition. In fact, conventional political discourse would be difficult without the implicit use of such models. Good explanatory theories are seldom abandoned simply because they do not fit the data. Spatial models may fit voters' perceptions in multi-party systems, although this has not been empirically demonstrated. There is undoubtedly wide variance in the saliency of particular dimensions in different countries and among voters in the same country.[7] However, with due caution concerning the existence of several ideological dimensions and ex-

[3] Spatial conceptions of parties assume that the parties contend for support along a given dimension; an ordered, measurable continuum, i.e., within a prescribed "space." For example, ideology can be conceived of as a liberal-conservative continuum with party attitudes and support proportionately distributed along it. Donald Stokes analyzes the assumptions underlying these models as they relate to parties in "Spatial Models of Party Competition" in Angus Campbell, Philip E. Converse, Warren E. Miller, and Donald E. Stokes, *Elections and the Political Order* (New York: John Wiley & Sons, 1966), pp. 161–179.

[4] Anthony Downs, *An Economic Theory of Democracy* (New York: Harper & Row, 1957). William Riker argues in *The Theory of Political Coalitions* (New Haven: Yale University Press, 1962) that parties seek a minimal winning coalition instead of maximum support. This important debate is not immediately relevant for our discussion.

[5] Stokes, *op. cit.*

[6] Donald Stokes, "Ideological Competition of British Political Parties," a paper presented at the 1964 Annual Convention of the American Political Science Association.

[7] Philip Converse, "The Problem of Party Distances in Models of Voting Change," in M. Kent Jennings and L. Harmon Zeigler, eds., *The Electoral Process* (Englewood Cliffs, N.J.: Prentice-Hall, 1966), pp. 175–208.

tensive political ignorance, spatial models are extremely useful for political analysis at the systemic level.

The theory referred to as the logic of collective action is of this third, formal type. It was developed in its present form by Mancur Olson, Jr.,[8] although many of its propositions have been current at least since Aristotle. It assumes that man in large organizations is the rational, calculating creature of classical economics. Unselfish action may be common in small and intermediate sized groups, but not in the large organizations that dominate politics at the systemic level.

Stripped of its symbolic formulation, the logic of collective action assumes that "unless the number of individuals in a group is quite small, or unless there is coercion or some other special device to make individuals act in their common interest, *rational, self-interested individuals will not act to achieve their common or group interest.*"[9] It may be summarized as "Let George do it" raised to an operating principle. The argument is as follows: Economic man exerts an effort in proportion to the return. In the case of collective goods (which benefit everyone), the contribution of the individual to the achievement is not crucial; yet because of the very nature of collective benefits, he will profit if the effort is successful. There are several propositions that derive from the above; not all are directly relevant to party democracy but they suggest some future applications of the theory.

One, there is a tendency "toward a suboptimal provision of collective goods."[10] "The larger the group, the farther it will fall short of providing an optimal amount of a collective good."[11] But other things being equal, a group whose members are of differing size "will show less of a tendency toward suboptimality . . . than an otherwise identical group composed of members of equal size."[12]

Two, this logic applies only to large groups. Small and intermediate groups are able to develop affective substitutes for individual, specific incentives (social status and social acceptance are individual, noncollective goods, and hence are

[8] Mancur Olson, Jr., *The Logic of Collective Action* (Cambridge: Harvard University Press, 1965).

[9] *Ibid.*, p. 2; italics in original.

[10] *Ibid.*, p. 28.

[11] *Ibid.*, p. 35.

[12] *Ibid.*, pp. 28–29.

important incentives in all groups). Olson also notes that some large groups are able, through subdivision or federation, to incorporate the dynamics of small groups.[13]

Three, group theorists of the "analytical pluralist school"—to employ Olson's label for Bentley, Truman, *et al.*—are incorrect in assuming that latent groups will mobilize simply because they have common interests to pursue. Olsen accuses the analytical pluralists of being guilty of the "anarchistic fallacy."[14] Latent large groups are in fact disadvantaged in competition with pre-existing small groups because of the high initial costs of organization; small political groups easily absorb these costs because of the "by-product" factor discussed below. Large groups are also disadvantaged because their collective interests, while substantial, bring a relatively small payoff to the individual compared with the return from noncollective and small group action.

Four, Olson develops the "by-product" theory of successful lobbying: the lobbies of the large economic groups are the by-products of organizations that have the capacity to "mobilize" a latent group with "selective incentives." To accomplish this they must "(1) have the authority and the capacity to be coercive, or (2) have a source of positive inducements that they can offer the individuals in a latent group."[15] He argues that lobbies such as unions, professional associations, and specialized industries originate as nonpolitical organizations, their noncollective activities attract membership.

Although Olson is developing a theory of interest groups, I see no reason why political parties should be excluded from these generalizations. At times, he appears to agree that his theory is relevant to parties.[16] Parties are viewed as organizations primarily oriented toward collective benefits. Since few people will work solely for collective benefits, most party duties are performed by those seeking selective, noncollective benefits —i.e., office-seekers. To him the political machine is a massive organizational structure that works for specific incentives (patronage and sometimes graft) rather than collective goods, which emerge as by-products if at all.[17]

[13] *Ibid.,* pp. 61–63.
[14] *Ibid.,* p. 131.
[15] *Ibid.,* pp. 132–133.
[16] *Ibid.,* pp. 163–165.
[17] *Ibid.*

In his analysis of political party organization, primarily in the United States, Schlesinger posits the search for public office as the goal of political parties.[18] Olson's insight suggests that, with a modification, Schlesinger's proposition can be applied to mass parties of the Socialist and Communist type, which often seem quite unconcerned with public office. This modification needs to be discussed in an extended digression.

The loose organizational structure of American parties enables the public officeholder to command a dominant position in the party except in areas controlled by a strong local machine. Perhaps, it is no accident that such machines are disappearing in the United States. A moderately educated, knowledgeable, and comfortable electorate has little need for their specific, noncollective benefits. But low political competence and the high cost of organization make spontaneous organization for collective action difficult for people of little education, political knowledge, and sense of efficacy. Successful political mobilization of such people requires competent leadership. Able representatives must be found in these or other groups and encouraged to devote their skills to collective action.

There are numerous ways in which this can be achieved. In polities where status distinctions are blurred, as in the United States, nonideological patronage-oriented machines, demagogues, patricians, and others may espouse collective action on behalf of groups of low political competence. But, as Olson's theory suggests, collective benefits are likely to be suboptimal. In highly stratified societies (which are usually also poor in resources and political competencies), such forms of mobilization seldom lead to the provision of any collective goods, regardless of the alleged policies of the leaders. There is little to distribute and few ways to hold leaders accountable, apart from overthrowing them.

The mass political party is a brilliant invention for mobilizing for collective action politically unsophisticated people in a highly stratified society. Lower strata can train and support

[18] Joseph A. Schlesinger, "Political Party Organization," in James G. March, ed., *Handbook of Organizations* (Chicago: Rand McNally, 1965), p. 768. This constitutes one of Bernard Hennessy's criteria for defining parties in his chapter in this volume. See the Hennessy chapter for an elaboration of his ideas and the Riggs chapter in this volume for comments on these criteria as well as a discussion of problems involved in identifying political parties as distinctive organizations.

their own leaders and recruit and control leaders from other strata by making *party position take primacy over public office.* Parties without substantial bureaucracies are usually controlled by officeholders. Since officeholders, motivated primarily by the desire to retain office, are often satisfied with noncollective rewards, there is an inherent danger of suboptimal provision of collective goods. The mass party, on the other hand, can at least try to insure that public office is subordinated to party office. In the Communist parties and the Socialist party I studied, there is no doubt that public office is a by-product of party position. There are differences, however, in the degree to which party influence is affected by public office: one obviously reinforces the other. Schlesinger's conception of the goal of the party as the assumption of public office thus needs to be modified. Only individuals have goals and these are, of course, seldom well-defined and differentiated. But if we can assume that the primary goal of the party leader is office, it will be public office in one system and private office in another. This is the modification that needs to be made in the proposition that the goal of the party is public office.

The logic of collective action suggests why formal organization is so important to lower strata. For upper strata with their multiple memberships and high political competence, politics is a by-product of other organizational activity. But for low status groups, the costs of initial organization are prohibitive unless skills can be purchased with specific benefits. Political organization becomes crucial for providing *and* controlling these specific benefits. It is not by chance that in those countries like Britain, where trade unions antedate the Left parties, the unions are still a dominant force in party politics and that in other highly stratified countries like Italy, union and party activity is mixed. The existence of either party or union reduces the initial costs of organization, as well as the independence, of the other.

Two important aspects of party organization in highly stratified societies need to be introduced here, though they cannot be analyzed in detail. The first is the division that often exists between parliamentarians and organizational politicians in parties of the Left. The second is the role of ideology.

The first aspect of party organization is evident in the French Socialist party (SFIO) and from time to time in the British Labor party. The division between parliamentarians and organizational politicians seems to reflect the inability of the party organization to dominate its public office holders; it stems from the dominance of public over party position, or at least the lack of dominance of the latter. The reasons for such a relationship vary. In France, it undoubtedly reflects the failure of the SFIO to maintain organizational bases in the milieu it once sought to mobilize: the parliamentarians may claim to represent the voters who elected them, while it is not easy to determine who organizational politicians represent beside themselves. If the organizational elites of mass parties are to remain strong, they must retain a mass organization for support; otherwise they become de facto parties of notables, despite taxonomic niceties.

In the British case, the electoral system, along with parliamentary tradition, appears to cause the tension between parliamentary and extra-parliamentary parties. The Labor party organization mobilizes too small a segment of the population to win election in the British single-member district system so that the electoral party (Parliamentary party) has to appeal to a wider latent group interest. The Labor party thus represents a mixture of elements of the mass party and an electoral machine.

An important question is, why are some parties content out of public office while others will make any compromise to win? The logic of collective action is insightful here. Noting the distinction between large and small groups as clarified by Olson, small groups can rely on incentives that emotionally tie the individual to the pursuit of collective goods. Political parties that are able to endure long periods out of public office seem to be those that rest on a highly structured system of face-to-face contacts.[19] Hence individuals can be tied through socialization and emotional relationships into a political subculture that fulfills most of their needs despite the absence of control over public policy. Communist, and sometimes Catholic, parties fall into this category, as do many Socialist parties. A general pattern is identifiable: a decline in the small-group and affective (nonrational) components of a party lead to an increase in the importance of public as opposed to party office. The experience of most European Socialist parties appear to support this contention. This prospect may also await current Western European Communist parties. Subcultural identification is facili-

---

[19] I speak here of all public office, not the situation where selective benefits may be available on the local or intermediate level for party leaders.

tated by wide divergences in status and poor lines of communication among groups in society. The narrowing of these gaps and improved communications tend to erode the affective basis of these parties. The process contributes to the apparent decline in ideological politics.

At present, the contribution of ideology to goal setting and the motivations of individuals in large organizations cannot be adequately assessed. I have argued elsewhere that ideology influences the behavior of elites directly, and mass publics are affected only through organizations dominated by ideologically motivated elites.[20] This conclusion is compatible with existing evidence, but the problem has not been adequately researched. If by ideology we mean an abstract ideational patterning of socio-political reality that imposes constraints on individual belief systems, it is probable that few large organizations consciously make decisions on the basis of ideology. More difficult to evaluate is the role of ideology in setting limits to the perception of alternatives and defining the reality of the situation itself. However, ideology is important here only as it relates to the logic of collective action. Its chief role is to justify, not initiate, collective action.

There are several ideologies that could serve to legitimate any particular pattern of collective action. The one that dominates is largely a function of historical tradition, organizational effectiveness, and—undoubtedly—chance. Ideology can serve as a capstone of the subcultural edifice, important as a basis for collective action. It is an important weapon in constructing a mass movement, in forging the linkage between the rational aims of the large organization and the socio-psychological needs of the individual in small groups. Yet, there is little evidence that ideology plays more than a supporting role in organizational politics at higher levels. Although ideology undoubtedly motivates many individuals, organizational considerations generally predominate: the history of mass movements is full of examples of the triumph of organizational technicians over ideologues.[21]

[20] Samuel H. Barnes, "Ideology and the Organization of Conflict: On the Relationship Between Political Thought and Behavior," *Journal of Politics*, 28 (August, 1966), pp. 513–530.

[21] The classification of conceptual levels is taken from the Survey Research Center's analyses of ideology. An "ideologue" is an individual "who . . . [relied] in some active way on a relatively abstract and far-reaching conceptual dimension as a yardstick against which political objects and their shifting policy significance over time were

Of course, not even tentative conclusions are possible concerning the role of ideology in organizations. I have introduced it to illustrate one possible pitfall in an uncritical acceptance of the theoretical assumptions of the logic of collective action. But, as will be demonstrated, it is remarkable that the more sophisticated members and leaders discussed below are able to maintain congruity between ideology and organizational needs while the less sophisticated cannot. This suggests the primacy of organization though of course it does not demonstrate it: causality is difficult to establish.

As a parting comment on ideology and organizations—large and small—some sources of the efficacy of the Communist party as an organizational weapon need to be mentioned. The party is able to combine the noncollective benefits of small organizations —such as comradeship, a sense of identity, and, often, self-respect—with the pursuit, on the systemic level, of collective benefits by an army of professionally able organizational technicians. On the mass level, this is accomplished by a network of cells and specialized structures providing many services—specific benefits—to members and supporters. The Communist elite can work for its vision of collective goals without succumbing to the lure of public office, thanks to the party's ability to provide income and status internally. The precise role of ideology in facilitating this achievement is unknown; it undoubtedly aids in uniting the two levels, and the vision of a future monopoly on public offices, no doubt, serves to make the often meager present financial rewards of party leadership more tolerable.

---

developed." The second level, or "near-ideologues," were those respondents "who mentioned such a dimension [e.g., liberal-conservative continuum] in a peripheral way but did not appear to place much evaluative dependence upon it or who used such concepts in a fashion that raised doubt about the breadth of their understanding of the meaning of the terms." The third level consisted of individuals who evaluated policies and parties in terms of their perceived effect on various social groups in the population. The fourth category was residual, included were those "who invoked some policy considerations in their evaluations yet employed none of the references meriting location in any of the first three levels [e.g., 'nature of the times,' or one isolated issue]." The fifth, and final, level included those whose evaluations "had no shred of policy significance whatever." These concepts are introduced and analyzed in Philip E. Converse, "The Nature of Belief Systems in Mass Publics," in David E. Apter, ed., *Ideology and Discontent* (New York: The Free Press of Glencoe, 1964), pp. 215–217. These terms are employed throughout this chapter. See, in particular, Table 3 below.

I have analyzed the Communist party because it is an example of what the Italian Socialist party (PSI) superficially appears to be, but actually is not. Although the PSI is a Marxist
party, it lacks the apocalyptic vision of its Communist rival, the
PCI. Certainly, few PSI members and leaders interviewed possessed that vision, but it is doubtful if the vision is widely shared
among contemporary Italian Communists. In the province under
study the Communists clearly possessed a more highly articulated organization than the smaller PSI. And, consequently, I
suspect that the Communist party could rely more heavily on
non-material, though still noncollective, rewards for its leaders.
With the data that follow I can be more specific, at least about
the PSI.

Costs, Benefits, and Participation in the PSI Federation

The major components of the logic of collective action have
been introduced and the possible relevance of the theory for
the study of political parties indicated. The usefulness of the
theory can now be evaluated. It would be presumptuous to claim
that I had tested the theory. Testing requires adequate controls
and more directly relevant data than is available. The data to be
presented were not collected within a framework designed to
operationalize Olson's ideas. But they illuminate several insights
derived from his theory and suggest how propositions which can
be widely applied may be derived from formal theory.

First, a brief introduction to the data is needed. They are
taken from a study of the internal politics of the PSI Federation
of Arezzo, a province in central Italy. The basic data consist of
58 interviews with all but one of the incumbents of Federation
posts, and 301 highly structured interviews with rank and file
members of the party in the commune of Arezzo. The study also
involved extensive work in party archives, observation of local
politics, and many long conversations with informants. Students
at the University of Florence conducted the interviews in March
and April of 1963. The particular measures employed will be
explained as the discussion progresses.

In 1963, the PSI was a two-party system.[22] Party elections

[22] It was the outward similarity between this two-party system and
that of the International Typographical Union, as reported by

were along factional lines at all levels and members were presented with a choice between alternative policy declarations and slates of convention delegates.

Examination of the history of the PSI suggests a recurring conflict between those Socialists who are dedicated to the complete revolutionary restructuring of Italian life and others who, while perhaps preferring such a solution, are prepared to advocate short-run reform of the present system in the meantime. There is an essential tension between revolutionaries and reformists. This is a situational division, there is little similarity between the Maximalist-Minimalist split of half a century ago and the Autonomist-Leftist division evident in 1963. Nevertheless, the results for the internal dynamics of the party are similar.

In 1963, the Antonomists favored independence from the PCI, the Communist party, and cooperation with the Center parties (Christian Democrats, Social Democrats, and Republicans).[23] The Leftists, fearing a loss of revolutionary fervor would result from cooperation with the Center, preferred continuing the PCI alliance. The Autonomists were the majority faction in 1963.

Superficially at least, clear-cut ideological differences separated the factions. When the structural basis of the cleavage is examined, however, ideological and policy differences can be separated from the specific benefits accruing to particular leaders.

Before analyzing leader gains, we must examine rank and file costs and rewards. The most important, yet least obvious, aspect of collective action is that participation costs vary greatly. The amount of effort required to accomplish a given task *may* be roughly the same for all members in terms of time and energy (although I suspect not), but the opportunity costs to the individual vary tremendously. This is a basic point that needs emphasis: the distribution of political competence is disproportionately located in the upper strata, a pattern especially pro-

---

S. M. Lipset, Martin Trow and James Coleman in *Union Democracy* (Garden City: Anchor Books, 1962), that first attracted me to the PSI.

[23] See Samuel H. Barnes, "Italy: Oppositions on Left, Right, Center," in Robert A. Dahl, ed., *Political Oppositions in Western Democracies* (New Haven: Yale University Press, 1966), pp. 303–331, for a discussion of Italian parties and politics. The party names and initials are listed on p. 304, footnote 1.

nounced in highly stratified societies. This is not to maintain that lower strata have no political ability. We speak of *average* levels, not absolutes; and there is convincing evidence that in the party analyzed here, and elsewhere, lower strata are disadvantaged in competition with higher.[24] The major asset of the lower strata is their numbers. But numbers are meaningless unless mobilized and the logic of collective action suggests that the size of the potential group acts as a handicap to its organization.

The effort required by some people to do what for others is routine is difficult to overestimate. Reading a newspaper, keeping records, addressing a meeting are tasks of no great effort for people of modest education; for the less educated they are often goals beyond reach. The PSI study concerned party members, people who were politically active to the extent they had at least taken a party card. Yet the average level of competence was exceedingly low—and directly related to a person's intensity of involvement.

Employing attendance at meetings and party work as criteria, there are four distinct levels of party participation; the categories correspond closely with conventional notions of participation. The *militant* (25 per cent of the party membership) is most active, the *participant* (27 per cent) somewhat less so, the *marginal* (34 per cent) has little to do with the party, and the *nominal* member (14 per cent) simply holds a party card.

I have demonstrated elsewhere that participation is closely associated with knowledge and efficacy, and that the association is strongest for those in the lowest educational level.[25] It appears that political participation provides an excellent opportunity for poorly educated people to develop some of the skills and attitudes that high status people acquire from extra-political sources. In the process, of course, the least able improve their own political competence. But, at any given level of participation, the poorly-educated can never match the individual skills of those more fortunate.

It requires a considerable effort for a person with a limited

24 For a discussion in detail of these findings, along with references to other studies on the subject, see Samuel H. Barnes, "Participation, Education, and Political Competence: Evidence From a Sample of Italian Socialists," *American Political Science Review,* 60 (June, 1966), pp. 348–353.
25 *Ibid.*

formal education to contribute extensively to party affairs. Yet, such people constituted a large proportion of the party membership. Only 17 per cent of the membership sample had more than five years of formal education, 37 per cent had less. Few were illiterate, but for many concentrated reading was difficult, or impossible. Even the party newspaper was ignored by a goodly number (41 per cent). Many scholars have noted the general political ignorance of Italians; this was certainly true of the PSI sample.[26] Also, a sense of political efficacy, the feeling of being able to exert a personal influence on political events, was not widespread in the party.[27] An examination of the distribution of the characteristics commonly associated with increased participation among the various membership categories (Table 1) reveals, in general, a positive correlation with involvement. Activists are better educated, more knowledgeable, and feel more efficacious. Many members do not possess the rudimentary skills necessary for meaningful participation. While party activity might contribute to an increase in knowledge and sense of efficacy, many refuse to become involved. For those who do, the effort is worthwhile; for others, the initial costs are probably too great.

As Table 1 illustrates, in addition to the positive association between education, knowledge and efficacy, intensity of participation increases among those who belong to other groups (union or otherwise), those associated with a party faction, or those most keenly concerned about ideological issues.

There are other costs that cannot be adequately measured. Many members live quite a distance from their sections and attendance is physically taxing. It is even more difficult to evaluate the cost paid by a peasant in competing in party matters with a skilled worker, or, even more demanding, a middle-class professional. The skilled worker has many advantages here. He is generally better educated, he has work colleagues with whom he

[26] See, for example, Gabriel Almond and Sidney Verba, *The Civic Culture* (Princeton: Princeton University Press, 1964), p. 96.

[27] The concept of "sense of political efficacy" was developed by the Survey Research Center at the University of Michigan. It is explained in Angus Campbell, Gerald Gurin, and Warren E. Miller, *The Voter Decides* (Evanston, Ill.: Row, Peterson and Company, 1954), pp. 187–194. See also for a discussion of this and related concepts, Angus Campbell, Philip E. Converse, Warren E. Miller, and Donald E. Stokes, *The American Voter* (New York: John Wiley & Sons, 1960).

TABLE 1

PARTY INVOLVEMENT AND PARTICIPATION VARIABLES, BY
MEMBERSHIP CATEGORY

Variables that Correlate with Participation	Membership Category			
	Nominal	Marginal	Partici-pant	Militant
Five Years or Less of Formal Education	93%	86%	81%	77%
Low Efficacy Score (0–1 on Index)	70	60	57	39
Low Knowledge Score (0–1 on Index)	72	54	40	18
Member of Union	20	40	55	60
Member of Party Faction	12	26	47	77
Ideologue or Near-Ideologue	5	9	11	30
Member of at Least One Organization in Addition to Party	24%	55%	66%	77%

can discuss matters, and he is a part of the larger world beyond the farm. The peasant lives a lonely existence. The legacy of the politically isolated peasant is passed on through the family, and is evident in the participation patterns of the next generation. Table 2, for example, illustrates differences between party members whose fathers were in agricultural occupations and those who were not.

A peasant's family and social life may be warm and satisfying, but his political life usually does not exceed the party ties he develops.[28] One thing that strikes me about Italy, some-

[28] Converse, *op. cit.*, pp. 252–254, discusses some of the problems implicit in peasant attachments to politics. For an analysis of farm-rural participation patterns in the United States, see Campbell *et al.*, *The American Voter*, *ibid.*, pp. 402–440.

TABLE 2

PARTY MEMBERS: SUBCULTURE OF YOUTH, BASED ON
FATHER'S OCCUPATION

Selected Variables	Father's Occupation	
	Agricultural	Non-Agricultural
Ideologue or Near-Ideologue	7%	31%
No Efficacious Response	33	15
One or No Answers Correct on Eight Knowledge Questions	57	23
Militants in Level of Participation	21	35
Fathers Not Interested in Politics	70	42
Education		
Less than 5 Years	51	19
5 Years	45	46
5 Years or More	4	35
Social Class		
Lower-Lower	72	25
Upper-Lower	24	34
Middle	4%	41%

thing largely ignored in the literature, is that many Italians are politically alienated without being personally or socially alienated. Alienation, like ideology, has its dimensions. Those who wonder at the survival of the Italian polity despite widespread political apathy need look at the tight networks of family and friends that surround the individual and provide the cement of the society. Against this background, political associations are of secondary importance. Personal and social networks are more amenable to clientelistic forms of political mobilization than to the specific, rational, organizational structures usually associated with the developed polity. However, clientelistic patterns of mobilization may be a substitute for, not a precursor of, rational organizational forms. Certainly clientelistic patterns are quite compatible with the mobilization of politically unsophisticated people, perhaps more so than rational organizational forms.[29] But, of course, clientelistic relationships lead to individual, non-collective benefits. The reality of widespread clientelism permeating even the rational organizational structures, including all political parties, affects the achievement of collective ends within the polity. Clientelism permeated the PSI.

This extended aside was intended to emphasize (1) the existence within the PSI of alternative organizational forms, and (2) the coexistence within the PSI of political apathy and warm inter-personal relationships. Many of the nominal and marginal members appear to join the party for affective reasons. If these types are active at all in party work, it is likely to be at the local level. Olson's theory would lead us to expect nonrational motivations to be most prominent here. This appears to be the case, although it can only be demonstrated obliquely. For example, 67 per cent of the nominal members had other members of their family enrolled. This figure compares with 36 per cent of the militants. The large percentage of militants proportionate to other members of the party may indicate that they recruit many of the more marginal types. Women ranked low in party involvement, 44 per cent being classified as nominal and 41 per cent as marginal members. Apparently, affective reasons are important in their recruitment. In the personal interviews, a much higher percentage of nominal and marginal members than others cited the influence of family and friends as motivating their political involvement. A great emphasis, then, was placed on affective reasons rather than considerations of individual or collective material gains.

It is revealing to ask what group benefits mean to people who do not think in terms of collectivities. As has been indicated, many members are politically naive, ranking extremely low on measures of knowledge, education, sense of efficacy, and other variables. Particularly striking is the poorly developed ideological

---

[29] For this argument concerning clientelism in Italy and a discussion of the concept in general, see Jane Catherine Schneider, *Patrons and Clients in the Italian Political System,* Ph.D. Dissertation in Political Science, The University of Michigan, 1965.

sensitivity evident among members. The measure of ideology employed in this study reflects the respondents' ability to impose an abstract, ideational understanding on political events.[30] Judged in this light, a small proportion of the sample evidenced ideological sophistication (Table 3). Only half the answers to a series of open-ended questions on political parties and problems of Italian politics exhibited any ideological superstructure *or* contained references to the collective interests of groups. The latter category was broadly interpreted to be as inclusive as possible. It is difficult for people to work consciously for group benefits if they are unaware of collectivities. Group action may result in a by-product of action undertaken for other ends, but this alters somewhat our conventional notions of the mass political party.

TABLE 3

PARTICIPATION AND IDEOLOGICAL SENSITIVITY*

Level of Ideological Awareness (In Ascending Order of Sophistication)	Membership Category			
	Nomi-nal	Mar-ginal	Partici-pation	Mili-tant
I. Personalities: Goodness and Badness of Times	47%	49%	46%	23%
II. Specific Group Benefits	26	22	21	31
III. General Group Benefits	19	18	19	17
IV. Ideologue and Near-Ideologue	8	11	14	29
	100%	100%	100%	100%
N	26	83	63	75

* Uncodable responses are excluded.

One final bit of evidence suggests that nonrational small group dynamics increase the participation of low status members. Smaller sections have consistently higher turnouts in party elections. The product moment correlations between section

[30] See Converse, *op. cit.*, and footnote 21 above.

size and turnout are negative for the five party elections for
which section voting data for the province are available. As the
smaller sections rank low on variables associated with high participation, this finding is surprising. Nonrational factors, such as
stronger social ties and controls in the small community, are undoubtedly involved in the higher rates of voting.

Table 4 cross-tabulates variables associated with increased
political involvement with the size of the sections.

The relationship between section size and general party
participation is less clear than the association between size and
voting.[31] While voting turnout is higher in the smaller sections,
broader party involvement is less common. Apparently, it is
easier to mobilize members to vote in party elections than it is
to stimulate them to participate in other varieties of party activity. Voting is the one act that members must be called upon
to perform, it cannot legitimately be executed on their behalf
by professional party workers. In short, activists do most of the
party's work, but they must mobilize the entire rank and file for
elections.

Olson has noted that affective considerations are more important in small groups, rational (in the economic sense) in
large organizations. Support for the applicability of this contention to the PSI comes from an analysis of votes for the opposing
factions in party elections. In the four competitive postwar elections (the fifth was not contested) in the provincial PSI, larger
sections consistently generated more competition (Table 5).

Further evidence for this interpretation emerges when the
potential basis of support for the Left is compared with the portion of party members *actually* identifying with the Left. A Leftist position on party policies combined with an expression of
dissatisfaction is employed as a measure of the faction's potential. By this gauge, the most impressive showing is found in the
largest section (Table 6).

In the biggest of the sections (200+), the percentage identifying with the Left is similar to the percentage dissatisfied; in
the smaller sections, there are far fewer Leftists than dissatisfied members. The most likely explanation—although not the

[31] Indeed, when controls are instituted for other factors using an
analysis of variance program, Multiple Classification Analysis, the
impact of section size on participation (as measured above, that is,
not mere voting) is much reduced, while education and other variables retain their influence.

TABLE 4

SIZE OF SECTION AND VARIABLES ASSOCIATED WITH PARTICIPATION

Variable	Size of Section				
	Less Than 40	40–49	50–59	100–199	200+
Political Efficacy Above Median	38%	19%	50%	54%	41%
Lower Middle or Middle Class	8	0	8	10	33
More than 5 Years Formal Education	17	0	10	10	29
More than One Correct Response to Knowledge Questions	62	28	52	45	71
Ideologue or Near-Ideologue	16	—	11	11	26
Belonging to More than One Non-Party Organ	30	6	14	19	37
Father PSI Member	41	53	50	57	62
Father Apolitical or Father's Politics Unknown	51	47	40	32	26
Other Members of Family Enrolled	32%	44%	40%	58%	39%
N	37	32	52	62	117

TABLE 5

VOTING FOR THE OPPOSITION AND SIZE OF SECTION
IN SELECTED POSTWAR FEDERATION ELECTIONS*

	Size of Section				
Year	Less than 40	40–49	50–99	100–199	200+
1948	53% (17)	100% (4)	43% (23)	75% (12)	86% (7)
1949	21 (28)	29 (7)	66 (9)	82 (11)	84 (6)
1961	69 (46)	78 (9)	87 (23)	100 (12)	100 (5)
1963	79% (47)	85% (13)	95% (19)	100% (13)	100% (6)

* Per Cent of Sections in which the Opposition received at least one
vote: number of sections is in parentheses.

TABLE 6

SIZE OF SECTION AND FACTIONAL DIFFERENCES

Size of Section	Per Cent Satisfied (Extremely or Moderately) with Party Policies	Per Cent Leftist (Extreme or Moderate) on Index of Programmatic Position	Per Cent Leftist in Factional Identification
Less than 40	81%	43%	8%
40–49	81	44	6
50–99	81	40	8
100–199	81	60	13
200+	74%	52%	22%

only one—for the decline of opposition in the smaller sections is that opposition and factionalism are incompatible with the achievement of social solidarity and group cohesiveness, a major appeal of socialism at this level. In the larger sections, where identification with a part rather than the whole can be achieved, conflict between subgroups does not interfere with group solidarity to the same extent. However, a number of respondents opposed factions precisely because they did disrupt party energies and resulted in conflicting loyalties. For many of these respondents, unity was the paramount value, and whether the Leftists or Autonomists dominated was a secondary concern. These findings support Olson's distinctions between the dynamics of large and small groups.

Although this discussion could be extended, the main point has been made as strongly as the data permit: collective action is extremely difficult for people with the limited experience of the low status PSI members. And many low status individuals seek affective rather than "rational" collective benefits from party membership.

Having discussed the costs of participation, let us now inquire into the rewards. Unfortunately, the data are more limited for dealing with rewards. But evidence is available to support the contention that those who participate more share disproportionately in the party's noncollective benefits. As will be shown, party leaders, in particular, do very well.

The relationship between participation and employment is revealing. Short of investigating each separate case, there is no way to prove that employment is related to party activity. In a few cases it is obvious, the jobs concerned are acknowledged to be patronage positions. This is true of most communal posts, for example, and some provincial posts. In other public positions, political ties are useful, at times essential, for promotion, good working conditions, and other such noncollective benefits. It is difficult in Italy for a public employee to be deeply involved in politics without it affecting his career. And, no phase of this study revealed any instance where a PSI party position hurt a public employee.

Party members who are not public employees may also occupationally benefit from their political affiliations. The beneficial relationship between law and politics is often stressed. Political ties can also reward various types of tradesmen. While I do not suggest that PSI members join for material or status reasons, still there are subtle noncollective benefits to be derived from party membership. Ordinarily, individuals also run a risk of being occupationally penalized because of their party connections. But this possibility is less in Arezzo. The Socialist and Communist parties dominate all provincial and most communal positions, including those in the commune of Arezzo itself. In fact, *not* having an entrée with a Leftist party could prove a substantial handicap to some tradesmen and professional people in the province.

Public employees are apparently more adept at relating collective goals to individual rewards. This point can be demonstrated by an analysis of policy preferences of communal employees. Respondents were asked whether they strongly agreed, agreed, were indifferent, disagreed, or strongly disagreed, with each of five questions relating to current policy disputes that sharply divided the two party factions. The membership was Leftist in its responses, despite the fact that the Autonomist was the majority faction (and the Rightists in the party conflict). Leftists were strong supporters of their faction's policy positions; Independents, those identifying with neither faction, were likewise Leftist in policy preferences; and the Autonomists were divided (Table 7).

TABLE 7

PARTY FACTION AND POLICY POSITION

Policy Orientation	Factional Indentification		
	Independent	Leftist	Autonomists
Strong Left	12%	35%	4%
Left	39	46	33
Indeterminate	12	12	11
Right	29	5	39
Strong Right	8	2	13
	100%	100%	100%
N	155	43	84

For a substantial number of Autonomists, therefore, factional loyalties and policy preferences are incongruent. Strong evidence indicates patronage appointees accurately perceive the association between policy and factional divisions. Twenty-four rank and file members worked for the commune; eight of these individuals were divided evenly between Left and Right policy positions. None of the eight reported any factional loyalties. Of the remainder, thirteen were Autonomists and three Leftists; and all sixteen were consistent in their policy preferences. The Autonomists took a Rightist stance, the Leftists an opposing position on issues. This does not, of course, demonstrate that specific rewards are the cause of this consistency; but it is suggestive.

The logic of collective action is more suitable for explaining the behavior of party leaders than members; one reason why it is difficult to analyze the rank and file in these terms. Those supporters who do contribute a great deal to the party eventually emerge as leaders. The result is that the ranks are filled with budding leaders as well as the more conventional nonmobile types. While it can be inferred that noncollective benefits motivate the mass membership, the evidence is more specific for the leaders.

Party work is a career for many, for some others it is an important adjunct to a principal nonparty occupation. The career aspect of party work is widely recognized, and much of the confusion which arises from intraparty politics is understandable when viewed from this perspective. The motives of Socialist leaders are, of course, mixed. Idealism cannot be discounted; but it is equally true that PSI leaders have personal ambitions and material needs, and that these must be satisfied.

Party positions do not pay well. There are at least two side benefits however. The first is the status that the positions bring. Most leaders are emotionally committed to the party. Although status and affective rewards taken alone are not sufficient to explain political involvement, the small group dynamics discussed by Olson are an important consideration in understanding the behavior of the core leadership group. The status associated with party office is partial compensation to leaders of middle-class origins for the loss of social standing that can accompany class disloyalty. Party office offers working-class leaders one of the few paths available for upward social mobility.

The second type of side benefit consists of nonparty positions. Prominent party leaders dominate the PSI representation in communal and provincial elective and appointive office. A PSI deputy was Federation secretary.[32] Three members of the

---

[32] The only Federation leader not interviewed was a PSI senator from Tuscany who was given a position on the Directing Committee of the Federation although he resided outside the province and took little

large Directing Committee were mayors of their communes, one of Arezzo itself, six were communal assessors (i.e., members of the *giunta*, selected from the elected council, that serves as the administrative board or cabinet for the commune), and three were provincial assessors. An additional seven were members of communal or provincial councils. Thus, 19, or 44 per cent of the total, held communal or provincial offices, and another member was a deputy to the national parliament. Four representatives to the Federation Directing Committee were school teachers, at least two of whom held administrative positions apparently gained through political influence. Potential benefits also may have accrued to the five businessmen and two lawyers in the sample. Finally, most of the eight clerks in the leadership group appeared to hold posts related to their party activity.

A sharp distinction must be made between two levels and types of leaders. The secretaries of the local section are mostly of lower class origins; their party activity seldom leads to higher office. The absence of longitudinal data prohibits a definitive statement on this point, but of the sixteen secretaries, thirteen held no higher position. The remaining three were secretaries of the larger sections, one of Arezzo itself.

The Federation considered the Arezzo section crucially important and resisted all attempts to subdivide it. The section contained roughly one-third of the total PSI membership in the commune and represented the largest organization of its type in the province. At first blush, its secretary would appear to be an important figure in the party's inner circle. In reality, a member of the Federation Executive Committee was assigned to act as secretary. The party leaders were reluctant to permit this vital local section any independence. The Arezzo secretary was atypical therefore.

The secretaries of the two other larger sections had achieved higher positions and thus were exceptions to the general rule stated above. But it appears that their appointments to the Directing Committee were intended to round out factional strengths. They lacked individual influence and they were not destined to advance further. Indeed, they would be fortunate to maintain their present assignments.

---

part in provincial politics. He was, in a sense, imposed on the Federation by the national party—a reasonable act given the electoral system, but one that gave him little standing within the Arezzo Federation.

Most of the thirteen remaining secretaries of party sections fit a common pattern.[33] Virtually all were lower class, poorly educated, and advancing in years. They were chosen for their probity and devotion to the party rather than for any individual political skills or future promise. Their posts, especially in smaller sections, did not demand much bookkeeping or campaigning. The important considerations were that the men be reliable, respected in their immediate environment, and fitting symbols of the party at the grass roots level. Most of the secretaries were party members of long standing. A few obtained employment through the party, and all worked during elections as paid organizers. Overall though, financial opportunities were irregular and the rewards slight. These men demonstrate the importance of nonmaterial—but still individual—rewards. While monetary gain is limited, the status and respect gratifications received from party work should not be underestimated. These men had few opportunities to command attention in their localities. None of the thirteen, for example, had a white-collar background, five were unskilled workers, four skilled workers, three pensioners, and one a sharecropper. Thus, party office rewarded these men with a position of eminence they could not have hoped to achieve otherwise.

Although I did not secure ideological measures for the leaders, in my interviews with the secretaries I was impressed by their pragmatic, nonideological approach to politics. When I asked one secretary of a section why he was a Socialist rather than a Communist, he responded that the Communists were against private property, wanted to nationalize shops and farms etc.! The best that the one leader could do who spoke in ideological terms was to quote clichés, probably borrowed from a party manual and only indirectly related to the issues discussed. The ties of these activists to the party were primarily emotional or, in Olson's terms, nonrational. It should be emphasized that the majority of their work was done in small groups. At this level, socialism, widely interpreted to mean assistance for collective action, is as much an ethical norm as an economic philosophy. Comradeship counts for a great deal; and self-sacrificing idealism is not outdated. At the local level, a small group of militants are the heart of the party, the secretary its soul.

[33] Actually, the latter two secretaries referred to above who had attained higher positions on the Directing Committee fit this pattern also.

At higher leadership levels, idealism is taken for granted; it is assumed yet seldom articulated. Here the logic of collective action is not as applicable. The top party leaders have a near monopoly of advanced political skills within the Federation and they dominate the noncollective benefits that accrue to the party.

Motivation is difficult to establish. Obviously, party leaders have the same financial obligations as others, and idealism alone is not enough to sustain most men. Sooner or later, the party worker must evaluate his long-range financial prospects. At this point, noncollective benefits assume great importance. Such considerations became evident in the interviews. One of the leaders noted, for example, that initially he worked through the party for social revolution, disdaining personal gain. After the 1948 elections, and after acquiring a wife and family, he accepted the possibility that the revolution might be far in the future. Consequently, he became more active in seeking short-run gains, joining with other party workers to demand social insurance programs and other party employee benefits.

The leaders acknowledged that paid party workers were constrained in their behavior. They were under substantial pressure to emerge on the winning side of intraparty disputes; a miscalculation could mean loss of office. Middle-class leaders were at something of an advantage in their internal disputes. Nonparty positions such as lawyer or school teacher alleviated some of the financial insecurity associated with factional politics. Leaders of either working class backgrounds or those in the middle-class who had never finished their education, becoming politically active at an early age, were in a more tenuous position. They had nowhere else to turn. Correspondingly, established middle-class leaders had less to lose through internal party democracy than others. In this perspective, the social basis of factional divisions and attitudes toward party democracy acquires new meaning.[34] Many apparent ideological questions are grounded on very personal, and practical, considerations; specifically, the benefits accruing to the particular leaders.

As noted, the Autonomists were the majority faction in 1963. The secretary and the four paid functionaries of the Federation were Autonomists, as were numerous and important

[34] This phenomenon of the greater dependence of working-class leaders on the party was noted by Gabriel Almond in *The Appeals of Communism* (Princeton: Princeton University Press, 1954), pp. 191–194.

government office holders. The mayor of Arezzo and several assessors were included in the latter group. The mayor, who depended upon Communist party (PCI) support in the communal council, was conciliatory towards the minority and served as a bridge between the warring factions.

The trade union movement, dominated by the Communists, provided minority faction leaders with non-party positions. The support given opposition leaders secured democracy within the party. All Socialist trade union activity was exercised on behalf of the CGIL (*Confederazione Generale Italiana di Lavoro*) and its affiliates. Socialists, however, were decidedly less influential than the Communists within these trade unions. Communist dominance was virtually complete and no Socialist could hold a union position without Communist acquiescence. Yet, the PCI in this province proved to be most accommodating. As a result, the Socialists held influential offices within the provincial unions disproportionate to their number in the electorate or their organizational strength. One PSI leader was secretary of the provincial Chamber of Labor; reputedly, one of two Socialists in Italy to hold the most prominent provincial labor post. Six provincial PSI leaders were paid full-time trade union officials. All of the union party leaders were Leftists. When these are accounted for, there are only seven additional Leftists remaining in the top leadership group. The ability of the opposition leaders to take refuge in posts which the PSI majority leadership could not control formed the basis for democracy within the PSI. Without this independence, a formal opposition would have difficulty surviving. The union positions permitted opposition leaders to maintain close ties with the rank and file as well as support themselves and their families.

The division between majority and minority within the PSI thus involved several dimensions. The ideological differences between factions were genuine enough; the policy debate likewise reflected basic cleavages. But the noncollective benefits underlying these differences are crucially important. If the majority policy had led to a breakdown in the good relations with the Communists, the minority position would have been untenable. The out-faction leaders could have expected to lose their union positions, or, at the very least, to have found themselves precariously employed. Consequently, their concern with the implications of Autonomist policies was understandable.

A secure party post has a strong attraction in troubled political times. Take, as evidence, the following incident. The

Autonomists induced the second ranking man in the opposition
to desert his faction, and the unions, for an official party post.
This tactic of divide and conquer was successful. It shattered
the unity of the Left and salvaged for the Autonomists a talented
leader. Within a year, the minority Left faction formally withdrew from the PSI and established a rival Socialist party. The
defection of the factional leader was widely believed to be a
power play in which a high party post was used to bribe an opposition leader. It could also be interpreted as the flight into
orthodoxy of a long-time leader who feared the consequences
of continued cooperation with the Communists, a relationship
made sensitive by the PSI's turn toward the center in national
politics. The defection was facilitated, not induced, by material
rewards.

Several other aspects of party matters could be introduced
into a discussion of the costs and benefits of party participation,
but at this point they would be redundant. It is evident that the
costs of participation differ greatly, that the contributions of the
membership vary likewise, and that those who assume the major
responsibilities for carrying on the party's work receive in turn
most of the non-collective benefits that result. The principal
costs of organization are borne by a few activists. While their
primary objective may be to achieve collective benefits for the
Italian working man, their party activity, nonetheless, provides
them with many material gratifications. It is incorrect to assume
that party leaders do not work for collective benefits. Yet, it is
equally unjustified to ignore the role noncollective rewards play
in the internal politics of the party.

Party Democracy and the Logic of Collective Action

There are many views of democracy and the organizational
process within mass parties. These include the Marxian argument that leaders form the vanguard of the proletariat, the belief that the party elite inevitably coalesces into a ruling oligarchy, and the view that the party is a machine for achieving
public office for leaders. The first school of thought has little
meaning in any empirical sense, the second is at best a vast
oversimplification, and the third is, in many cases, untenable.

If one defines democracy in Marxian terms, then the precise nature of the internal party process—whether it is demo-

cratic in the sense used in this paper or not—is largely irrelevant. In some areas, interparty competition may render a measure of organizational democracy, or at least its façade, desirable. But this is a tactical problem, not a theoretical one.

The Iron Law of Oligarchy deserves more attention than it can receive here. I must content myself with two observations. First, if by oligarchy we mean merely that minorities rule, then the law is irrefutable; but it is also trivial and tautological.[35] Second, if we mean that elites rule in their own interest counter to those of the masses, then we have a more complicated problem. It is in part a normative question whether the "real" interests of the masses are being advanced by a particular course of action. And, even if we were to agree on normative criteria, we still have the empirical problem of measuring whether particular elites act in opposition to mass interests. It would take a rash scholar to maintain that elites consistently subvert broader group objectives. But the fundamental question remains, when do they act as oligarchic and when as democratic leaders? Scholars concerned with party oligarchy have chosen an important subject to investigate, but an oligarchical model is not the best theoretical device for attacking the problem.

Those who seek to explain internal party dynamics in terms of the pursuit of public office by party elites employ a more promising focus.[36] At least in the United States, and perhaps in other two-party systems, this approach has several advantages: it is empirical and can be disproved; it has a reasonably close approximation to the data; and it is not difficult to operationalize. Its chief weakness is its lack of universality; it does not apply to a number of party systems. Also, its insights into organizational processes, the concern of students of structural oligarchy, are necessarily restricted.

The logic of collective action holds promise for reconciling all these approaches. Although the theory was designed to facilitate an understanding of pressure group activity, it has a remarkably good fit with the PSI data. Olson's distinction between large and small organizations is extremely useful. Obviously, many members, including some leaders at the local level, obtain no material rewards from their activity. It is less certain that they do not receive noncollective benefits. Status

---

[35] Dahl, *op. cit.*, p. 369.
[36] Again, the Riggs and Hennessy pieces in this volume also directly address themselves to this point.

within the party and the community is a noncollective gratification of considerable importance. Family and friendship bonds, and other nonrational stimulants, appear decisive in the recruitment of many members. Apart from voting in party elections, few members have either the time or the competence to make major contributions to the party. Most organizational work is conducted by a small number of activists and leaders. This core group does receive extensive (at least as viewed from the local perspective) noncollective benefits for their efforts.

Noncollective rewards are most prominent at the Federation level. Federation politics can be meaningfully interpreted in terms of the specific benefits accruing to particular leaders. This phenomenon should not be viewed cynically. Politicians, like anyone else, have material and ego-enhancing needs. The crucial problem for mass political parties is to harness these energies to the achievement of party goals. The highly structured mass party has several advantages over its more loosely organized American counterpart in mobilizing large numbers of politically unsophisticated people. The mass party can offer specific incentives, e.g., status and moderate financial returns, to prospective leaders. At the same time, it can assure that these rewards accrue to leaders who work for the achievement of collective goals. When a party loses sight of its collective objectives, when it becomes an electoral machine dedicated to supporting particular politicians, then it forfeits its status as a mass party.

The rank and file "keep the leaders honest." The definition of party goals emerges from the competition among leaders and the interplay between the Federation and local levels of the organization, another form of leadership competition. In democratic parties, leaders must compete for the support of the membership, and the nonrational motivations of most rank and file members require that leaders reinterpret their own disputes in collective terms. In short, the necessity of appealing to the party membership forces leaders to sublimate the noncollective dimensions of their struggle and consequently—and perhaps as a by-product—to seek collective ends as the price for achieving their own specific goals. I repeat: this is not to deny importance to ideological and altruistic leadership motives, but rather to point out that these provide limited explanations of elite behavior.

The necessity to appeal to the rank and file is thus the principal reason for the sublimation of the noncollective aspects of elite conflict. This does not account, however, for the existence of internal party democracy. It is possible for party elites to unite against outsiders, coopt their successors, effectively monopolize all elite positions, and completely dominate party elections. Such a pattern is, in fact, a common occurrence in organizations, and is the basis for much of the debate over oligarchy. Party elections may therefore be considered a necessary but, by themselves, insufficient precondition for the existence of internal party democracy.[37]

Democracy within the PSI Federation was possible because there were two distinct, and independently powerful, factions within the party who pursued their own specific benefits. The PSI party system rested upon these two leadership sets. The personal interests of the leaders of the factions were tied to the divisive policy considerations that underlay the fight for dominance between the groups. The minority Leftist faction was intensely concerned with party policy, fearing a move toward the center would jeopardize the faction's good relations with the trade unions and would deprive the leaders of their extra-party posts. The Leftists devoted much of their energy to countering the rightward drift of the party under the Autonomists. The differences between the faction, of course, also represented basic disagreements on ideology. Yet, the factional cleavage was not broad enough to prevent the second ranking Leftist leader in the province from joining the Autonomists when the opportunity arose.

The lesson to be learned is obvious: it is unreasonable to expect rational men to act counter to their own interests, and if one wishes to maximize the democratic potential of an organization, one must find ways to secure specific benefits for those who are willing to oppose the majority. Structural independence is very important to the procurement of these benefits. This is the insight of those who view such devices as pluralism and federalism as conducive to democracy. There are several functional equivalents to pluralism and federalism within organizations, including the independence of levels, multiple hierarchies, and periodic elections. The latter method has its weaknesses; organizational elites can often dominate elections unless a structural independence supporting an opposition's quest for specific benefits is also present.

There are, of course, many other bases for party democracy.

---

[37] Linz, *op. cit.*, makes this point.

Middle class groups normally are not dependent on politics for their sustenance and consequently can afford the risks involved in opposition. Politically competent groups can also pay the initially high, and continuing, costs of organization. But financial security and high political competence are precisely what low status groups lack, one reason for the mass party in the first place. The argument presented here is not that specific benefits must be provided the opposition, but rather that the provision of such incentives facilitates internal party democracy. As the logic of collective action suggests, party democracy in the case studied was a by-product of different leaders pursuing their individual noncollective benefits.

The logic of collective action has been very useful in achieving a theoretical formulation of the bases of democracy in the PSI Federation of Arezzo. It has encouraged us to look behind the ideological and policy differences between the two factions and to seek to understand them in terms of specific and noncollective benefits. It enables us to understand and reconcile the differences between the rational (in the economic sense) activities of the elite and the largely nonrational behavior of the rank and file. It also suggests a possible reconciliation between approaches to the study of party organization that view the goal of political parties as the achievement of public office and those that see parties as pursuing their own particular vision of a collective good. The logic of collective action suggests that both approaches can be subsumed under one that asks, what are the specific noncollective benefits accruing to party participants? The differences between the two approaches derive from different sources of specific benefits.

As a theory of politics, the logic of collective action was designed to refine group theory. It was not elaborated as a theory of political parties. However, it holds great promise as a theory able to explain—perhaps elegantly—patterns of behavior in organizations that are currently viewed as too disparate to permit meaningful comparison.

FOUR

Candidate Selection and Party Cohesion in Britain and the United States*

Austin Ranney

University of Wisconsin

FOR NEARLY A CENTURY, American political scientists have studied the British party system, not only for its intrinsic interest but also as a way of better understanding and evaluating the American system. In 1879, Woodrow Wilson first used British parties as the standard for judging their American counterparts.[1] And many others, from A. Lawrence Lowell and Henry Jones Ford in Wilson's time to Samuel Beer, Harry Eckstein, Leon Epstein, Roland Young, and others in our own, have found the study of British ways useful for appraising American.

British scholars have been less inclined to reverse the process; but British politicians—from the organizers of the registration societies in the 1830's, through Joseph Chamberlain's development of the Birmingham Caucus, to Harold Wilson's attentive reading of White's *The Making of the President, 1960*—have picked up useful pointers by studying American practices.

* This is a revised version of a paper delivered at the Annual Meeting of The American Political Science Association, Washington, D.C., September, 1965. I am grateful to Dean Leon D. Epstein and Professor Warren E. Miller for their comments on the first draft.

[1] See his articles, "Cabinet Government in the United States," *International Review*, 7 (August, 1879), pp. 146–163; and "Committee or Cabinet Government?", *Overland Monthly*, Series 2, 3 (January, 1884), pp. 17–33; and his famous doctoral dissertation, *Congressional Government* (Boston: Houghton, Mifflin and Co., 1885).

American scholars have explored many aspects of British party politics,[2] but the feature intriguing them most has been the parliamentary parties' cohesion—their ability to muster all or almost all their M.P.s in the division lobby stipulated by the whips on any issue the party leaders direct. We may date American investigation of this phenomenon from Lowell's influential pioneer study of party voting on both sides of the Atlantic. To evaluate the charge, often heard in the 1890's, that American party "bosses" regularly "dictate" how their legislators vote, Lowell tabulated roll calls in seven sessions of the House of Commons, six sessions of Congress, and one session each in five state legislatures. He found a much higher incidence of "true party votes" (i.e., roll calls in which more than 90 per cent of the members of one party vote Yea, and more than 90 per cent of the members of the other party vote Nay) in Britain than in the United States, and thus first documented a characteristic of British parties that has fascinated Americans ever since.[3]

In 1928, Stuart Rice published his "index of cohesion," a somewhat more refined measure than Lowell's "party vote."[4] Since then, a number of political scientists have applied the Lowell and/or Rice measures to Congress and state legislatures, and most have contrasted the high cohesion of British parties to the substantially lower cohesion of American parties.[5]

There are several good reasons why students of American politics should try to understand the degree, causes, and consequences of British party cohesion. The most obvious is its central role in the doctrine of responsible party government. This doctrine, first developed by Woodrow Wilson and ably advocated in our time by E. E. Schattschneider, Stephen Bailey,

[2] The late Lord Morrison of Lambeth once complained to me, "There are so many of you American chaps clogging our corridors and anterooms asking questions, it's hard to get any work done!"

[3] "The Influence of Party upon Legislation in England and America," *Annual Report of the American Historical Association for the Year 1901* (Washington, D.C.: Government Printing Office, 1902), 1, pp. 321–542.

[4] *Quantitative Methods in Politics* (New York: Alfred A. Knopf, 1928), pp. 208–209.

[5] E.g., Julius Turner, *Party and Constituency* (Baltimore: The Johns Hopkins Press, 1951); David B. Truman, *The Congressional Party* (New York: John Wiley & Sons, Inc., 1959); and Malcolm E. Jewell, "Party Voting in American State Legislatures," *American Political Science Review,* 49 (September, 1955), pp. 773–791.

and James Burns,[6] holds party cohesion in government to be the chief prerequisite for creating parties that are programmatically effective and democratically responsible. And while their ideal party system is not necessarily an exact duplicate of British practices, the fact that, in their view, each British party is cohesive and therefore collectively responsible for its stewardship of the government shows that the ideal of responsible party government is no mere academic fantasy. Clearly, then, the wellsprings of British cohesion are of the highest interest for scholars of this persuasion; for if they can learn how the British get the job done they will know better what must be done here.

But even we who are unconvinced of the feasibility or desirability of Anglicizing American parties find the difference in cohesion of great interest. It is, after all, a difference that seems to affect the two governing systems profoundly. If we can advance our understanding of its root causes we will not only learn a good deal about Britain and the United States but about the process of government in any modern mass democracy.

Where, then, should we look? One possibility which has received relatively little attention is the two countries' procedures for selecting national legislative candidates. And here I should note the first thing I learned about American politics by studying Britain: the utility of distinguishing between "candidate selection" and "nomination." Like most Americans, I was accustomed to using the two terms interchangeably to denote the whole politico-legal process by which particular persons emerge from the general population to appear on general-election ballots either as party standard-bearers or as "finalists" in nonpartisan elections.[7] But I found that in Britain "nomination" denotes only the legal proceeding by which eligible per-

[6] See Schattschneider, *Party Government* (New York: Farrar and Rinehart, 1942); Bailey, *The Condition of Our National Parties* (New York; Fund for the Republic, 1959); Burns, *The Deadlock of Democracy* (Englewood Cliffs, N.J.: Prentice-Hall, Inc., 1963); and my *The Doctrine of Responsible Party Government* (Urbana: University of Illinois Press, 1962).

[7] For examples of this usage, see Austin Ranney and Willmoore Kendall, *Democracy and the American Party System* (New York: Harcourt, Brace and Co., 1956), pp. 265–267; V. O. Key, Jr., *Politics, Parties, & Pressure Groups* (5th ed.; New York: Thomas Y. Crowell Co., 1964), pp. 370–371; and Hugh A. Bone, *American Politics and the Party System* (3rd ed.; New York: McGraw-Hill Book Company, Inc., 1965), Ch. 11.

sons are formally designated "candidates" and have their names accepted by public authorities for printing on election ballots. The extralegal process by which each party decides whom it will support is generally called "candidate selection." These differences in usage no doubt stem from the fact that under America's direct primary laws the final legal process for designating candidates for the ballot and the final party process for choosing standard-bearers are one and the same, whereas in Britain, as in most other democracies, they are quite separate.[8]

If we adopt this distinction, as I believe we should, then clearly we are interested in the relation of "candidate selection," not "nomination," to party cohesion in the two nations. But why should we hypothesize that one materially affects the other? I see at least two reasons. First is the general proposition stated by Schattschneider and supported by most students of parties that

> The nominating [i.e., candidate selecting] process . . . has become the crucial process of the party. The nature of the nominating procedure determines the nature of the party; he who can make nominations is the owner of the party. This is therefore one of the best points at which to observe the distribution of power within the party.[9]

If the candidate selecting process is indeed so central to party structure and activity, then the differences in the two nations' modes of choosing candidates must surely affect the cohesion of their legislative members.

The second reason is the widely-held belief that British national party agencies so closely control the selection of parliamentary candidates that they can both "place" especially loyal and desirable candidates in safe seats and "veto" the readoption of especially disloyal and undesirable M.P.s. This, of course, is in sharp contrast with the American national party agencies' almost total lack of control over congressional nominations. The

---

[8] Some writers on American parties have employed a comparable distinction without making it as explicit as I am suggesting here: cf. Avery Leiserson, *Parties and Politics* (New York: Alfred A. Knopf, 1958), pp. 100–101; and Frank J. Sorauf, *Political Parties in the American System* (Boston: Little, Brown & Co., 1964), pp. 98–104.

[9] *Op. cit.*, p. 64.

British arrangement, some believe, almost guarantees cohesive parliamentary parties, while the American almost precludes cohesive congressional parties.[10]

Whether these are good reasons or bad, they prompted me, as an "Americanist" especially interested in the doctrine of responsible party government, to study candidate selection in Great Britain.[11] With generous support from the Social Science Research Council, I spent 1961–1962 in Britain interviewing national and local party leaders, candidates, and aspirants, and collected socio-economic data about the candidates and the constituencies in which they stood in the general elections of 1951, 1955, 1959, and 1964, and in all by-elections from 1951 to 1961.[12] The purpose of the present paper is to report some reflections about candidate selection and party cohesion in the United States suggested by my study of their British counterparts.

I

Figure 1 outlines the main features of the British and American processes for selecting parliamentary and congressional candidates. A glance at it discloses several similarities and two particularly striking differences.

[10] Two leading academic statements of this view are: Schattschneider, *op. cit.*, pp. 99–100; and Herman Finer, *The Theory and Practice of Modern Government*, rev. ed. (New York: Henry Holt and Co., 1949), p. 243. It is impossible to say exactly how prevalent this belief is; some scholars of British politics have advised me that no one of any stature holds so extreme a view. But I have encountered it often in discussions with scholars and politicians on both sides of the Atlantic, and my impression is that it is the prevailing, not to say the only, view.

[11] There are several useful but brief descriptions available, notably Robert T. McKenzie, *British Political Parties* (2nd ed.; London: Mercury Books, 1964), pp. 241–253, 549–558; Peter G. Richards, *Honourable Members* (London: Faber & Faber, Ltd., 1959), Ch. 1; Martin Harrison, *Trade Unions and the Labour Party since 1945* (London: George Allen & Unwin, Ltd., 1960), pp. 80–88, Ch. 6; and several articles in the *Political Quarterly*, 30 (July–September, 1959). But there is no comprehensive analysis comparable to David Butler's study of the electoral system.

[12] The results are published in *Pathways to Parliament* (Madison: University of Wisconsin Press, 1965) and (London: Macmillan and Co., Ltd., 1965).

FIGURE 1

CANDIDATE SELECTION PROCEDURES IN BRITAIN AND THE UNITED STATES

Selection Stage	British Procedures	American Procedures
1. Preliminary local party selection.	1. "Short lists" drawn up by small screening committees after considering and/or soliciting possibilities. Almost always done in secret.	1. Where local parties are strong, organization's choice is made after considering and/or soliciting possibilities. Almost always done in secret. Where local parties are weak, changing congeries of local factions push several different aspirants, and there is no organization choice.
2. Final local party selection.	2. By small representative councils elected by dues-paying local party members. Usually done in secret. (Conservatives also have final ratification by a meeting of all local dues-paying members.)	2. Same as 4.
3. National party endorsement.	3. A national agency must endorse the local selection before he or she may appear publicly as the party's official candidate.*	3. None.
4. Legal nomination.	4. Nomination paper entered with constituency returning officer; ten signatures of qualified voters in constituency required; £150 deposit, returned if candidate polls over 1/8 of general election vote; no party designations on the ballot.	4. Winner of each party's direct primary election in state or district automatically goes on the ballot as his party's official nominee. (Four states nominate senatorial candidates by state conventions of locally selected delegates.)

* In the Conservative and Labour parties, but not in the Liberal party.

The first difference is in stage two. In the United States most final local party selections are made simultaneously with the legal nominations in direct primaries by procedures almost identical with those used in general elections. The rules are laid down by the state, not the parties; the aspirants' campaigns are conducted openly and resemble general-election campaigns; any eligible voter can participate no matter how little commitment he may have to a party; the party leaders have no effective control over who participates; public, not party officials, count the ballots and report the results; and the procedures are enforced by courts of law. The whole system is based upon the belief, deeply held by the Progressive authors of direct primary legislation, that a political party is not a purely private organization, but at least quasi-public; therefore, its mode of selecting candidates, like its ways of getting and spending campaign funds, should be regulated by law—and regulated so as to transfer control of candidate selection from the "party bosses" to "the people."

In Great Britain, on the other hand, the final local party selections are made by rules and procedures drawn up and enforced entirely by party agencies; such campaigning as the aspirants may attempt is conducted almost entirely out of the general public's gaze; the selections are made in secret by small bodies of local dues-paying party activists; local party officers count the ballots and report the results; and deviations from the prescribed procedures are appealed to national party officials, not to the courts or other public authorities. The British system rests upon the prevailing belief that political parties are purely private associations, like garden clubs or societies to end cruel sports; hence their internal affairs, such as the way they select their parliamentary candidates, are no concern of the law or general public. Moreover—and the contrast here is even more striking to an American observer—the British news media have long respected the parties' privacy far more than have their American confreres; only occasionally have reporters pried into local selection controversies and published their findings—all of which considerably complicates scholarly data-gathering.[13]

---

[13] One aspect of the recent "Americanization" of British politics and society is that this seems to be changing: I found substantially more newspaper accounts of local candidate selections for the period 1959–1965 than for the period before 1959.

Let us label these two modes of candidate selection "open" and "closed," referring to the substantially different proportions of the general electorate having direct access to the selection process. How different are they in terms of the way most candidates are actually selected? There is no doubt that a hard-fought American primary—e.g., Kennedy v. McCormack, Salinger v. Cranston, Blatt v. Musmanno—is in many respects very open indeed. It is fought largely in public; great sums are spent on mass-media propaganda for the contenders and the decision is formally left to people who have made and intend to make little or no contribution to the party beyond giving it their vote in the general election—if that.[14] It is far more open than even the most contentious and publicized selection controversy in Britain.

But how frequent are such free-for-alls in American elections? Recent studies of our primaries have found that such contests are by no means the rule. Their frequency depends in part upon the party's presumed chances of winning the general election (the greater its chances, the more likely are contests in its primaries), and in part upon the state or district organization's ability to foreclose contests by convincing the aspirants it has passed over that they cannot successfully challenge its choice. Hence, in many instances the candidate is, in fact if not in form, selected by the local party leaders in private conclave quite as closed as any in Britain, and their choices encounter only token opposition or no opposition at all in the primaries.[15]

So it must be said that while most American selections are *de jure* open and all British are *de jure* closed, many American selections are *de facto* quite as closed as any in Britain. But what, if anything, does this tell us about party cohesion in the two countries? Implicit in some of the responsible-party-government literature is the assumption that open candidate selection tends to produce low cohesion and closed selection high

---

[14] Although there is some evidence that primary electorates far more than those in general elections are made up of the most partisan, active, and loyal segments of each party's following: see Austin Ranney and Leon D. Epstein, "The Two Electorates: Voters and Non-Voters in a Wisconsin Primary," *Journal of Politics*, 28 (August, 1966), pp. 598–616.

[15] Cf. Key, *op. cit.*, Ch. 16; and Sorauf, *op. cit.*, pp. 98–104. See also Sorauf's *Party and Representation* (New York: Atherton Press, 1963), Chs. 3–5.

cohesion. Presumably the winner of a primary who has defeated the several contenders by his own efforts owes the party organization nothing, and, if elected, is more likely to vote as he pleases, not as the party leaders wish. Conversely, a legislator who owes his nomination and election to the party organization is more likely to heed its desires. Hence the closed primary is better than the open primary, and by extension, the closed British system is better than the open American system.[16]

Plausible though this reasoning may appear, American experience does not support it. Ira Ralph Telford, for example, reports that from 1945 to 1960 United States Senators from states with open primaries in the legal sense had slightly *higher* party-unity scores than Senators from closed-primary states.[17] The Sorauf and MacRae studies of the Pennsylvania and Massachusetts legislatures found that substantially more of the variance in legislators' party unity could be explained by the socio-economic character of their constituencies than by their selection by open or closed methods as we are using the terms.[18] Accordingly, the generally greater prevalence of open candidate selection procedures in the United States than in Great Britain tells us very little about why British parliamentary parties are more cohesive than American congressional parties.

Another line of inquiry is suggested by the observations of Huitt, Key, Sorauf, and others that American state and congressional district party organizations are quite separate—and see themselves as quite separate—from the congressional party organizations. Thus a Senator's or Representative's loyalty to his local party in gratitude for past support and hope for more of the same in the future is not automatically translated into

[16] No advocate of responsible party government puts the argument as badly as in the text, but it seems implicit in, e.g., the claim of the American Political Science Association's Committee on Political Parties that "the question of open versus closed primaries needs to be considered from the angle of strengthening rather than weakening party cohesion and responsibility. The closed primary deserves preference because it is more readily compatible with the development of a responsible party system": *Toward a More Responsible Two-Party System* (New York: Rinehart & Co., 1950), p. 71.

[17] "Types of Primary and Party Responsibility," *American Political Science Review*, 59 (March, 1965), pp. 117–118.

[18] Cf. Sorauf, *Party and Representation, op. cit.*, pp. 133–144; and Duncan MacRae, Jr., "The Relation between Roll-Call Votes and Constituencies in the Massachusetts Legislature," *American Political Science Review*, 46 (December, 1952), pp. 1046–1055.

loyalty to the national legislative party even though they bear the same label. Indeed, loyalty to the local party may *require* disloyalty to the national. When this is the case, the local loyalty is usually the more powerful, for it more directly affects the congressman's ability to get himself renominated and re-elected.

If this is so, then perhaps the cohesion of British parties rests on a relationship between national and local party agencies very different from that in the United States.

II

The second major difference in the two systems of candidate selection lies in the national party agencies' formal powers over local selections. In both nations the final selections of national legislative candidates are made locally—by state and district primaries (and, in a few states, conventions) in the United States, and by constituency party organizations in Britain. American national party agencies have no formal powers over local selections; the winner of a party's state or district primary automatically becomes its legal nominee no matter how distasteful he may be to the President or the national committee or the party's congressional leaders.

On the other hand, the Conservative and Labour national agencies' formal powers over local candidate selections[19] are most impressive to American eyes. Both party headquarters maintain lists of nationally-approved candidates and urge the constituency organizations to choose from them; the absence of a local-residence rule for M.P.s permits the national leaders to place particularly desirable aspirants in safe seats with little regard for their geographical backgrounds; both national offices employ full-time regional representatives to see that the local organizations follow proper procedures and to press the causes of nationally-favored aspirants; and both enjoy the power to veto any undesirable local choice and thereby effectively deny him the party label. Labour's supervisory powers are even more elaborate than the Conservatives', but both parties' powers fulfill every requirement of the responsible-party-government model.[20]

[19] The Liberals' national agencies have almost no formal power over local candidate selection.

[20] The formal powers are reviewed in detail in *Pathways to Parliament, op. cit.*, Chs. 2 and 5.

Yet, each British party's *actual* central control is substantially weaker than one would suppose from reading its rules. It is important to understand why.

First, conflict between national and local party organizations over candidate selection is—in Britain as in the United States—endemic. It stems from certain inherent differences in outlook familiar on both sides of the Atlantic. On the one hand, the national leaders view the candidature[21] of any particular constituency as merely one local element in a much broader national operation, and they want it to contribute to the national effort. Thus, they want their national roster of candidates to be "representative," that is, to include persons from all major segments of society—the British version of the "balanced ticket"; they want persons with the talents and expertise needed by the parliamentary party placed in the safest seats; and they want candidates in all constituencies (but especially in the winnable ones[22]) who will give loyal support to the party's national leaders and program.

On the other hand, a constituency organization is likely to see its candidature from a more local perspective. Most of its activists are well aware that selecting the parliamentary candidate is the only real power they have left (resolutions at annual party conferences, as McKenzie has shown, are more rituals than decisions).[23] If they surrender it they accept completely the status of local servants of national masters, which is not the best psychological base for doing the hard work of canvassing and fund-raising that the local party demands and the national party finds useful. But in none of the three British parties are they willing to do so; rather, most are extremely jealous of their prerogative to select the candidate and quick to resent any effort to interfere by the national leaders.

Second, this means that national headquarters cannot, as some suppose, "place" any candidate—or even type of candidate

[21] The term "candidature" refers to the position of official party nominee for a specified electoral district.

[22] In this essay and this volume "winnability" (or "winnable") has a specific meaning. It refers to the politicians' estimation of their party's chances of success in given constituencies. The assessment is based on the party's poll (vote) in the previous general election and an evaluation of current public opinion trends. For a further discussion of the concept, see Ranney, *Pathways to Parliament, op. cit.*, pp. 286–287.

[23] McKenzie, *op. cit.*, Chs. 4, 8, 10.

—in any constituency they wish. In party "law" and political fact the final selection belongs to the local organization, and headquarters can arrange the adoption of a favored aspirant only by enlisting the cooperation of the local leaders, never by issuing orders. Indeed, if an aspirant, however attractive, becomes locally known as "Central Office's man" or "Transport House's candidate," that in itself is usually enough to eliminate him. ("Carpetbagger," I was surprised to learn, is a term often used by local party leaders in Britain.) Significantly, such guidance as the national agencies do manage comes mainly through the efforts of the area agents and regional organizers; and while these are national party employees with national obligations, their effectiveness depends on how well they know the constituency leaders and hold their confidence.

Third, the national agencies' veto powers have played only a minor role in the disciplining of rebel M.P.s. The Conservatives have used their veto only once since 1945, and then not against a maverick M.P. but against a "crypto-fascist" who had been selected in a marginal Labour seat. Even more striking is the fact that although a number of Conservative M.P.s have defied and/or resigned the whip since 1945, not one has had his re-adoption even challenged, let alone denied, by Central Office. Indeed, on more than one occasion Central Office leaders have publicly declared that, as a matter of principle, the selection of candidates—and therefore the decision as to whether a rebel M.P. should be readopted—is a matter for the constituency associations, not Central Office.[24]

A brief review of the circumstances in which Conservative associations have and have not refused to readopt their M.P.s is instructive. I found a total of 18 instances between 1945 and 1964 in which Conservative M.P.s' readoptions were seriously challenged, including 12 in which readoption was denied. Half the cases involved local objections to the M.P.s' personal deficiencies (e.g., excessive age, divorce, or failure to render adequate local services) and had no ideological or programmatic overtones. The other half arose because some association "influentials" objected to their M.P.s' defiance of the whip. Most of the latter cases resulted from the parliamentary party's split over the Eden government's military intervention in Suez in 1956. The split and its consequences have been well told else-

---

[24] *Pathways to Parliament, ibid.*, pp. 42–51.

where,[25] but the essentials are worth recounting here. Eight "left-wing rebels" abstained from voting on Labour's motion of no-confidence in the government and thereby gave aid and comfort to the opposition at a time when feelings on both sides ran high. The constituency associations of all eight expressed strong disapproval of their M.P.s' abstentions, demanded an accounting, and seriously questioned whether the rebels should be readopted. Three were directly denied readoption, two resigned their candidatures without a fight, and the other three managed to survive. A year later eight "right-wing rebels" resigned the whip to protest the Macmillan government's decision to accept Nasser's control of the Canal. Six of the eight explained their resignations to their constituency associations, and all received near-unanimous votes of confidence and public statements upholding "the right of an M.P. to disagree with the Government on any issue and to abstain from voting if he so wishes"[26]—a principle hardly appropriate for the presumed working model of responsible party government! The other two did not even bother to justify their actions, but received strong votes of confidence anyway.

In short: since 1945, various Conservative M.P.s have strayed from the party line on one occasion or another. The national party leaders have had ample formal power to veto the rebels' readoptions, and these are precisely the circumstances in which, according to the doctrine of responsible party government, the power should have been used. Yet in not one case did headquarters attempt or even contemplate any such action. On the other hand, *certain kinds* of rebellion provoked some constituency associations into denying readoptions. The rebel M.P.s who took positions to the left of the national leaders and nearer Labour's stand were subjected to severe questioning by their constituency associations, and five lost their seats. But none of the rebels taking positions to the *right* of the national leaders—the "true Conservative" position as seen by the local activists—was disciplined by his constituency association in any way. Several, indeed, were even lauded for their "independence" in ringing phrases familiar to American ears.

[25] Notably by Leon D. Epstein, "British M.P.s and Their Local Parties: The Suez Case," *American Political Science Review,* 54 (June, 1960), pp. 374–390; and *British Politics in the Suez Crisis* (Urbana: University of Illinois Press, 1963), Ch. 6.

[26] Quoted in *Pathways to Parliament, op. cit.,* p. 84.

The Labour party's situation has been somewhat different. I found a total of 16 instances between 1945 and 1964 in which Labour M.P.s' readoptions were seriously challenged, and in 12 readoption was denied. Three main patterns were evident. (1) *Central challenge:* in four instances, all involving left-wing critics of the Labour government's anti-Communist foreign policy in the late 1940's, the National Executive Committee took the initiative by expelling rebel M.P.s from the party, thereby automatically disqualifying them for readoption. In three of the four cases the constituency Labour parties tried to resist, but were forced to capitulate by the NEC's threat to expel anyone who supported the rebels. (2) *Local challenge and central acquiescence:* in six instances local Labour parties denied readoption to their M.P.s and national headquarters acquiesced. Two were dismissed for parliamentary deviations—one right-winger (Alfred Edwards) who voted against the party's iron and steel nationalization bill in 1948, and another right-winger (Stanley Evans) who spoke against and abstained from Labour's censure of Eden's Suez venture. The others were dismissed for, respectively, excessive age, personal dishonesty, heavy drinking, and failure to provide adequate local services. (In four instances challenged M.P.s rallied enough local support to win readoption and retain their seats.) (3) *Local challenge and central resistance:* in two cases Bevanite constituency parties tried to force out right-wing M.P.s, but were prevented from doing so by the NEC's threat to expel anyone who supported such a move. So Labour constituency parties, like their Conservative opposite numbers, have been very tolerant of left-wing deviations (away from the Conservatives and toward "true socialism"), but very severe on right-wing deviations toward the Conservatives' position. Thus in both parties not all breaches of party discipline have been frowned on—only those which supported the opposition's position.

The NEC has also refused endorsement to five locally-selected candidates who were not M.P.s. Four of the five were highly visible leaders of the party's left wing, and the fifth had supported an Independent against the party's official candidate in the preceding general election. In all instances the constituency parties complained, but nevertheless adopted new and more acceptable candidates.

Thus Labour's NEC has used its veto power noticeably more than Conservative Central Office, and perhaps more nearly fits the responsible-parties model. But at least as significant for the present discussion is the much larger number of instances in which the NEC has *not* expelled rebel M.P.s or vetoed left-wing candidates. In 1955, for example, the Parliamentary Labour Party withdrew the whip from Aneurin Bevan and seven of his most intransigent followers, and the NEC seriously considered expelling them from the party. But the Bevanites were strong in many constituency parties, and they were not pro-Communist like the M.P.s punished so severely in the late 1940's. Consequently, things were patched up, the eight rebels were readmitted to the parliamentary party, and the NEC did not have to face the formidable challenge of trying to force their constituency parties not to readopt them. In 1961, the PLP withdrew the whip from five left-wing M.P.s for voting contrary to the party's position; but one of the first things Harold Wilson did on assuming the leadership in 1963 was to restore the whip to them, and again the NEC was spared the task of trying to prevent their readoption.

From 1945, at least, to Hugh Gaitskell's death in 1963, Labour's national candidate-supervising machinery was firmly controlled by the party's right wing. Yet during that time a substantial number of left-wing candidates—some of whom made no secret of their aversion to the party's official policies and leaders—were adopted *and* endorsed by the NEC. Many were, of course, in hopelessly Conservative constituencies where they were relatively harmless from the NEC's point of view. But enough were in marginal and safe seats that some believe the PLP in the mid-1960's has a higher proportion of left-wing M.P.s than it had in the 1940's and 1950's.[27]

In short: while Labour's national leaders have controlled local candidate selections somewhat more closely than have their Conservative counterparts, the two parties' similarities are far greater than their differences. And while both parties' national agencies play distinctly more active roles than their American analogues in candidate selection, the great majority of the choices are in fact made by the constituency organizations. Hence, the differences between the central supervision of candidate selection in Britain and the absence of such supervision in the United States accounts for very little of the differences in the two systems' legislative party cohesion.

[27] See the evidence cited in Leon D. Epstein, "New M.P.s and the Politics of the PLP," *Political Studies*, 10 (June, 1962), pp. 121–129.

III

The foregoing suggests that while candidate selection in Britain is both more closed and more centralized than in the United States, the behavioral differences are not as great as some suppose and certainly do not account for the differences in the cohesion of their legislative parties. Yet British parliamentary parties *are* more cohesive than American congressional parties. Evidently, then, even though Central Office and Transport House do not and cannot force them to do so, Conservative and Labour constituency organizations nevertheless choose candidates who, when elected, dutifully vote as the whips direct in all but the most exceptional circumstances.

Why? In my opinion the principal causes of British party cohesion have already been identified by Epstein, McKenzie, and others,[28] but perhaps I can add something from my study of candidate selection.

First, as Epstein and McKenzie point out, the British version of parliamentary government demands team play from its parties while the American version of presidential government does not. In the British system, if the majority party loses a vote on a major issue, either the opposition must take over the government or a new election must be called which the opposition might win. Thus each parliamentary vote has electoral as well as programmatic consequences; it is a vote not only on whether the particular measure should be passed, but also on whether the party controlling the government should continue to do so. This means that if a majority party M.P. opposes his leaders on a particular issue, voting against them is no mere registration of his dissent on that issue alone with no implications about whether they should continue in office; it also means—and there is no way he can escape it—that he is willing to see his party turned out of power and the other side put in as the price of defeating the particular bill. This is a choice few are willing to make no matter how much they oppose a particular party stand.

No such dilemma confronts a legislator in the American system. The President, Senators, and Representatives all con-

<hr>

[28] See particularly Leon D. Epstein, "Cohesion of British Parliamentary Parties," *American Political Science Review,* 50 (June, 1956), pp. 360–377; and McKenzie, *op. cit.,* Ch. 11.

tinue in office until their constitutional terms expire regardless of what happens to the administration's legislative program. Hence the only direct and immediate consequences of congressional votes are programmatic, not electoral. If a Democratic Senator, say, votes against the administration's foreign aid bill, he is voting on that issue alone; he certainly is not voting to replace Lyndon Johnson with Barry Goldwater or Democratic committee chairmen with Republican.

Now, if the British and American major parties are first and foremost agencies for winning elections and only secondarily agencies for pressing particular programs or philosophies—and surely they are far more alike than different in this respect—then their differences in cohesion are more easily understood. American parties can tolerate legislative rebellions because they do not pose immediate electoral threats, while British parties cannot tolerate more than a few occasional individual aberrations; anything more creates a clear and present electoral danger. This explanation is confirmed, as Epstein has shown, by the fact that Canadian parliamentary parties, operating in a British-type parliamentary system, are highly cohesive despite the fact that many other aspects of their environment (e.g., federalism and intense local loyalties) make for low cohesion.[29]

Second, while, as I have suggested, there is plenty of "localism" in British party politics, it is not quite the same kind we are accustomed to in the United States. Like ours, it requires non-programmatic local services from its legislators—e.g., appearing at local party dances, bazaars, and other social affairs. It even requires an M.P. to hold periodic "surgeries" to let the local voters tell him their troubles. But unlike ours, it does not require him to vote against official party policy in Westminster to advance local interests. A British constituency party exists to elect one national public official, its M.P.; it is not involved in electing slates of local or regional officials, as state and even district organizations often are in America. It is manned by activists whose ideological and programmatic loyalties belong to the *national* party's leaders and cause. The local activists know that when their M.P. takes his seat he cannot be an inde-

[29] Leon D. Epstein, "A Comparative Study of Canadian Parties," *American Political Science Review*, 58 (March, 1964), pp. 46–59. See also Allan Kornberg, "Caucus and Cohesion in Canadian Parliamentary Parties," *American Political Science Review*, 60 (March, 1966), pp. 83–92.

pendent operator like an American legislator. Effective power lies in the ministries and the Cabinet, and the only way the backbencher can change the course of public policy is to persuade the governing party's leaders to change their program. Voting with the opposition is voting to put the other party team ahead of his own, and, as the Suez cases suggest, most local activists feel that giving aid and comfort to the opposition is the most heinous of political sins. Hence they are quick to call to account the M.P. who breaks party ranks to support the opposition, but benignly tolerant of one who deserts the parliamentary party when its leaders take a weaker anti-opposition line than he (and the local militants) think "true conservatism" or "true socialism" demands. So for the most part the national party agencies do not need to discipline rebel M.P.s by denying readoption; the local party organizations are, at least in the circumstances just noted, only too eager to do the job for them —indeed, often far more eager than the national leaders would prefer. On the few occasions in which the local organizations are prepared to resist the national party line to the end, the national agencies' power to bring them to heel is well short of absolute.

Third, central supervision of candidate selection in Britain is clearly not a major cause of the parliamentary parties' cohesion. Lowell's study showed that cohesion was already high by the 1890's, but the present centralization of candidate selection goes back only to the mid-1930's. Both the Conservative and Labour parties adopted the new procedures not so much to keep rebel M.P.s in line as to prevent local parties from adopting candidates of inferior personal quality or extreme views who might tarnish the parties' national images and damage their chances of winning national majorities. Moreover, the Liberals' national supervision of candidate selection has always been much weaker than the Conservatives' or Labour's—indeed, little greater than the Democrats' or Republicans'; yet the few Liberals in Parliament have been no less cohesive than their rivals. So if we in the United States want British-style party cohesion, the evidence suggests that copying British methods of selecting candidates is not the way to get it.

Finally, neither the British mode of selecting candidates nor the cohesion of British parties are separate political tools individually available for export. Each is a strand interwoven with the whole British socio-political fabric. If we really want the cohesion part, we will have to import the whole package:

parliamentary government, co-optative selection of leaders by small groups of party activists, the conduct of most party affairs secretly by party rules rather than openly by public laws, the reduction of the ordinary legislator from the status of "independent operator" to that of "lobby fodder"—and the whole body of beliefs about majority rule and minority rights on which, as I have argued elsewhere, it rests. And whether we can, or should, do *that* is another question.

FIVE

Retrieving Information for a Comparative Study of Political Parties

Kenneth Janda

Northwestern University

THIS CHAPTER describes plans for a comparative study of virtually all the world's established political parties in the period 1950–1962. Data for the study will be derived from the vast published literature on political parties which has been produced since 1950. The broad methodological problem that confronts the study is to gather, process and analyze the enormous amount of information to be found in the literature. This chapter reviews the history and background of the project and sets forth the various information retrieval techniques proposed for assembling the data.

History and Background

Interest in conducting a world-wide comparative study of political parties resulted from my experience in teaching the undergraduate course on parties at Northwestern University.[1] Many instructors restricted their undergraduate course to the study of political parties in the United States. The fine texts on American parties, the students' inherent interest in learning about the Democratic and Republican parties and the realistic time limitations of a one-term course which restrict the

[1] I want to thank Richard C. Snyder, former Chairman of the Political Science Department at Northwestern University, for stimulating and encouraging my interests in teaching the parties course in a comparative framework.

subject-matter to be covered all contribute to the American focus.

These factors notwithstanding, a comparative perspective has advantages. Not only would students learn about party politics in foreign countries—a worthy objective in itself—but they would also learn more about *American* party politics through cross-national comparisons. True, students would acquire less detailed knowledge about party operations in the United States, but details are most likely to be forgotten within a few weeks after the course has ended. On the other hand, cross-national comparisons would call attention to the basic nature of American parties as non-membership, decentralized, loosely disciplined organizations and would promote a better— and more lasting—understanding of the American party system. To me, the promised benefits of comparing different party systems seemed to outweigh the advantages of studying the American party system in depth.

A major problem in teaching a comparative parties course, however, is the scarcity of suitable text material. There are many fine texts on American political parties and a number of very good books on party systems in other countries. But works that attempt genuine cross-national comparisons of political parties are almost non-existent. Maurice Duverger's relatively young, already classic, and much-critiqued book, *Political Parties*, is the only comprehensive comparative analysis available.[2] Despite the criticisms leveled against it,[3] *Political Parties* presents a useful set of concepts for studying political parties and actually *compares* parties across nations. From the standpoint of establishing the validity of its analysis, however, Duverger's *Political Parties* suffers greatly from a lack of data on which to base its comparisons.

[2] Sigmund Neumann's *Modern Political Parties* (Chicago: University of Chicago Press, 1956) fails to qualify as a truly comparative text because it is essentially a collection of case studies on the party politics of individual countries. Thomas Hodgkin's *African Political Parties* (Baltimore: Penguin Books, 1961) is comparative in nature but is restricted to African politics.

[3] For reviews of Duverger's *Political Parties* (New York: John Wiley, 1959) see the following: Aaron B. Wildavsky, "A Methodological Critique of Duverger's *Political Parties*," *Journal of Politics*, 21 (May, 1959), pp. 303–318; Frederick C. Englemann, "A Critique of Recent Writings on Political Parties," *Journal of Politics*, 19 (August, 1957), pp. 423–440; and Samuel H. Beer, "*Les Parties Politiques*," *Western Political Quarterly*, 6 (September, 1953), pp. 512–517.

In applying his concepts and drawing his comparisons, Duverger displays an amazing breadth of knowledge about party systems on the European and American continents. He frequently buttresses his remarks with charts and figures on election returns, membership reports, legislative representation, and so on. But despite his heroic attempts to document general propositions, he never provides adequate data. His supporting evidence consists of a series of selected examples, sometimes one or sometimes several, but never approaching a full presentation of the relevant cases. He simply does not have the data required for testing his theoretical statements.

To take one example, Duverger suggests a relationship between the "basic elements" of party organization and the activities carried out by the party. Parties organized on a "caucus" basis are more likely to restrict their activities to contesting elections than are "branch-based" parties, which also perform political education and social welfare functions. "Cell" and "militia" parties are even more likely to exercise welfare functions than branch parties. Duverger supports these propositions by citing specific caucus, branch, cell, and militia parties and describing their activities. But he does not provide the reader with a general overview of the relationship between these concepts for all or a large sample of the world's parties. He lacks the data needed for filling in the cells of a table, similar to Table 1, that relates these concepts.

Despite its limitations, Duverger's insightful book remains the best available, and I adopted it as one of the basic texts in my parties course. It then occurred to me that my students could collect data to test some of Duverger's propositions more thoroughly. Individual students were, in fact, assigned different countries from which to collect information relating to several of Duverger's key concepts. Their assignment was facilitated and their results made comparable by the use of special data recording forms. The students thus acquired genuine research experience relating directly to their course work while producing a body of data that could be used in the closing days of the course to validate textbook assertions.

The experiences of three years of teaching the parties course to students who were conducting coordinated research are reported in another paper.[4] Suffice it to say that, on the

---

[4] Kenneth Janda, "A Methodological Approach to the Comparative Study of Political Parties." Paper delivered before the Seminar on Comparative Politics, University of Michigan, November 18, 1964.

TABLE 1

RELATIONSHIP OF BASIS OF ORGANIZATION TO FUNCTIONAL
ORIENTATION OF ACTIVITIES

	Caucus-Precinct	Branch	Cell-Militia
Party Activities:			
Contest elections (only)	xx	xx	xx
The above and educates politically	xx	xx	xx
The above and serves welfare role	xx	xx	xx
	100%	100%	100%
(Total number of parties)	( )	( )	( )

basis of experience, the research instructions and data gathering instruments underwent considerable change before the students were able to produce usable data. By the end of the third year, however, data of varying degrees of quality were available on some 277 parties in 77 countries.

The nature of the data gathered by the students was determined by the data recording forms. Each student was provided with a set of forms for data on the political system of the country assigned to him and a different set of forms for data on each of the parties in that country. A separate page in each set was reserved for a different variable, and all variables were pre-coded as much as possible for keypunching and subsequent computer analysis.

Students were instructed to check the coded categories on their forms that most closely described the variables relating to their countries and parties. Each coding decision had to be documented with the page number and information source, which was keyed to a bibliography submitted with the data. In addition, students were encouraged to use the remainder of the coding page for a written statement about the information requested. Inconsistencies among sources of information and inadequacies in the codes were to be noted in these statements.

To indicate the nature of the data gathered by the students, two of the coded variables will be presented below. (More complete information on variables and codes is contained in Appendix A of this chapter.) The variables chosen for presentation relate to the party's "basis of organization" and its "functional orientation."

Codes	*Basic element of organization*
1	Caucus: no party membership and officials not chosen by party voters
2	Precinct: no party membership but officials chosen by party voters
3	Branch
4	Cell
5	Militia
6	Other: _____

Codes	*Functional orientation of party*
1	Restricted to nominating candidates and contesting elections
2	Includes the above and undertakes programs of political education
3	Includes the above and provides for social welfare
4	Other: _____

Working mostly with published literature, my 1963 parties class coded, in full or in part, some 205 parties in 55 countries. The data they produced permitted a test during the last class meeting of Duverger's proposition that parties organized on a "caucus" basis are more likely than "branch-based" parties to restrict their activities to contesting elections. Table 1 presented a framework for testing this proposition, given the necessary data. Table 2 is an exact reconstruction of Table 1 except that Table 2 contains data collected for the 87 parties which were coded on both concepts by the students. Assuming their validity for the moment, the data on these parties clearly support Duverger's proposition in a much more conclusive manner than evidence based on a few selected cases.

The data reported in Table 2 are "soft" at best. The information was collected by students whose competencies and motivations varied. But the quality of these data is not at issue. Table

TABLE 2

RELATIONSHIP OF BASIS OF ORGANIZATION TO FUNCTIONAL
ORIENTATION OF ACTIVITIES

Party Activities:	Caucus-Precinct	Branch	Cell-Militia
Contest elections (only)	68	2	5
The above and educates politically	32	85	35
The above and serves welfare role	0	13	60
	100%	100%	100%
(Total Number of Parties)	(22)	(45)	(20)

2 is presented only to illustrate what the results of a systematic
and comprehensive survey of party characteristics might be.

The research project outlined in this paper proposes a
similar survey, but one that would produce reliable data. My
previous experience with student research has convinced me of
the value of approaching the study of political parties through
an exhaustive analysis of secondary sources. The problem with
this approach, of course, is in organizing the relevant literature
in order to extract the necessary information.

At least five major information handling problems confront a researcher who proposes to conduct systematic and comprehensive research on the world's political parties by mining
existing literature. These are:

1. developing an effective method for retrieving information
   from the parties literature,
2. locating literature which contains relevant information on
   parties in the study,
3. building an inventory of propositions and theories about
   political parties and party systems,
4. operationalizing variables in the propositions with reference to information from the literature, and

5. analyzing data for hundreds of parties coded according to variables included in the study.

To some extent, these problems confront almost every research project. The scope of the proposed survey, however, magnifies the tasks far beyond what is conceivable with traditional methods of research. The demands of this project require the utilization of modern information retrieval and information processing technology. A variety of specific techniques are proposed as solutions to the information handling problems presented above. Each of the proposed solutions will be discussed in turn.

Retrieving Information from Parties Literature

In the early stages of the comparative parties project, considerable attention was given to the development and application of computer techniques for retrieving information from political parties literature. The fundamental drawback in using computer techniques for a project of this scale, however, was the tremendous amount of keypunching required to put the literature in machine-readable form. Keypunching costs would go down, of course, if one chose to punch only abstracts of literature rather than entire texts. But this decision would result both in less information going into the system and higher costs in preparing the information for keypunching. At least until optical scanners of printed texts become both practical to use and economical to operate, computer techniques of information retrieval seem unsuited for handling the thousands of books and articles that will eventually form the input to the parties project.

A far more effective method for harnessing this vast literature was found in the MIRACODE system, developed by Recordak, a subsidiary of the Eastman Kodak Company. MIRACODE is an acronym for "Microfilm Information Retrieval Access CODE." The basic components of the MIRACODE system are a special 16 mm. microfilm camera and microfilm reader. The system can retrieve individual pages of microfilmed documents according to one or more three-digit numbers which are used to tag information on each page. These numbers are then transformed into a machine-readable binary code.

Input to the MIRACODE system is in the form of pages from books and articles which are marked with code numbers in the margins corresponding to information contained in the text. A sample page taken from material coded for microfilming is given in Figure 1, which shows a page from a book an Japanese political parties.

While the pages are photographed, the MIRACODE camera translates the written code numbers into a machine-readable binary code of clear and opaque rectangles on the film next to the page image. The page image and the codes are recorded on the film in accordance with the schematic diagram in Figure 2.

Using photography instead of keypunching saves a tremendous amount of time and expense. The entire text is recorded in seconds without need for proofreading and corrections. Along with this advantage, the MIRACODE system has the great virtue of being able to retrieve information from microfilm with code numbers written in the margins and recorded on film. Information is retrieved from microfilm with the use of the MIRACODE reader. A film magazine is placed in the reader and code numbers corresponding to the inquiry are entered into the keyboard on the MIRACODE console (see Figure 3). The MIRACODE reader searches the binary code patterns on the film and stops when the code matches the number or numbers entered on the keyboard. The retrieved page image is projected on a large viewing screen for study. If the first page retrieved does not yield the information, the search can be continued through the rest of the reel, which may contain up to 100 feet of film and several hundred pages of material—depending upon how deeply the information is coded. A full reel of film can be searched in ten seconds. If desired, black-and-white prints can be made of anything projected on the screen simply by pressing a button on the reader.[5]

Obviously, it is crucial that proper code numbers be entered in the page margins for effective retrieval of information about political parties. Rules and instructions are being devised to maximize intercoder reliabilities and promote the retrieval ob-

[5] A more complete description of the MIRACODE system is contained in Kenneth Janda, "Political Research with MIRACODE: A 16 mm. Microfilm Information Retrieval System," *Social Science Information,* 1967. I wish to thank the Research Committee of Northwestern University for supporting my work with MIRACODE equipment.

FIGURE 1

SAMPLE PAGE TAGGED WITH CODE NUMBERS AND READY FOR
MICROFILMING

Yanaga, Chitoshi, *Japanese People and Politics,*   069
New York: Wiley, 1956

278   Japanese People and Politics

of every 4. This was 2.6 times the next largest group, Waseda
University, which was represented by 47 members or 1 out of
36- 10. Even in the Socialist parties the Tokyo University group was
the largest, with Waseda University coming second.[44]

There is a striking social disparity between the members of
the Diet and the rank and file members of the party outside the
32- parliament. This is true of all the parties but is more clearly
demonstrated in the conservative parties as can be seen by the
educational background of the members who come from the
upper and upper middle classes. Within the parliamentary
parties themselves, however, there is remarkable educational-
level homogeneity.

As compared with the British Labor Party members of
Parliament in 1950, of whom about 4 out of 11 or better than
 one-third had some kind of university education, the overwhelming majority of Socialist Party members of the Diet, to the extent
of 80 to 84 percent, had some kind of college or university education. This gives quite an intellectual flavor to the leadership
in their activities.

Occupation

Occupational breakdown presents a difficult problem since
accuracy in classification categories becomes almost impossible.
However, an analysis can provide a useful basis for understanding the bias of the Diet. Table V represents the occupational
distribution of the members of the House of Representatives
who were elected in the General Election of April 19, 1953.

Several generalizations can be made from the figures given
above. "Big business" has the biggest representation, taking up
well over one-third of the entire House of Representatives membership on their side. This compares with the conservative
parties in which 3 in every

[44] The preponderance of Tokyo University graduates was maintained
in the Diet as the result of the House of Representatives election of
April 19, 1953, though there was a slight decrease in the total number. The educational background of the newly elected members was
as follows:

Tokyo University	113
Waseda University	50
Nippon University	34
Kyoto University	26
Chuo University	22
Other universities and colleges	141
Secondary education only	70
No mention	10
Total	466

FIGURE 2

SECTION OF 16 MM. MICROFILM CREATED FOR PAGE SHOWN
IN FIGURE 1

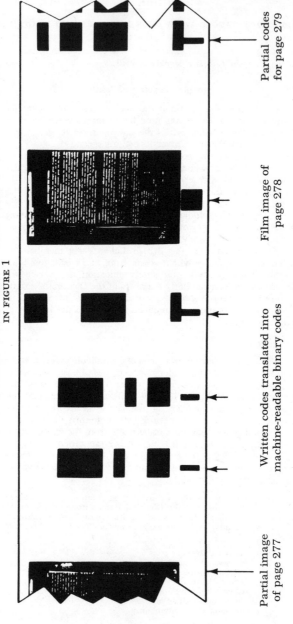

Partial codes
for page 279

Film image of
page 278

Written codes translated into
machine-readable binary codes

Partial image
of page 277

168

FIGURE 3

"MIRACODE" READER-PRINTER AND KEYBOARD CONSOLE

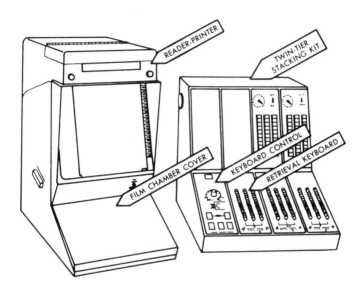

jectives,[6] which are to retrieve (1) descriptive information for operationalizing variables on political parties, (2) explicit statements of theory or propositions about political parties, and (3) descriptive information about methodologies in the study of political parties. These objectives are incorporated into the coding categories being developed for the project.

[6] The average intercoder reliabilities calculated over 186 pages from 19 articles on Japanese political parties were .73 for party codes and .50 for substantive codes. Coding reliabilities are expected to increase considerably as instructions and codes are revised and as coders acquire experience.

Two different sets of numbers are used in coding the political parties literature. One set, consisting of three-digit numbers from 000 through 999, is used exclusively as *identification codes* for specific parties. The other set, consisting of two-digit codes from 00– to 99–, is used to index *substantive information* about parties.[7]

IDENTIFICATION CODES: The party identification codes are organized on the basis of ten broad cultural-geographical categories. The first digit of the three-digit code stands for each main division as follows:

Code   *Cultural-geographical division*

0—   Anglo-American political culture

1—   West Central and Southern Europe

2—   Scandinavia

3—   South America

4—   Central America and the Caribbean

5—   Asia and the Far East

6—   Eastern Europe

7—   Middle East and North Africa

8—   West Africa

9—   Central and East Africa

The second digit of the three-digit code stands for a particular country within each division. This scheme permits recording up to ten countries within each division, thus accommodating a maximum of 100 countries. Although there are about 115 countries in the United Nations alone, the coding scheme is adequate for the purposes of the parties project, which includes some 92 nations.

The number of countries included in the study is limited due to the project's definition of a political party, which is any political organization whose electoral candidates won at least five per cent of the membership of the lower house of the na-

---

[7] The MIRACODE system has the capability of distinguishing between similar numbers in different coding sets by means of the value of a "utility bit" associated with each number. For further information, see the paper cited in Footnote 5.

tional legislature in two successive elections in the period 1950–1962. While this may seem like a restrictive definition, it produces some 260 political parties for comparative study. The complete list of parties presently identified for inclusion in the project is given in Appendix B.[8]

It should be understood that the project defines a universe of parties and not a universe of countries from which parties are selected. Countries enter the universe only on the backs of parties, so to speak. No code number is assigned to a country unless it has at least one party under the above definition, and, for any country in the study, only those organizations meeting the definition are included in the code.

Organization of the party codes by area and country merely reflect the way literature on parties is organized. Insofar as possible, literature dealing exclusively with the same parties will be grouped together to form separate film magazines. Literature dealing with more than one party in the same countries will form film magazines on parties in general. Finally, writings comparing parties across countries will form magazines of comparative parties literature.

Party identification codes are used to tag places in texts where information about specific parties is presented. The *substantive* nature of the information is recorded by means of information codes.

INFORMATION CODES: The MIRACODE system can deal with three-digit codes, and the party identification codes are, in fact, three-digit numbers. The initial set of information codes for the project were also three-digit numbers. Our experience in applying three-digit codes to selected articles on political parties, however, revealed that these codes were too detailed. Coding the material with 1000 coding categories required far more

---

[8] Most of the preliminary research done to identify the parties (and thus countries) to be included in the project was the product of two Northwestern students. Miss Cathy Jennings identified 160 parties in 58 countries outside of Africa. Mr. Roger McClure identified 43 parties in 20 countries in West, Central, and East Africa. Professor Gwendolen Carter furnished helpful information for my decisions to exclude certain African parties in countries for which there was little or no written material available. The list of parties identified for study at this stage of the project is subject to revision as detailed research gets underway. The list published in Appendix B, however, probably is close to what the final listing will be.

time than anticipated. Moreover, coders often agreed about the first two digits, but not the third.

Upon re-examination of the nature of the codes and the objectives of the project, the decision was made to discontinue making the fine distinctions that the third digit required and to code only at the two-digit level. This scheme provides 100 coding categories for information on political parties and, at the same time, leaves room for expansion of the code (by activating the third digit) to accommodate up to 1000 categories, should the finer distinctions prove necessary. Because of technical considerations in the MIRACODE system, the two digit codes are recorded with "–" as a dummy third digit.

The information codes have been organized to answer several basic questions about political parties. Each of these questions encompasses up to ten coding categories. The first digit of the information codes stands for a given question.

Code	Questions about political parties
0–	What is a political party?—Definition, function, theory
1–	How do political parties begin?—The origin of parties
2–	What does a party do?—Party activities
3–	Who belongs to the party?—Party composition
4–	How is the party organized?—Party structure
5–	What does the party seek to accomplish?—Party goals
6–	Under what conditions does the party operate?—Political environment
7–	Under what conditions does the party operate?—Social, economic and geographical environment
8–	Are there any other parties in the country?—Party system
9–	How have parties been studied?—Methodology

Each of the code divisions has been subdivided into a maximum of ten concept categories. The complete set of codes as it stands in the present stage of the parties project is given in Appendix C.[9]

[9] Charles Baer, Barbara Lewis, Jean Jacobsohn, Gary Rader, Roger McClure, Eila Cutler, Fred Hartwig, and Margaret Ferguson assisted me in developing the present coding categories. The coding process is still under development, and the codes may yet undergo considerable revision.

This sketches out the process by which the MIRACODE system will be used to retrieve information from the political parties literature. Identification and selection of the literature to be coded will be discussed in the following section.

Locating the Relevant Literature

One of the underlying assumptions of the comparative parties project is that most of the necessary information about the world's parties and party systems can be found somewhere in the enormous literature on foreign and comparative government. Some idea of the size and diversity of this literature can be gained by browsing through the "Foreign and Comparative Government" bibliographies published regularly in the back pages of the *American Political Science Review*. The September 1964 issue, for example, contained brief reviews of twenty-three books and citations to more than one-hundred and forty selected articles and documents on politics abroad. Lists like this have been published for years in every quarterly issue of the *Review*, and, of course, the items in those lists represent only part of the total literature. The comparative parties project must try to cull relevant information out of this vast literature. The first step in this task is to identify books, articles, papers, and documents dealing with foreign parties and party systems. This is an old-fashioned problem of preparing a comprehensive bibliography, but its magnitude demands new and better methods of handling it.

Bibliographies have traditionally been prepared by building up index card files of entries usually arranged by author and, in some cases, cross-indexed by subject. The card file itself usually constitutes the working bibliography for the individual scholar. If it is to be used by other researchers, the bibliography must ordinarily be re-typed from the cards. There are several disadvantages with this procedure for compiling and distributing bibliographies. Re-typing is costly and subject to error; lists of items arranged by author obstruct retrieval of the information by subject; and cumulating the bibliography after new items have been added seems scarcely worth the effort.

The demands of the comparative parties project cannot be met with traditional methods that were barely suitable for individual scholars operating with smaller bodies of literature. The project needs working bibliographies of thousands of items that can be furnished at low cost to many researchers. It needs a method for compiling, revising, and continually updating this bibliography. The problem calls for solution through mechanized means of document retrieval.

To many students in the behavioral sciences, computer techniques for information or document retrieval may seem like promises of the future, still on the drawing board and hardly operational. To be sure, many exciting techniques are still in the process of development, but there are also some tested methods ready for practical application to literature problems in the behavioral sciences. The most popular computer method of document retrieval, keyword indexing, has already been used to compile a cumulative index for more than 2,500 titles published during the first 57 years of the *American Political Science Review*.[10] Keyword indexing is also suggested for preparing bibliographies to be used in the project.[11]

The methodology of keyword indexing is a subject in itself and will not be discussed here.[12] In outline form, the system operates as follows. Citations to the literature, complete with author, title, and publication information, are punched on IBM cards. A computer reads these cards and, by referring to a predetermined set of keywords (or *non*-keywords) prepares an alphabetical listing of all the keywords in the titles. The complete citation in which the keyword appears is printed also, and it is reprinted for each appearance of a keyword in the title. The indexing technique can best be understood by looking at the finished product in Figure 4, which shows a partial printout from a computer listing of keywords contained in 928 entries for "Africa" and "The Middle East" that were reported in

[10] Kenneth Janda, *Cumulative Index to the American Political Science Review, Volumes 1–57; 1906–1963.* (Evanston: Northwestern University Press, 1964.)

[11] "KWIC," or "Key-Word-In-Context," indexing was used to prepare the *Cumulative Index to the American Political Science Review.* The technique proposed for use in the parties project is "KWOC", or "Key-Word-Out-of-Context," indexing. A discussion of the two techniques is contained in Kenneth Janda, "Keyword Indexes for the Behavioral Sciences," *American Behavioral Scientist*, 7 (June, 1964), 55–58.

[12] Additional applications of keyword indexing methodology are contained in Kenneth Janda, *Data Processing: Applications to Political Research* (Evanston: Northwestern University Press, 1965), Chapter VIII and the Index to the book itself.

the "Foreign and Comparative Government" bibliography of the
American Political Science Review from 1959 to 1963.

FIGURE 4

PARTIAL COMPUTER PRINTOUT OF KEYWORD INDEX TO
BIBLIOGRAPHY ON "AFRICA" AND THE "MIDDLE EAST"

THE MIDDLE EASTERN JOURNAL (SUMMER 1959)

1286 Turks   Karpat KH
                Young Turks Again. =
                Challenge March, 1961

079 Turmoil   Cate C
                Turmoil in Algeria. =
                Atlantic Monthly December, 1962

272 Turmoil   Cate C
                Turmoil in Algeria. =
                The Atlantic Monthly December, 1962

1988 Turmoil   Author Not Given
                South Africa in Turmoil—From Boycott to
                    Assassination. =
                Round Table June, 1960

2338 Turmoil   Richardson CB
                Nyasaland—Causes of Turmoil. =
                Foreign Policy Bulletin (May 1, 1959)

1744 Tyranny   Good RC
                Tyranny or Puritanism. Sekou Toure's
                    Guinea. =
                African Report October, 1960

085 UAR   Hoskins HL
                Arab Socialism in the UAR. =
                Current History January, 1963

439 UAR   Horton AW
                The Central Social and Political Problem of
                    the UAR—Part—3
                The Search for Popular Support. =
                New York—American Universities Field
                    Staff, 1962
                (American Universities Field Staff Reports
                    Service. Northeast Africa Series V. 9, No.
                    4, United Arab Republic)

440 UAR   Horton AW
                The Charter for National Action of the
                    UAR. =
                New York—American Universities Field
                    Staff, 1962

(American Universities Field Staff Reports
Service. Northeast Africa Series V. 9, No.
5, United Arab Republic)

1295 UAR   Vatikiotis PJ
Dilemmas of Political Leadership in the
Arab Middle East— The Case of the
UAR. =
International Affairs April, 1961

281 Uganda   Carter J
Independence of Uganda. =
World Today September, 1962

288 Uganda   Jesman C
Uganda—Background to Independence. =
British Survey October, 1962

291 Uganda   Low DA
Political Parties in Uganda 1949–62. =
Institute of Commonwealth Studies, Uni-
versity of London
London, Athlone Press, 1962

295 Uganda   Richards A
Constitutional Problems in Uganda. =
The Political Quarterly October–December,
1962

303 Uganda   Author Not Given
Uganda. =
New York, British Information Services,
1962

304 Uganda   Author Not Given
Uganda—The Making of a Nation. =
Central Office of Information, Reference
Division London 1962 (R.F.P. 5441)

At one level in the project, keyword indexing will be used
to prepare crude indexes to the thousands of items appearing
in both the "Foreign and Comparative Government" bibliographies and the listing of doctoral dissertations that have appeared in the *American Political Science Review* since 1950.
This job has already been done for bibliography items published
from 1959 to 1962. The resulting index contains more than
10,000 keyword entries from 2,500 items. The titles were
punched, processed, and indexed at a cost of less than $300.[13]
All titles punched to form the African bibliography were later

[13] I want to thank the Comparative Politics Program at Northwestern
University for making these funds available to me.

supplemented by entries from more recent issues of the *Review* to prepare a special index for my 1964 parties course, which was researching African parties.[14] Part of that index is reproduced in Figure 4.

At another level, keyword indexing will be used to prepare refined bibliographies of titles especially relevant to the comparative study of political parties. Before inclusion in the refined bibliography, citations will be checked for accuracy in spelling, pagination, etc. If needed, additional keywords can be enclosed within parentheses and placed after a title to improve its descriptiveness and hence its retrievability. If corrections or additions are not necessary, the citations need not even be repunched but can simply be taken from the crude bibliography file and entered at random in the refined file. The computer will take over from there to compile an alphabetized, updated, refined index of comparative parties literature.

In addition to the literature reported in the bibliographical section and dissertation notes of the *American Political Science Review*, more recent articles will be fed into the system by the Selective Dissemination of Information (SDI) system established for the Intersocietal Studies group at Northwestern University.[15] Briefly, SDI operates as follows. Individual users of the system prepare lists of key terms describing their specific research interests. These lists are stored on magnetic tape and constitute the "interest profiles" for each user. As each new issue of a selected number of social science journals dealing with intersocietal or cross-national studies comes into the library, it is processed for input to the computer and the SDI system. The processing involves keypunching the author, title, journal, and —unless an abstract is available—the first and last paragraphs of every article.

[14] I am indebted to the Program of African Studies at Northwestern University for supporting this phase of my research.

[15] Mr. Gary Rader served as an invaluable research assistant during the initial stages of the SDI project. The program employed in the project was written by William H. Tetzlaff and is the same as the program referred to in Footnote 16. I want to thank Professor Richard D. Schwartz and the Council for Intersocietal Studies at Northwestern University for supporting the SDI pilot project. The SDI project is discussed in more detail in Kenneth Janda, "Information Retrieval: Applications to Bibliographies on International and Comparative Politics," prepared for delivery at the Computers and the Policy Making Community Institute, Lawrence Radiation Laboratory, Livermore, California, April 4, 1966.

The input is recorded on magnetic tape for computer processing. At the end of every two-week period, the computer compares the users' interest profiles with the information that has been keypunched for each article. When an abstract is found that contains sufficient terms that appear in a user's interest profile to satisfy a certain "hit" level, the computer prints the name of the user and the information on the article. The citations and abstracts retrieved by the system are then mailed to the user, notifying him of the library's acquisition of pertinent material. In this way, an SDI system, as its name implies, aims at the *selective* dissemination of information.

For the parties project, the SDI system will examine incoming journals for articles dealing with the following terms: "party," "parties," "partisan," "political groups," and the names of all the countries with parties in the study. With the help of Northwestern's Intersocietal SDI system, the project should be able to keep fully abreast of the current literature on political parties.

Building a Propositional Inventory

The original purpose of the comparative parties project was to gather data for testing propositions about parties and party systems. It is essential, therefore, that attention be given to inventorying propositions within the literature. The method for building a usable propositional inventory will involve the use of yet another information retrieval technique in conjunction with the parties literature coded for the MIRACODE system.

Information code "03–" will be used to index theoretical and propositional statements in the parties literature. By entering this code in the keyboard of the MIRACODE retrieval station, one can locate every theoretical discussion coded on the film magazines. But to construct a propositional inventory, it is not enough merely to locate theoretical discussions. Once the statements are retrieved, additional information processing is required, because different writers often use different terms to discuss the same phenomena. The simple notion of "enfranchisement," for example, can be expressed in terms of "extension of the suffrage," "providing new classes of the population with the right to vote," and "increasing the electorate." In this example, different wording may not trouble the interpretation because the idea is relatively clear. But political concepts are not always clear; a "centralized" party may or may not mean the same thing as a "cohesive" party. Furthermore, there is no guarantee that writers who use identical terms are, in fact, applying them to the same concepts.

Terminological differences between authors are ordinarily resolved by an implicit process of "translation." The parties project proposes to make this process explicit by translating major propositions into a basic "language" of party variables. The vocabulary of this language will be codified into a thesaurus of terms. By itself, successful translation of propositions into a basic language should produce clarified concepts, sharpened theories, and improved comparisons within the literature. As a by-product of the translation, the thesaurus should provide a means of access to the inventory of propositions extracted from the literature.

Propositions in the literature that are indexed with the "03–" code will be retrieved on the MIRACODE reader, copied, and recorded on punchcards for computer processing. The specific technique to be used in processing these propositions will be a computer program called "TRIAL," for "Technique to *Re*trieve *I*nformation from *A*bstracts of *L*iterature."[16] A complete discussion of this technique is, again, the subject of another paper, and only its main features will be sketched out here.[17]

TRIAL is a computer program for searching natural language text and retrieving information according to specified logical combinations of keywords. The input to the TRIAL program for the parties project consists of propositions about political parties. The propositions will be accompanied by a complete citation of the sources in which they appear, and each proposition will be represented in the input in its "translated" and "original" forms. The translation expresses the proposition in the basic vocabulary of the parties project. Immediately following the translation is the original statement, quoted from the text,

[16] My colleague, Lester Milbrath, first stimulated my thinking in using computers to process propositional inventories. See Lester W. Milbrath and Kenneth Janda, "Computer Applications to Abstraction, Storage, and Recovery of Propositions from Political Science Literature," paper delivered at the 1964 Annual Meeting of the American Political Science Association, Chicago, Illinois.

[17] Kenneth Janda and William H. Tetzlaff, "TRIAL: A Computer Technique for Retrieving Information from Abstracts of Literature," *Behavioral Science*, 11 (November, 1966), pp. 480–486.

which provides a check against the interpretation and accuracy of the translated statement.

Examples of translated propositions about political parties are given in Figure 5, which reproduces a printout of three propositions quoted from Samuel Eldersveld's *Political Parties: A Behavioral Analysis*[18] and translated into a simple statement involving "basic" vocabulary terms. Translating the proposition facilitates both its retrievability and its comparability with similar propositions by other authors. Terms in the translated statement, like "heterogeneous," "identifiers," "centralization," and "factionalism," are all *candidates* for a thesaurus of terms on party variables. They are only "candidates" because preparation of the thesaurus has barely begun, and subsequent experience with the literature may suggest better terms.

The researcher who wants to extract all propositions from the inventory that involve certain variables and concepts will look them up in the thesaurus, which will indicate the terms included in the vocabulary and those replaced with synonyms in the translations. He will then instruct the computer, operating under the TRIAL program, to search the propositional inventory with the proper terms from the basic vocabulary. TRIAL search instructions are communicated to the computer by specifying terms within parentheses and stating logical connections that must exist between the terms to retrieve a proposition.

The use of the standard logical operators: "not," "or," and "and" is inherent in the power of the search command. If the researcher wants to search the inventory for all statements about the relationship between "heterogeneity of party identifiers" and "factionalism," for example, he can construct the following command.

(/HETEROGEN/ .AND. IDENTIFIERS .AND. /FACTION/)

Placing a word between slashes defines it as a "root word," thereby retrieving any word that begins with the same root. Thus, /HETEROGEN/ would retrieve "heterogeneous" and "heterogeneity." Any number of "nests" of parentheses can be used with any combination of logical operators to permit more complex searches. The above command, however, would retrieve the first proposition in Figure 5, which would be printed out in conjunction with the citation to Eldersveld's book and the original phraseology.

[18] Samuel J. Eldersveld, *Political Parties: A Behavioral Analysis* (Chicago: Rand McNally, 1964).

FIGURE 5

PROPOSITIONS FROM SAMUEL ELDERSVELD, *Political Parties: A Behavioral Analysis* (Chicago: Rand McNally, 1964), TRANSLATED INTO BASIC TERMS AND REPRODUCED IN THE TRIAL FORMAT

Statement of Proposition . . .

The more socially heterogeneous the party identifiers, the less centralization of control, the more factionalism, the less operating efficiency, and the more conflict over goals and ideology.

"The party is always 'potential-clientele' conscious. It is open at its base to new recruits for party work as well as to nonactivist supporters. It is often open at the higher levels also, indeed, sometimes at the elite apex, if such a strategy will profit the party's power aspirations. Thus it is permeable and adaptive. . . . Where adaptation is maximal, internal managerial control is difficult, factional pluralism multiplied, operational efficiency likely to be impaired, and goal orientations and ideological consensus highly noncongruent, where adaptation is minimal, such consequences for internal control and perspectives will doubtless be less severe." (pp. 5–6)

Statement of Proposition . . .

Party structures absorb conflict between the group goal and coalition goals.

"The subcoalitions within the party may be identified variously—in terms of geographical boundaries, on the basis of organizational status, as demographic or social categories, or on the basis of ideological division. . . . Conflict within the party must be tolerated. As a power-aspiring group, 'greedy' for new followers, the party does not settle conflict, it defers the resolution of conflict. The party is thus no genuine mediator; it seeks to stabilize subcoalitional relationships and interactions so that these multiple interests will remain committed to the organization . . . (pp. 6–7)

Statement of Proposition . . .

Control in the party structure is not centralized in an elite, as assumed by the "Iron Law of Oligarchy."

". . . we take issue with the necessity of one crucial assumption in that 'Iron Law,' the assumption that control of the party structure is inexorably concentrated in the hands of a single leadership corps, the top, elite, managerial nucleus of the structure." (p. 8)

Operationalizing Party Variables

The results of the propositional inventory will serve to determine the variables that need to be measured or "operationalized" to test theory. Operationalization of variables dealing with political phenomena is often a difficult task, especially when the underlying concepts do not invite quantitative expression. One important factor in the strategy of operationalization is knowledge of different interpretations of the concept. Knowing the various ways in which the concept has been used can often inspire the development of imaginative techniques for identification and measurement. Having the parties literature coded and indexed for retrieval enables one to make a quick review of previous uses, which should disclose essential factors that might be operationalized in terms of quantitative scales or qualitative coding categories. Operational measures devised for all the variables in the study will then be incorporated into printed forms for evaluating individual parties on every variable. These forms will presumably be similar to those used by students in my parties classes and presented in Appendix A for purposes of illustration.

Each party will be coded on every variable with the use of the MIRACODE retrieval station. To illustrate the process, coding the Italian Socialist Party on the "party membership" variable might proceed as follows. The "Italian Socialist Party" film magazine would be inserted into the MIRACODE reader and the code number "32–" would be entered into the keyboard. The film would be searched for coded references to membership in the party. Every time code number "32–" was encountered by the microfilm reader, the image of the corresponding page would be projected on the screen for examination. In a matter of minutes, the coder would be able to review what the literature had to say about membership requirements in the Italian Socialist Party. Agreement or disagreement among authors could easily be noted, permitting judgments to be made about the validity of conflicting information.

Disagreement between sources might be resolved by also searching the film prepared on "Italian Parties: General." In this case, the code number "153," which identifies the Socialist Party, would be entered into the keyboard in addition to number "32–," the membership code. The reader then would stop only to display pages that discussed party membership *and* the Socialist Party. If the disagreement remained unresolved, a coding judgment would be made and the discrepancy noted. A written record of the judgment underlying each difficult coding decision will be helpful later in resolving differences between *coders,* for each party will be coded by at least two different people, providing a measure of intercoder reliability at this stage of the project as well. The objective of the reliability checks is to produce the highest quality data the literature will allow for testing propositions about parties.[19]

Analyzing the Data

The comparative parties project will ultimately generate scores of variables on hundreds of political parties in almost one hundred countries. Electronic data processing methods will be employed to analyze these data effectively. Depending upon the level of measurement used to operationalize specific variables, several different techniques of statistical analysis may be re-

[19] There is good reason to question just what *is* the quality of the information contained in the parties literature. Undoubtedly, some of the information would, because of poor research or biased observation, bear little resemblance to the state of affairs pertaining to the parties or countries under study. Speaking very frankly, my data will enable me to test propositions not with actual *data on* parties but with what people *say about* parties. The two are clearly quite different, and I have written about the study as if I were collecting data *on* parties primarily for stylistic reasons.

Despite the differences that most certainly occur between what the literature *says* about parties and what actually *exists,* we would expect a high, albeit not perfect, correlation between the two. To some extent, we will be able to identify and investigate biases, omissions, and systematic errors in the literature through use of our methodology categories, particularly the data quality control codes (see Raoul Naroll, *Data Quality Control.* New York: The Free Press of Glencoe, 1962). Nevertheless, the basic presumption of the project is that political parties exist and operate largely as people say they do.

Even if our experience with evaluating the literature and the criticisms of others ultimately force rejecting this presumption, I contend that learning the shape and extent of reliable knowledge about political parties is in itself a worthwhile objective. And analyzing existing research literature to learn about parties appears to be far less costly than conducting coordinated field research at hundreds of sites throughout the world.

quired to validate the propositions. Because most of the variables
are likely to be measured on nominal or ordinal scales, however,
cross-tabulation of variables is apt to be the basic type of
analysis employed in the project. The specific computer program
that will be used for cross-tabulating the variables is Northwestern University's NUCROS.

NUCROS is described elsewhere;[20] only its main features
are presented here. In its present form, the NUCROS program
can process up to 40 variables on a maximum of 9,999 cases for
the purposes of preparing up to 72 contingency tables. Each
table can consist of simple bivariate cross-tabulations (illustrated in Tables 1 and 2) or involve third and fourth variables
introduced as "controls." The program provides for automatic
recoding of data, automatic identification of tables with names
of variables involved in the cross-tabulation, and optional calculation of percentages, chi-square values, and other non-para-
metric statistics.

The NUCROS program was used to process the data presented in Table 2, which illustrated how one of Duverger's propositions might be tested by cross-tabulating two variables. While
the data will be used primarily to validate propositions about
parties, a somewhat more basic analysis will determine the
distribution of party characteristics throughout the world. The
students' data will be used to illustrate this level of analysis.

Duverger discussed different types of party origins; some
parties had been formed inside parliament by legislators with
similar interests and others were originated outside parliament
by social organizations. Of course, he lacked the data which
would disclose how frequently each type of origin occurred.
Some indication of the distribution of occurrences, however,
can be gleaned from the data my students collected on 277
parties. Their data were processed by the NUCROS program
and, for illustrative purposes, were separated into African and
non-African parties. These data, presented in Table 3, show
the percentage distribution for frequency of occurrence for 72
African and 205 non-African parties.

According to the data in Table 3, African parties are more
likely to originate outside of parliament, where they are organized by regional or ethnic leaders. The quality of the student-

[20] Kenneth Janda, *Data Processing: Applications to Political Research*
(Evanston: Northwestern University Press, 1965), Chapter VI and
Appendix C-1.

TABLE 3

DISTRIBUTION OF PARTY ORIGINS FOR AFRICAN AND
NON-AFRICAN POLITICAL PARTIES

	African	Non-African
Formed inside the legislature	3	9
Splinter group from another party	18	18
Merger of two or more parties	18	15
Organized by religious leaders	1	3
" " labor leaders		5
" " intellectuals	3	9
" " regional, ethnic leaders	25	3
" " promote specific issues	11	7
Other condition of origin	17	18
No information reported	4	13
	100%	100%
(Total number of parties)	(72)	(205)

collected data is admittedly suspect, but the information produced is plausible and encouraging. At the same time, however, attention must be called to the lack of information or the inability to classify 21 per cent of the African parties and 31 per cent of the non-African parties. Hopefully, the full-scale project will produce more and better information for coding parties and will develop more adequate operationalizations of the variables to increase the percentages that can be coded on the variables.

If the expected success is achieved on these dimensions, then the data produced in the project should merit serious consideration in accepting, rejecting, or revising propositions about political parties. To illustrate the strategy of using cross-tabulations in clarifying and revising theory, consider the data presented in Table 4, which is constructed to test Duverger's proposition that parties which originate inside parliament are more likely to be conservative in ideology than those originating outside parliament.

Only data on non-African parties were available for Table 4, and, of these, the students were able to code only 113 on both variables. Assuming again the validity of the data, the

TABLE 4

CONDITION OF ORIGIN BY IDEOLOGICAL ORIENTATION,
FOR NON-AFRICAN PARTIES ONLY

	Parliamentary origin of parties		
	Inside	Split/Merger	Outside
Leftist	31	46	53
Centerist	19	24	15
Rightist	50	30	32
	100%	100%	100%
(Number of parties)	(16)	(50)	(47)

pattern does not fully support Duverger's proposition. Perhaps his proposition could be revised by stating qualifying conditions and introducing additional variables. With more reliable data, one could examine the specific parties that deviated from the proposition, e.g., leftist parties formed inside parliament and rightist parties formed outside. Deviant case analysis might produce insights that will revise the original proposition.

Conclusion

A science never really matures until it develops powerful theories that explain its data. Within political science, the comparative study of political parties has as its ultimate objective the development of theory to explain and predict the behavior of parties and party systems across the world. The emphasis of this research project, however, falls primarily on collecting data and only secondarily on building theory. This choice of focus stems from the firm belief that adequate data are important ingredients in successful theory building. Whether data collection should precede theory building, or *vice versa*, is essentially a "chicken-and-egg" problem. Both are needed eventually, but one of the two must start the cycle somewhere. Although this study is not designed to make a frontal attack on the general problem of theory construction, it should contribute directly to the general assault by inventorying propositions, sharpening concepts, providing facts, and testing narrow-range hypotheses and middle-range propositions—the stuff from which bodies of theory are made.

Appendix A

The coding categories given below for data on countries and data on parties within countries were prepared for use by my 1964 undergraduate course on political parties. They may not resemble the coding categories developed from the parties project and are offered here simply to indicate how data on countries and parties might be recorded in punchcard form. The numbers under the heading "Card Columns" refer to the columns on an IBM card in which the information has been punched. The keypunch operator would punch into the card the code numbers checked off by the student researcher or numerical values—depending on the information that was provided.

The coding categories below are given in an abbreviated form. Space has not been reserved for comments on the categories, as it had been on the students' forms, and only the categories for the lower house of the legislature have been reproduced for the country codes. The upper house categories are virtually identical and were eliminated to save space.

Data on Countries

Student: _____ Country _____
Columns 7–8: ID# _____

Card Columns	Information and Codes
9–12	YEAR ADOPTING A POPULARLY ELECTED LEGISLATURE _____ Source: _____ Page: _____
13–16	YEAR ADOPTING PRESENT GOVERNMENTAL STRUCTURE _____ Source: _____ Page: _____
17	LEGISLATIVE-EXECUTIVE STRUCTURE (Banks and Textor) Source: _____ Page: _____ 1 Presidential 2 Presidential-Republican

3   Parliamentary-Republican
4   Pure Parliamentary
5   Parliamentary-Royalist
6   Monarchical-Parliamentary
7   Monarchical
8   Communist
9   Other (explain)

18 NATURE OF THE STATE Source: _____ Page: _____
    1   Unitary state
    2   Federal state
    3   Other

19 NUMBER OF CHAMBERS IN THE LEGISLATURE OR PARLIAMENT   Source: _____ Page: _____
    1   Unicameral
    2   Bicameral, but the lower chamber has little influence in legislating
    3   Bicameral, but the *upper* chamber has little influence in legislating
    4   Bicameral, and both are about equal in importance
    5   Other (explain)

20–22 NUMBER OF MEMBERS IN THE LOWER CHAMBER   Source: _____ Page: _____

23–25 NUMBER OF MEMBERS POPULARLY ELECTED   Source: _____ Page: _____

26 PERCENTAGE OF TOTAL MEMBERSHIP POPULARLY ELECTED   Source: _____ Page: _____
    1   No members of lower chamber are popularly elected
    2   Less than 25%
    3   25 to 49.9%
    4   50 to 74.9%
    5   75 to 99.9%
    6   100% —all members of lower chamber are popularly elected

34 ELECTIONS FOR PARLIAMENT OR LEGISLATURE   Source: _____ Page: _____
    1   Unicameral: all elected members chosen at same time
    2   ”   terms are staggered; only part elected at one time
    3   Bicameral: *all* elected members chosen at same time (both chambers)
    4   ”   all elected members of each house chosen separately
    5   ”   all elected members of *one* house

chosen at one time along with part of the elected membership of the *other* (US model)

6   "   all elected members of the lower house chosen at one time; upper house not popularly elected

7   "   terms of the lower house members are staggered; upper house not popularly elected

8 Neither chamber popularly elected

9 Other (explain)

35 MAXIMUM TIME ALLOWED BETWEEN ELECTIONS FOR LOWER HOUSE

Source: _____ Page: _____

1 One year

2 Two years

3 Three "

4 Four   "

5 Five   "

6 Six years or more

7 No maximum time; elections are not tied to calendar at all

8 Other (explain)

9 Not applicable: lower chamber not popularly elected

37–38 METHOD OF VOTING FOR LOWER CHAMBER

Source: _____ Page: _____

11 Proportional Representation: don't know what form

12   "   "   single transferable vote

13   "   "   simple list and national constituency

14   "   "   simple list 2 to 5 man districts

15   "   "   simple list 6 or more man districts

16   "   "   list & preferential voting within list

17   "   "   list & transferable vote between lists

| 18 | " | " | list and re-gional or na-tional pools of candi-dates |
| 19 | " | " | other (ex-plain) |

20	Minority Representation:		don't know what form
21	"	"	single non-trans-ferable vote
22	"	"	limited vote
23	"	"	cumulative vot-ing
24	"	"	point or fractional system
25	"	"	other (explain)

30	Majority Representation:		don't know what form
31	"	"	repeated ballot
32	"	"	second ballot—limited to top two candidates
33	"	"	second ballot—limited to those who stood on the first ballot, but not top two
34	"	"	second ballot—not limited to candidates on the first ballot
35	"	"	alternative vote
36	"	"	other (explain)

40	Simple plurality-single ballot:				don't know the type of dis-tricts
41	"	"	"	"	single-member districts pre-dominate
42	"	"	"	"	two-member districts pre-dominate
43	"	"	"	"	three-member districts pre-dominate

44   „   „   „   „   four-member
                            districts pre-
                            dominate
45   „   „   „   „   other num-
                            ber: _____
46   „   „   „   „   other (ex-
                            plain)

50   Combination of the above: proportional and
                            minority repre-
                            sentation
51   „   „   „   „   proportional and
                            majority repre-
                            sentation
52   „   „   „   „   proportional and
                            simple plurality
                            one ballot
53   „   „   „   „   minority repre-
                            sentation and
                            simple plurality
54   „   „   „   „   other (explain)
55   Other method of voting (explain)

41 ELECTORAL SYSTEM FOR PRESIDENT
                    Source: _____ Page: _____
    1 Not applicable: no president
    2 Indirectly elected, election not dependent on
       popular vote
    3 Electoral college tied closely to popular vote
       (US model)
    4 Popular vote
    5 Other (explain)
42 TERM OF PRESIDENT   Source: _____ Page: _____
    1 One year
    2 2 years
    3 3 years
    4 4 years
    5 5 years
    6 6 years
    7 7 years
    8 Other (explain)
    9 Not applicable: no president
43 NATURE OF DISTRICTS IN LOWER CHAMBER
    Predominant type   Source: _____ Page: _____
    1 Single member
    2 Two member
    3 Three member
    4 Four member

     5   Five member
     6   Other number: _____
     7   National constituency: all members elected
          at large

45–46   YEAR OF MOST RECENT ELECTION FOR LOWER
       HOUSE _____   Source: _____ Page: _____

47–48   NUMBER OF PARTIES GETTING AT LEAST 5%
       OF VOTES _____   Source: _____ Page: _____

49–50   NUMBER OF PARTIES GETTING ANY SEATS _____
                      Source: _____ Page: _____

  57   VOTING QUALIFICATIONS FOR LOWER HOUSE
       ELECTIONS   Source: _____ Page: _____
       1   Universal suffrage: Age _____
       2   Universal male suffrage: Age _____
       3   Male suffrage and property restrictions
       4   Male suffrage and other restrictions
       5   Other

59–60   PARTY SYSTEM: # OF PARTIES SEATED IN
       LOWER HOUSE   Source: _____ Page: _____
     01   One-party: after the most recent election
          studied, one party held at least 95% of all
          seats in the lower chamber
     02   Modified one-party: one party held from
          75% to 95% of the seats
     03   Two-party: the 2 largest parties held at least
          95% of the seats
     04   Modified two-party: the 2 largest held from
          80% to 95% of the seats
     05   Three-party: the 3 largest parties held at
          least 95% of the seats
     06   Modified three-party: the 3 largest held from
          85% to 95% of the seats
     07   Four-party: the 4 largest parties held at least
          95% of the seats
     08   Modified four-party: the 4 largest held from
          90% to 95% of the seats
     09   Poly-party: no fewer than 5 parties held at
          least 95% of the seats among themselves
     10   Other (explain)

Data on Parties

Student: _____   Country: _____
                           Columns 7–8:   ID# _____

Columns   Information and Codes

9–10   PARTY CODE# _____ Order in alphabetical listing of
       parties
              Party name: _____

11–14 YEAR OF ORIGIN OF PARTY: _____
                              Source: _____ Page: _____

15   CONDITIONS OF ORIGIN (explain classification
       below)   Source: _____ Page: _____
          1 Formed by parliamentary members with
             similar interests
          2 Formed as a splinter group from another es-
             tablished party
          3 Formed from a merger of two or more other
             parties
          4   "   outside of parliament: by religious
                                              leaders
          5   "   "   "   "   by labor
                                              leaders
          6   "   "   "   "   by intellectu-
                                              als or philo-
                                              sophical
                                              societies
          7   "   "   "   "   by regional,
                                              ethnic, or
                                              racial
                                              groups
          8   "   "   "   "   to promote a
                                              specific
                                              issue
          9 Other

16   ARTICULATION OF PARTY ORGANIZATION
                              Source: _____ Page: _____
          1 Weakly articulated: has co-opted party of-
             ficials
          2 Moderately articulated
          3 Strongly articulated: specified in detail how
             officials are selected and has not co-opted
             party officials

17   NATURE OF PARTY LINKAGE
                              Source: _____ Page: _____
          1 No clear lines of authority are drawn be-
             tween party organs
          2 Lines of authority are specified between
             some party organs, but the authority links
             are bifurcated or fragmented—some or-
             gans being formally independent of others
             supposedly their superior

     3   Lines of authority are clearly specified and there are not autonomous groups of party organs, but there are horizontal links between some party organs

     4   Lines of authority are clearly specified, there is no fragmentation of authority, and there are no horizontal links

     5   Other (explain below)

(Include a diagram if possible)

18   LOCUS OF INFLUENCE IN THE ORGANIZATION: NOMINATIONS   Source: _____ Page: _____

     1   Decentralized: nominations for the lower house determined locally

     2   Decentralized and centralized aspects (explain below)

     3   Centralized: nominations for the lower house approved nationally

19   LOCUS OF INFLUENCE IN THE ORGANIZATION: ELECTIONS   Source: _____ Page: _____

     1   Decentralized: financed by local organizations

     2   Decentralized and centralized aspects (explain below)

     3   Centralized: financial aid is given by national organization

20   BASIC ELEMENT OF ORGANIZATION   Source: _____ Page: _____

     1   Caucus: no party membership and officials not chosen by party voters

     2   Precinct: no party membership but officials chosen by party voters

     3   Branch

     4   Cell

     5   Militia

     6   Other: _____

21   BASIS OF PARTY AFFILIATION   Source: _____ Page: _____

     1   No formal membership: merely interest and support

     2   Formal membership: register as member or sign membership card *only*

     3   Formal membership: pay dues but *not* sign membership form

     4   ”   ”   sign membership form *and* pay dues

     5   ”   ”   sign membership

form, pay dues, *and* go through a probationary period or have application reviewed by party officials before membership is granted

6 Other (explain below)

22 FORM OF PARTY MEMBERSHIP
Source: _____ Page: _____

1 Indirect only: party "membership" comes with membership in some other organization

2 Mainly indirect, but there are some direct members

3 Membership is about equally divided between both

4 Mainly direct, but there are some indirect members

5 Direct membership only

6 Not applicable: no party membership

23 FUNCTIONAL ORIENTATION OF PARTY

1 Nominating candidates and contesting elections

2 Includes the above and undertakes programs of political education

3 Includes the above and provides for a variety of social needs for party identifiers

4 Other

24 MAJOR ISSUE ORIENTATION OF PARTY (Choose only one; explain your choice)
Source: _____ Page: _____

1 Anti-colonial

2 Ethnic, or regionalistic, or national minority

3 Pro-labor

4 Clerical

5 Anti-clerical

6 Land reform

7 Agrarian

8 Other: (explain)

9 No dominant issue orientation

25 IDEOLOGICAL ORIENTATION
Source: _____ Page: _____

1 Communist

2 Extreme Left

3 Left of Center

4 Center

5 Right of Center

6 Extreme Right

7   Fascist
8   Does not "fit" on an ideological continuum
9   Other (explain)

31 VOTING COHESION IN LOWER CHAMBER (Refer to average index if data are available)

Source: _____ Page: _____

1   Little or no cohesion—Average Index less than 25
2   Weak cohesion—Average Index from 25 to 49
3   Moderate cohesion—Average Index from 50 to 74
4   High cohesion—Average Index from 75 to 89
5   Very high cohesion—Average Index 90 or more
6   Other (explain)

33 METHODS OF DISCIPLINE

Source: _____ Page: _____

1   Withdrawal of membership
2   Withdrawal of financial support in elections
3   Failure to designate as party candidate
4   Both one and two
5   Both one and three
6   Both two and three
7   All of the above
8   None of the above
9   Other (explain)

34–35   YEAR OF MOST RECENT ELECTION FOR WHICH DATA ARE AVAILABLE:
ELECTION TO *LOWER* CHAMBER: _____

Source: _____ Page: _____

36–38   % OF POPULAR VOTE WON IN ELECTION _____

Source: _____ Page: _____

39–41   % OF SEATS WON IN *LOWER* CHAMBER _____

Source: _____ Page: _____

Appendix B

For the purposes of the project, a party is defined as any political organization whose electoral candidates won at least 5% of the membership of the lower house of the national legislature in two successive elections between 1950–1962. The list of parties was obtained by applying this definition to information contained in the following sources:

The Worldmark Encyclopedia of the Nations. (New York Worldmark 1960 and 1963.)

Keesing's Contemporary Archives, Volumes No. XII–XV, 1950–1962. (London: Keesing's Publications Limited.)

Segal, Ronald, *African Profiles.* (Middlesex: Penguin Books, 1963.)

Mallory, Walter H. (ed.), *Political Handbook and Atlas of the World.* (New York: Harper & Row, 1950–1963.)

The Europa Year Book, Volumes I and II. (London: Europa Publications Limited, 1950–1964.)

The Middle East and North Africa, 11th edition. (London: Europa Publications Limited, 1964–1965.)

Africa Report, 8 (November, 1963).

Considerable disagreement over party names, election results, and election dates was encountered sometimes among these sources. The listing of parties given below, therefore, will undoubtedly be corrected and refined in the course of detailed research within the literature of each country, and this list should be regarded only as a preliminary definition of the universe of parties.

0	ANGLO-AMERICAN POLITICAL CULTURE
000	AUSTRALIA
001	Labour
002	Liberal
003	Country
010	CANADA
011	Liberal
012	Progressive Conservative
013	Cooperative Commonwealth (New Democrat After 1961)
014	Social Credit
020	IRELAND
021	Fianna Fail

022   Fine Gael
023   Labour
030   NEW ZEALAND
031   National
032   Labour
040   RHODESIAN AND NYASALAND FEDERATION
041   United Federal Party
050   SOUTH AFRICA
051   National
052   United
052   Republican
060   UNITED KINGDOM
061   Labour
062   Conservative
070   UNITED STATES
071   Democrat
072   Republican

1   WEST CENTRAL EUROPE
100   AUSTRIA
101   People's (Osterreichische Volkspartei)
102   Socialist (Sozialistische Partei)
103   League of Independents (Liberal After 1955, Aus-
         trian Freedom in 1962) (Freiheitliche Partei
         Osterreichs)
110   BELGIUM
111   Christian Social (PSC)—Formerly Catholic (Social
         Chretien, Kristelijke Volkspartij)
112   Socialist (Socialiste Belge, Belgische Socialistische,
         PSB)
113   Liberal (Liberty and Progress Freedom and Progress)
         (De La Liberte Et Du Progres, PLP, Partij Vour
         Vrijheiden Vooruitgang, PWW)
120   FRANCE
121   Popular Republican Movement (MRP, Mouvement
         Republicain Populaire)
122   Republican Radical and Radical Socialist (RGR)

123	Socialist (SFIO) (Section Francaise De L'Internationale Ouvriere)
124	Union for the New Republic (UNR) (Union Pour la Nouvelle Republique)
125	Communist
130	FEDERAL REPUBLIC OF GERMANY (WEST GERMANY)
131	Christian Democratic Union (CDU/CSU—Bavarian Wing) (Christlich-Demokratische Union, Christlich-Soziale Union in Bavaria)
132	Social Democrat (SPD) (Sozialdemokratische Partei Deutschlands)
133	Free Democrat (FDP) (Freie Demokratische Partei)
140	GREECE
141	Liberal (Komma Phileleftheron)
142	National Progressive Union of Center (EPEK)
143	Greek Rally
144	National Radical Union (ERE) (Ethniki Rizospastiki Enosis)
145	United Democratic Left (EDA) (Ellniki Dimokratiki Aristera)
150	ITALY
151	Christian Democrat (DC) (Partito Democrazia Cristiana)
152	Communist (PCI) (Partito Communista Italiano)
153	Socialist (PSI) (Socialista Italiano)
160	LUXEMBOURG
161	Christian Social
162	Socialist Labour
163	Democratic (Groupement, Parti Democratique)
164	Communist
170	NETHERLANDS
171	Roman Catholic People's (Katholieke Volkspartij)
172	Labor (Partij Van De Arbeid)
173	Liberal (People's Party for Freedom and Democracy) (Volkspartij Voor Vrijheid En Democratie)
174	Anti-Revolutionary (Anti-Revolutionaire Partij)
175	Christian Historical Union (Christelijk-Historische Unie)

176   Communist (Communistische Partij Van Nederland)
180   PORTUGAL
181   National Union (Uniao Nacional)
190   SWITZERLAND
191   Radical Democratic (Radikal-Demokratische, Frei-
           sinnig-Demokratische)
192   Socialist, Social Democrats (Sozialdemokratische)
193   Swiss Conservative People's, Catholic Conservative,
           Conservatives   (Konservativ-Christlichsoziale
           Volksparter Der Schweiz)
194   Farmers (Peasants), Artisans and Middle Class
           (Bauern, Gewerbe und Burger)
195   Independents' (Landesring der Unabhaengigen)

2   SCANDINAVIA
200   DENMARK
201   Social Democratic (Socialdemokratiske)
202   Moderate Liberal (Agrarian) (Venstre)
203   Conservative (Konservative)
204   Social Liberal (Formerly Radical Union) (Radikale
           Venstre)
210   FINLAND
211   Agrarian (Maalaisliitto)
212   Social Democratic (Sosiaalidemokraattinen Puolue)
213   Finnish People's Democratic Union (Communist)
           (FDPU) (Suomen Kansan Demokraattinen Liitto,
           SKDL)
214   National Coalition, Conservative (Kansallinen Ko-
           koomus)
215   Swedish People's (Ruotsalainen Kansanpuolue)
216   Finnish People's (Suomalainen Kansanpuolue)
220   ICELAND
221   Independence (Formerly Conservative) (Sjalfstaed-
           isflokkurinn)
222   Progressive (Framsoknarflokkurinn)
223   People's Union (Socialist Unity, Labor Alliance, Com-
           munist) (Althydubandalag)
224   Social Democrat (Althyduflokkurinn)

230   NORWAY
231   Labor (Arbeiderpartiet)
232   Conservative (Hoire)
233   Liberal (Venstre)
234   Center (Formerly Agrarian) (Senterpartiet)
235   Christian People's, Christian Democrat (Kristelig Folkeparti)
240   SWEDEN
241   Social Democrat (Socialdemokratiska Arbetarepartiet)
242   Center (Formerly Farmers' Agrarian) (Centerpartiet)
243   Liberal (Folkpartiet)
244   Conservative (Hogerpartiet)

3   SOUTH AMERICA
300   ARGENTINA
301   Popular Union (Peronistas)
302   Radicals (UCR)
303   Intransigent Radical Civic Union (UCRI) (Union Civica Radical Intransigente)
304   People's Radical Civic Union (UCRP) (Union Civica Radical Del Pueblo)
310   BOLIVIA
311   National Revolutionary Movement (MNR) (Movimiento Nacionalista Revolucionario)
312   Socialists (FSB) (Falange Socialista Boliviana)
320   BRAZIL
321   Social Democratic (PSD) (Partido Social Democratico)
322   National Democratic Union (UDN) (Uniao Democratica Nacional)
323   Labor (PTB) (Partido Trabalhista Brasiliero)
324   Social Progressive (PSP) (Partido Social Progressista)
325   Republican (PR) (Partido Republicano)
330   CHILE
331   Liberal (PL) (Partido Liberal)

332	United Conservative (Formerly Traditionalist Conservative) (Partido Conservador Unido) (PCU)

332   United Conservative (Formerly Traditionalist Conservative) (Partido Conservador Unido) (PCU)

333   National Popular (Became National Democratic, Formerly Ag. Labor)

334   Christian Democratic (Formerly Social Christian) (PDC) (Partido Democrata Cristiano)

335   Radical (PR) (Partido Radical)

336   United Socialist

337   Communist

340   COLOMBIA

341   Liberal

342   Conservative

350   ECUADOR

351   National Velasquista Federation (FNV) (Federacion Nacional Velasquista)

352   Conservative

353   Radical Liberal, Liberal Radical (Partido Radical Liberal)

354   Socialist (PSE)

360   PARAGUAY

361   Democratic Colorados (National Republican) (Associacion Nacional Republicana, Partido Colorado)

370   PERU

371   Movement of National Unification (Democratico Peruano Unificacion Nacional, Movimiento De Unificacion Nacional)

372   Christian Democratic (PC) (Partido Democrata Cristiano)

380   URUGUAY

381   Colorados (Partido Colorado, Gestidos, Lealtad y Unidad Batallista, Independientes)

382   Blancos (Partido Nacional, Union Blanca Democratica) (Includes Orthodox Herristas, Herristas, and Ruralistas)

390   VENEZUELA

391   Republican Democratic Union (URD) (Union Republican Democratica)

392   Christian Social (COPEI) (Partido Social Cristiano)

393   Democratic Action (AD) (Accion Democratica)

4   CENTRAL AMERICA AND THE CARIBBEAN

400   Costa Rica

401   National Liberation (PLN) (Partido Liberacion Nacional)

402   National Union (PUN)

403   National Republican (PRN, Calderonista) (Partido Republicano Nacional)

410   Cuba

411   Cuban Revolutionary (PRC(A)) (Revolucionario Cubano (Authenico))

412   Liberal

413   Democratic (Democratas)

420   Dominican Republic

421   Dominican Party (Partido Dominicano)

430   El Salvador

431   Revolutionary Party of Democratic Unification (PRUD) (Partido Revolucionario Unificacion Democratica)

432   Party of the Renewal Action (PAR) (Partido Accion Renovadora)

440   Guatemala

441   Nationalist Democratic Movement (Movimiento Democratico Nationalista) (MDN)

442   Christian Democratic of Guatemala (Democracia Cristiana) (DCG)

443   Revolutionary (Revolucionario) (PR)

444   National Democratic Reconciliation (Reconciliacion Democratica Nacional, Redencion) (PRDN)

445   National Renovation or Renewal (Renovacion Nacional) (RN)

446   Revolutionary Action (Revolutionare Action) (PAR)

450   Honduras

451   Nationalist (Nacional Conservador De Honduras) (PNCH)

452   Liberal (Liberal De Honduras) (PLH)

453   Reformist (Movimiento Nacional Reformista) (MNR)

460   Mexico

461   Revolutionary Institutional (Revolucionaria Institu-
         tional) (PRI)
470   NICARAGUA
471   Nationalist Liberal (Liberal Nacionalista) (PLN)
472   Nicaraguan Conservative (Conservador Nicrag-
         uense) (PCN)
480   PANAMA
481   National Patriotic Coalition (CPN) (Coalicion Pa-
         triotica Nacional)
482   National Liberal (Liberal Nacional)

5   ASIA AND THE FAR EAST
500   BURMA
501   Anti-Fascist People's Freedom League (AFPFL)
502   People's Democratic Front
503   National United Front (NUF)
510   CEYLON
511   SRI Lanka Freedom
512   United National
513   Federal (Tamil Group)
514   People's United Front (Mahajama Eksath Permuna,
         MEP)
515   Social Equality ((Nara) (Lanka) Sama Samaja,
         Trotskysist)
520   CHINA
521   Communist
530   INDIA
531   National Congress
532   Communist
540   JAPAN
541   Progressive (Kaishinto)
542   Left-Wing Socialist (Saha Shakaito)
543   Right-Wing Socialist (Uha Shakaito)
544   Liberal Democratic (Jiyu Minshuto)
545   Socialist (Shakaito, Social Democratic before 1955)
550   SOUTH KOREA
551   Liberal

552	Democratic (Democratic Nationalists before 1955)
560	NORTH KOREA
561	Korean Workers' (Communist)
570	LAOS
571	Rally of the Lao People (Rassemblement Du Peuple Lao, Laotian People's Party, Neutralist Party)
572	Peace Party (Neo Lao Hak Sat, Pathet Lao, Pro-Communist Party)
580	MALAYA
581	Alliance (United Malays, Malayan Chinese Association, Malayan Indian)
582	Pan-Malayan Islamic (PMIP)
583	Socialist Front (People's Party–Party Ra'ayat, Labour Party)
590	PHILIPPINES
591	Nationalist (Nacionalista)
592	Liberal
593	Democratic Nationalist (Democratic-Nacionalistas)

6	EASTERN EUROPE
600	ALBANIA
601	Albanian Party of Labor (Partija E Punes)
610	BULGARIA
611	Communist (BGP)
612	National Agrarian Union (BZN)
620	CZECHOSLOVAKIA
621	Communist Party of Czechoslovakia (KSC)
622	Communist Party of Slovakia (KSS)
623	People's (CSL) (Christian)
624	Socialist (CSS)
625	Slovak Freedom (SSS)
626	Slovak Reconstruction (SSO)
630	GERMAN DEMOCRATIC REPUBLIC (EAST)
631	Socialist Unity (SED) (Sozialistische Einheitspartei Deutschlands)
632	Christian Democratic Union (CDU) (Christlich-Demokratische Union)

633   National Democratic (NDPD) (National-Demokratische)

634   Liberal Democratic (LDPD) (Liberal-Demokratische)

635   Democratic Peasants (DBD) (Demokratische Bauernpartei)

640   HUNGARY

641   Socialist Workers (MSZMP) (People's Patriotic Front) (Magyar Szocialista Munkaspart)

650   POLAND

651   United Workers (PZPR) (Polska Zjednoczona Partia Robotnicza)

652   United Peasants (ZSL, Zjednoczone Stronnictwo Ludowe)

653   Democratic (SD, Stronnictwo Demokratyczne)

660   RUMANIA

661   Workers (PMR)

670   UNION OF SOVIET SOCIALIST REPUBLICS

671   Communist

680   YUGOSLAVIA

681   League of Communists (LCY) (Savez Komunista Jugoslavije)

7   MIDDLE EAST AND NORTH AFRICA

700   MALI

701   Union Soudanaise (US)

710   MAURITANIA

711   Union Progressive (UPM) (Parti Du Regroupement Mauritanienne, PRM Merged UPM and Entente Mauritanienne)

720   MOROCCO

721   Istiqlal

722   National Union of Popular Forces (Union National Des Forces Populaires) (UNFP)

730   SOMALIA

731   Somali Youth League (SYL) (Liga Dei Giovani Somali)

732   Independent Constitutional (Costituzionale Independente, HDMS)

740   SUDAN
741   National Unionist
742   People's Party (UMMA)
743   Southern (Liberal)
750   TUNISIA
751   National Front or Union (Neo-Destour)
760   LEBANON
761   Rashid Karami Group
762   Constitutionalist
763   El-Assaad Group
764   Phalangist (Kata'eb)
765   National Bloc
770   IRAN
771   People's (Mardom)
772   National (Melliyun)
780   TURKEY
781   Republican People's (CHP)
782   Democratic
790   ISRAEL
791   Israel Labor (Mapai, Mifleget Poalei Eretz Israel)
792   Freedom Party (Herut)
793   General Zionist (Merged with Progressives to form Liberal)
794   Religious National (Hapoel, Hamizrahi, and Mizrahi
795   United Workers (Mapam, Mifleget Hapoalim Hameuchedet)
796   Unity of Labor (Achdut Avodah (Poalei Zion))
797   Religious Front (Agudat Israel and Poalei Agudat Israel or Labor)

8   WEST AFRICA
800   DAHOMEY
801   Dahomen Party of Unity (Parti Dahomeen de L'Unite, PDU)
810   GHANA
811   Convention People's Party (CPP)

812   Northern People's Party (NPP, United Party after
         1957, UP)

820   GUINEA

821   Democratic Party of Guinea (Parti Democratique de
         Guinee, PDG)

830   IVORY COAST

831   Democratic Party of Ivory Coast (Parti Demo-
         cratique, PDCI)

840   LIBERIA

841   True Whig

850   NIGER

851   Nigerian Progressive Party (Parti Progressiste Ni-
         gerian, PPN)

860   NIGERIA

861   Northern People's Congress (NPC)

862   National Council of Nigeria and the Cameroons
         (NCNC)

863   Action Group (AG)

870   SENEGAL

871   Senegal Progressive Union (Union Progressiste Sene-
         galaise, UPS)

880   SIERRA LEONE

881   Serra Leone People's (SLPP)

882   All People's Congress

890   TOGO

891   Committee of Togolese Unity (Comite or Parti de
         L'Unite Togolaise, CUT or PUT)

892   Movement of Togolese Youth (Mouvement de La
         Jeunesse Togolaise, Juvento)

893   Democratic Union of the Togolese Populations
         (Union Democratique des Populations Togolaise,
         UDPT)

894   Togolese Popular Movement (Mouvement Populaire
         Togolaise, MPT)

9   CENTRAL AND EAST AFRICA

900   CAMEROUN

901   Camerounian Union or Movement of Camerounian
         Union (Union Camerounaise, Mouvement d'Union
         Camerounaise, UCUR, MUC)

902	Cameroun Democratic (PDC, Parti Democrates Camerounais) (DC)
903	Union of the Cameroun Peoples (UPC) (Union des Peuples Camerounais)
904	Kamerun National Democratic (KNDP)
905	Cameroons Peoples National Convention
910	CENTRAL AFRICAN REPUBLIC
911	Movement of Social Evolution of Black Africa (Mouvement d'Evolution Sociale de L'Afrique Noire, MESAN)
920	CHAD
921	Chadian Progressive Party (Parti Progressiste Tchadien, PPT)
930	CONGO—BRAZZAVILLE
931	Democratic Union for Defense of African Interests (Union Democratique de Defense des Interets Africains, UDDIA)
932	African Socialist Movement (Mouvement Socialiste Africain, MSA)
940	CONGO—LEOPOLDVILLE
941	National Congolese Movement (MNC) (Mouvement National Congolais, both Lumumba and Kalonji Wings)
942	Bakongo Alliance or Association (Alliance Bas-Congo) (ABAKO, Association des Bakango)
943	National Solidarity Party (Party Solidaire Africain) (PSA)
944	CONAKAT (Confederation des Associations Tribales de Katanga)
950	GABON
951	Gabonese Democratic Bloc (Bloc Democratique Gabonais) (United Front)
952	Gabonese Democratic and Social Union (United Front) (Union Democratique et Sociale Gabonaise)
960	KENYA
961	Kenya African National Union (KANU)
962	Kenya African Democratic Union (KADU)
970	TANGANYIKA
971	Tanganyika African National Union (TANU)

Appendix C

CURRENT SET OF CODES FOR SUBSTANTIVE INFORMATION

0   *What Is a Political Party—Definition, Functions, Theory*
00   Definition of a Political Party
01   Typology of Parties (Specific Reference to Typology)
02   Purpose of Studying Parties—Why Interested in Study-
            ing Parties
03   Theory About Parties
04   Functions of Parties
05
06
07
08
09

1   *How Does a Political Party Begin—The Origin of Parties*
10   When Was It Formed
11   Who Formed It
12   Why Was It Formed—What Were Its Goals (Ideology)
13   How Was It Formed
14   What Was Its Group Support
15   History of Party
16
17

18

19

2   *What Does A Political Party Do—Party Activities*

20   Selects Candidates or Officials

21   Conducts Election Campaigns

22   Formulates Party Policy (e.g., Process of Platform, Resolutions)

23   Influences Government Policy (Inc. Legislative Voting, Intro. of Bills)

24   Propagandizes Its Goals and Activities

25   Discipline—Punishments or Rewards

26   Raises Funds

27   Causes Demonstrations, Riots, Assassinations, etc.

28   Intercedes in Government Action on Behalf of Citizens

29   Social Functions (e.g., Education, Recreation, Social Welfare)

3   *Who Belongs to the Party—Actors and Supporters*

30   Party Supporters (Identifiers and Usual Voters)

31   Party Contributors (Money)

32   Party Members

33   Party Workers or Activists

34   Party Leaders and Officials

35   Party Candidates

36   Party Members in Government Posts (Includes Legislators)

37   Group Support (e.g,. Votes or Funds)

38   Organizational Support (e.g., Endorsements, Votes, or Funds)

39   Party Factions (i.e., Organized and Continuing)

4   *How Is the Party Organized—Party Structure*

40   Local Party Organization (e.g., Branch, Precinct, Ward)

41   Constituency Party Organization (e.g., Cong. Dist. in U.S.)

66   The Executive (e.g., President, Prime Minister, Cabinet)

67   The Legislature

68   Government Structure and Political History (Inc. Colonial Experience, Democracy, Totalitarianism)

69   Geographical Allocation of Powers—Federalism

7   *Under What Conditions Does the Party Operate—Social, Economic, Geographic*

70   Economic

71   Geographic Divisions—Regional or Sectional Characteristics

72   Social

73   Religious

74   Social Norms and Attitudes

75   Activities of the Military (Inc. Veterans)

76   Student Activities

77

78

79

8   *Are There Any Other Parties—Party System*

80   Number of Parties

81   Election Results (General Elections, Presidential, Parliamentary)

82   Stability of Parties in the Party System

83   Interparty Competition (Use for Relative Strength)

84   Interparty Cooperation—Coalition Behavior, Electoral Alliances

85   Origin, Support and History of the Party System

86   Status of the Party in the Party System (Inc. Legal and Functional Status)

87   Typology of Party Systems

88

89

9   *How Have Political Parties Been Studied—Methodology*

90   Data Sources

900   Sample Surveys of Individuals

901   Election Returns or Census Data

902   Newspapers, Books or Journals

903   Government Publications or Party Documents
904   Interviews With Party Officials or Leaders
905   Roll Calls
906   Personal Experience
907
908
909   No Data Sources Given
91   *Scope of Study*
910   Single Case Study—Country
911   Single Case Study—Party
912   Area Survey
913   Purposive Sample Survey of Parties
914   Probability Sample Survey of Parties
915   General Theory
916   Comparison of Case Studies—Countries
917   Comparison of Case Studies—Parties
918
919
92   *Focus of Study*
920   Methodology in the Study of Political Parties
921   Party Origin
922   Party Activities
923   Party Composition
924   Party Structure
925   Party Goals
926   Political Environment of the Party
927   Economic, Social, Geographical, and Religious Environments
928   Party Systems
929
93   *Date of Data (Not Necessarily Publication Date)*
930   Prior to World War II (1939 or Earlier)
931   1940–1944
932   1945–1949
933   1950–1954
934   1955–1959

935   1960–1962
936   1963–
937
938   Post World War II
939   No Specific Time Period
94   *Data Quality Control—Language and Nationality*
95   *Data Quality Control—Academic Background, Data Collection Role*
96   *Data Quality Control—Research Methods*
97   *Data Quality Control—Participation in Political System*
98   *Data Quality Control—Theoretical Orientation*
99   *Data Quality Control—Literature Source*

SIX

Toward a Functionalist Theory of Political Parties: Inter-Party Competition in North Carolina*

Douglas S. Gatlin

Florida Atlantic University

ALTHOUGH TWO GREAT POLITICAL PARTIES dominate the vast majority of elective offices in the United States, wide variations in degrees of party competition have been observed among states and smaller constituencies. In many districts, the electorate sustains a monolithic one-partyism unmarred by the election of a second party candidate for generations, while in other districts, party control of offices alternates frequently and elections are regularly decided by a mere handful of votes. In recent years, such variations in party competition in the United States have been subjected to painstaking, and sometimes intricate, measurements.[1] However, improved methods of measuring

* This paper is a revision of part of the author's doctoral dissertation in Political Science at the University of North Carolina (1964). Professors Donald R. Matthews and James W. Prothro were generous with their counsel on the dissertation. Invaluable advice on statistical matters was given by Professor Daniel O. Price, then of the University of North Carolina, and Professor Allen Nash of Florida Atlantic University. The dissertation was supported in part by the Southern Fellowships Fund. Neither this organization nor the gentlemen mentioned should be held responsible for any errors in this study.

[1] In the professional literature, the writer has discovered twenty-two methods of measuring inter-party competition. Each uses measurement procedures different in some respect from all the others, but they all testify to an extreme variety of competitive patterns. Perhaps the most familiar measures are those in Austin Ranney and Willmoore Kendall, "The American Party Systems," *American Politi-*

party competition have surpassed advances in our ability to explain the recognized variations.

This paper will present a theory designed to explain variations in competition within a two-party framework as related to variations in the complexity of the social and economic environments of election constituencies. Anticipating our conclusions briefly, empirical tests of this theory will show a close association between environmental heterogeneity and inter-party competition at the polls. But our data will also indicate the partial adequacy of a purely socio-economic approach to understanding variations in party competition. The data will suggest the strategic importance of local party organizations in the aggregation of environmental conflicts in the party system. In summary, we will show that variations in party competition are a function of environmental group and class conflicts as mobilized through the activities of party organizations.

Several concepts borrowed from systemic or structural-functional analysis will appear in the ensuing discussion, e.g., inputs, interest aggregation, function, and dysfunction.[2] Strictly speaking, the theory below does not logically require the use of any of these concepts. Its essential elements are hypotheses about operational, quantifiable factors: inter-party competition in elections, social and economic characteristics of constituencies, and party organizational activity. But the advantage of supplying a functionalist interpretation of these hypotheses is that it emphasizes their significance for the political order in a broader context. Thus, in the treating of quantitative co-variations between intra-party competition and ecological factors, we will simultaneously be in a realm of discourse about a fundamental problem for political analysis—the channeling of social forces into the stream of influences shaping public policy. In systemic terms, this is a question of inputs from society to polity, or of the party system as a structure of interest aggregation. And a brief look at empirical relations between party organizational activity and party competition in elections will

---

cal Science Review, 48 (June, 1954), pp. 477–485, and in Joseph A. Schlesinger, "A Two-Dimensional Scheme for Classifying the States According to Degree of Inter-Party Competition," *American Political Science Review*, 49 (December, 1955), pp. 1120–1128.

[2] The pioneer functionalist treatment of political parties is Theodore Lowi, "Toward Functionalism in Political Science: The Case of Innovation in Party Systems," *American Political Science Review*, 57 (September, 1963), pp. 570–583.

further suggest that party organizations can be usefully studied from the viewpoint of their role in the mobilization of environmental forces into the party system, of the consequences of their activities for effective linkage between society and polity. To attempt a full-blown functionalist theory of political parties would be premature. Yet there is a need for some such overarching conceptual framework for the comparative study of state and local party systems so diverse in their formal organizational structures and informal practices, patterns of competition, elite recruitment, traditions and the like. At least, therefore, functionalism can serve at present to locate empirical studies within a comprehensive theoretical framework and can orient research in new and productive directions.

A Theory of the Environmental Bases
of Party Competition

In complex modern nations such as the United States, the environment of the polity contains many interest groupings (social classes, religious, ethnic, occupational groups) exerting demands on the polity for decisions protecting or advancing their interests. In turn, political parties penetrate the environment and link it with the polity. One of the primary functions of the party system is presumably the aggregation of environmental demands and their transmission to points within the polity where authoritative decisions can be made with respect to them. As a consequence of presenting a limited set of choices in elections, the party system facilitates a more direct and efficient flow of interest from society to polity than might otherwise be possible and thereby affords a measure of responsibility, integration, and stability to the political system. Generally speaking, the American party system is a major input structure for combining and channeling a wide range of group interests to the polity. Yet it must operate within a great number of separate constituencies—states, congressional districts, counties, cities—which vary considerably in the complexity of their social and economic characteristics and, therefore, in their potential for interest aggregation by the party system. According to our major hypothesis, inter-party competition among these constituencies varies with environmental complexity. A politically divided electorate is, therefore, unlikely in a constituency uniform in its economic, social, racial and religious attributes; it is quite probable that its dominant communal values will include a political conformity which reduces partisan struggle, if it exists at all, to a matter of personalities, of *ad hoc* cliques of friends and neighbors within a single party. In short, the one-party system is functional to the homogeneous community. At the opposite extreme, a single party will seldom be able to contain the conflicting interests and values emerging along many lines in the economically advanced, socially heterogeneous society. The interplay of a variety of socio-economic groups provides the aggregative potential for a viable two-party system. If this theoretical interpretation of the function of the party system is valid, then the degree of inter-party competition in elections depends upon the existence and intensity of conflicting environmental demands: *In any constituency, the greater the socio-economic diversity of the electorate the greater its tendency to divide its votes equally among the candidates of two parties; conversely, the greater the socio-economic homogeneity of the electorate the greater its tendency to polarize its votes around the candidates of one party.*

But it would be folly to expect an exact correspondence between the degree of environmental group conflict and the intensity of inter-party competition. The inertia of traditional party loyalty will divert the expression of group interests through the party system; the appeals of candidates above party, compelling domestic or international issues and other more-or-less momentary phenomena will upset predictions based on our theory. But for present purposes, our attention is especially drawn to party organizations in their hypothesized role as structures of interest aggregation. The ineffectiveness or the occasionally deliberate inaction of party cadres in election campaigns will impede the processes through which the aggregation of interests becomes an empirical reality—or, at least, so we hypothesize. The major hypothesis above portrayed inter-party competition as a dependent variable, more-or-less passively affected by environmental group forces. This hypothesis is now qualified by the proposition that party organizational activity is itself an independent variable affecting the division of party votes at the polls. In theoretical terms, party organization thus becomes a mediating structure or catalyst between society and polity. The mobilization of group interests into the party system depends in part on the success of party cadres in recruiting candidates, in informing the electorate of programmatic alternatives and in mobilizing group support through active campaigning. Environmental complexity is a necessary but insufficient condition of a competitive party system. If party organizations do not carry out their partisan roles, conflicts of social and economic interests probably cannot be fully and effectively channeled through the party system. For theoretical clarity and research convenience, we initially posited an unconditional association between environmental complexity and inter-party competition. Following the empirical analysis of this proposition, however, we will investigate the further hypothesis that variations in party competition are a function of environmental group and class conflicts in so far as the latter are politically mobilized through the activities of party organizations.

We now proceed to a more thorough theoretical development of the initial major hypothesis above, that the degree of party competition in elections varies directly with the environmental complexity of the party system. This proposition is too general to be immediately amenable to empirical research, but its very generality permits the development of a number of more limited hypotheses which can be operationalized and tested. Several hypotheses relating specific characteristics of the social and economic environment to the degree of party competition have been collated from the literature of political science. All of them, logically catalogued under the broader proposition above, can be tested empirically and, in turn, the validity of the more general hypothesis can be judged. In their original forms, all of the hypotheses to be outlined below were the result of scholarly observation and reflection. Thus, the strategy of theory construction employed here is the marshalling of a number of fugitive hypotheses from many sources, old and new, and their reformulation within a single deductive framework.

A search of the literature produced twelve theoretically relevant and empirically testable hypotheses. In some instances, a hypothesis was not stated explicitly in the original source but seemed implicit in a discursive argument; in such cases, a hypothesis was synthesized from suggestive passages. In each case, the methodological problem was one of selecting a hypothesis expressed more or less directly in the original source, reformulating the latter within the logic of the theory above, and expressing it operationally through quantitative data on voting and socio-economic factors. The tests of the hypotheses are limited to the one hundred counties of North Carolina and for elections between 1944 and 1956, as part of a larger study of party politics in that state; thus, the usual precautions about generalizing to a larger universe must be observed. The method of measuring inter-party competition will be discussed presently.

The methods of quantifying the social and economic factors are reported under each of the hypotheses below. Census and other published sources of data for 1950, the mid-point of the election years, were used in quantifying the socio-economic variables derived from the literature. Occasional distortions of the original authors' intentions may have occurred in the process of translating literary passages into operational indices. Still, the advancement of many disciplines has been based on the recasting and recodification of such knowledge as existed at the moment. The resulting compendium of hypotheses is not exhaustive. It does, however, constitute a group of theoretical propositions with which to begin the empirical analysis of the environmental bases of inter-party competition.

I. Economic class conflict as the basis of political conflict is a venerable idea in political science—as old as Aristotle, more recent than Marx. While present-day social scientists have vested the concept of class not only with economic but also with socio-psychological content, the unadulterated economic approach to describing classes has still remained a staple category in attempted explanations of behavior. Perhaps more succinctly than any other American writer on politics, James Madison in *The Federalist, No. 10*, posited the idea that economic competition, more than any other set of conflicting environmental demands, is the most general and fundamental source of political conflict.

> . . . the most common and durable source of factions has been the various and unequal distribution of property. Those who hold and those who are without property have ever formed distinct interests in society. Those who are creditors, and those who are debtors, fall under a like discrimination. A landed interest, a manufacturing interest, a mercantile interest, a moneyed interest, with many lesser interests, grow up of necessity in civilized nations, and divide them into different classes, actuated by different sentiments and views. The regulation of these various and interfering interests forms the principal task of modern legislation, and involves the spirit of party and faction

in the necessary and ordinary operations of the government.[3]

That "the various and unequal distribution of property" is the fundamental source of "factions" supports the notion that party conflict is one expression, at the political level, of the environmental conflict of economic classes. By inference (and ignoring for the moment the impact of other social or economic factors) the relative absence of inequalities in wealth, objectively-measured, will result in a single party system; conversely, the presence of a class system based on the differential ownership of wealth will result in an electorate polarized into two competing parties.

The relationship between economic classes and party conflict can be operationalized through the medium of census data on income for 1950, in which the number of families and unrelated individuals were reported for a number of income categories. It is the dispersion of a county's population across these income categories that is pertinent to the hypothesis; the concentration of population in any one of the three would signify the near absence of economic class differences. The standard deviation is a simple statistical measure of dispersion that can be applied to these income categories. A high standard deviation will reflect a relatively wider range in income across a population while a lower measure will indicate a relatively homogeneous economic class. Stating the hypothesis in operational terms:

1. *Party competition varies directly with the standard deviation of income groups.*

II. Madison's principal concern in the familiar passage from *The Federalist, No. 10* is to explain the genesis of political conflict. He finds it in the conflicts of environmental "factions." Madison's definition and use of the latter term evidently extends not only to social classes but also to groups with economic interests cross-cutting class lines. American political researchers have employed the class concept in discussing voting behavior more than any other sociological category, but there have been occasional suggestions that class conflict may often be submerged in a common adherence to some over-arching eco-

[3] James Madison, "The Federalist, No. 10," in Alexander Hamilton, John Jay, and James Madison, *The Federalist* (New York: Modern Library, 1937), p. 56.

nomic interest uniting rich and poor. "The effect of common interest in uniting different classes of voters" was noted by Key in his discussion of regional voting differences.[4] Macmahon concluded that "the real party division in the United States has been based on the reality of conflict between wealth in the land and wealth seeking outlets in industry,"[5] while Binkley asserts even more firmly that the basis for two-party alignments has been the "mercantile-financial" versus the "independent farming" interests.[6] The theoretical implication of these ideas is that political conflict is in part rooted in the conflict of industrially centered groups for governmental favor. Any constituency having a uniform economic base from which is drawn the livelihood of a large majority would be united politically in defense of its economic interest and, conversely, a constituency with a highly diversified economy will contain a number of conflicting economic interests which cannot be accommodated by a single party.

In operationalizing this hypothesis, census data on the number of persons employed by industry categories were inspected for each county, and the number in the most heavily populated category was expressed as a percentage of the total employed labor force in the county. As this percentage increases (as the economic base becomes more homogeneous), the degree of inter-party competition should decrease according to the reasoning above:

> 2. *Party competition varies inversely with the per cent of the labor force employed in the dominant industrial category.*

III. Madison further develops his theory of political conflict by superimposing an areal dimension upon the economic sources. One of his leading arguments in favor of a large federal union was that it "renders factious combinations less to be dreaded."[7] That political power in the hands of a single faction would be tyrannical he did not doubt, but this danger could be

---

[4] V. O. Key, Jr., *Politics, Parties, and Pressure Groups* (4th ed.; New York: Thomas Y. Crowell, 1958), p. 269.

[5] Arthur W. Macmahon, "Parties, Political: United States," *Encyclopedia of the Social Sciences*, Vol. II (New York: Macmillan, 1933), p. 598.

[6] Wilfred E. Binkley, *American Political Parties* (New York: Alfred A. Knopf, 1943), p. viii.

[7] Madison, *op. cit.*, p. 60.

averted by incorporating a larger number of factions within the political system.

> The smaller the society, the fewer probably will be the distinct parties and interests composing it; the fewer the distinct parties and interests, the more frequently will a majority be found of the same party; and the smaller the number of individuals composing a majority, and the smaller the compass within which they are placed, the more easily will they concert and execute their plans of oppression. Extend the sphere, and you take in a greater variety of parties and interests.[8]

Thus, the "smaller society" will tend to be more homogeneous in its interests while a more densely populated area will probably be an environment of plural and conflicting groups. Note that Madison does not allude to urbanization *per se* but to the size of a population relative to the area it occupies, i.e., to population density whether urban, rural, or mixed. Thus the third Madisonian hypothesis can be directly operationalized:

> 3. *Party competition varies directly with population density.*

IV. Contemporary political scientists have used the concept of urbanism in two somewhat different ways to explain competitive variations. First, environmental conflict *within* metropolitan areas is said to increase with their size and, therefore, the city itself is posited as the source of a heightened inter-party competition. Second, the presumed differences of rural *versus* urban interests may also provide the foundation for political conflict. These explanations will be developed in this and the following hypothesis.

A number of the literary sources agree that small-town politics is characteristically one-party politics and that there is a mounting tendency toward two-partyism as cities increase in size. In smaller cities, latent differences are presumably submerged in a "highly integrated community life with a powerful capacity to induce conformity."[9] In a similar vein, Berelson *et al.* concluded that a class-conscious vote was inhibited in the small

[8] *Ibid.*, pp. 60–61.
[9] V. O. Key, Jr., *American State Politics* (New York: Alfred A. Knopf, 1956), p. 227.

city of Elmira by "the dominant community ideology centered in the middle class and its rural forebears."[10] Epstein carries these notions to a more complete explanation based upon his studies of party competition in Wisconsin:

> Political issues do not so clearly divide the small city or village, and elections tend to be contested within a single party on the basis of rival personal claims either to popularity or administrative efficiency. . . . What this view suggests is that reinforcing the political traditionalism of smaller places . . . is a relative homogeneity associated with their size. Class-consciousness is not entirely absent, but it is easy to believe that working-class consciousness is inhibited in smaller as compared with larger cities by the more readily available personal and social channels for communicating middle-class values. There is a greater opportunity for those values to pervade and dominate.[11]

We shall employ the number of persons in the largest town as an indirect indicator of potentialities for class and group conflict. Logic requires us to recognize the possibility that some metropolitan election districts might be socially and economically homogeneous; in such cases a high empirical index of urbanization would be a spurious measure of their potential for group conflict. But as the sources suggest, it seems reasonable to assume that more heavily urbanized districts will contain more opportunities for voters to perceive differences of interest and value, and our operational hypothesis follows theirs:[12]

[10] Bernard R. Berelson, Paul F. Lazarsfeld, and William N. McPhee, *Voting* (Chicago: University of Chicago Press, 1954), p. 57.

[11] Leon D. Epstein, *Politics in Wisconsin* (Madison: University of Wisconsin Press, 1958), pp. 68–69.

[12] This hypothesis requires a measure of "urbanism" with a zero-point reflecting the existence of a wholly rural population and the size of the smallest as well as the larger centers. By the census definitions of urbanism, many American counties have no urban population though they have small towns and villages. Thus, instead of the census figures on the "per cent urban" by county, we employ the raw number of persons living in the county's largest town, however small, better to capture the theoretical idea of a continuous function between size of place and party competition. Also, the raw figures are used in preference to percentages of the county popula-

4. *Party competition varies directly with the size of the largest town.*

V. According to the last hypothesis, one source of inter-party competition lies in the environmental conflicts arising within towns and cities, but the literature also implies that divergent interests and values between city and countryside are a base for political conflict. According to Key:

> One of the most common foundations for two-party competition within individual states is that of the metrop-olis against the countryside . . . the typical pattern is that more than half the metropolitan electorate leans in one direction, whereas more than half the rural population leans in the other.[13]

And Key concludes this passage by suggesting that the "ways of life" of city and countryside are somehow different enough to serve as an environmental basis for aggregation by competing parties. A related theme from sociological theory has been the social structural difference between *gemeinschaft* and *gesellschaft,* with the former connoting a rural communal society in which action is oriented to the feeling of the actors that they belong together in contrast to the rationally motivated adjustment of interests attributable to an urban life. Tending to support the concept of the communal rural society is the empiri-cal finding of Campbell *et al.,* that "contact with modern urban life increases the likelihood of class awareness. The level of awareness . . . is particularly low among people in farm occu-pations."[14] In theory, then, to speak of the rural society is to imply a political homogeneity of values which may foreclose aggregative opportunities by more than one party.

To remain as close as possible to the theoretical references above, the rural farm population as a percentage of the county population will be used as a measure having at least face validity

---

tion living in the largest town, since the latter figure would reflect an urban-rural proportion unsuitable for operationalizing the idea of environmental conflict *within* towns and cities.

[13] Key, *op. cit.* (1958), p. 325.

[14] Angus Campbell, Philip E. Converse, Warren E. Miller, and Donald E. Stokes, *The American Voter* (New York: John Wiley and Sons, 1960), p. 369.

as an indicator of the aforementioned economic and social characteristics of ruralism. As this figure declines, it is assumed that the interests and values attributed to an urban industrial-associational society would become predominant. The theoretical sources imply that as the rural farm population increases, both social and economic forces would pull a society in the direction of political homogeneity:

   5. *Party competition varies inversely with the rural farm population as a percentage of the total population.*

VI. Madison, much like Marx, viewed class as a direct manifestation of economic cleavages. However, modern social research has shown that social stratification in the United States is better described by socio-psychological than by economic criteria—that the consciousness of class is more a matter of subjective attitudes than of objective economic determinants. For example, the sociologist, Charles H. Page, observed two decades ago that in this country class, described economically, is not identical with the kind of stratification reflected by "common values, attitudes, and aspirations."[15]

Furthermore, Arthur Holcombe suggested that those who hold middle class values have displaced the conflict of rich against poor so greatly feared by Madison and his contemporaries; Holcombe held that this middle class, now primarily urban, is politically moderate and subject to the blandishments of both parties.[16] The middle class's moderation (or perhaps more precisely its vacillation) in political attitudes was also noted by C. Wright Mills, who found that white collar workers in middle-sized cities were not establishing their own value orientations but were torn between the big business group on the one hand and organized labor on the other.[17] Strong support to this line of reasoning is also supplied by Richard Centers' research on the characteristic attitudes of the urban middle class, occupationally defined; those near the middle of his array of occupational statuses were often "of different minds" on matters of political policy while those in the highest and lowest statuses

[15] Charles H. Page, "Social Class and American Sociology," in Reinhard Bendix and Seymour Martin Lipset, eds., *Class, Status and Power* (Glencoe: The Free Press, 1953), p. 48.

[16] Arthur N. Holcombe, *The Middle Classes in American Politics* (Cambridge, Mass.: Harvard University Press, 1940), p. 219.

[17] C. Wright Mills, "The Middle Classes in Middle Sized Cities," *American Sociological Review*, 11 (October, 1946), pp. 528–529.

tended to have clearer polar attitudes.[18] Finally, and with particular reference to the South, Alexander Heard has followed the Holcombe thesis in predicting that the development of a Southern urban middle class would hasten the rise of the minor party, giving it a potential source of votes from which it might eventually approach competitive equality with the major party.[19] These writers lead directly to the hypothesis that, in any constituency, the greater the proportion of the population holding middle class values, the greater the tendency toward polarization of the electorate into two parties.

The demographic data available for North Carolina counties do not permit this hypothesis to be operationalized precisely in accord with the ideas of these writers, because so few counties in the state have "urban" populations according to the census definitions thereof. It will be necessary, therefore, to depart slightly from these writers' stress on the urban locus of this class and cast our operational hypothesis simply in terms of non-farm middle-class occupations. The effect of this change is to assume that the middle-class values expressed in such a measure will roughly approximate the urban references of the hypotheses in the literature. Social scientists have most often utilized occupation categories as the best objective indicators of subjective class consciousness, and we follow Millls and Centers in adopting them. Middle class will be defined in terms of the following occupational categories for counties in the 1950 census: professional, technical and kindred workers; managers except farm; clerical and sales. Our operational hypothesis, therefore, is formulated as follows:

> 6. *Party competition varies directly with the per cent of the labor force in non-farm middle class occupations.*

VII. Madison's view of economic class conflict has been interpreted here to mean that where any one of the three income categories becomes a strong majority party competition will decline, but the particular role of a uniformly poor population vis-à-vis political conflict has occasionally been alluded to by social scientists. Lipset suggests that stable poverty is symptomatic of the communal society, whose values are determined by

---

[18] Richard Centers, *The Psychology of Social Classes* (Princeton: Princeton University Press, 1949), p. 108.

[19] Alexander Heard, *A Two-Party South?* (Chapel Hill: University of North Carolina Press, 1952), pp. 247–248.

tradition and whose political expression is a uniform conservatism. In areas where poor farmers and workers predominate . . .

> the positions of rich and poor are defined as the
> natural order of things and are supported by personal,
> family, and local loyalties rather than viewed as a product
> of impersonal economic and social forces, subject to
> change through political action.[20]

At another point, Lipset cites Marx's pessimism about the
lower class as a radical political force. The poor, Marx believed,
would probably be often characterized by "false consciousness"
because they accept the traditional structure of social relationships; their acceptance of the established order is reinforced by
the major value-creating social institutions.[21] In studies of
American politics a similar theme has appeared. The paradoxical attachment of some poor counties in the border states to
the Republican party was attributed to a conservatism among
their large low-income populations which was instilled by local
commercial elites.[22] The decline of agrarian radicalism in
Arkansas, according to V. O. Key, Jr., may have been partly due
to the reduction of many commercial farmers to the status of
low-income subsistence or tenant farmers, the assumption being that "when an owner becomes a tenant he loses his spunk
and his concern about public affairs."[23] These ideas lead to the
hypothesis that predominantly poor areas will tend toward one-
partyism.

In operationalizing this hypothesis, it will be necessary to
utilize economic data to describe a presumed state of mind;
there is no necessary logical relationship between the two, and
a high correlation between poverty and one-partyism would
constitute only presumptive evidence of a socio-psychological
state. Operationally, "lowest income category" refers to families
and unrelated individuals reporting $999 or less yearly income
in census reports:

[20] Seymour Martin Lipset, *Political Man* (Garden City: Doubleday
and Company, 1960), p. 259.

[21] *Ibid.*, p. 280.

[22] John H. Fenton, *Politics in the Border States* (New Orleans:
Hauser Press, 1957), pp. 214–215.

[23] Key, *op. cit.* (1949), p. 185n.

7. *Party competition varies inversely with the per cent of
the population in the lowest income category.*

VIII. Increasing levels of educational attainment have
been found to be associated with a greater sense of political
efficacy, "sense of citizen duty" and familiarity with political
issues, and with a greater degree of political activity above and
beyond the act of voting.[24] Such findings suggest a more dynamic political system with a greater potentiality for competitive parties. Moreover, education has been discovered to be itself a significant indicator of class, apart from other dimensions
such as occupation and income, and "class voting" may be a
function of the more general political sophistication that presumably accompanies higher levels of formal education. Conversely, the political homogeneity of the static society may be
in part due to its generally low level of education, as Leon
Epstein has hypothesized with reference to Wisconsin's rural
counties.[25] Census data on the size of the lowest educational
category can be used in setting up an operational hypothesis
following these ideas:

8. *Party competition varies inversely with the per cent of
all persons twenty-five years and older with less than a
fifth grade education.*

IX. Class awareness may also be a function of age. Leon
Epstein theorizes that an aging population is symptomatic of a
static society in which values tend to be settled and homogeneous, dulling political conflict.[26] A constituency with a large
proportion of voters in the upper age brackets might, therefore,
be expected to tend toward one-partyism. The authors of *The
American Voter*, however, suggest a different conclusion with
respect to the impact of the class awareness of an aging population on party conflict.

> Across a fair portion of the age continuum we find
> rising awareness with increasing years. . . . The age group
> in which [class] awareness is most prevalent includes those
> individuals who were in their twenties and thirties during
> the depths of the Great Depression, a generation long as-
> sumed to have been strongly affected by economic events.[27]

[24] Campbell *et al., op. cit.,* pp. 175, 412–413, 476–477.

[25] Epstein, *op. cit.,* pp. 15–16.

[26] *Ibid.*

[27] Campbell *et al., op. cit.,* p. 357.

If awareness of class differences constitutes a basis for environmental conflict, then a greater tendency toward political polarization might be expected in a constituency with a large fifty-year-old-and-over age bracket.

Though apparently contradictory, each of these ideas is reasonable: on the one hand, the picture of an aging population as conducive to a static society is compatible with widely-held sociological stereotypes; on the other hand, the life experiences of the now older generation may lend it a political sensitivity uncommon to younger age groups. Avoiding ratiocination about their relative validity, the following empirical hypothesis should tend to support one or the other when tested:

9. *Party competition varies inversely with the per cent of the population fifty years old and over.*

X. The sixth hypothesis above referred to the role of an urban middle class vis-à-vis party competition. However, the role of the rural middle class in the party system merits special attention. Arthur Holcombe asserts that through most of American history the rural middle class, rather than the urban, was the balance wheel of the party system.

My thesis is that for a larger part of our national existence that class [which holds the balance of power] was the rural middle class and that increasingly in our time it tends to become the urban middle class. . . . At present the system of presidential elections tends more and more to shift the balance of power to the urban middle class.[28]

Holcombe suggests that, with the rise of an urban middle class, the rural middle class was displaced as the most dynamic voting group. In predominantly rural states, however, the rural middle class may still play the dominant role ascribed to it by Holcombe. If the second Holcombe thesis is valid, then the presumably moderate values of the state's rural middle class may yet contribute to the existence of a more competitive party system. Again operationalizing middle class in occupational terms as in the sixth hypothesis:

[28] Quoted in Samuel J. Eldersveld, "The Influence of Metropolitan Party Pluralities in Presidential Elections Since 1920: A Study of Twelve Key Cities," *American Political Science Review,* 43 (December, 1949), pp. 1189–1206.

10. *Party competition varies directly with the per cent of the rural population in middle class occupations.*

XI. In addition to the familiar industrial sources, politics itself may provide an important element in the economic base of governmental districts. In so far as politics is a major source of income, it may exert a special influence on the intensity of political party competition.

> Finally, another variation in economic structure must be mentioned—the variation between towns dominated by business interests and those dominated by political authority (through control of patronage, road contracts, and other local governmental contracting). In the latter, found most often in the non-industrialized south, the absence of industry and the dominance of politics makes concern with politics much greater, and increases the likelihood that politically related incidents will set off controversy.[29]

The rationale behind the second hypothesis was that a uniform economic base would tend to produce political consensus, and the same reasoning applies in this case. The "dominance of politics" of which Coleman writes connotes intense identification with the dominant party by those whose livelihood depends in some measure on its continued success: office-holders, appointees, holders of patronage and their employees, their families and associates. Key has shown that in North Carolina the "organization faction" of the dominant state party elicits strong allegiance from its beneficiaries in these counties[30]—at least inferential support for the proposition that politics as a source of income may result in a more wide-spread party identification. As the income from political sources becomes a greater proportion of the economic base of a community, therefore, tendencies toward one-partyism should increase.[31]

[29] James S. Coleman, *Community Conflict* (Glencoe: The Free Press, 1957), p. 7.
[30] V. O. Key, Jr., *Southern Politics in State and Nation* (New York: Alfred A. Knopf, 1949), pp. 223–228.
[31] Necessary income data were obtained from Walter Allen Spivey, "An Analysis of Per Capita Income in the States and Regions of the United States, 1929–1953, with Special Reference to North Carolina," unpublished Ph.D. dissertation, University of North Carolina, 1956, pp. 171–174.

11. *Party competition varies inversely with the per cent of income payments from government.*

XII. Finally, the importance of racial and cultural minorities to environmental conflict is too well-recognized to require extensive documentation; the following statement of the idea by Key is concise and to the point:

> Anthropologists tell us that in primitive cultures the cohesion of social groups is mightily promoted by the proximity of unlike groups. If that phenomenon occurs generally, it would be expected that the strongest roots of southern unity would be found in those parts of the South in which Negroes constituted a large part of the population. On the other hand, it might be supposed that the bonds of southern unity would be weakest in those areas with fewest Negroes.[32]

Generally speaking, "unlike groups" which Key speaks of may be any racial, cultural or ethnic minorities in the areas under investigation. In North Carolina, the site of this research, the only such groups of any size are Negroes and American Indians, both of which are designated by the Census as "nonwhite," therefore:

12. *Party competition varies inversely with the per cent non-white of the total population.*

In reprise, each of these twelve testable hypotheses is a statement about inputs from the environment into the party system. If one of the functions of parties is interest aggregation, and if the environment ranges from homogeneity to heterogeneity of interest, then variations in party competition are related to the degree of environmental conflict of interest among election constituencies.

Patterns of Inter-Party Competition in North Carolina

The term party competition, as used here, refers only to the division of popular votes in elections for the candidates of the

[32] Key, *op. cit.* (1958), pp. 263–264.

two major parties, and our measurements of competition follow straightforwardly from this definition. There is no plea that the method presented here is qualitatively any better than many other ways of measuring party competition, or even that it is particularly original. The only argument that needs to be presented in its favor is that this method of measurement is directly appropriate to testing the theory.

The districts chosen for testing the theory are the one hundred counties of North Carolina during the dozen years from 1944 to 1956, a span of time probably long enough to minimize or "balance out" the effect of any unusual elections in measuring party competition. For each county, three separate measurements of party competition were calculated: (1) for president of the United States; (2) a combined measure for governor and U.S. senator; (3) a combined measure for county sheriff, county commissioners, and county representatives to the lower house of the state legislature.[33] To compute these rates of party competition, the mean percentage vote for the party winning the most elections at each ballot level was determined and, by simple arithmetic procedures, was converted to a scale having limits of 1.000 and .000; the former figure corresponds to a fifty per cent mean vote for both parties, or perfect competition as here defined, and the latter figure corresponds to a one hundred per cent mean vote for the candidates of one of the parties, or a total absence of party competition at the polls.[34]

As the table shows, therefore, these one hundred counties proved to be quite diverse in competitiveness—sufficiently so to meet the test requirement of a wide range in the dependent variable, party competition. With regard to their environmental characteristics, there is considerable diversity among these counties on all of the independent variables specified in the

[33] Only votes for the major parties were used in these calculations. Write-in votes bearing no party designation were disregarded, as were votes for candidates of the Dixiecrat and Progressive parties of 1948, whose combined vote did not exceed 9.3% of the total at any level of the ballot.

[34] For example, the Republican party won a majority of all the elections for governor and U.S. senator in Watauga county between 1940 and 1960, and the mean percentage vote for the majority party's candidates was .504. To transform this figure to the more convenient zero-to-one scale, the mean was multiplied by two and subtracted from two, resulting in a rate of party competition for this county at the state level of .992—very near the perfect competition rate of 1.000.

TABLE 1

FREQUENCY DISTRIBUTION OF NORTH CAROLINA COUNTIES
BY RATES OF PARTY COMPETITION FOR PRESIDENTIAL, STATE,
AND LOCAL BALLOT LEVELS

Rate of Competition:	Pres.	State	Local
High (.750–1.000)	44	30	27
Moderately High (.500–.749)	17	20	11
Moderately Low (.250–.499)	33	20	12
Low (.000–.249)	6	30	50
Total counties:	100	100	100
Range of rate of competition:	.990 to .114	.992 to .068	.992 to .000
Mean rate of competition:	.642	.510	.375

hypotheses with the exception that they contain no very large metropolitan areas. However, the environmental diversities among them are sufficient to permit tests of the hypothesized co-variations between the dependent and independent variables.

Statistical Tests of the Theory

The twelve hypotheses were tested by using the three indices of party competition as the dependent variables respectively in three separate multiple regression analyses, with the independent variables being the twelve environmental factors spelled out in the hypotheses. Coefficients of multiple correlation (R) will measure the degree of association between party competition and the twelve independent variables considered simultaneously. Further, multiple regression analysis permits the assessment of the relative contribution to the multiple R's of each of the twelve predictor variables. In Table 2, these beta values are the standardized coefficients of the regression equations and are statistically comparable with each other.[35] Thus the betas which are larger made a stronger contribution to the total association, and the hypotheses corresponding to these betas can be accorded a higher measure of validity.

As Table 2 shows, the multiple correlation coefficients at each level of the ballot were above .85, a high figure indicating that the twelve hypotheses together were quite successful statistically in explaining variations in party competition. For each R, the possibility that so large a figure could have occurred by chance was less than .001 ($F_{12, 87}$). Coefficients of determination (R^2) indicate that approximately seventy-five per cent of the variance in competition was accounted for at each ballot level. Thus the regression analyses strongly support the theory stated in the beginning of this study—that the basis of inter-party competition at the polls lies in the conflicting values of environmental groups. The greater the environmental heterogeneity of the party system, the greater the degree of party competition, while the one-party system is a function of the homogeneous community. The magnitude of the multiple correlation coefficients affords a strong impression of the party system as an effective structure of interest aggregation.

So far as the twelve hypotheses are concerned, no firm conclusions about their individual validity are warranted beyond the geographical boundaries of our research. For North Carolina, the values of the regression parameters in Table 2 add substance to the impression of one-partyism as rooted in the static rural *gemeinschaft,* whose party orientation congealed generations ago and where the level of political interest and information is probably low. Yet the rather high eleventh beta suggests a more pragmatic basis of one-partyism; balanced party competition declines as there is an increase in the percentage of persons whose livelihood depends largely on the continued power of the dominant state party. Therefore, in the South as presumably in the rest of the nation, many areas contain social

[35] The formula for standardizing beta coefficients is reported in Mordecai Ezekiel and Karl A. Fox, *Methods of Correlation and Regression Analysis* (3rd ed.; New York: John Wiley and Sons, 1959), p. 196.

TABLE 2

STANDARDIZED REGRESSION COEFFICIENTS FOR PREDICTING RATES OF PARTY COMPETITION

Predictor Variables:	President	State	County
1. Income classes	.1230*	.0757	.0516
2. Economic base	−.0436	−.0119	.0095
3. Population density	−.0616	−.0979	−.0969
4. Size of largest town	.2540**	.2596**	.1374
5. Rural farm population	−.2737**	−.1796*	−.5242**
6. Urban middle class	−.3453**	−.3982**	−.2966*
7. Working class	.1716*	.1995*	.1716*
8. Low education	−.2707**	−.1819**	−.1467*
9. Aging population	−.0490	−.0847	−.1198*
10. Rural middle class	.0726	.0782	.0613
11. Government income	−.2578**	−.2682**	−.2931**
12. Non-white	−.6641**	−.7838**	−.7728**
Multiple Correlation Coefficient	.8742	.8869	.8512
Coefficient of Determination (R^2)	.7642	.7866	.7245
Standard Error of Estimate	13.6205	15.0377	20.8299

*Significant at the .20 level.
**Significant at the .05 level.

and economic forces sufficiently uniform and pervasive to virtually preclude the aggregation of conflicting interests by a two-party system. But the distinctive basis of most Southern one-party systems is powerfully underscored by the twelfth beta; its very high magnitude echoes the conclusion of so many studies, that the typical source of Southern one-partyism is white solidarity in the presence of large non-white populations.

Apparently, then, one-partyism in the American political system may be a function of not one but several environmental group configurations, and the same is true of competitive party systems. The first beta in the Table indicates that party competition increases in the presence of a class system based on the differential ownership of wealth. For North Carolina, this Madisonian, economic class conflict was a more powerful contributor to the total association than was the pluralistic economic group conflict referred to in the second hypothesis. Two-partyism is also largely an urban phenomenon, though not entirely absent from the countryside as suggested by the tenth beta, and tends to increase with the size of the working class. Rather surprisingly, the regression coefficients for the sixth hypothesis indicate a strong and negative association between urban middle-classness and party competition. Urban white collar voters in North Carolina did not comprise a balance wheel of the party system during the period covered in this study. Yet the betas for hypotheses one, seven and ten suggest dual party systems based in part on the aggregation of class interests.[36]

Party Organizations and Interest Aggregation

The theory of environmental conflict and party competition has been strongly supported by the empirical data for North Carolina. In a sense, the preceding section was a statistical portrayal of interest aggregation in a two-party framework. But

---

[36] One pitfall in this type of analysis is the possible reification of demographic aggregates into "real" groups having a consciousness of kind and an awareness of other groups with opposing values. Still, the high magnitude and levels of significance of some of the betas seem to imply a social reality beyond mere statistical categories; also, the failure of some hypotheses to produce significant regression parameters may mean that their socio-economic indices measured only the size of demographic sets, not groups in the socio-psychological sense.

interest aggregation is not an automatic output of a mechanistic system. It is a theoretical construct deriving empirical reality only from behavioral processes—from actions by and among flesh and blood actors. From a functionalist framework, a party organization can be viewed as a configuration of actions, the purpose of which is to marshall environmental interests and values as inputs into the polity. In large measure, the mobilization of group interests depends on the efficiency and effectiveness of party leaders and workers. But organizational activities implementing aggregation are carried out with greater or less vigor from district to district. And the data presented below will at least imply, if they do not demonstrate, that in the absence of such activities, interest aggregation falls short of the potential that might be realized by party systems.[37]

We will attempt to trace the effect of organizational activity first by isolating deviant cases—those counties which stray from the generally close association between socio-economic factors and inter-party competition. Multiple regression analysis provides an estimating equation for calculating the exact degree of inter-party competition that would be expected in each county on the basis of the overall association between the dependent and independent variables. The observed degree of party competition in any given county, based upon the original election data, can thus be compared with the degree of competition statistically predicted from its socio-economic characteristics in the light of the total relationship for all of the counties. Applying the estimating equations to each county, the deviant cases are those counties with higher residuals (differences) between the observed and predicted rates of competition. These calculations showed that for half or more of the counties at each ballot level, the statistically predicted rates of competition were within 10 points, plus or minus, of the rates observed from the election data. In these counties, the party system seems to have been a reasonably effective structure for aggregating environmental conflict. Still, the residuals for almost half of the counties at each ballot level exceeded 10 points. The hypothesis is that these higher residuals are due in part to variations in party organizational activity.

Politicians of the weaker party in North Carolina bewail

---

[37] Data not reported here also indicate a traditionalism in party voting that is purely political, not explainable by group or class characteristics. In counties where this is in evidence, the observed rates of competition fell considerably below that predicted statistically.

their difficulties in recruiting dedicated and resourceful party workers at the grass roots level. Moreover, the minor party has often been unable even to recruit candidates to run in local races. There were twenty-one North Carolina counties in which no Republican candidates whatever ran for sheriff, county commissioner, or member of the lower house of the state legislature during the entire period under investigation. If a local party organization does not even recruit candidates, then it very probably does not perform other functionally relevant activities. Conversely, where there is a full slate of party nominees for offices at this lowest level of the ballot, local party cadres are probably better geared to all of these activities. Therefore, a simple but useful indicator of county party organizational activity may be the frequency with which the party's candidates run for office at the county level. The one hundred counties were thus divided into two categories: counties in which the minor party ran candidates in half or more of the elections for county offices are classed as having "active" organizations, while the "inactive" group of counties is comprised of all those in which minor party candidates ran in less than half of the elections for these offices. This dichotomous scale relates closely to the residuals between the observed and predicted rates of competition, as shown in Table 3.

Here is strong evidence that, in the presence of inactive local party organizations, the degree of competition actually registered at the polls is less than that predicted by our theory; conversely, in the presence of active local party organizations, the degree of inter-party competition sometimes exceeds that which was theoretically predicted on the basis of environmental factors. There is a significant relationship, therefore, between party organizational activity and the fulfillment of the aggregative function. Notice that where one of the party organizations does not produce candidates for *county* offices, its potential vote for candidates at the presidential and state levels is not likely to be realized either. Evidently, if a party is to mobilize environmental stresses in state and national elections, the efforts of campaigners at these higher levels must be supplemented by working organizations at the county level.

According to several recent studies, the formation of public opinion is greatly affected by local influentials who interpret the information supplied by the mass media to the voters. The individual voter often apparently finds it difficult to understand a campaign in terms of his own position in society without the

TABLE 3

ACTIVITY OF LOCAL PARTY ORGANIZATIONS AND RESIDUALS
AT PRESIDENTIAL AND STATE BALLOT LEVELS BY
NUMBER OF COUNTIES

A. PRESIDENTIAL BALLOT LEVEL

Residuals
(Difference between Observed and Predicted
Rates of Competition)

Local Party Organization	Observed less than Predicted			Observed more than Predicted	
	10 points or more	5 to 9 points	±5 points	5 to 9 points	10 points or more
Active	4	3	19	10	15
Inactive	15	4	23	4	3
(N)	(19)	(7)	(42)	(14)	(18)

$x^2 = 17.42$ d.f. $= 4$ P $< .01$

B. STATE BALLOT LEVEL

Residuals
(Difference between Observed and Predicted
Rates of Competition)

Local Party Organization	Observed less than Predicted			Observed more than Predicted	
	10 points or more	5 to 9 points	±5 points	5 to 9 points	10 points or more
Active	6	5	14	7	19
Inactive	16	8	17	5	3
(N)	(22)	(13)	(31)	(12)	(22)

$x^2 = 17.47$ d.f. $= 4$ P $< .01$

aid of these local opinion leaders. An inference from Table 3 is that local party activists are an important link in this "two-step flow of communication." The weakness of local party organizations may redound on elections at the higher ballot levels because it constitutes a breakdown in communication between the voters and the state and national candidates.

Again, Table 3 strongly suggests the importance of local party activists for the input of environmental conflicts into the party system at all ballot levels. Where one, or even both, of the party organizations is only a paper organization, where its candidates are unknown, unattractive, or even non-existent, its potential voting support cannot be realized in any races. Socio-economic conflicts cannot be effectively aggregated through the party system if party cadres do not carry out their partisan activities. Perhaps some inefficiency in interest aggregation by parties promotes the stability of a democratic political system in an environment of conflicting factions. On the other hand, there is some point at which the empirical inefficiencies of party cadres become a matter of concern to the democratic order. A reasonable efficacy in the functioning of these structures on the boundaries between the polity and the environment is vitally important to a system which values governmental responsiveness to the electorate and the creative discussion of policy alternatives. Where the party leadership is delinquent, there are, perhaps, other boundary structures aggregating environmental interest more or less efficiently. Nevertheless, both for the empirical theory and out of normative concern, it is an important question whether or to what extent legitimate environmental demands are mobilized and reflected in the polity when party leaders do not carry out the aggregative function.

Conclusions

There are obvious pitfalls for the unwary in the interpretation of correlation coefficients, especially when the latter are high and significant. The point is an elementary one in statistical induction but perhaps bears repeating at this point, that no conclusions about causality are warranted from measures of statistical association. In this analysis, inter-party competition has been treated analytically as a dependent variable. However, we should not ignore the possibility that party competition might itself be an independent variable stimulating changes in the degree of environmental conflict, considered as a dependent variable. In fact, one consequence of a more competitive party system may be to draw the lines of environmental conflict more clearly, to make manifest and dramatize differences of interest and value among various publics and, thereby, to arouse the latter politically. One of the common criticisms of traditionalistic one-party systems in the South is precisely that their campaign appeals have failed to activate the latent political interests of race and class. Conversely, a competitive politics may have the effect of maintaining and re-inforcing the group divisions upon which it feeds. It is safe to assume that there is a complex interplay between socioeconomic conflict, organizational activity and party competition at the polls; we cannot yet speak of active or passive roles for these factors in a causal sense. Further, we have scarcely scratched the surface of what might be "intervening variables." It is probably rare that party organizations are the only structures in a constituency having aggregative functions for the system; candidate (as opposed to party) organizations presumably will play such a role, as may some associational groups without continuous or manifest political functions. And within our limited theoretical framework, no attempt has been made to encompass the myriad personal and situational factors of the moment which, no doubt, would often confound statistical prediction. Finally, of course, the North Carolina counties are in no sense a sample of American election constituencies. In effect, all of these cautionary remarks on statistical interpretation constitute questions for further theoretical explication and empirical research.

But with all of these qualifications in mind, the tests of our data still lend strong statistical support to the theory that the party system effectively aggregates environmental conflicts, for variations in the degree of party competition are closely associated statistically with the complexity of environmental interests. The single-party system is a function of the homogeneous environment, while two-party systems are reflections of environmental conflicts of interests and values. But the data also indicate the partial adequacy of an explanation of variations in party competition which ignores the impact of organizational activity. The potentialities for interest aggregation by the party system are unlikely to be realized in the absence of active local party organizations. Passivity among party cadres has dysfunctional consequences for the aggregation of latent environmental interests. The data imply the importance of local party organizations as catalysts between society and polity.

What this analysis suggests is that the study of political party organizations could be approached profitably from the standpoint of the functional consequences of their structural and behavioral characteristics. Past studies of party organizations, however well conceived and executed, have often dealt with rather "low range" hypotheses about factors internal to organizations, without suggesting their implications for the broader processes of the political system. Indeed, a *political* theory of party organizations can hardly be said to exist. The signal advantage of the functionalist approaches is that they suggest what is worth studying about party organizations and why, from the standpoint of the system as a whole, and that they provide a unifying focus around which theories might be constructed. Vagaries in the institutional and behavioral characteristics of state and local party organizations call for some such focus as a precondition for their systematic comparative analysis. To conceptualize the types of actions relevant to aggregation, communication, integration, and for the transmission of demands and supports from environment to polity, would be a useful beginning in itself; it would also serve to locate party organizations within a larger conceptual framework and orient research on their consequences for the political system.

Our analysis is by no means offered as a finished piece, either theoretically or methodologically. Hopefully it may be a step toward a more refined, empirically based theory in a functionalist framework and it outlines a general strategy of theory-research interaction that may contribute to that end. The results of the study suggest that a process of this kind may indeed prove fruitful. More sophisticated and conclusive studies will depend upon the development of more refined instruments of measuring and testing, but even more on theoretical labor in extending and refining the number and quality of testable hypotheses. The problem is at once theoretical and methodological; advances in one must be accompanied by advances in the other if we are to approach a body of reliable knowledge of the American party systems.

SEVEN

The Party Organization
and Its Activities

William J. Crotty
Northwestern University

THERE ARE two prominent themes in the folklore of American politics as it relates to political parties. One stresses the potentially decisive effects of activities conducted by the local units of the parties. Practicing politicians in particular emphasize the strategic importance of the lower levels of the party hierarchy in influencing the outcome of elections. The better mobilized the precincts and the party organizations just above them—ward, city, county—the more promising the possibility of winning office. At least, this is the message carried by the candidate to party workers.[1]

Both academicians and political practitioners agree on the second point: party structure in the United States lacks cohesion and centralization. On an organizational chart, the party structure represents something close to an ideal model of organization. There are (or appear to be) identifiable lines of communication, unity of command, clear responsibility for decision-making, centralization of resources, and a division of

[1] A report distributed by the Republican National Committee can serve as testimonial to the pervasiveness of this belief. See *The 1960 Elections* (rev., 3rd printing; Washington, D.C.: Prepared by the Research Division of the Republican National Committee, August, 1961), especially pp. 42-44. Consult also Ivan Hinderacker, *Party Politics* (New York: Henry Holt and Company, 1956), pp. 491–492, for other illustrations.

labor. Unfortunately, one learns very little from a formal organizational chart about the actual nature of the parties.[2]

Clinton Rossiter underscores the point. After describing
the organization of American parties as "pluralized, dispersed,
. . . fractured," he goes on to argue that the most appropriate
word with which to characterize the parties and their organization is feudal. Yet, as Rossiter notes, the state of party organization may be closer to anarchy than feudalism.[3]

Most American political scientists share Rossiter's senti-
ments. There is some controversy however. The nature of the
disagreements and the state of present parties' research can
best be illustrated by reference to the Report of the Committee
on Political Parties of the American Political Science Association,
Toward a More Responsible Two-Party System.[4] Its assumptions
can be briefly summarized. First, it argued that the major goal
of the party should be the presentation of meaningful policy
alternatives to the electorate and the enactment of the winning

[2] Samuel J. Eldersveld addresses himself to this problem in his *Political Parties: A Behavioral Analysis* (Chicago: Rand McNally and
Company, 1964), pp. 4–5.

The reference to organization in this report is to the conventional
party units on the various federated levels of the electoral system
(precinct, ward, county, district, state, national) that have a formally
prescribed party structure (e.g., precinct committee and chairmen;
county committee, chairmen, auxiliary workers and units, etc.). The
activation of the organization is noted through measures of the
number of such units manned by party activists and engaging in
identifiable bureaucratic activities, *e.g.*, record keeping, holding
meetings, attempting to effectuate group goals.

[3] Clinton Rossiter, *Parties and Politics in America* (Ithaca: Cornell
University Press, 1960), pp. 12–13. For another presentation of this
point of view, see: V. O. Key, Jr., *Politics, Parties and Pressure
Groups* (5th ed.; New York: Thomas Y. Crowell, 1964).

[4] American Political Science Association, *Toward a More Responsible
Two-Party System* (New York: Rinehart and Company, Inc., 1950), p.
25. (Hereinafter referred to as the Report.) The implications of the
centralization-decentralization debate far exceed the empirical, or-
ganizational focus that is the basis for the present discussion. A few
of the more prominent works of relevance to the controversy are:
Stephen K. Bailey, *The Condition of Our National Political Parties*
(Santa Barbara, Calif.: The Fund for the Republic, 1959); Murray
S. Stedman, Jr., and Herbert Sonthoff, "Party Responsibility—A
Critical Inquiry," *Western Political Quarterly*, 4 (September, 1951),
pp. 454–486; E. E. Schattschneider, *Party Government* (New York:
Rinehart & Company, Inc., 1942; and Austin Ranney, *The Doctrine
of Responsible Party Government* (Urbana: University of Illinois
Press, 1962).

party's program. And second, it suggested that the most immediate means for realizing the objectives envisioned was through a series of structural modifications designed to make the party more internally cohesive and, ultimately, more accountable for its actions.

The Report sparked a wide debate among political scientists over the utility and organization of the parties.[5] Yet by necessity, the debate had to take place without access to a large pool of reliable "hard" data on, for example, the interrelationship of the formal and informal party organization, the nature of the party's functions and their *relative* systemic importance, and the effectiveness of the party in achieving its self-perceived, and attributed, objectives. Data, in other words, of accepted validity concerning the most fundamental of questions in parties' research were not available.

The intention of the present research is to indicate the utility of developing and applying empirical indices of the bureaucratic organization of the party, potentially of much value in analyzing the party and its activities. In the process, it is hoped that the description of party activities in one state can serve as a referent for similar investigations in other localities.[6] Perhaps the needed systematic knowledge of the party

---

[5] *Ibid.* More recent critical assessments of the party responsibility dialogue and other literature citations are available in: Allan P. Sindler, *Political Parties in the United States* (New York: St. Martin's Press, 1966), pp. 91–107; and Frank J. Sorauf, *Political Parties in the American System* (Boston: Little, Brown and Company, 1964), pp. 116–134. See also Ranney's discussion of party responsibility in his chapter in this volume.

[6] There are a number of comparative works on state politics which either have a different focus or are meant to serve as an introduction to political practices in a given state and, therefore, are not suitable for present purposes. The flavor of these comparative works can be gained by sampling the following: V. O. Key, Jr., *Southern Politics* (New York: Vintage Books, n. d. [originally published in 1949]); Key, *American State Politics: An Introduction* (New York: Alfred A. Knopf, 1956); Duane Lockard, *New England State Politics* (Princeton: Princeton University Press, 1959); John H. Fenton, *Midwest Politics* (New York: Holt, Rinehart and Winston, Inc., 1966); Frank Jonas, ed., *Western Politics* (Salt Lake City: University of Utah Press, 1961); Fenton, *Politics in the Border States* (New Orleans: The Hauser Press, 1957); Edgar Litt, *The Political Cultures of Massachusetts* (Cambridge: M.I.T. Press, 1965); and the selections by Austin Ranney (pp. 61–99) and Lester Milbrath (pp. 25–60) in Herbert Jacob and Kenneth H. Vines, eds., *Politics in the*

and its operations will ultimately emerge from such work.[7]

The presentation is divided into four general areas: (1) a systematic comparison of the organization of the two parties at the local level, i.e., precinct and county organization in the state, North Carolina, in which the research was done; (2) an analysis of the party organization's involvement in candidate recruitment; (3) the efforts of the party organization in contesting elections, with an indication as to relative effectiveness; and (4) organizational differences in collecting and distributing funds.

Methodology

The data used in this analysis were collected in the fall and winter of 1962–1963, primarily through a mail survey of the 195 (100 Democratic, 95 Republican) county chairmen in North Carolina. The questionnaire was lengthy: seven and one-half pages, forty-eight questions. The questionnaire was supplemented through personal interviews with party organizational personnel (county chairmen, precinct workers, precinct chairmen, the state chairmen of the two parties, and party office-workers), attendance at organizational meetings, interviews with political observers, primarily newspaper men, and through the use of census data, library materials, and relevant scholarly works.

American States (Boston: Little, Brown and Company, 1965). A scattering of representative monographs on the politics of individual states can be found in the series partly done under the auspices of the National Center for Education in Politics. Representative examples are: Earl Latham and George Goodwin, Jr., *Massachusetts Politics* (Medford, Mass.: The Tufts Civic Education Center, 1960); Austin Ranney, *Illinois Politics* (New York: New York University Press, 1960); and Daniel M. Ogden, Jr. and Hugh A. Bone, *Washington [State] Politics* (New York: New York University Press, 1960).

[7] There are notable beginnings towards such a data pool. See Eldersveld, *op. cit.*; and Leon Epstein, *Politics in Wisconsin* (Madison: University of Wisconsin Press, 1958). Other works with a more specialized focus but in line with the approach argued as desirable in this report are those by Katz and Eldersveld, Frost, Lipset, Trow and Coleman, and the series of articles by Rossi and Cutright all listed in the Hennessy bibliography following Chapter I. Citations to most of the relevant literature can be found in: Joseph A. Schlesinger, "Political Party Organization," in James G. March, ed., *Hand-*

There was a return rate on the mail survey of 89 per cent for the Democratic chairmen and 87 per cent for the Republican chairmen. The total return percentage of useable questionnaires was 88 per cent. The completion ratio of items on the questionnaire was over 96 per cent.[8]

Party Organization

A DESCRIPTIVE INTRODUCTION   Political parties in North Carolina have at least a nominal organization in virtually every one of the one hundred counties in the state (the Democrats are represented in all, the Republicans in 95).[9] Most of these county organizations (92%) were active in some capacity in the two general elections, the 1960 presidential-gubernatorial election and the 1962 off-year elections, that immediately preceded the study.

There was an implicit expectation that factional divisions within the majority Democratic party, in part fostered by its long hegemony in state politics, would be shown in lax party organization and sporadic and indifferent campaign efforts by a number of the county committees. This did not prove to be the case. While major divisions within the Democratic party are undeniable, the party norms emphasize that all activists are expected to work in behalf of official party nominees. This is an

---

book of Organizations (Chicago: Rand McNally and Company, 1965), pp. 764–801. In "Political Parties: Problems of Intranational Comparison" (Mimeo.: Presented at the Midwest Conference of Political Scientists, 1966), Donald P. Kommers and William T. Lui discuss their attempt to replicate Eldersveld's Detroit study in South Bend. An imaginative functional theoretical approach to county party organization is contained in: Marvin Harder and Thomas Ungs, "Notes Toward a Functional Analysis of Local Party Organizations" (Mimeo.: Presented at the Midwest Conference of Political Scientists, 1963).

[8] An extended discussion of the methodology involved in the study can be found in: William J. Crotty, "The Utilization of Mail Questionnaires and the Problem of a Representative Return Rate," *Western Political Quarterly*, 19 (March, 1966), pp. 44–53.

[9] The five counties in which the Republicans have no formal organization are all non-competitive, Democratic. In the most recently contested elections (1960–1962) for offices at all levels (local, county, state, and national), the Democrats received an average of 92 per cent of all votes cast.

understood precondition for accepting a post such as county chairman. Personal or policy differences must be subordinated to the major aim of winning office. Parenthetically, there is a reciprocal expectation that prospective office-seekers who receive official endorsement will coordinate their campaigns through the established party organs. There are, of course, mutual advantages to both the nominee and the party in such an arrangement. The candidate has access to a ready-made organization, experienced professionals to guide the campaign, and funding. The party in turn keeps local units in fighting trim. Eventual public office-holders develop a sense of obligation to the party that helped elect them. The arrangement also reinforces an identification among local party workers and candidates with the state party organization and the other county parties and their problems. Finally, it enables the Democratic party continually to develop a reservoir of skilled professional talent upon which to draw in future elections.

Perhaps a better indication of the thoroughness of party organizations than the number of county organizations manned or at work during election periods is the percentage of actively organized *precincts* in each of the counties. By this measure, the Democrats are more impressively organized. Every county in the state has at least some of its precincts organized by the Democratic party and three-fourths (76%) have all of their precincts actively organized. The Republicans, in comparison, have 13 counties (this number includes the five with no formal county organization) in which none of the precincts are activated; in only 35 per cent of the counties are all the precincts fully organized. These findings, then, suggest a much stronger state-wide Democratic organization.

When a number of other organizational variables are considered in addition to precinct organization, the primacy of the Democrats is not as apparent. Republicans excel in some measures of organizational vitality, Democrats in others. Table 1 presents a summary analysis of the comparative bureaucratic emphases of the two parties.

A few examples will suffice to indicate the nature of the differences between the two parties (Appendix A presents these in more detail). Precincts in the last majority of counties (62%) maintain files of various kinds: registration records, voter reference cards, lists of prospective contributors and workers, minutes of meetings, and other such forms of potential use to the party in organizing and campaigning. Republican precincts (better than half the counties report 60% or better

TABLE 1

PARTY PREDOMINANCE IN SELECTED ORGANIZATIONAL VARIABLES

Organizational		Party Predominant	
Level	Variable	Demo-crats	Republi-cans
Precinct	% Organized	+	−
	% Maintaining Records	−	+
	% Fully Represented at County Conventions	+	−
County (County Committee)	% Organized	+	−
	% Maintaining Records	+	−
	% Campaigned Last Election	+	−
	Number of Committee Meetings, Election Years	−	+
	Number of Committee Meetings, Non-Election Years	−	+

of their precincts maintaining such files) rely on this type of organizational activity more than Democrats. On the county level, slightly more Democratic (72%) than Republican chairmen (64%) utilize records, some quite elaborate, analogous to those kept by the precincts. Democrats, on the other hand, have a greater number of precinct organizations—twice as many as do Republican—in full attendance at their county conventions. To illustrate: ninety-five per cent of the Democratic county chairmen report that 50 per cent or more of their precincts are completely represented by delegates and alternates at these conventions. Republican county conventions are less well attended. Roughly one-quarter of the counties (27%) have less than half of their precincts at these affairs; 10 per cent of the counties have no precincts represented at the county convention.

The frequency with which county committees meet also varies. Some county committees meet on a weekly basis, others average one meeting a month and some do not schedule any formal sessions. Two general patterns are apparent. More county committee meetings are arranged during election years than in non-election years and Republicans meet with greater regularity than Democrats in both election and non-election years.

Certain types of organizational activity, formal meetings of the party personnel for example, may well assume more importance for an emerging minority party than they do for a well-established majority party. The greater regularity of Republican county committee meetings could be a function of the relative inexperience of incumbent chairmen, the higher incidence of troublesome organizational problems, the need for collective decision-making, or an attempt to institutionalize and formalize communication channels. The relative frequency of meetings also could be a function of the county chairman's unfamiliarity with the response patterns of his party colleagues—here primarily the precinct chairmen who constitute the major portion of the county committee—and hence an inability to predict their likely reactions. The newer the organization and the more unsure it is of itself, the greater the emphasis on formal meetings to resolve its problems. Or, and it must be admitted beforehand that the weight of the findings in this study make this alternative appear unlikely, the higher incidence of Republican county committee meetings could be simply an indication of superior coordination.

In sum, the foregoing indicates that there are differences in the emphases of the two parties. Still, it does not present any clear picture of the nature of the disparities in organization between the parties and, in some respects, it leads to confusion.

A BUREAUCRATIC SCALE OF PARTY ORGANIZATION   The need at this point for a more systematic analysis of the two party organizations can be satisfied by devising through Guttman scaling techniques a cumulative scale with which to compare the parties. The Party Organization Scale (POS) as constructed is based on five of the items previously employed in describing the organization of the two parties (see Appendix A, Table A.5).

The composite groupings of counties on the scale divide into three categories: those evidencing "high party organization," 41 counties or 25 per cent of the total; those scoring as "medium party organization," 57 counties or 39 per cent of the total; and those exhibiting "low party organization," 64 counties or 40 per cent of the total (Table 2).[10] The differences in dis-

[10] Ten counties were not scalable, i.e., two or more of the items included in the scale were left unanswered. There are problems involved in scaling non-attitudinal data taken from a mail question-

tribution between the parties are significant.[11] Relatively few Democratic county organizations are clasified as either high or low in party organization. Substantially more Democratic county organizations than Republican are found in the medium party organization category. The Democratic party then by this measure is more *consistently* organized on the local level throughout the state than is its Republican counterpart. The Republican party tends in turn to polarize with a large proportion of their counties evidencing either very high or very low levels of organization.

TABLE 2

DISTRIBUTION OF PARTIES ON PARTY ORGANIZATION SCALE

Party Organization	Dem.	Rep.	Total
High	19.3%	31.7%	25.3%
Medium	44.6	25.3	35.2
Low	36.1	43.0	39.5
Total	100.0%	100.0%	100.0%
N	83	79	162

P < .05, V = .21

naire. Questions or portions of questions used in the scale but not answered on the questionnaire were treated as scaling errors, which lowered the coefficient of reproducibility. There is good reason to believe that the majority of the questions on organization that were not answered were left so because the particular county did not employ that specific form of organizational activity. If this could have been proven, there would have been more flexibility in structuring the scale. In attitudinal questions the individual usually has more options relative to the degree to which he agrees or disagrees with a particular statement. In this study, if the question did not relate to the conditions of the chairman answering, it was left blank. This suspicion was supported by the comments on the questionnaires and in the personal interviews.

[11] The standard chi square test is used in this report with the level of acceptance P ≤ .05. The test of association employed is Cramer's V. Using this measure, .20–.29 will be considered a moderate relationship, .30–.39 a moderately strong relationship, and anything equal to or above .40 as a strong relationship.

The Democratic party is organized well enough to accomplish its immediate ends, electing fellow Democrats to office. The Republican situation is more fluid. The party is attempting to develop vigorous organizations in precincts and counties that have no previous history of Republican organization or in which "patronage Republicans"[12] never seriously contested elections. The process of rebuilding dormant local parties or extending the party organization into virgin territory is a gradual one. The local units in which the state and national parties have invested their resources and in which local activists have shown some enthusiasm for the job score impressively high on the Party Organization Scale. In other counties in which the same combination of factors has yet to materialize or in which the revitalization of moribund local parties has just begun, the traditionally inactive organizations persist.

The Democratic party is subject also to different environmental pressures. Even in safe areas in which the primacy of the local party is not open to serious challenge, the party leaders are obligated both to clientele groups within the county and to the state party to maintain at least a minimally active organization. The nature of the demands made by the state party headquarters and, more indirectly, the more competitive counties upon the party in one-party dominant counties will become clearer in the discussion below of fund-raising and the need to maintain a winning margin of statewide races.

The Republican party is acutely aware of the limited utility of prematurely investing resources in localities in which there is little real chance of mobilizing a substantial party vote. The costs involved in "showing the flag," to borrow Austin Ranney's phrase,[13] are greater than the party can presently afford.

The expectation is that a growth in Republican organization at the local level will be slow but inevitable. The results of the increasing Republican emphasis on county and precinct organization will become apparent as a higher proportion of the Republican county parties enter the medium and high categories on the Party Organization Scale. It can be hypothesized that the attention paid by the Republican party to organization will stimulate more Democratic organizational developments at the

---

[12] Key, *Southern Politics*, *op. cit.*

[13] Austin Ranney, *Pathways to Parliament* (Madison and Milwaukee: University of Wisconsin Press, 1965), pp. 248–249.

local level and thus an eventual statewide increase in organizational activity for both parties.

Some corroborating evidence for the above points is supplied by the county chairmen.

From the Republican county chairmen:

> Prior to my time, my impression is that such [Republican] party organization as existed was held together because of the possibility of obtaining federal offices under a Republican president. I have tried to increase party registration and interest by appeals to individuals interested in sound government.
>
> Virtually dead since the 1920's the _____ county GOP is being rebuilt and reorganized. Last candidate of GOP to run for public office in this county was in 1936. This year (1962) there are three and each has a chance of being successful.
>
> Poor Republican showing in _____ county can be attributed to: (1) complete lack of organization and planning, (2) no Republican works for the state or county, (3) defeatist attitude of old Republicans, (4) iron curtain between congressional Republicans and precinct workers. Precinct Republicans get immediate hearing by Democrat congressman . . . . . . We are working on it.

From the Democratic county chairmen:

> Our county never has had serious Republican effort. Therefore our County Democratic Committee is very lax —we are interested in the candidates and the primary. The election "goes Democratic."
>
> Traditionally in eastern North Carolina, the organization of the Democratic party has not been too active, since it took no official part in Democratic primaries, which for all practical purposes *were* the real elections. In the future, the formal party organization in eastern North Carolina will become increasingly important.

PARTY ORGANIZATION AND ELECTORAL COMPETITION   The explanation of the difference found in party organization between the two parties assumes a correlation between party organization and competition in a given locality. This relationship can be more systemtically explored by introducing a measure of party competition. The index of party competition employed is based on the winning party's margin of victory for three levels of competition—county, state, and national—at the last election at which the offices (sheriff, state representative, state senator, governor, and president) included in the computations were contested (1960 for governor and president, 1962 for the others). The mean victory percentages for the offices used in the index were computed and the counties were then grouped into high competition (34) and low competition (66) categories, depending on whether the mean percentage of the county's vote came within 10 percentage points of an even division.[14]

The argument above receives support from the analysis. There is a decided affinity between the strength of the local party organization as measured by the Party Organization Scale and the closeness of electoral contests in a county. The findings are more significant, however, when the relationship between rate of party competition and amount of organization is examined for each of the parties individually (Table 3). Although there are significant relationships between degree of organiza-

---

[14] To compute the actual rate, the party's mean percentage for the offices included in the index was doubled and the sum was subtracted from 2.000. The resulting number is the "rate of party competition at the last election." The range of possible scores varies from .000 (no competition, one party averages 100% of the vote) to 1.000 (perfect competition, an average 50% division of the vote). This manner of presenting the rate of party competition was developed in Douglas Gatlin's "Rates of Party Competition for North Carolina Counties" (unpublished, n.d.) and his chapter in this volume. It is similar to the party competition rate for a twenty year period employed in part in the analysis. The association between the twenty year rate of party competition and the rate for the last election, using the Pearsonian product-moment correlation, is quite high (Pr = .999), indicating that the 1960–1962 elections are not aberrations but rather that they reflect competitive trends. The rate of competition at the last election when utilized was done so because it includes the elections closest to the period in which the data were collected and because, although the mean percentage for all the counties is negligibly higher than the mean percentage for all counties over the twenty year period, there is a more even distribution of the vote and a greater number of counties (34) falling within 10 per cent of an even division of the votes cast. The twenty year figures cover the period 1940–1960 or 1940–1962 depending on the office being contested. The three levels of competition included the percentage distribution of the vote for the following offices: "National"—president of the U.S.; "State"—U.S. Senator, N.C. governor; and "County"—sheriff, representative to the lower house of the state legislature, county commissioner.

tion and electoral competition for both of the parties, the correlation between the variables is much higher for the Democrats. Apparently, the Democrats increase their emphasis on organization and their activity in proportion to the threat posed by the opposition; the more competitive the county, the greater the amount of Democratic organization. It is hypothesized then that high instances of Democratic organization on the Party Organization Scale are a product of, and response to, strong Republican organization and the number of votes the Republican party can muster in elections.

In one respect, the Republicans have more leeway. The Republican party is interested in building its local organizations, often quite weak, in as many counties as possible. As these renovated Republican organizations acquire the resources to contest elections, it can be expected that the Democratic organizations in turn will more closely resemble competitive party machines.

TABLE 3

PARTY ORGANIZATION AS IT RELATES TO PARTY
COMPETITION AT THE LAST ELECTION, BY PARTY

Party Organization	Dem.[a]		Rep.[b]		Composite[c]	
	Party Competition		Party Competition		Party Competition	
	High	Low	High	Low	High	Low
High	34.5%	11.1%	48.4%	20.8%	41.7%	15.7%
Medium	55.2	38.9	25.8	25.0	40.0	32.3
Low	10.3	50.0	25.8	54.2	18.3	52.0
TOTAL	100.0%	100.0%	100.0%	100.0%	100.0%	100.0%
N	29	54	31	48	60	102

[a]$P < .001$, $V = .42$.
[b]$P < .02$, $V = .32$.
[c]$P < .001$, $V = .36$.

Party Organization and Candidate Recruitment

Candidate recruitment is one of the more important functions performed by the party that has both extra-organizational and intra-organizational consequences. The party in recruiting candidates determines the personnel and, more symbolically, the groups to be represented among the decision-making elite. Through recruitment, the party indirectly influences the types of policy decisions to be enacted and the interests most likely to be heard. Candidate recruitment then represents one of the key linkages between the electorate and the policy-making process.

For the party organization, the major concern of this study,[15] candidate recruitment also has pronounced implications.

[15] One organizational activity included in the original analysis but omitted from this report relates to patronage (defined as jobs made available through the party organization to the local party personnel). The meagre number of positions secured from any source by the Republican party made an extended comparative analysis of limited value. One finding should be noted however. The Democratic party had extensive patronage resources available from county, state and federal sources (see below). The pattern of patronage distribution among the counties in the Democratic party showed no significant correlation with either party organization (POS) or party competition. This could mean that, regardless of the extent of the Republican threat in an individual county or the degree of Democratic organization, an apparent effort is made to reward all party committees in such a manner as to weld relatively coherent and committed organizations in all areas.

The breakdown in difference of sources by party is as follows:

Political Appointment	Dem.	Rep.	Total
Federal	34.2%	87.5%	37.6%
State	34.2	0.0	32.0
County	24.8	0.0	23.2
City	1.7	0.0	1.6
Private Business or Industry	5.1	12.5	5.6
Total	100.0%	100.0%	100.0%
N	117	8	125

$P < .001$, $V = .30$

For other accounts relevant to the organizational deployment of patronage, see Sorauf, "The Structure of Incentives," *Political Parties in the American System, op. cit.*, pp. 81–97; and the articles by Sorauf, J. Q. Wilson, Wilson and P. Clark, Wilson and D. P. Moyni-

The quality of candidates presented to the electorate, and for a minority party the consistency with which candidates are placed before the voters, does much to determine the overall success of the organization in achieving its stated objective, winning office.

FIELDING A SLATE OF CANDIDATES   A political party with a good chance of winning elections should have little difficulty in finding people to run for office. If anything, there should be a surplus of available talent. Apparently, this is the case. There are pronounced differences between the parties in both the availability of candidates and the extent to which the county chairmen become involved in the process of seeking people to run for office (Table 4). Democratic chairmen have little trouble finding prospective office-seekers, and a large number of them apparently do not perceive this as an integral part of their duties. For such offices as justice of the peace, superior and state supreme court justices, and for congressional candidacies, virtually no Democratic chairmen experienced any problems in putting forth candidates. More troublesome were candidatures for town and city office and county commissioner. Still, only an average of 10 per cent of the Democratic chairmen reported that filling these places on the party ticket was "very" difficult. In contrast, three to four times this proportion of Republican chairmen faced a "very" great challenge in filling these candidacies with party nominees.

Depending on the office involved, anywhere from one-fifth to one-half of the Democratic chairmen were not extended in securing willing recruits. The Republican chairmen were not as fortunate. At the most, roughly one-fourth of the chairmen experienced no difficulties in candidate recruitment. Expressed in starker terms, from 30 to 75 per cent of the Republican chairmen did face obstacles of varying degrees of severity in finding people to run for office on the party ticket.

The Republican chairmen encountered the most resistance in encouraging potential candidates to seek the positions of sheriff, town or city elective office, and judicial posts. The sheriff's of-

---

han, and P. Cutright listed in the bibliography following Chapter I. Earlier, and now dated, emphases on the value of patronage to party organization are: Harold F. Gosnell, *Machine Politics: Chicago Model* (Chicago: University of Chicago Press, 1937); and Sonya Forthal, *Cogwheels of Democracy* (New York: William-Frederick Press, 1946).

TABLE 4

DIFFICULTY IN SECURING CANDIDATES TO SEEK OFFICE, BY PARTY

Level of Difficulty	1	2	3	4	5	6	7	8
Democrats								
Very difficult	8.3%	11.0%	2.4%	3.8%	5.0%	0.0%	0.0%	1.4%
Somewhat difficult	20.0	17.1	6.1	1.4	8.7	1.3	0.0	2.7
Not very difficult	20.0	34.1	48.8	39.2	42.5	35.9	35.5	24.7
Chairman takes *no* part in selection process	51.7	37.8	42.7	55.6	43.8	62.8	64.5	71.2
No candidate offered	0.0	0.0	0.0	0.0	0.0	0.0	0.0	0.0
N	100.0% 75	100.0% 82	100.0% 82	100.0% 79	100.0% 80	100.0% 78	100.0% 76	100.0% 73
Republicans								
Very difficult	43.5%	36.0%	50.7%	43.9%	38.2%	42.6%	37.3%	31.8%
Somewhat difficult	20.3	38.7	18.7	26.0	28.9	22.1	22.7	11.1
Not very difficult	13.0	18.7	24.7	16.4	23.7	7.4	16.0	14.3
Chairman takes *no* part in selection process	18.8	5.3	4.6	8.2	6.6	23.5	20.0	34.9

TABLE 4 (*Continued*)

	1	2	3	4	5	6	7	8
No candidate offered	4.4	1.3	1.3	5.5	2.6	4.4	4.0	7.9
N	100.0% 69	100.0% 75	100.0% 75	100.0% 73	100.0% 76	100.0% 68	100.0% 75	100.0% 63

Total

	1	2	3	4	5	6	7	8
Very difficult	25.7%	22.9%	25.5%	23.0%	21.2%	19.9%	18.5%	15.4%
Somewhat difficult	20.1	27.4	12.1	18.5	18.6	11.0	11.3	6.6
Not very difficult	16.7	26.8	36.3	28.3	33.3	22.6	25.8	19.9
Chairman takes *no* part in selection process	35.4	22.3	25.5	27.6	25.6	44.5	42.4	54.4
No candidate offered	2.1	0.6	0.6	2.6	1.3	2.0	2.0	3.7
N	100.0% 144	100.0% 157	100.0% 157	100.0% 152	100.0% 156	100.0% 146	100.0% 151	100.0% 136

Key: 1. Local (town or city) candidates
2. County Commissioner
3. Sheriff
4. Other County Offices (Register of Deeds, Coroner, etc.)
5. State Legislators (House and Senate)
6. Judicial candidacies (Justice of the Peace, Superior Court Justice, Supreme Court Justices)
7. U.S. Congressional candidacies (House and Senate)
8. Governor

fice is one of great power within a county and it is often closely
identified with an individual incumbent. Strictly speaking, it is
not a partisan position and it would appear reasonable that there
are few individuals anxious to contest the incumbent. The Republican party has controlled a number of the mountain counties in the western part of the state, a tradition that has per-
sisted since the Civil War. In these counties, the party finds
candidates willing enough to run for sheriff, should there be a
vacancy. This accounts for an apparent paradox, namely, the
sheriff's position is the single most difficult office for the vast
majority of Republican county parties to contest and yet represents one of the two offices for which one-fourth of the Republican chairmen have the least difficulty in recruiting.

Municipal elections and those for lesser county offices in
North Carolina are often considered non-partisan; primarily because of the overwhelming superiority of the Democrats in these
contests. Partisan or not, these are the type of races in which
a minority party should experience the most resistance in challenging the majority party. The Democratic party is entrenched
most solidly at the community level.

Election returns help to illustrate the magnitude of the
problem facing the Republicans. The Republican party in the
South has made its best showing in the presidential vote, where
there has been a decided increase in the proportion of Republican voting since 1948. The party has not been able to transfer
this support for presidential candidates, however, into immediate votes for state and local party nominees. There is a major
psychological jump, and hence a greater challenge to the voter's
fundamental identification with the Democratic party, in translating a refusal to support the national party and its nominees
into a similar reaction against the state and local parties and
their candidates.[16] The transference of presidential support into

---

[16] The time lag and the problems encountered in translating Republi-
can presidential support in the South to local Republican support
are treated by Philip E. Converse in "A Major Political Realignment
in the South?" in Allan P. Sindler, ed., *Change in the Contemporary
South* (Durham, N.C.: Duke University Press, 1963), pp. 195–222.
See also: V. O. Key, Jr., *Southern Politics, op. cit.;* James W. Prothro,
"Two-Party Voting in the South: Class Versus Party Identification,"
American Political Science Review, 52 (March, 1958), pp. 131–139;
Avery Leiserson, ed., *The American South in the 1960's* (New York:
Frederick Praeger, 1964); Donald S. Strong, *Urban Republicanism in
the South* (University, Ala.: Bureau of Public Administration, 1960);

local party votes will require a good deal of effort on the part of Republican activists. Meanwhile, the party should continue to confront the short-run difficulties indicated in presenting candidates to the electorate for county and municipal offices.

Finally, the Republican problems in convincing people to seek judicial positions were anticipated. These offices are not highly competitive for the most part. Many of the more prestigious judicial offices are in the federal court system and thus are not open to electoral decision. Some of the lesser offices such as justice of the peace are not perceived as party offices. In many cases, these positions are closely associated with a community's power structure, in particular, its law enforcement agencies. And an analysis of the occupational and educational backgrounds of the Republican chairmen indicates that relatively few have legal experience and that a good proportion come from the lower socio-economic groups in the locality.[17] The Republican party may simply have trouble in finding people with the necessary prerequisites for offices such as district solicitor and superior court judge.

Overall, there is a slight inverse relationship between the level of office sought and the difficulty of finding candidates to contest for it—the higher the office, the more willing a number of individuals are to run for it.

Two other points are of interest. All of the Democratic chairmen indicated that candidates were offered for *all* offices. This is surprising. Even in the Republican one-party dominant counties, the Democrats at least go through the motions of contesting offices; one testimonial to the pervasiveness of Democratic party organization and its persistence in performing its electoral duties. Republicans in predominantly one-party Democratic areas are not as active. Anywhere from one to five per cent of the Republican chairmen indicate that specific offices were not contested in their counties.

There is one other quite noticeable difference between the Democratic and Republican chairmen in relation to their ability

---

and the major contribution of Donald R. Matthews and James W. Prothro to the clarification of political restructuring in the South, *Negroes and the New Southern Politics* (New York: Harcourt, Brace and World, 1966).

[17] William J. Crotty, "The Social Attributes of Party Organizational Activists in a Transitional Political System," *Western Political Quarterly*, 20 (September, 1967).

to enlist candidates. Democratic chairmen are much more inclined to stay out of the selection process, regardless of the
level of office analyzed.[18] Anywhere from 38 to 71 per cent of
the Democratic chairmen, depending on the office category, do
not take part in the recruiting process. Democrats are more inclined to seek candidates for county and state legislative positions than they are for local offices, judicial positions, congressional races, or gubernatorial contests. The most pronounced
withdrawal from the selection process is at the top of the hierarchy—that for governorship. Republicans, in contrast, take a
relatively active part in all levels of candidate selection. Their
rate of recruitment activity declines for the same categories of
office as in the case of the Democrats—local, judicial, congressional, and gubernatorial. But for every office, far more of the
Republican chairmen are active in the recruitment process.

There are several explanations for the differences. The
larger number of potential candidates available to the majority
party limits what a Democratic county chairman can do. Ordinarily, in his official capacity as county chairman, it is not
his duty to seek out and actively support candidates of his
choice. Rather, he is expected to remain relatively neutral in the
selection of candidates and the primary battle that follow. His
energy is concentrated on the general election. While it may
also be important for a Republican chairman to remain uncom-
mitted to an individual or a party faction in a primary battle,
the nature of the minority party situation compels him to be
more aggressive. The Republican chairman who intends to
contest elections is forced to seek out those willing to make what
in all probability will be a futile race.[19]

[18] Comparative findings can be found in: V. O. Key, Jr., *Politics,
Parties, and Pressure Groups, op. cit.,* chs. 14, 16; and Lester Selig-
man, "Political Recruitment and Party Structure: A Case Study,"
American Political Science Review, 55 (March, 1961), pp. 77–86.
Seligman has contributed the most original theorizing on the im-
portance of recruitment to the political system. See his *Political
Recruitment* (Boston: Little, Brown and Company, forthcoming).
On legislative recruitment, some of the better studies are: Seligman,
Leadership in a New Nation (New York: Atherton Press, 1964);
Ranney, *Pathways to Parliament, op. cit.;* Frank J. Sorauf, *Party and
Representation* (New York: Atherton Press, 1963); and James David
Barber, *The Lawmakers* (New Haven: Yale University Press, 1965).
[19] Samuel C. Patterson in his "Characteristics of Party Leaders,"
Western Political Quarterly, 16 (June, 1963), pp. 332–352, makes a

The office for which both party chairmen have the least voice in initial candidate sponsorship is for that of governor. Nevertheless, there is a 36 per cent differential between the parties in the number of chairmen taking part in the selection process. This is definitely not a duty of the Democratic chairmen. Conceivably, within the smaller core of activists constituting the minority party, the Republican chairmen have more say in sounding out and deciding upon those available to head the statewide ticket.

The correlation of the difficulty involved in coopting candidates with other possible influencing factors—party, degree of party competition in the county, and the extent of county party organization—results in distributions that are highly unlikely to have occurred by chance (for all the cross-tabulations, $P < .001$). Using Cramer's V as the test of significance, there is low relationship between degree of difficulty in finding amenable candidates and either party organization ($V = .12$) or office sought ($V = .14$), a moderate relationship between difficulty in candidate procurement and party competition ($V = .22$), and an exceptionally high ($V = .58$) correlation between facility in recruiting candidates and party. By far the most important factor of those tested in influencing the ease or difficulty in seeking potential candidates is the party engaged in the recruiting. The high correlation between party and effort in securing candidates lends substance to the dissimilarities in role perception and role-playing indicated above.

CONSCRIPTING CANDIDATES   Drafting candidates to run for office, i.e., convincing reluctant individuals to make elective races, is more a Republican than a Democratic phenomenon. In 1962 as an example, twice the number of Democratic as Republican chairmen did not draft *any* candidates. Overall, the Republicans held better than a two-to-one edge in the total number of candidates drafted. In 1960, although the differences did not equal this 2:1 ratio, the trend was the same—one-third again as many

distinction between organization-oriented and campaign-oriented chairman roles. Some indication of the differences suggested by these categorizations is relevant to the present analysis. Patterson's broad contrasts in role behavior however need refinement. See also his (with Phillip Althoff) "Political Activism in a Rural County," *Midwest Journal of Political Science*, 10 (February, 1966), pp. 39–51.

Democratic chairmen as Republican chairmen did not draft candidates, one-third again as many Republican candidates were drafted as were Democratic candidates. The differences between the parties are statistically significant ($V = .24$, $P < .01$).

Individuals are pressured into running for office when the party wants to offer a full slate of candidates to the electorate and needs someone to contest the more unattractive positions or when the minority party in a given locality desires to contest specific positions, usually with the long-run objective of building a winning coalition.

The extent of party organization and the amount of electoral competition in a given county both correlate positively with the number of candidates drafted by the parties in the previous two elections. Party organization appears to be of somewhat greater importance however. The greater the level of party organization in the county and the more competitive the county, the more likely the party is to draft candidates for office. The correlations respectively are $V = .35$ and $V = .26$ with both well below the .05 level of significance.[20]

There is a good deal of similarity in the arguments used by the party chairmen to persuade individuals to seek office. When Kendall's Tau is employed to test the associations between the emphasis of arguments resorted to, a strong positive relationship is found between high and low competition areas ($T = .86$) and counties with varying degrees of party organization ($T = .82$). The least similarity in the tactical arguments favored is the correlation between the rankings of those employed by each of the two parties ($T = .60$).

The differences in the types of arguments put forward in highly competitive as against non-competitive counties and in well organized as against poorly organized counties can be quickly sketched. First, an emphasis on the individual's civic duty is apparently the most persuasive of arguments. In highly competitive counties, the chance to hold public office is next in line. In low competition areas, the potential contribution of the

[20] When the county organizations that did draft candidates are run against the Party Organization Scale, no significant relationship emerges ($V = .14$, $P < .50$). This controls for party and means that the relationship of those county organizations drafting candidates to the level of party organization is not significantly different in either party. The better organized they are, the more likely they are to draft candidates.

individual to the eventual creation of a two-party system moves into second place and the possibility of winning the election drops to third. In high and medium party organization counties there is a perfect positive correlation between the rankings of the arguments used. Also the differences in arguments used between these two levels of party organization and low party organization counties are not great. The introduction of two ties between alternatives accounts for the slight variation.

Differences in the nature of the arguments most likely to be employed by each of the two parties require exploration (Table 5). Democrats are more inclined to emphasize citizen obligation, the probability of winning elections, loyalty to the party and the need to make individual political races more competitive. Republicans stress the desire for a two-party system first, citizen duty second, chance of winning third, and loyalty to the Republican party fourth. Both parties give little attention to patronage considerations or other selling points.

The arguments of prime importance to the parties reflect the nature of the North Carolina political situation. Both parties find the emphasis on the individual's sense of duty to his community rewarding. Beyond this, Democrats have success with arguments suggesting their electoral primacy in the state—the opportunity to win office and the individual's loyalty to a party with which he more than likely grew up. Republicans resort to an emphasis on the need for a two-party system—an argument that also proves effective in enticing people to assume the responsibilities of Republican county chairman.[21] Interestingly, party loyalty for Republicans ranks fourth. Given the fact that the Republican party as a large-scale, statewide organization is a relatively new phenomenon, the majority of citizens could not be expected to have strong emotional ties to it.

Party Organization and Campaign Activities

Campaigning produces the most direct linkages between the party organization, its clientele groups, and its assumed objec-

[21] These findings compliment the results of an analysis of the data on the motivational gratifications sought in party service by the North Carolina county chairmen. Altruistic appeals in general and,

TABLE 5

ARGUMENTS* EMPLOYED IN CONSCRIPTING CANDIDATES,
BY PARTY

Arguments	Dem. Per Cent	Dem. Rank	Rep. Per Cent	Rep. Rank	Composite Per Cent	Composite Rank
It is your obligation as a citizen to run for office when you are needed.	42.7%	1	30.3%	2	34.8%	1
We have an excellent chance of winning this time.	22.0	2	17.9	3	19.4	3
You are a loyal party member, you have not run yet and it is your turn to run.	19.5	3	9.7	4	13.2	4
Your help is needed in the interests of a two-party system in this area.	7.3	4	34.5	1	24.6	2
"Other" (any not included on suggested list).	6.1	5	6.2	5	6.2	5
We are going to have some federal (state, local, etc.) patronage, and we will remember our friends.	2.4	6	1.4	6	1.8	6
Total	100.0%		100.0%		100.0%	
N	83		145		228	

* The chairmen were asked to check the 3 most effective arguments
they used in drafting candidates.

tive, the winning of public office. For this reason, the campaign periods have been objects of concern both to the academician and the practitioner. In the terminology of the social scientist, the major purposes of the campaign are to activate latent support and reinforce inclinations among sympathetic voters to support their party and its candidates.[22] More simply, in the view of the professional politician a concerted effort during the campaign period is the best guarantee of winning elections.

The campaign is actually divided into at least three different periods, each with its own demands and limitations that, in turn, set the framework in which the politician must act. These different, and identifiable, campaign cycles are distinguished by the mood of the groups with which the party must work. It is the party leader's job to evaluate the receptivity of the electorate and the nature of the investment of organizational resources he has at his disposal (time, money, individual effort, patronage) that should return the greatest profit. The type of activities a party chairman could engage in are extensive, varying from more indirect appeals for public support and attempts to bolster morale among party members, to holding rallies, parades, and barbecues, a well-received and commendable Southern tradition, and eventually to the direct transportation of voters to the polls on election day. The party professional tailors his activities to the responsiveness of the voters and, of course, the needs and resources of the organization.

To give an illustration, the two year period (in North Carolina) beginning the day after an election and ending with the stretch-drive push that precedes the next election by a few months is characterized by a general disinterest in politics by

---

for Republicans, the need for a two-party competitive system proved to be important in motivating the chairmen to accept their positions. These are also similar to the reasons found effective by a cross-section of Democratic party leaders in analyzing their own recruitment. Gordon L. Lippitt and Drexel A. Sprecher, "Factors Motivating Citizens to Become Active in Politics as Seen by Practical Politicians," *Journal of Social Issues*, 16 (1960), pp. 11–17.

[22] This discussion of the effects of campaigning is found in Paul F. Lazarsfeld, Bernard R. Berelson, and Hazel Gaudet, *The People's Choice* (2nd ed., New York: Columbia University Press, 1948), pp. 73–100. It omits, of course, the reference to conversions. See also: Angus Campbell, Phillip E. Converse, Warren E. Miller and Donald E. Stokes, *The American Voter* (New York: John Wiley and Sons, 1960).

the majority of voters.[23] The party chairmen take this fact of life into account and the nature of activities engaged in reflects both the apathy of the voters and the relative position of the parties in the North Carolina electorate. For example, Democrats concentrate more during this particular cycle of the campaign period on keeping up personal contacts and doing what they can to alleviate any discontent that might arise in party ranks. The Republican party does not neglect personal contacts. Still, it places a greater emphasis on seeking potential recruits from those previously inactive or, possibly, on converting voters from the opposition party. The Republican party also spends more time registering voters. The respective party emphases in the two other campaign cycles—the three to six months immediately preceding an election, or the regular campaign period, and election day—also vary with the objectives of the party and the attentiveness of the public.

To simplify the scope and variety of the material and to order these more systematically, the party organization activities emphasized in each of the three campaign cycles—between-elections, the regular or more visible campaign period preceeding the election, and election day—have been scaled through the use of Guttman techniques. The campaign effort scales constructed in this manner are the Inter-Campaign Activities Scale (ICAS), the Campaign Activities Scale (CAS), and the Election Day Activities Scale (EDAS). The correlation among the scales is low, suggesting that these represent different measures of campaign effort.[24]

The expectation is that neither the type of activity nor the extent of party effort is randomly distributed among county parties. Rather, two hypotheses will be offered at this point. These are: (a) that campaign activity will correlate positively with the degree of party organization in a county, i.e., the greater the degree of party organization, the larger the number

---

[23] Campbell, *et al., ibid.;* and Lester W. Milbrath, *Political Participation* (Chicago: Rand McNally and Company, 1965).

[24] Similar to any statistical measure, the Inter-Campaign Activities Scale, the Campaign Activities Scale, and the Election Day Activities Scale, as well as the Party Organization Scale, are indices of relative value useful within the confines of this study and, therefore, adequate for present needs. The range of activities sampled, the questions used to solicit the information, the specific items employed in the scales and the distribution of the county parties on the three campaign scales can be found in Appendix B.

of specific activities in which the party will engage; and (b) that campaign activity will evidence a strong, positive correlation with party competition, i.e., the more competitive the area, the greater the campaign effort expended by the parties.

CAMPAIGN EFFORT BY PARTY, PARTY COMPETITION, AND PARTY ORGANIZATION   Contrary to expectations, the hypotheses stipulating associations between party organization and electoral competition and campaigning require extensive modification. No significant differences are found between the two parties in their reliance on either between-election activities or in their campaign period emphasis. Neither the Inter-Campaign Activities Scale nor the Campaign Activities Scale correlate positively with competition or the extent of Democratic or Republican party organization in the county. Evidently, there is a general reliance on a pattern and scope of activities in the interim period between campaigns and during the traditional campaign period that is not directly related to either of the two parties or the amount of competition in the county or the strength of the party's organization.

The same findings do not hold true for election day. There is a good correlation ($V = .30$, $P < .01$) between the Election Day Activities Scale and the political parties involved. The Republicans have a slightly greater number of counties evidencing a high EDAS score and twice as many counties as the Democrats in the low EDAS category. The Democrats in turn are over-represented in the medium EDAS category with two and one-half as many counties as their opponents.

The EDAS pattern is reminiscent of variations in the degree of party organization between the two parties. Again it appears that the Democratic party engages in a consistent number of campaign activities (e.g., telephoning voters, providing transportation to the polls, etc.) on a statewide basis while the local Republican party organizations either undertake a large number of activities, many more than the Democrats normally would, or virtually none at all. The Election Day Activities Scale has a low to moderate, but still less than acceptable, relationship ($V = .19$, $P < .05$) to party organization and, as was the case with the other two scales, no relationship to the measure of electoral competition.

The Republican county organizations that fall at either end of the continuum (a great deal of election day activity or little to none) can be isolated and examined.[25] Competitive counties show a borderline association with the amount of election day activity that is not significant at the .05 level ($V = .22$, $P < .20$). There is a strong relationship ($V = .37$, $P < .05$) however between Republican organization and the number of activities conducted on election day. Organization then appears to be *the* most significant variable of those tested. The better organized the Republicans are in a county, the more likely they will be to engage in a large number of election day activities.

CAMPAIGN ACTIVITIES AND VOTER REGISTRATION   The amount of campaign activity in a county may be a function of the number of eligible voters in a community. To test this possibility, the three scales of campaign effort were compared with the voter registration totals for each of the counties in 1960. In addition, the Party Organization Scale (POS) was run against voter registration to find if there were any significant relationships between the two (Table 6). The Election Day Activities Scale does show a strong relationship to the number of voters registered in a county. There is a moderate relationship between voter registration and both inter-election campaigning and party organization, and there is no relationship between registration and either party competition or general campaign activities (CAS). Thus, regardless of intensity of party competition or the activities conducted during the nominally prescribed campaign period, parties in counties with high voter registration will engage in more election day activities in an attempt to increase their proportion of the vote. Also, the counties with higher voter registration are more inclined to have strong party organizations and they are more likely to engage in a number of activities to bolster party strength in the between-elections period. There is a reciprocal relationship among these variables. For example, it is probable that in counties in which the voter registration is high, between elections the party is more concerned with strengthening the organization, in attempting to win new converts, and in placating old adherents. It is also quite possible that where there is concentrated activity during the inter-campaign period, one of the chief concerns would be

---

[25] Those falling in a medium EDAS category are omitted for analytic purposes because of their small number.

with registering new voters which in turn would be evidenced by a higher voter registration for the county. The process is self-sustaining. The more voters registered, the greater the pressure for party activity. The more party activity in the inter-election span, the more voters that will register. The fact that there is also a positive correlation between the number of voters registered and party organization would lend some substance to this point. Finally, the party organization would go all out on election day in seeing that the potential voters they had encouraged to register, and, for that matter, all eligible party supporters, went to the polls.[26]

TABLE 6

THE RELATIONSHIP OF THREE SCALES OF CAMPAIGN EFFORT,
THE PARTY ORGANIZATION SCALE, AND THE RATE OF
PARTY COMPETITION AT THE LAST ELECTION TO
VOTER REGISTRATION

Scale	Cramer's V Test of Relationship[a]	Chi Square Test of Significance[b]
ICAS	.24	P < .01
CAS	.13	P < .30
EDAS	.39	P < .001
POS	.26	P < .01
Rate of Party Competition	.07	P < .50

[a] Level of acceptance, V = .20.
[b] Level of acceptance, P ≤ .05.

CAMPAIGN ACTIVITIES AND VOTER TURNOUT   North Carolina had a statewide turnout of 54 per cent of the eligible adult population in the 1960 general election—not high when compared with the 64 per cent average turnout for the nation as a

[26] This analysis is concerned only with campaign procedures and their relation to registration. For a more extended discussion of 21 socio-economic variables and 10 political variables and their rela-

whole, but impressive when North Carolina is compared with her southern neighbors.[27] Fifteen counties in the state had exceptional turnouts of 90 per cent or better.

A multitude of factors influence election turnout—socioeconomic conditions, individual personality composition, tradition, and sectional idiosyncrasies—to suggest a few broad categories of contributing variables. Religious and racial considerations, particularly as associated with the Democratic presidential candidate, introduced an element into the 1960 elections in the South which no doubt had important electoral repercussions.[28] These are not of concern here. What is of importance is whether or not the varied types of campaign activity had any relationship to the turnout of voters in a community. In other words, is there any evidence that campaigning of and by itself is associated with a significantly higher voter turnout?[29] To ascertain this, the three scales of campaign effort and the Party Organization Scale were run against the percentage turnout of the eligible adult population in each of the counties.

The high priority placed by professional party politicians on the value of good organization is evidently well-founded. Party organization had by far the best relationship ($V = .32$, $P < .001$) of the variables tested to the turnout of eligible voters. The EDAS produced the best correlation ($V = .20$, $P < .05$) of the various indices of campaign activity. The party activities conducted on election day to deliver voters to the polls pay the highest dividends in terms of the actual number of

---

tionship to voter registration in the South, see: Donald R. Matthews and James W. Prothro, "Social and Economic Factors and Negro Voter Registration in the South," *American Political Science Review*, 57 (March, 1963), pp. 24–44; and Matthews and Prothro, "Political Factors and Negro Registration in the South," *American Political Science Review*, 57 (June, 1963), pp. 335–367.

[27] For a discussion of turnout in North Carolina see: *Equal Protection of the Laws in North Carolina*, Report of the North Carolina Advisory Committee on Civil Rights, 1959–1962 (Washington, D.C.: U.S. Government Printing Office, 1962), pp. 38–47.

[28] Phillip E. Converse, Angus Campbell, and Warren E. Miller, "Stability and Change in 1960: A Reinstating Election," *American Political Science Review*, 55 (June, 1961), pp. 269–280.

[29] It must be understood, of course, that these tests of relationships do not indicate the direction of causality. However, there may be clearer grounds for *inferring* the direction in this case than in some others.

people who vote. This is reasonable. Effort expended during the interim election period does not greatly influence the actual turnout on election day. In many ways, this is the form of activity most removed from the act of actually getting to the polls. Inter-campaign activities may be important in formulating attitudes or reinforcing commitments but this would be more apparent in party or candidate preference than it would be in the turnout.

Perhaps a reminder is in order here. The Campaign Activities Scale measures levels of *organizational* activity. It is not concerned with the quality and attractiveness of candidates, individual personalities, or campaign issues, all of which may have a more direct affect on the election. The CAS is concerned only with the *volume* of campaign activity, it has no relation to the *content*. Thus, if it is clear that the CAS is a gauge of organizational activity only, some of the previous correlations are placed in a better perspective. Even a small correlation under these conditions is impressive. Also, it seems logical that those organizational activities performed on election day and directly concerned with inducing the citizen to perform the physical act of voting should have the greatest success. In this regard, there is an increasingly positive relationship between types of organizational campaign efforts and the proximity of the election (i.e., ICAS, V = .06, CAS, V = .12, EDAS, V = .20).

CAMPAIGN ACTIVITIES AND EFFECT ON THE VOTE   The number of county committees which campaign for various offices differs according to the office or levels of office sought (Table 7). The office for which most county committees exert some campaign effort is president. Of those offices elected either from within the county or using the county as the electoral unit, more local party organizations campaigned for the state representative from their county than for any other office.[30]

The 1960 vote for president and the 1962 vote for state representative were run against the three scales of campaign activity to determine if any relationship existed between campaign activity and an increase or decrease in the proportion of

[30] There were 120 state representatives and 100 counties in North Carolina. At the time of the study, each county was entitled to at least one with the extra 20 being divided among the most populous counties.

the vote received by the party. The projected vote is based on the relative division of the county vote in the twenty year period preceding the elections analyzed. The mean vote was calculated for competitive and non-competitive counties and deviations from the mean vote in the individual elections (1960, 1962) were correlated with campaign effort to see if any relationships

TABLE 7

OFFICE COUNTY ORGANIZATIONS CAMPAIGNED FOR, BY PARTY*

| Office | Per Cent of County Organizations Campaigning | | |
	Dem.	Rep.	Total
Local	22.4%	19.4%	21.0%
County Commissioner	47.1	58.3	52.2
County Sheriff	41.2	30.6	36.3
Other County Offices	40.0	38.9	39.5
State Legislature	52.9	62.5	57.3
Judicial	22.4	5.6	14.6
U.S. Congress	69.4	68.1	68.8
Governor	84.7	76.4	80.9
President	85.9%	81.9%	84.1%
N	85	72	157

* Most county organizations campaigned for more than one office. Therefore, the total percentage does not equal 100.0%.

were apparent.[31] The expectation was that for both parties the three scales of campaign effort would show a consistently higher

[31] More specifically, the rates of party competition (which is the mean of the winning party's majority) for the tweny year period preceding the election used in this analysis (1936–1956 for president, 1940–1960 for state representative) were calculated. The

relationship to deviations in the projected vote than to variations in the presidential vote. This was not entirely the case (Table 8).

TABLE 8

THE RELATIONSHIP OF SCALES OF CAMPAIGN EFFORT TO
HIGH AND LOW VOTE FOR PRESIDENT (1960) AND
STATE REPRESENTATIVE (1962), BY PARTY

Level of Competition	Scale of Campaign Effort	Democrat Cramer's V[a]	Chi Square[b]	Republican Cramer's V[a]	Chi Square[b]
		PRESIDENT, 1960			
Competitive	ICAS	.40	P < .10	.40	P < .10
	CAS	.07	P < .95	.23	P < .50
	EDAS	.04	P < .99	.26	P < .50
Non-Competitive	ICAS	.36	P < .10	.26	P < .30
	CAS	.13	P < .70	.08	P < .95
	EDAS	.28	P < .20	.38	P < .10
		STATE REPRESENTATIVE, 1962			
Competitive	ICAS	.28	P < .70	.23	P < .70
	CAS	.22	P < .70	.14	P < .90
	EDAS	.27	P < .70	.23	P < .70
Non-Competitive	ICAS	.35	P < .02	.26	P < .20
	CAS	.10	P < .80	.34	P < .10
	EDAS	.30	P < .30	.42	P < .02

[a] Level of acceptance, V = .20.
[b] Level of acceptance, P ≤ .05.

counties which were competitive (within 10% of an even division of the vote) over the twenty year period for each of the offices were isolated from the non-competitive counties. The mean vote was tabulated for the election in question (the 1960 presidential and the 1962 state representative races) for competitive counties, one-party Democratic counties and the small number of one-party Republican counties. (For analytic purposes the latter two categories

There is a high relationship between the ICAS and deviation from the mean presidential vote in competitive counties for both parties. For Republicans, there is a moderate relationship between presidential vote fluctuations in competitive areas and the other two classifications of campaign activity. Further, in non-competitive counties there is a good relationship for Democrats between the ICAS and the vote and for Republicans between the EDAS and the vote and a moderate relationship between the Democratic EDAS and, for Republicans, the ICAS and changes in the presidential vote. Unfortunately, although all of the foregoing indicate a relationship, none is significant at the .05 level of acceptance. In the majority of these cases the N is too small for computing a reliable chi square. The findings then can only be suggestive.

A few observations can be offered if the above limitation is kept firmly in mind. The amount of work done between elections in competitive counties—the Democrats by showing an interest in their supporters, the Republicans by recruiting new members and building party organizations—should have a bearing on the partisan distribution of the vote in presidential elections. A greater Republican effort in each of the campaign cycles is associated with an increase in the proportion of the vote they can expect to receive. The pattern is not repeated for Democrats in competitive counties.

In non-competitive counties, inter-campaign and election day efforts apparently have a greater influence on the presidential vote for both parties than does strictly campaign effort (CAS). The findings are reversed here for each of the parties. Although both of these forms of activity evidently influence the presidential vote, inter-campaign activities appear more fruitful for Democrats than election day activities. The exact opposite is the case for Republicans—election day effort appears to have a much greater return for them than does between-election campaigning. This would seem appropriate. The vast majority

---

were grouped together under the heading non-competitive counties.) All counties which fell above the mean were classified as having a "higher than expected vote" and all counties which fell below the mean were considered as counties that had a "lower than expected vote." These "plus" and "minus" counties were then compared as to their campaign efforts to see if campaign activities had any significant relationship to an increase or decrease in the anticipated percentage division of the vote between the parties.

of the non-competitive counties are Democratic. The more the Democrats can do between elections to keep party supporters content and party morale high, the better the results on election day. Conversely, there are severe limitations as to what the Republicans can do between elections—they have little patronage or other tangible rewards to bolster party spirit, they have few party members to contact and encourage, and appeals to the general public through the mass media would appear inappropriate and expensive. However, if Republicans concentrate on getting a good turnout of the faithful on election day and on wooing undecided or weakly committed Democrats, they should achieve a greater return. Actually, the crucial focus of the presidential campaign for both parties in the months immediately preceding the election is outside of the one-party areas. There is no good reason for either of the two major parties to invest their limited resources in great quantity in counties where the outcome of the presidential balloting is seemingly foreordained.

In the race for state representative in competitive districts, although none reaches a level of significance, all forms of campaign effort, with the exception of the Republican CAS, show a moderate relationship to an increase or decrease in the party vote. It may be necessary for county committees in highly competitive areas consistently and continuously to campaign in one way or another to keep the other party from increasing its share of the vote. Campaigning in these counties represents a sustained fight between two evenly matched opponents, a struggle which does not end at election day and in which neither party relies on any one activity or form of activity to influence the electorate.

Another point should be noted. The race for state representative in the individual counties should be more nearly indicative of the actual political campaigns than is the presidential contest. That is, since each North Carolina county in 1962 elected at least one representative, the county committee and the precinct committees and their pre-election activities should be more intimately related to the candidate and his campaign and thus should more directly reflect this emphasis than would a presidential race in which the candidate and his policies are alien to the county. In the presidential campaign the county committee is working *for* the national party and its candidate. In the contest for the state's lower house, the party organization is working *with* a candidate and, if elected, the results in both prestige and tangible rewards will be much more visible and immediate. This emphasis would explain in part a more consistent overall effort by the parties in areas in which they had a real chance of capturing the seat—that is, in two-party competitive counties.

Some more pronounced and less evenly distributed relationships are shown in non-competitive areas between forms of campaign activity and changes in the vote for state representative. There is a good correlation between the ICAS and increases in the Democratic vote and an even higher correlation between the Republican EDAS and increases in their party's vote for state representative. Both relationships are significant at the .05 level and both are similar in emphasis to the trend in non-competitive counties in the presidential voting. The explanation offered previously now has some corroborating evidence. There is a relatively higher payoff for Democrats than Republicans in keeping the party members happy and aware of party activity between elections. On the other hand, Republicans have some success with last-second appeals. This represents a rational investment of energy by the minority party, given the overwhelming one-party Democratic orientation of most of these counties. There is no relationship between campaign activity (CAS) and an increase in the vote for Democrats. There is a good, although not significant, relationship for Democrats between party effort on election day and the vote. For Republicans, there is a moderate to high relationship (only one of which passes the chi square test of significance) between vote increases and the three phases of campaign activity—a relationship which increases with the proximity of the election. That is, there is a three-step pattern beginning with electioneering in the interim campaign period (moderate relationship), progressing through the campaign period (moderately high relationship), and climaxing with the election day activity (high relationship), that show a positive, increasingly higher association with a larger partisan percentage of the votes cast. Although all categories of Republican campaign activity show a relationship, the closer the category of campaign activity to the election, the greater the potential payoff for Republicans.

The relationship of party organization, independent of campaign effort, to the voter registration and voter turnout was not entirely anticipated. Perhaps even more surprising is the moderately strong relationship of party organization, again independent of campaign activity, to the party vote (Table 9). It cannot be reemphasized strongly enough that the N in these tests is small enough to make the chi square questionable. Any findings then can only be indicative of future avenues of exploration. An examination of party organization and changes in either party's proportion of the vote can be approached if this restriction is accepted.

There is no relationship of any importance between party organization and the presidential vote for the Republicans, in either competitive or non-competitive counties, or for the Democrats in non-competitive counties. There is a high, significant relationship between party organization and the Democratic vote in competitive counties. It is possible that this finding is

TABLE 9

THE RELATIONSHIP OF THE PARTY ORGANIZATION SCALE TO
HIGH AND LOW VOTE FOR PRESIDENT (1960) AND
STATE REPRESENTATIVE (1962), BY PARTY

Level of Competition	Scale	Democrat		Republican	
		Cramer's V[a]	Chi Square[b]	Cramer's V[a]	Chi Square[b]
PRESIDENT, 1960					
Competitive	POS	.45	P < .05	.08	P < .90
Non-Competitive	POS	.07	P < .90	.08	P < .90
STATE REPRESENTATIVE, 1962					
Competitive	POS	.46	P < .20	.38	P < .30
Non-Competitive	POS	.39	P < .01	.59	P < .001

[a] Level of acceptance, V = .20.
[b] Level of acceptance, P ≤ .05.

relevant, in such a pronounced manner at any rate, only for the 1960 presidential election. The Democrats in 1960 felt that the party's presidential nominee had little appeal for the mass

of North Carolina voters. During the campaign there was specu-
lation that the state might vote Republican, at least on the
presidential level. The Democratic party took the Republican
challenge seriously and attempted to increase the party's vote
in the areas where it would do the most good. It could be that
the party leaders chose to bolster their organizations in competitive areas in the belief that, although their majority might drop
in the heavily one-party Democratic counties, it would not dip
below a winning percentage. If so, then the relationship between
party organization and competitive counties for the Democrats
is explainable. Whether this finding represents only the campaign strategy in one election is not known. Seemingly, such an
allocation of priorities would be a rational strategy for both
parties and thus a continuing phenomenon, but the absence of
anything approaching a meaningful relationship between Republican party organization in competitive districts and increases in their proportion of the presidential vote casts some
doubt on this inference.

Party organization in the race for the office of state representative shows a high to very high correlation with increases in
the party's proportion of the vote, although not all correlations
are significant. There is a high correlation for both parties in
competitive areas between an increase in the vote and party
organization. The Democratic correlation is higher than the
Republican correlation and equivalent to that found for competitive districts at the presidential level. Neither relationship
however is significant at the .05 level.

Perhaps the most interesting finding is the good, significant
correlation between party organization and the vote for state
representative in one-party areas. These figures can be viewed
with a little more assurance since the N is higher and hence
the chi square test more reliable. In these non-competitive counties there is a strong correlation between party organization and
an increase in the party's vote for state representative for the
Democrats and an exceptionally high correlation between party
organization and a larger proportionate share of the vote for
Republicans. It would appear that an efficient party organization
for both parties has an effect on the vote in competitive and
non-competitive areas. A strong relationship between good
organization and an increased share of the vote is especially
noticeable, however, in non-competitive counties in races of particular importance to the county (state representative). This

positive association between high levels of organization and a larger percentage of the vote is even more striking for the minority Republican party than it is for the majority party.[32]

A few generalizations now are in order. Campaign activity shows a more consistent relationship to the contest for state representative than it does to that for president. This was anticipated. What was not expected was the consistency in the relationship of some of the campaign measures to increases in the proportion of the presidential vote for both parties, the strength of some of these measures of association, and the overall relationship of Republican campaigning (with one exception) in both competitive and non-competitive counties to a higher percentage share of the presidential vote. As Table 8 indicates, there is a good to high relationship between year-around campaign effort and proportionate increases in the presidential vote for both parties. In competitive areas, between-election campaigning appears a necessity. In competitive and non-competitive counties, inter-election activity appears to produce greater dividends for the majority party. The Republicans —and this is especially true in one-party areas—receive better mileage from last minute appeals to receptive voters. The Democrats are in the position of conducting a holding operation— for the most part this party attempts to shore up the strength it has. Republicans, conversely, have the greatest success, at least in their present stage of development, in reaching those Democrats alienated in one manner or another from the party or those whom the party fails to reach or motivate strongly. These weakly committed voters could well be the element the Republicans most effectively proselytize on election day.

An unexpected finding was the positive relationship between the level of party organization and both voter registration and voter turnout. Although this is not confined to one-party areas, the relationship between party organization and party vote —especially in state representative races—was particularly sig-

---

[32] The results of the Rossi and Cutright, Eldersveld, and Katz and Eldersveld studies cited above and in the bibliography following Chapter I, although confined to electorates and party organizations in urban centers and although employing a somewhat different gauge of the organization and its effects, can be used for comparative purposes. In general, for example, it was found that organizational strength does have an independent relationship to the party vote.

nificant in non-competitive counties, and even more so for the minority party. The extraordinary across-the-board importance of party organization is accentuated by these findings. In studying campaigning, the role of the party organization as an independent variable should not be overlooked. Finally, it can be concluded that, although organizational activities during the varying campaign periods can conceivably be important in and of themselves, their influence in large part depends on the office sought, the category of campaign effort, and the relative position of the parties in the electorate.

Party Organization and Financing

There are noticeable differences between the two parties in a.) the financial sources they rely on and in b.) the manner in which the money obtained by the parties is deployed within the state.[33] For example, while three-fourths (71%) of all funds raised by the county organizations for both the political parties came from people and groups within the county, the Republicans unlike the Democrats were almost totally restricted to these sources. In 1960, their most successful year in soliciting financial support from agencies outside of the county, the Republican county parties were able to collect on the average only 17 per cent of their total funds from these non-county groups.

The Democratic situation offers some contrasts. Slightly better than one-half (55%) of all Democratic party funds in both the presidential-gubernatorial year of 1960 and the off-year elections of 1962 came to the local Democratic parties from sources within their county lines. There were potential outside funds available to Democrats in some situations, however, that could be called upon. These funds could prove important in specific counties in helping the local Democratic organization

[33] Works generally relevant to the focus of this analysis are: Alexander Heard, *The Costs of Democracy* (Chapel Hill: University of North Carolina Press, 1960), pp. 282–318; and John P. White and John R. Owens, *Parties, Group Interests and Campaign Finance: Michigan '56* (Princeton, N.J.: Citizens' Research Foundation, 1960); and more indirectly, "Comparative Studies in Political Finance," *Journal of Politics*, 25 (November, 1963), pp. 646–811; and Herbert E. Alexander, ed., *Studies in Money in Politics* (Princeton, N.J.: Citizens' Research Foundation, 1965).

to meet its responsibilities; particularly, in subsidizing a more concerted campaign effort. A common practice in the Democratic party involved the routing of outside, i.e., non-county, money through the state party headquarters to counties of its choosing. This had the dual effect of aiding the local party and of contributing to statewide organizational coherence by enabling the state headquarters to exercise some primacy over its local units.

The *non-county* sources available to the two parties differ. The Democratic county committees depended on, in order, the state party, candidates for public offices that were based on electoral units comprising more than one county, and private individuals. The Democratic county chairmen received virtually no money directly from national party committees. What financing that did come from national groups was routed through the state party headquarters or candidates seeking individual offices.

In contrast, the Republican county organization did receive some direct help from national party headquarters. About one-fifth (21%) of the extra-county funds came from this source in the presidential election year of 1960. The Republican party organizations also depended more heavily on private individuals outside the county to help subsidize party expenses. In 1960, 90 per cent and, in 1962, 75 per cent of the county parties received money from these individuals and volunteer groups. Non-county business organizations and candidates for offices that were not solely decided within the county were of more limited financial assistance to the local Republican parties.

An analysis of the financial sources available to the parties *within the county* illustrates the inherent advantages enjoyed by a well entrenched majority party. During campaign periods, the Democratic party exploits its influence with political appointees. From one-third (36%) in 1960 to almost one-half (45%) in 1962 of the Democratic county organizations drew upon state and local government employees for contributions to meet operating expenses (Table 10). This same source was denied to the vast majority (87%) of Republican county parties.

As Table 10 shows, sixty per cent or more of the Democratic county parties could count on receiving donations in 1960 from the following groups and individuals within the county: personal friends, businessmen, professional people, party drives for small contributions, and candidates for office at the county level.

TABLE 10

MAJOR SOURCES OF EXTRA-COUNTY AND INTRA-COUNTY FUNDS
IN 1960 AND 1962, BY PARTY

Extra-County Sources

Source	1960		1962	
	Dem. (N = 38)	Rep. (N = 19)	Dem. (N = 43)	Rep. (N = 28)
State Party Organization	76.3%	15.8%	76.7%	21.4%
Candidates for Office (i.e., Gubernatorial, Congressional, etc.)	76.3	31.6	69.8	32.1
Individuals	65.7	89.5	69.8	75.0
Business Organizations	23.7	52.6	30.2	32.1
Volunteer Groups	23.7	42.1	23.3	35.7
National Party Organizations	2.6	21.1	0.0	3.6
Other	28.9% [a]	42.0% [b]	32.5% [c]	46.4% [d]

TABLE 10 (Continued)

Intra-County Sources

Source	1960		1962	
	Dem. (N = 86)	Rep. (N = 79)	Dem. (N = 86)	Rep. (N = 79)
Personal Friends	65.1%	69.6%	83.7%	86.1%
Businessmen	64.0	60.8	81.4	78.5
Professional People	59.3	43.0	72.1	55.7
Party Drives for Small Contributions	59.3	41.8	72.1	59.5
Candidates for County Office	59.3	31.6	74.4	44.3
Farmers	52.3	53.2	65.1	68.4
Government Employees or Wives	36.0	13.9	45.3	13.9
Other	55.9% [e]	63.5% [f]	93.2% [g]	101.7% [h]

[a] Largest single source accounted for 18%, $\overline{X} = 7.2\%$.
[b] Largest single source accounted for 16%, $\overline{X} = 11.5\%$.
[c] Largest single source accounted for 19%, $\overline{X} = 8.1\%$.
[d] Largest single source accounted for 18%, $\overline{X} = 11.6\%$.
[e] Largest single source accounted for 33% (party dinners), $\overline{X} = 10.6\%$.
[f] Largest single source accounted for 38% (party dinners), $\overline{X} = 10.4\%$.
[g] Largest single source accounted for 55% (party dinners), $\overline{X} = 15.5\%$.
[h] Largest single source accounted for 61% (party dinners), $\overline{X} = 17.0\%$.

289

The Democratic county committees relied even more heavily on the same sources in 1962.

The top three sources of contributions from within the county for Republicans in 1960 were personal friends, businessmen, and farmers. The priority ordering of sources remained the same in 1962 while the percentage of counties depending on these sources increased.

From a party organizational standpoint, the characteristics of the counties that are able to attract outside financing—primarily from the state party and candidates for office for Democrats and from private individuals for Republicans—are perhaps of more interest.

The extent of party organization is a factor. The better the party is organized in a given county, the greater its chances of having its expenses subsidized by outside interests ($V = .23$, $P < .05$). The correlation of organization with non-county funding is higher for Democratic county parties ($V = .34$, $P < .02$) than it is for the smaller number of Republican county parties ($V = .29$, $P < .10$) that receive such help.

Non-competitive counties are unlikely to receive money from beyond their borders. The Republican party does not have the surplus funds available to support county organizations in areas in which there is little chance of immediate electoral success, regardless of how beneficial activities such as campaigning and personal recruitment might prove over the long-run.

The Democratic situation in one-party counties is more complex. A Democratic party that dominates a county should experience little trouble in financing its activities. The assurance of victory at the local level and the high probability of the party winning statewide should encourage businessmen, government employees, and others who wish access to those in power to contribute generously to party coffers. Also, it could be argued that not only would the funds be plentiful, a realistic appraisal of conditions, but that the party in these areas would need a minimum amount of money to contest elections in which there is often little to no Republican opposition.

Appearances can be deceiving. While comparatively little is spent on general election campaigns, party committees in non-competitive Democratic areas are still called upon to raise substantial amounts of money. The state headquarters of the Democratic party, similar to its Republican counterpart, assesses its county organizations' annual financial quotas. The Democratic county quotas are substantial, averaging better than twice as much as the corresponding Republican levies. The most demanding quotas are assigned to the *one-party* Democratic counties—not, as is the practice with the Republican party, to the two-party competitive areas. The Democratic state headquarters in turn routes a large portion of the money thus received to the counties in which the local party is experiencing the greatest challenge from its Republican adversaries.

Such procedures have a number of objectives. Assistance is given to the county parties most in need of help; a strategic deployment of the organization's resources. Second, the primacy of the party in one-party areas and the potential of its position of power in the locality and the state is intelligently exploited to maintain its overall dominance. Third, in areas in which, due to the lack of any strong opposition, there is little ostensible need for party organization, the party continues to work to both further its own interests and, more importantly, those of the party statewide. And finally, state party channels are employed to encourage a degree of organizational cohesion and a sense of commitment on the part of all the county committees to the broader goals of the organization.

The explanation advanced for the pattern of deployment of the party's financial resources is supported by the evidence. The counties in which the Democratic party in 1960 was forced to be competitive showed a high association, and one unlikely to have occurred by chance ($V = .55$, $P < .001$), with ability to attract outside financing. There is no significant correlation ($V = .04$, $P < .80$) between Republican party competition in 1960 and extra-county funding.

The same pattern is repeated in 1962. Democratic party organizations in competitive counties could expect to receive the major share of outside funds; Republican organizations in similar circumstances were not as fortunate. There is an exceptionally strong association ($V = .65$, $P < .001$) between party competition and the proportion of Democratic funds from outside sources and again no association ($V = .07$, $P < .70$) between competition and Republican extra-county financing.

One other point deserves to be mentioned. In assigning the counties their specific quotas, the Democratic state headquarters showed a realistic appreciation of what each of the counties could be expected to pay. Each of the 100 county organizations contributed almost precisely what it was assessed; only four counties returned slightly more, and two counties slightly less than that asked.

The Republican state party evidenced no such sensitivity to county finances. Although the county quotas averaged less than one-half that of the Democrats, and although the total percentage completion of the quotas averaged higher than that for the Democrats, 116 per cent to 102 per cent respectively, only one-fourth (25%) of the Republican county committees met the exact sum assessed, one-half (54%) of the county committees returned less than their full share (some as little as one-sixth or one-third), and one-fifth (21%) of the county committees contributed more than the requested amount (some as much as 9 to 10 times that expected). This would indicate, among other things, that communication channels among county units and between the Republican state party and its local appendages are not as well developed—nor do they serve the needs of the party as adequately—as those of the Democrats.

The financial resources of the Republican party in North Carolina are limited. The scarcity of money plus the embryonic nature of Republican party organization at the state level restricts the amount of funds the party is able to accumulate and thus what it can make available to the more competitive local parties. In fact, the Republican party organizations in the most highly competitive areas are asked to contribute disproportionately large sums to subsidize the upkeep and activities of the state party headquarters. Also, those minority parties struggling to survive in one-party Democratic areas can expect to receive no financial assistance whatsoever from either the state party or the other potentially more affluent county organizations.

The financial strain placed upon Republican county parties which are competitive, the inability of the state Republican party to draw large sums from or to direct funds to party organizations in one-party areas, the skill of the Democratic party in realizing the most from the one-party areas it controls and the deployment of the funds thus gained to meet the challenge of the Republican party in the most competitive districts all serve to emphasize the difficulties faced by a minority party in challenging a well established and intelligently mobilized majority party.

Conclusion

To encourage comparisons, the major findings of this study are presented as propositions, adaptable for testing in other localities. These are as follows:[34]

I. Differences between the two parties in party organization.

1. The majority party in a modified one-party state will be more consistently organized statewide on the county and precinct levels than will the minority party.

2. The minority party will be over-represented among those county parties in the state with either (a) the weakest organizations or (b) the best organized and most active local units.

3. The minority party organization statewide will draw closer to the mean Democratic organization as the competition evidenced in presidential elections becomes more common in elections for all offices at all levels.

4. The most difficulty in both contesting for office and maintaining active year-around party organizations for the minority party will occur at the local level.

5. A developing minority party will put a higher priority on formal organizational devices (e.g., bureaucratic records, formal meetings) than will the majority party.

6. As the minority party increases its organization, the majority party will strengthen its organization as a countermove.

7. Over the long run, there will be an increase in statewide organization at the county and local levels by both parties.

8. The strength of the majority party's local organization in any given locality is positively correlated with the competition provided by the minority party.

[34] At some points, the propositions are stated with a greater assurance than the analysis of the data warrants. The limitations of the statements can be found in the more extended interpretations found in the body of the report.

II. Differences between the two parties in candidate recruitment.

 1. The number of potential candidates available to a party for nomination for office is positively associated with the party's chance of winning.

 2. The higher the office, the less difficulty both parties have in finding nominees.

 3. The minority party has the most difficulty in finding candidates for (a) local offices and (b) offices that require special skills or previous training.

 4. The minority party has the least difficulty in finding candidates for the more visible and more important state and federal offices.

 5. As the number of available potential candidates increases, the county chairmen of the party will become more neutral in the selection process.

 6. The county chairmen in the state's majority party will be less active in candidate selection, with the percentage of chairmen withdrawing from the processes increasing with the importance of the office being sought.

 7. The state's minority party chairmen are much more active in seeking candidates for office at all levels than are the state's majority party chairmen.

 8. The county chairmen of both the majority and minority parties are less active in seeking candidates for offices that are not decided within the county.

 9. The minority party conscripts more candidates to seek office than the majority party.

 10. Parties in the more competitive counties will conscript more candidates for offices (especially offices that hold little intrinsic attraction) than will parties in less competitive counties.

 11. The better organized a county party is, the more likely it is to draft candidates for office.

 12. The arguments used in drafting candidates reflect the relative positions of the parties in the electorate: the majority party places heavier stress on chance of winning and party loyalty, the minority party on the need for a two-party competitive system.

III. Differences between the two parties in campaign activities.

1. The majority party will engage in a more consistent number of campaign activities statewide in any given election than the minority party.

2. The majority party will average a greater number of activities in all campaign cycles than will the minority party.

3. On election day, the activities of the minority party will tend to polarize, in comparison with those of the majority party, with local party units engaging in a large number of activities or few to none.

4. A strong minority party organization at the local level is more likely to engage in a greater number of election day activities.

5. A party organization in a county with high voter registration is more likely to engage in a large number of activities in the inter-election campaign period.

6. A party organization in a county with high voter registration is more likely to engage in a greater number of election day activities.

7. Strong party organization is correlated with a higher turnout of voters on election day.

8. The closer the campaign activities conducted by the party organization are to the election, the more likely they are to correlate with a higher voter turnout.

9. The election day activities conducted by the party organization have the highest correlation with voter turnout.

10. Activities conducted by the local units of both parties in competitive counties during the inter-election campaign period will show a positive correlation with increases in the party's proportion of the presidential vote.

11. The volume of minority party campaign activities conducted in competitive counties on election day will correlate positively with an increase in the party's proportion of the presidential vote.

12. In non-competitive counties, the number of inter-campaign activities conducted by the majority party will correlate positively with an increase in the party's proportion of the presidential vote.

13. In non-competitive counties, the number of election day activities conducted by the minority party will correlate positively with an increase in the party's proportion of the presidential vote.

14. In non-competitive counties, the number of election day activities conducted by the majority party will show a modest correlation with an increase in the party's proportion of the presidential vote.

15. In non-competitive counties, the number of activities conducted by the minority party in the inter-election campaign period will show a modest correlation with an increase in the party's proportion of the presidential vote.

16. In non-competitive counties, the volume of activities conducted during the regular campaign period by both parties will show the least relationship to a change in the party's proportion of the presidential vote.

17. In competitive counties, the volume of campaign activities engaged in by either of the parties in any of the campaign periods will *not* show a high correlation with an increase in the party's proportion of the vote for state representative.

18. In non-competitive counties, the number of inter-campaign activities engaged in by the majority party will show a positive correlation to increases in the party's proportion of the vote for state representative.

19. In non-competitive counties, the number of activities engaged in on election day by the minority party will show a strong correlation with increases in the party's proportion of the vote for state representative.

20. For the minority party in non-competitive counties, the volume of activities in each of the campaign periods will correlate with increases in the party's proportion of the vote for state representative, but the closer the campaign period is to the actual election, the higher the correlation will be.

21. Strong party organization will be correlated with a higher voter registration in a county.

22. Strong majority party organization in competitive counties will be correlated with an increase in the party's proportion of the presidential vote.

23. Strong party organization in competitive and non-competitive counties for both parties will be correlated with an increase in the party's proportion of the vote for state representative.

24. The relationship between party organization and an increase in the party's proportion of the vote for state representative will be particularly pronounced for the minority party in non-competitive counties.

IV. Differences between the two parties in fund-raising and deployment.

1. County organizations of the majority party in the state will have more non-county fund raising options open to them than will the local organizations of the minority party.

2. Private individuals will represent the primary financial source outside of a county available to a local organization of the minority party.

3. The county organizations of the majority party can expect to receive considerably more non-county financial assistance from their party's state headquarters and candidates for district and statewide office than can the local units of the minority party.

4. Acquaintances and businessmen will represent the top financial sources for both parties within the county.

5. Professional people, candidates for county office, and party drives for small contributions will prove to be more profitable sources of funds for the local organizations of the majority party than for those of the minority party.

6. Government employees and their wives will represent a source of funds available to the local organizations of the majority party, but one of limited usefulness to the local organizations of the minority party.

7. Farmers will contribute proportionately more to the minority party than the majority party.

8. The stronger the local party organization, the more likely it will be to receive non-county financial help.

9. The relationship between party organization and the attraction of non-county financial assistance will be more pronounced for the majority party than for the minority party in the state.

10. Local organizations in non-competitive counties will be unlikely to receive non-county financial assistance.

11. The local organizations in the non-competitive counties in which the majority party in the state predominates will raise funds to help the local organizations of the party in the more competitive counties.

12. The local organizations of the state's majority party in non-competitive counties will be more heavily assessed to support the operations of the state party's headquarters than will the local organizations in the more competitive counties.

13. The local organizations of the state's minority party in competitive counties will be more heavily assessed to support the operations of the state party's headquarters than will the local units in the non-competitive counties.

14. The more competitive the county, the more likely the local organization of the majority party will be to receive non-county financial assistance.

Appendix A

Indices of Party Organization in North Carolina

TABLE A.1

PERCENTAGE OF PRECINCTS IN COUNTY WITH
ACTIVE ORGANIZATIONS, 1962

Per Cent of Precincts in County Organized	Per Cent of Counties		
	Dem.	Rep.	Total
0.0%	0.0%	10.0%	4.8%
1–49%	3.5	16.3	9.5
50–99%	20.4	38.7	29.2
100% (all)	76.1	35.0	56.5
Total	100.0%	100.0%	100.0%
N	88	80	168

TABLE A.2

PRECINCTS KEEPING RECORDS

Precincts Keep Records	Dem.	Rep.	Total
Yes	63.5%	60.2%	61.9%
No	36.5	39.8	38.1
Total	100.0%	100.0%	100.0%
N	85	83	168

Per Cent of Precincts Keeping Records	Dem.	Rep.	Total
0–19%	9.4%	8.3%	8.9%
20–39%	26.4	14.6	20.8
40–59%	26.4	25.0	25.8
60–79%	5.7	10.4	7.9
80–99%	3.8	8.3	5.9
100%	28.3	33.4	30.7
Total	100.0%	100.0%	100.0%
N	53	48	101

TABLE A.3

PERCENTAGE OF PRECINCTS SENDING A FULL SLATE OF
DELEGATES TO COUNTY CONVENTION

Per Cent	Dem.	Rep.	Total
0.0%	2.3%	9.6%	5.7%
1–49%	2.3	17.8	9.4
50–99%	50.0	50.7	50.3
100%	45.4	21.9	34.6
Total	100.0%	100.0%	100.0%
N	86	73	159

TABLE A.4

MEAN NUMBER OF COUNTY COMMITTEE MEETINGS IN ELECTION
AND NON-ELECTION YEARS, BY PARTY

Party	Election Years	Non-election Years
Dem.	6.5	2.0
Rep.	10.6	3.8
Composite	8.6	2.9

TABLE A.5

UNIDIMENSIONAL SCALE OF PARTY ORGANIZATION

Scale Type	1.	2.	3.	4.	5.	Per Cent	Cumulative Per Cent
High	+	+	+	+	+	9.9%	9.9%
	+	+	+	+	−	15.4	25.3
Medium	+	+	+	−	−	35.2	60.5
	+	+	−	−	−	14.8	75.3
Low	+	−	−	−	−	8.5	83.8
	−	−	−	−	−	16.2%	100.0%
N							162

Items: 1. Some of precincts in county actively organized.
2. County chairmen keep records for campaign and organizational purposes.
3. Some of precincts in county maintain files, records, etc.
4. County committee held four or more meetings in non-election years.
5. All of precincts in county keep precinct records.

Cr = .91

Note: If a county had two or more NA's to scale items, the county was not scalable. Ten counties were not scalable.

Appendix B

Variables Used in Three Scales of Campaign Activity

INTER-CAMPAIGN ACTIVITIES SCALE (ICAS). The question on which this scale was based is as follows:

Q. 38. In securing voting support, in which of the following areas is the *greatest* amount of effort concentrated? (Please check the 3 most important.)

_____ Registration—increasing numerical strength

_____ Party morale—that is, keeping the party regulars aware and enthusiastic through public appeals to them

_____ General public appeal—that is, radio, TV and newspaper appeals to the public, regardless of party

_____ Personal contact with party members

_____ Other (please specify: _____
_____)

_____ No effort to secure support is being made at the present time.

The items used in the Inter-Campaign Activities Scale and the frequency distributions are as follows:

TABLE B.1

ITEMS USED IN INTER-CAMPAIGN ACTIVITIES SCALE*

Scale Type	1.	2.	3.	4.	Per Cent	Cumulative Per Cent
High	X	X	X	X	4.9%	4.9%
	X	X	X	—	29.3	34.2
Medium	X	X	—	—	33.5	67.7
Low	X	—	—	—	24.4	92.1
	—	—	—	—	7.9%	100.0%
N						164

Items: 1. Other (some other activity from those listed in question).
2. Public appeal.
3. Registration.
4. Personal contact.

Cr = .90
* Eight chairmen did not answer the question and thus were not included in the scale.

CAMPAIGN ACTIVITIES SCALE (CAS). The question on which this scale was based is as follows:

Q. 14. Listed below are campaign activities that have been employed by some county committees in general elections. Please indicate whether your county committee *often* uses, *sometimes* uses, or *never* uses each activity. Does it:

_____ 1. Employ movie advertisements

_____ 2. Organize door to door canvassing

_____ 3. Organize rallies

_____ 4. Arrange barbecues and chicken fries

_____ 5. Employ radio time in county campaigns

_____ 6. Prepare press releases

_____ 7. Employ television time in county campaigns

_____ 8. Buy newspaper space for county campaigns

_____ 9. Mail circulars and letters

_____ 10. Distribute throw-aways

_____ 11. Organize telephone campaigns

_____ 12. Put up billboards or posters

_____ 13. Bring in special speakers

_____ 14. Emphasize personal contact, word of mouth campaigns

_____ 15. Other (please specify: _____)

The items used in the Campaign Activities Scale and the frequency distributions are as follows:

TABLE B.2

ITEMS USED IN CAMPAIGN ACTIVITIES SCALE*

Scale Position	1.	2.	3.	4.	5.	6.	Per Cent	Cumulative Per Cent
High	X	X	X	X	X	X	25.5%	25.5%
Medium	X	X	X	X	X	—	39.9	65.4
Low	X	X	X	X	—	—	20.2	85.6
	X	X	X	—	—	—	6.5	92.1
	X	X	—	—	—	—	4.6	96.7
	X	—	—	—	—	—	3.3%	100.0%
N								153

Items: 1. TV
2. Throwaways
3. Door to door canvassing
4. Press releases
5. Rallies
6. Personal contact

Cr = .92
* Nineteen chairmen had 3 or more NA's and were not scalable.

ELECTION DAY ACTIVITIES SCALE (EDAS). The question on which this scale was based is as follows:

Q. 19. In approximately how many of the precincts, if any, were the following election day activities carried on in the last general election (1960)? (Please check the box closest to the per cent of precincts engaging in the activity)

1. Transporting voters to and from the polls
2. Poll watchers
3. Providing baby sitters
4. Passing out literature and throw sheets
5. Employing sound trucks
6. Phoning registered voters reminding them to vote
7. Last minute newspaper, radio or TV advertising
8. Parades or motorcades
9. Other (please specify: ───────────────────)

    The items used in the Election Day Activities Scale and the
frequency distributions are as follows:

TABLE B.3

ITEMS USED IN ELECTION DAY ACTIVITIES SCALE*

Scale	Type of Activity				Per	Cumulative
Type	1.	2.	3.	4.	Cent	Per Cent
High	X	X	X	X	17.2%	17.2%
	X	X	X	—	23.9	41.1
Medium	X	X	—	—	32.1	73.2
Low	X	—	—	—	17.9	91.1
	—	—	—	—	8.9%	100.0%
N						134

Items: 1. Sound trucks
       2. Parades
       3. Newspapers
       4. Transporting voters

Cr = .94
* Thirty-eight chairmen had 2 or more NA's and were not scalable.

EIGHT

Application of the Attribution Model to the Study of Political Recruitment: County Elective Offices

Thomas M. Watts

University of Pennsylvania

Everywhere in Indiana, the formal party organization remains the center of partisan activity. In some other states the legal party structure has become a derelict, exercising no real political power while other organizations make the important decisions in politics and carry on the significant political activity. This is nowhere true in Indiana. (Frank Munger, 1955).[1]

THE FORMAL PARTY organization referred to in the above quotation is the regularly elected personnel of the legally stipu-

[1] Frank Munger, "Two-Party Politics in the State of Indiana" (Harvard University, Unpublished Ph.D. Dissertation, 1955), p. 151.
In Indiana, the formal organization is provided for in a detailed election code. It comprises a hierarchy of committees ranging from precinct committees at the base to the state central committee at the top. Except for state convention delegates, the only party official elected directly by the people is the precinct committeeman. The committeeman is elected by the votes of his party every two years in the primary election preceding the general election. He in turn appoints a vice-committeeman (of the opposite sex) and together with their counterparts in all other precincts in a county, they comprise the county committee. This committee meets for organization on the Saturday following the primary and selects a chairman, a vice-chairman (of the opposite sex), a secretary, and a treasurer. The following week the congressional district committees meet to organize. The district committee is composed of the chairman and vice-chairman of the county committees within the congressional district. The district chairman and vice-chairman make up the state central committee which meets to organize during the following week.

lated party structures. The study the selection is borrowed from views auxiliary associations as exerting limited influence on party affairs. It concludes that law, tradition, and practice have made the formal organization powerful—and, therefore, the chief prize in intra-party contests.[2]

At the local level in Indiana, most of the formal power in the party organization rests in the hands of two people, the county chairman and vice-chairman. In practice, the chairman alone is usually the dominant force. There are, however, little understood *informal* positions of influence, not included within the officially prescribed party structures, yet closely allied to them. A knowledge of these informal centers of power and their influence on party activity is a necessary prerequisite for an understanding of the politics of the Indiana, or for that matter any, party system.

To gain an appreciation of the inter-relationship of formal and informal organizational within the party, this report will focus on party nominations for elective office. Essentially, the questions to be answered are: Who determines party nominations? What, if any, influence do "informal" party leaders exercise in this process? And, who are these informal leaders?

Background

There is an expanding body of literature concerned with political recruitment processes and personnel. Participation— the broader category of which recruitment is one aspect—spans a continuum from limited involvement, e.g., talking politics, voting, to extensive political commitment, e.g., holding public or party office. The factors leading to increased participation are not clearly understood. Nonetheless, the broad classification scheme employed by Milbrath—social, environmental (and family), psychological, and political factors—in his propositional inventory of studies dealing with participation can serve as a convenient point of departure for the present discussion.[3]

---

[2] Munger, *ibid.*

[3] Lester W. Milbrath, *Political Participation* (Chicago: Rand Mcnally and Co., 1965). See particularly chs. 2–5. Also, Lewis Bowman and G. R. Boynton present a recruitment model that is developed from similar categories. See their "Recruitment Patterns among Local Party Officials: A Model and Some Preliminary Findings in Selected Locales," *American Political Science Review,* 60 (September, 1966), pp. 667–680.

Robert Lane, drawing on his analytic synthesis of the relevant literature, has advanced the general proposition that upper status people participate more in politics, a contention supported by the findings of many studies.[4] Matthews, in his analysis of the social background of decision-makers, shows that high echelon political offices draw individuals from the best educated and occupationally most prestigious groups in the society.[5] For example, using father's occupation as an index of class origin, the decision-makers were, with few exceptions, sons of professional men, business officials, proprietors, and, atypically, but understandable in light of the time periods covered, farmers. Few officials came from families of wage earners, low salaried workers, or farm laborers. The higher the political position, the more impressive the social characteristics of the occupants.

Efforts have been made to connect social and electoral cleavages with political activists. Lipset cites some "skimpy evidence" to show that office-holders reflect their electorates— at least in community politics. Lipset notes in Munger's study on Indiana, introduced above, the close correspondence between leader and voter characteristics. Three-fourths (76%) of those seeking Republican party nominations were in professional or business-managerial occupations; forty-two per cent of those desiring Democratic nominations were manual workers.[6] In a somewhat better known study, Epstein found that 54 per cent of the leaders in the local Democratic party in Milwaukee were manual workers, or sales or clerical personnel. This compared with a corresponding Republican figure of 10 per cent. Republican party officials were primarily drawn from those in professional careers or those who ran business concerns.[7] Crotty, in an

[4] Robert E. Lane, *Political Life: Why People Get Involved in Politics* (Glencoe, Ill.: The Free Press, 1959), ch. 16. See also, for example, Julian L. Woodward and Elmo Roper, "Political Activity of American Citizens," *American Political Science Review*, 44 (December, 1950), p. 877; and R. Agger and V. Ostrom, "Political Participation in a Small Community," in H. Eulau, S. Eldersveld, and M. Janowitz, eds., *Political Behavior* (Glencoe, Ill.: The Free Press, 1956), pp. 138–148.

[5] Donald R. Matthews, *The Social Backgrounds of Political Decision Makers* (New York: Random House, 1954), p. 28. Matthews does not include data below the level of state legislatures.

[6] Seymour Martin Lipset, *Political Man* (New York: Doubleday and Co., Inc., 1960), pp. 288–299; and Munger, *op. cit.*, p. 240.

[7] Leon D. Epstein, *Politics in Wisconsin* (Madison: University of Wisconsin Press, 1958), p. 89.

analysis of *party* leader-follower-community characteristics in a modified one-party state, refines these contentions somewhat. Party activists reflect their *immediate* constituencies. As a result, the characteristics of party organizational personnel need not coincide with national party images of group support. The traditionally noncompetitive nature of some areas structures the environment from which each of the parties can draw activists, resulting in atypical, for the nation or for more competitive constituencies, leadership profiles.[8]

A different perspective on the association between status and public office is offered by Jacob. He contends that occupational *role*, rather than status per se, is the decisive factor. He distinguishes what he calls "broker" roles, i.e., those which place a premium on bargaining among equals in search of mutually satisfactory agreements. Those in broker positions would include lawyers, insurance salesmen, realtors, merchants, undertakers, farmers, plumbers, and bankers.[9] When considerations arising from Weber's conception of "role dispensability" are added to delimit the political relevance of the occupations, the remaining ones would serve as important gateways to politics.

Milbrath categorizes three types of political participants: *gladiators*, those who work in campaigns, contribute money, or seek party and public office; *spectators*, those who acquire information, discuss politics, or vote; and *apathetics*, those who do not engage in any political activities. Respectively, each category constitutes roughly one-twentieth, two-thirds, and one-third of the electorate.[10]

Social status factors are important correlates of spectator activities, less important for understanding gladiatorial roles. The latter appears to be a product of more personal considerations and one with far greater individual ramifications than, for example, the less strenuous commitment implicit in communicating with government leaders or voting.

[8] William J. Crotty, "The Social Attributes of Party Organizational Activists in a Transitional Political System," *Western Political Quarterly*, 20 (September, 1967).

[9] Herbert Jacob, "Initial Recruitment of Elected Officials in the U.S.: A Model," *Journal of Politics*, 24 (November, 1962), pp. 709–711. Jacob suggests that the esteem in which a community holds political office constitutes a filter determining which potential politicians seek elective office.

[10] Lester W. Milbrath, "Predispositions toward Political Contention," *Western Political Quarterly*, 13 (March, 1960), pp. 5–18; and Milbrath, *Political Participation, op. cit.*, pp. 16–38.

One conditioning experience predisposing an individual to be politically active is the socialization he undergoes. The family is a particularly important source of stimuli here. The Wahlke *et al.* study of legislators in four states, as an illustration, presented detailed evidence on the large number of representatives who came from politically active families.[11] Schooling, peer groups, and occupational associates are also of great importance in the process.[12]

Psychological factors are of greater help at present in understanding mass behavior patterns, e.g., voting, than they are in identifying those most likely to assume gladiatorial roles. Milbrath, who has done research of his own in the area, considers personality variables, expecially sociablility, to be important for explaining intensive involvement.[13]

Finally, the argument that the political setting is an important consideration in recruitment is usually concerned with the relative competition between parties in an area or the strength of local party organization. V. O. Key, for one, argues that the primary competition within a party varies with the probability of success in the general election; the greater the possibility of winning the office, the more competitors seeking the party nomination. In one-party dominant areas, there are few primary contests. Rather, the minority party is faced with the problem of actively seeking candidates to contest for office in order to put forward a full slate in the general election. Further, in safe districts, Key finds that incumbents who seek re-nomination normally face little primary opposition.[14]

[11] John C. Wahlke, Heinz Eulau, William Buchanan, and LeRoy C. Ferguson, *The Legislative System* (New York: John Wiley and Sons, 1962), ch. 4.

[12] An introduction to political socialization in general and useful guides to the literature can be found in: Herbert Hyman, *Political Socialization* (New York: Free Press, 1959); and Roberta Sigel, ed., *Political Socialization: Its Role in the Political Process* (Philadelphia: The Annals of the American Academy of Political and Social Science, September, 1965).

[13] Milbrath's review of the literature relating personal factors to participation covers the relevant research. *Political Participation, op cit.,* pp. 48–89. For data on the effects of party organizational efforts in the development of attitudes predisposing citizens favorably toward accepting activist and leadership positions within the party, see Samuel J. Eldersveld, *Political Parties: A Behavioral Analysis* (Chicago: Rand McNally and Co., 1964), ch. 17.

[14] V. O. Key, Jr., *Politics, Parties, and Pressure Groups* (4th ed.; New York: Thomas Crowell Co., 1958); and Key, *American State*

In a study of Indiana primary elections for Prosecuting Attorney and House and Senate candidacies for the General Assembly, Standing and Robinson did indeed find strong support
for the proposition that more candidates entered the primary
of the dominant party. The combined total number of con-
testants, however, did not vary with the competitiveness of the
general election.[15]

Key offers some plausible explanations for the large incidence of uncontested primaries, in addition to the party's
chances of success. Many contenders for a party nomination
could be interpreted as disapproval of a slate of candidates endorsed by a formal party committee. Primary competition, also,
is likely to be futile in a situation in which a well-financed organization unites behind its choices. Or, serious nomination
fights could reveal disagreements among party factions.[16]

In many primaries, there are no official, or unofficial, organization contenders for party endorsement. Rather, a number
of individuals enter the party contests, hoping to capitalize on
specialized followings, ethnic identifications, family support, a
popular name, or some other personal asset to capture the
nomination. In such contests, there may be no leadership group
within the party with the capacity to control the nominating
process. Professional organizational personnel, however, can
enter the primary fight in the form of a multiplicity of leadership clusters formed around individually favored candidates or
focused on given offices.[17]

In a study of state legislative recruitment in Oregon, Lester
Seligman makes a convenient distinction between the *certifica-*

Politics (New York: Alfred A. Knopf, 1956), pp. 175–177. Key
analyzes data from Missouri and Ohio legislative districts. The
Crotty chapter in this volume also treats party recruitment of candidates, in this instance in North Carolina, and reports findings supportive of Key.

[15] William H. Standing and James A. Robinson, "Inter-Party Competition and Primary Contesting: The Case of Indiana," *American
Political Science Review,* 52 (December, 1958), pp. 1066–1077. Also,
consult the early study by Charles S. Hyneman, "Tenure and Turnover of the Indiana General Assembly," *American Political Science
Review,* 32 (April, 1938), pp. 320–321. His data suggest a relationship between fear of defeat and the tendency to seek re-election by
Indiana legislators.

[16] Key, *Politics, Parties, and Pressure Groups, op. cit.,* pp. 418–419.

[17] *Ibid.,* p. 420.

tion and *selection* stages of the nomination process.[18] Certification includes the type of concerns predominant in the work of Milbrath, Matthews, Lane and, to an extent, Marvick in this volume. That is, this first step would include the social screening, environmental channeling and, potentially at least, psychological stimuli that culminate in eligibility for candidacy. The second stage, selection, is reminiscent of the points raised by Key. This aspect of the process is concerned with the political structures and considerations that result in the actual choice of candidates to represent the parties in the general election.

The present study will deal with questions of certification, but its primary focus will be on considerations of selection. In passing, though, social characteristics, motivational factors, and environmental stimuli will be treated.

Before leaving the Seligman study, a few of his additional contributions to the study of recruitment should be noted. For example, individual candidacies are conceived of in two phases: *instigation,* i.e., the events and relationships that affect the decision to file; and *reinforcement,* i.e., the process through which support for a candidate is enlisted.

From his analysis of the effect of political factors on legislative recruitment, Seligman found:

1. In safe districts, majority party officials were least active in instigating or supporting candidates.
2. In safe districts, the organizational personnel of the minority party actively sought potential candidates. The least interest-group intervention and the only examples of fully centralized party recruitment were found in these areas.
3. In competitive districts, candidacy was open and there was no evidence of centralized party control.[19]

The study also found differing party patterns. Organizational instigation was more frequent among Democrats; interest

[18] Lester G. Seligman, "Political Recruitment and Party Structure: A Case Study," *American Political Science Review,* 55 (March, 1961), pp. 77–78. See also the distinctions noted by Ranney in his chapter in this volume.

[19] This conclusion was highly qualified. Also, it should be noted that although Oregon has a closed primary, under Oregon laws, unlike Indiana, the official party organization must observe strict neutrality in the primary contests.

groups and voluntary associations more often actively influenced Republican party nominations.

Finally, based on the findings, four role types for behavior
at the instigation stage were constructed: (1) party *conscrip-
tion*, a candidate is recruited by the party, normally where
chances of success in the general election are minimal; (2)
self-recruitment, a situation in which a candidate seeks nomination without any clearance from party leaders; (3) *cooptation*,
a candidate not explicitly associated with the party is induced
to run to enhance public support; and (4) *agency*, a candidate
committed to an organized interest group enters the race.[20]

The Seligman and Key work reflect the more recent, and
imaginative, thinking on political recruitment. The research reported here elaborates on questions explored by these, and
other, students of political parties. Its principal contribution lies
in the focus on informal centers of power of potential importance in influencing party nominations and in the methodological techniques employed.

Method of Inquiry

To identify forces affecting party nominations, a methodological tool more commonly associated with analyses of community power structures—the power attribution, reputational,
or elitist model—was adapted for the research.[21]

Few hypotheses are more difficult to test than those which
relate decision-making to clique structure. Since Floyd Hunter's

---

[20] *Ibid.*, pp. 85–86.

[21] Support for portions of the research was supplied by Indiana
University and the Relm Foundation in the form of fellowships and
research grants. I am particularly indebted to Professors Charles S.
Hyneman and David R. Derge of Indiana University for their aid
and suggestions at all stages of the project. For detailed presenta-
tion of data and analysis, see my unpublished Ph.D. dissertation,
"Indiana Primary Elections: The Selection of Candidates and the
Distribution of Power" (Indiana University, 1963).

In part my interest in the relation between formal and informal
party organizations resulted from my own political experience. During the period from 1953 to 1959, I served at the local level in
Indiana in various party organizational capacities, including precinct committeeman, city chairman, and county chairman.

classic study of "Regional City,"[22] however, researchers have been trying to perfect economical tools for identifying and describing power structures. Such studies have generated much comment. Extensive criticism, especially that from the "pluralist" school, has been directed at the practice of attributing influence to individuals without adequately testing for involvement with outcomes of issues. Dahl, Polsby, and others, for example, have argued that rather than the "single pyramid of power" found in some of these studies, a more accurate reflection of reality might be a series of power clusters, or "pyramids of power," within the broader community, each focusing on different policy areas.[23]

The application of the attribution model in the present study was designed to correct for some of the major weaknesses associated with it. First, party nominations were selected as an *issue* to be analyzed.[24] In this case, the issue outcome is, in part, an independent decision by a candidate to seek official endorsement and, in part, a reflection of the response of others to a potential candidacy. It is, therefore, possible to evaluate the influence of attributed power-wielders by comparing their reputed influence with actual nominations. And, the generalizations derived from the analysis are limited to one institutional segment of a community, the *political*.[25]

Two considerations underlying the model require comment. Conceptually, power and influence are used inter-changeably in the analysis. Second, the fundamental assumption in research of this nature is that certain groups or individuals *do* exercise

22 Floyd Hunter, *Community Power Structure* (Chapel Hill: University of North Carolina Press, 1953).

23 For a comprehensive discussion of the earlier studies and their relevance for political science, see Lawrence J. R. Herson, "In the Footsteps of Community Power," *American Political Science Review*, 55 (December, 1961), pp. 817–830. For a critique of both "Elitist" and "Pluralist" Models, see Peter Bachrach and Morton Baratz, "Two Faces of Power," *American Political Science Review*, 56 (December, 1962), pp. 947–952. Consult also Nelson W. Polsby, *Community Power and Political Theory* (New Haven: Yale University Press, 1964); and Robert A. Dahl, *Who Governs?* (New Haven: Yale University Press, 1961).

24 Nominations have been treated as issues in other studies. See, for example, Dahl, *ibid.*

25 Other institutional sectors in communities might include business, culture, education, industry, labor, religion, mass communication and welfare.

a great deal of political, and perhaps economic and social, power in communities, and that these *can* be identified. The problem here, then, is to specify those influential in the nominating process, examine the interactions among influentials, and then explore the communications between this group and those seeking party endorsement. Two basic questions need to be answered: the extent to which the influentials act in concert, as groups, or elites, with distinctive structures, cohesiveness, and solidarity; and the inter-relationship between these non-party groups and the nomination process.

Finally, it should be noted that the model employed in this study offers exciting possibilities for the study of informal leadership structures and their relation to the party organization and its activities, an area that has received little attention to date.[26]

The Data

This report concentrates on party nomination practices at the county level. The data were gathered primarily from interviews with the following:

1. Thirty-one candidates for county elective office in one Indiana county (Howard);[27]
2. Nineteen reputationally selected political leaders of both parties in the county; and

[26] A major exception is Frost's 1957 study of "real" county leaders in eight New Jersey counties. Nominations were secured from municipal and district leaders, state party officials, and county leaders. Sixty "real" leaders were identified and fifty-seven interviewed following the general election. Robert T. Frost, "Stability and Change in Local Party Politics," *Public Opinion Quarterly*, 25 (Summer, 1961), pp. 221–235.

[27] In any given election year, the offices to be filled vary somewhat in different counties, but the following were included for this study: county clerk, auditor, sheriff, assessor, recorder, judge, county commissioner, and prosecutor. The regular term for these offices is four years, and, except for the last three, they do not have special educational or residential requirements. Aspirants for these offices face the voters in the spring of each year in which there is to be a general election in the fall. Indiana has a closed primary, requiring a record to be kept of whether a voter votes a Democratic or a Republican ballot.

3. Twenty-seven county chairmen of both parties in fifteen additional counties.[28]

At the time of this study in 1962, Howard County and its central city, Kokomo, had populations of 69,509 and 47,197 respectively. The County is situated in the rich agricultural lands of northern Indiana some fifty miles north of Indianapolis and 156 miles southeast of Chicago. Although it has a substantial rural population, eighty-two per cent of the area's income comes from industrial manufacturing. Similar to all Indiana cities and counties, Kokomo has a mayor-council plan of government and Howard County a three man board of commissioners. Politically, the County is characterized by vigorous party competition. Nominally Republican until 1930, the County has changed to the point that the Democratic party was dominant in 1962.

Three criteria—population, location, and party competition—were employed in selecting fifteen other Indiana counties for comparison with the findings in Howard County. The counties selected were in the population range of forty to one hundred thousand. Location of the counties was included as a consideration in order that the findings might be generally indicative of the state. To improve geographic representation, two considerably larger counties, one in the northeast and one in the southwest, were included among those analyzed. And the counties sampled represented one-party Democratic and Republican and two-party competitive areas.[29]

In Howard County, the candidates were questioned concerning the manner in which they were recruited and the contacts they made, the leaders about their role in recruiting candidates, and the county chairmen on leadership groups in

[28] The other counties in the study were: Allen, Bartholomew, Cass, Clark, Floyd, Grant, Henry, Knox, Kosciusko, Laporte, Monroe, Porter, Tippecanoe, Vanderburgh, and Wayne.

[29] Party classification for all counties in this study was determined on the basis of state representative races according to the Schlesinger two-dimensional scheme. Joseph Schlesinger, "A Two Dimensional Scheme for Classifying the States According to Degree of Inter-Party Competition," *American Political Science Review*, 49 (December, 1955), pp. 1120–1128.

Fifteen counties do not constitute a representative sample for a heterogeneous state of 92 counties and generalizations suggested must be treated with appropriate caution.

their respective counties as well as on their own recruitment
activities. The information collected from candidates included
the names of all persons with whom they were in contact at
various recruitment stages and the nature of each contact. Data
were also sought as to who initiated the contact and for what
purpose. Members of the leadership group, selected on the basis
of a party issue different from nominations, were questioned
about their interests in the primary, meetings they attended,
the direct and indirect contacts they made, and the nature of
those contacts. Data from these schedules were compared in
the analysis.[30]

The Party Elites

Three working hypotheses were constructed to guide the
analysis. These are:

1. There is a small informal group of persons within the
   general structure of each political party who work closely
   with the formal leaders and make the key decisions;
2. Decisions made by this leadership group concern primarily
   party matters and seldom broader community questions
   which do not directly affect the party;
3. Where leadership groups of the parties are active in the
   selection of candidates, aspirants favored by them will file
   their candidacies and successfully win nomination.

In support of the first hypothesis, quite clearly identifiable
leadership groups were found in Howard County and in twenty-
six of twenty-seven party organizations investigated in the other
fifteen counties.
   Within each Howard County leadership group, to be referred to as *Top Influentials*, a much smaller, but also well
defined, group of leaders, to be called *Key Influentials*, was iso-

[30] This report is concerned primarily with evidence supporting the
elite hypothesis. Data were also collected on the recruitment activity
of other groups, interests, and newspapers, but since their overall
involvement was found to be comparatively limited, the procedures
and findings are not included.

lated.[31] The Top Influential groups in each party were located by securing nominations from informants according to an adaptation of techniques suggested by Hunter and refined by other reputational researchers.[32] The Republican list contained twenty-five names, the Democratic thirty-nine. Interviews were conducted with as many as possible of those rated by judges as generally "most influential" on each of the lists. The Key Influential groups were identified by analysis of the completed schedules. As a first step, each leader was asked this question:

> If you felt responsible for influencing a party policy in this county (such as who should be the next county chairman should a vacancy occur), which ten on this list would presently be most helpful to you, regardless of whether they are known personally to you or not?

The entire list of Top Influentials was submitted to respondents who were asked to identify the ten men they considered most prominent in their party. The number was arbitrary. The respondents were encouraged to modify it as they felt appropriate. From this appraisal, four Republicans and one Democrat were added to the original list. A consensus emerged from the tabulation of the "votes" in both parties as to who were the party influentials. From the initial list of 29 Republicans, thirteen principal leaders emerged, and from the initial 40 Democrats, ten (Table 1).[33]

Next an attempt was made to determine if the influentials functioned as "groups." Each Key Influential interviewed was given the original list and asked to indicate the extent to which he was acquainted with each of the other leaders.[34] An analysis

[31] This terminology was adapted from a discussion in William H. Form and Delbert C. Miller, *Industry, Labor, and Community* (New York: Harper & Brothers, 1960), pp. 444–447.

[32] *Ibid.,* pp. 697–701.

[33] An individual had to be named by at least half of the respondents for his party to be included as a Key Influential. This dividing point is somewhat arbitrary. However, the next lower names on both lists were named by considerably fewer than half of the respondents. For further comparative purposes, when Top Influentials are referred to as a group, the Key Influentials will be excluded.

[34] Of the nineteen Top Influential leaders interviewed (eleven Republicans and eight Democrats), ten Republicans and five Democrats were also Key Influentials. These fifteen schedules provided the basis for this analysis.

TABLE 1

NUMBER OF PERSONS REPUTED TO BE MOST INFLUENTIAL
IN PARTY DECISION-MAKING

(Howard County, Indiana, 1962)

Top Influentials

Republicans	Democrats
29	40

Key Influentials

13	10

of the results found that the principal leadership groups in each party were better acquainted with those at the same level than with the others on the list.[35]

Of course, by itself, these findings do not establish a collective identity for the group or show that the leaders operated as a unit. All leaders, therefore, were asked to elaborate on the following question:

In your judgment, is the following statement true or false? "There is a small crowd of persons within your party who pretty much work together and make the big decisions."

All of the respondents agreed that such groups existed, although the description of the two varied by party.

The informal Republican group met when elections were imminent, but seldom at other times. The group was relatively stable and included all of the Key Influentials.[36] It concerned

[35] That the Key Influentials have more contact with one another suggests a likelihood that they therefore have more opportunity to discuss political issues, though nothing in the acquaintanceship pattern alone demonstrates that this in fact happens.

[36] The term "stable" here means that the group has a more or less constant membership during its tenure. It is possible, however, that a large part of a group's membership might be altered when one party faction replaces another.

itself primarily with party affairs—that is, raising finances, selecting county chairmen, "filling the ticket" (nominations), recommending major appointments, arranging meetings, preparing for campaigns, and, occasionally, discussing campaign issues (Table 2). The meeting agenda was kept "fluid," different things were discussed at different times. Civic issues apparently did *not* come before the group. When action on community matters was desired, it was accomplished outside of the group structure, either through word of mouth contact among interested members or individual action initiated by the persons concerned.

The pattern of deliberations of the Democratic leadership group in Howard County was similar to the Republicans: the group also restricted itself to considering party matters (Table 2).

TABLE 2

THE SALIENCY OF HOWARD COUNTY PARTY ISSUES
ACCORDING TO LEADERS' RANKINGS, BY PARTY (1962).

Issue	Party			
	Republican (N = 11)		Democrat (N = 8)	
	Rank	$\overline{X}$ Score	Rank	$\overline{X}$ Score
Election of a County Chairman	1	1.63	1	1.25
Nomination of County Candidates	2	2.63	2	2.00
Raising Campaign Funds	3	3.00	4	3.75
New School Board Appointments	4	4.13	3	3.60
Approval of City Budget	5	4.38	5	5.25
Finding a New Plan Commission Director	6	5.41	6	4.50
Obtaining a New Street Parking Lot	7	6.85	7	5.75

Informal leadership groups were also reported by twenty-six of the twenty-seven chairmen in the other counties. Within the other twenty-six informal groups, in fewer than half were election issues reportedly discussed with any frequency and in only five were civic problems mentioned. The chairmen in these counties reported that interest in civic issues represented individual concerns.[37] They were seldom discussed by the party leadership groups. When exceptions to the general rule arose, they involved issues likely to grow into sources of community conflict, e.g., urban renewal. Yet, even in such cases, group discussions were more concerned with the potential effect the issue might have on the organization, rather than how the party might become involved in promoting or opposing it. The group reaction was essentially defensive. All policy concerns, also, were of a local nature: the party chairman did not report any discussions of state or national issues at their meetings. No discernible differences were apparent between Republican and Democratic groups as to the nature or the attention given to non-party concerns. Overall, there is little evidence of programmatic activity at this level of the party organization.

The Democratic party in Howard County was divided into three distinct factions and each met separately. The members of the Democratic Key Influential group, which included the county chairman, were all from the same faction. The meetings of this "in group," when held, tended to be smaller and more informal than those of the corresponding Republican group, although the size fluctuated depending on the issue being considered. Low cohesiveness combined with party factionalism made it difficult for the group to exert any sustained control over party affairs. One participant, for example, described the group as "fuzzy," and its sessions as lacking a fixed agenda.

The average size of the informal leadership groups in the twenty-six other counties was about the same for the two parties, 9.4 members for the Republicans and 9.6 for the Democrats; figures virtually identical to those for Howard County (Table 3). Nineteen of these informal consultative groups had a stable composition and met at regular intervals. The remaining seven had a more fluid membership, relying to a greater extent on

---

[37] An election issue was one in which the party might take an open stand in a forthcoming election; a civic issue is one in which party leaders may use their influence to promote or block a project which may or may not become an election issue.

TABLE 3

SIZE, MEMBERSHIP, AND MEETING CHARACTERISTICS OF
TWENTY-SIX INFORMAL LEADERSHIP GROUPS IN FIFTEEN
SELECTED INDIANA COUNTIES, BY PARTY (1962)

| Characteristic | | Party | | |
		Republican (N = 13)	Democratic (N = 13)	Total
Size	1–6 Members	2	1	3
	6–10 Members	7	5	12
	10–20 Members	4	7	11
Group Stability	Stable	7	11	18
	Fluid	5	2	7
Group Meetings	Holds Formal Meetings	8	11	19

informal contacts. All of the groups were consulted by the chairmen on important party problems. There were no apparent distinctions in patterns of group associations in one-party dominant or two-party competitive areas.

Lawyers, bankers, insurance men, and public officials are represented about equally in the consultive groups in both parties (Table 4). Manufacturing executives, however, are over-represented among Republican group members. In contrast, the Democratic party groups showed an equally disproportionate favoritism for farmers. No union officers were included in the Republican groups and only five in the Democratic, a small representation considering the importance of organized labor in most of the counties studied and the influence attributed to labor in Democratic party activities.[38]

In Howard County, the Republican group consisted of four attorneys, two newspapermen (an editor and publisher), three

[38] For an assessment of the role of labor in Indiana politics at the state level see Melvin A. Kahn, "Labor and the Law-making Process: the Case of Indiana," (Indiana University, Unpublished Ph.D. Dissertation, 1964).

TABLE 4

OCCUPATIONS OF INFORMAL LEADERS IN TWENTY-SIX PARTY GROUPS
IN FIFTEEN SELECTED INDIANA COUNTIES, BY PARTY (1962).

Occupations	Party	
	Republican	Democratic
Lawyers	16	14
Farmers	8	18
Bankers	7	6
Insurance Representatives	4	3
Manufacturing Executives	18	5
County or City Office Holders	8	8
Contractors	4	1
Union Officers and Stewards	0	5
Miscellaneous (all others)	18	21
Total reported	83	81

elective officials, an insurance man, a farmer, a manufacturer, and a public appointee. The Democratic group contained three farmers, one elected official, a farmer-teacher, a banker, an attorney, a housewife, a school principal, and an insurance agent. The average age for Democrats was 56.2, Republicans 51.6. The youngest Key Influential was forty-three, the oldest seventy-one. All were residents of the County for at least thirty years. Apparently, positions in both Howard County Key Influential groups were earned over long periods of time by people with deep roots in the locality.

The Howard County Key Influentials were active in many aspects of politics. For both parties, almost all contributed money to the party, passed out literature, contacted voters, gave speeches and managed campaigns. Nearly all had themselves been candidates for public office at some point in their political careers, and ten had held elective public office.[39]

A composite portrait of the "average" Howard County Key Influential would be as follows: male, in his early to middle fifties, Protestant, and a county resident of long standing. He is probably the offspring of a politically active family, becoming personally involved in politics in his late twenties or early thirties. He is above average in occupational and educational status. Although he and his associates may operate quietly as a group, he is likely to have been publicly associated with the party for many years, probably even having sought elective office under party auspices. If a Democrat, more than likely he matured within the party organization, holding a series of party positions at various points in his career. For both parties, his present position results from a long and continued involvement in some area of party affairs. Personally, the Key Influentials appear to possess those elusive leadership qualities that have gained them respect and success in their non-political as well as political pursuits.

Many reasons were advanced by candidates, county chairmen, and other informants to explain the power and prestige of the party leaders. The most frequently volunteered of these was expertise, characterized as specialized skills in given areas, extensive knowledge, or particular insight into the political process. Also, almost all in the leadership groups were believed to be perceptive men of sound judgement. Several members of the party groups were credited with exceptional abilities to accomplish specified goals, e.g., raise money. All were believed to be strongly motivated. A number of the leaders were successful office-holders with their own followings within the party. Many members—and in particular, the formal party personnel—had patronage resources; they could award or, in some cases, remove people from jobs. In general, party organizational personnel, public officeholders, and respected citizens in the local community were found serving in the party leadership groups. This calibre of personnel permitted the groups a certain legitimacy in decision-making and the control of the formal party machinery when needed to enforce their decisions.

The data, then, support the first two hypotheses: there

[39] Frost, *op. cit.,* reported similar findings in his New Jersey study, where 93% of the county leaders interviewed had held appointive or elective office.

were informal leadership groups within the Howard County parties and in most of the other county parties studied, and these
groups primarily concern themselves with questions directly
affecting the party organization.

Instigation

To add perspective to the recruitment process, the decision-
making process of the individual candidates needs some elaboration. Each of the contenders was asked to assess his own political objectives and his immediate reasons for seeking the party
nomination. Responses to this question varied widely, but one
pattern did emerge. Most individuals reported that their desire
to receive party endorsement was not the product of an isolated
or impulsive act. Rather, their decision to enter the primary
had taken shape over a period of years.

Such a decision-making process frequently results in a
commitment to political office per se, rather than a desire to
seek one office to the exclusion of others. The decision to file
in a party primary for nomination for a specific office is dic-
tated by a potential candidate's assessment of the amount of
competition he will face, the strength of his likely opponents,
his own assets in the given contest, the effect of the race on his
long-run ambitions, and ultimately, of course, his chances of
success in the primary and the general election to follow. Before the filing deadline, the individual goes through a period
of acquiring and sifting information, and evaluating the intentions of others. Even among self-starters, there are few quick
decisions to file for office. The process of deciding is usually slow
and painful.

The specific reasons given for seeking party nomination
varied from the more general contentions such as "desire to
serve the public," found to be important among campaign
workers and convention delegates in the Marvick chapter in this
volume, to more personal incentives, the noncollective rewards
that Barnes argues help explain the political involvement of
party organizational personnel. The surprisingly few references
to broader objectives, the "community good" or a desire to
"straighten things out," lends support to the contentions of
Barnes in his chapter in this volume. The more common reasons
given for running were greater income or improved personal

position. One factory worker, for example, related an increase in his salary to his holding political office. A farmer, injured in an automobile accident, wanted another job with less physical demands than his previous one. Political considerations were also important. One candidate entered the race as a decoy, feeling his candidacy would stimulate others to run and would result in greater representation for his section of the county. Two incumbents, one inclined to seek reelection, the other reluctant, were, in their words, "nudged" into the race. And one incumbent accepted it as a matter of course that he, the office-holder, should file for renomination.

Candidates were also questioned concerning the groups most likely to be of assistance in winning nomination. Ranks were computed for a range of reference group alternatives. These evaluations were compared for the successful and unsuccessful candidates by party (Table 5). Respondents generally perceived business and professional groups to represent the greatest asset to their campaigns. Friendships with politically prominent individuals was next in order of importance. It is likely that candidates sought the advice of individuals in these areas when deciding whether to file, and probably during the campaigns also. As it turned out, contacts with politically important individuals occurred more frequently than those with any other possible category.

In relation to instigation stage contacts, it is difficult to fit each of these candidates into the Seligman typology, i.e., self-starter, party conscriptee, coopted candidate, or interest group advocate. In most cases, the recruit represented a combination of types. Some 74 per cent, twenty-three of the thirty-one Howard County candidates, were initially approached by others.[40] Of all the candidates for both of the parties, only the successful Democratic incumbents for sheriff and clerk reported no contacts at the instigation stage. None of the other candidates filed without first discussing their prospects with at least

[40] Each candidate was asked to name those who came to him about the nominations and those he himself sought out before he actually filed his candidacy. These were to be persons having some importance beyond being part of his immediate family or of holding only a potential vote. This 74% may be to some extent compared with what Bowman and Boynton, *op. cit.*, p. 675, and Eldersveld *op. cit.*, pp. 126–127, found in their respective studies of North Carolina and Massachusetts and of Detroit area party officials. Both studies reported over 50% more or less drafted into politics as a result of "outside influences."

TABLE 5

CANDIDATES' EVALUATION OF FACTORS CONTRIBUTING TO WINNING
NOMINATIONS, BY CANDIDATE SUCCESS AND PARTY.
(HOWARD COUNTY, INDIANA, 1962)

	Successful Candidates		Unsuccessful Candidates	
	Rep.	Dem.	Rep.	Dem.
Factor	Average Rank (N)	Average Rank (N)	Average Rank (N)	Average Rank (N)
Business or Professional Connections	1.4(5)	2.1(7)	2.1(7)	1.7(10)
Personal Friendships with Persons Prominent in Politics	2.2(6)	2.1(8)	2.0(6)	2.3(8)
Community Service Rendered (e.g., Community Chest Drives)	2.8(4)	3.6(5)	3.3(3)	3.8(4)
Church Connections and Activities	3.5(6)	4.3(4)	5.0(2)	2.7(7)
Family Connections	4.0(3)	4.0(2)	2.5(2)	2.8(4)
Military Record or Connection with Veterans' Organizations	4.7(3)	5.0(2)	4.0(3)	3.0(2)
Connections with or Activities in Service Clubs	4.0(1)	3.7(6)	2.3(3)	4.0(1)
Prominence in Politics of Family Members	5.0(1)	3.5(2)	3.0(2)	3.0(1)
Affiliation with Labor Organizations or Activities	5.0(1)	2.0(1)	4.0(1)	2.5(2)
Identification with a Nationality Group	0.0(0)	0.0(0)	0.0(0)	0.0(0)

two other people felt to be important. With the exception of
two unsuccessful candidates, all of the Republicans were approached by one or more persons before filing. Only six Democrats fit the pattern, and four of these lost (an incumbent

sheriff and clerk were the exceptions). The advice and support of others was an important consideration in a candidate's decision to run for office. All of the eventual winners reported others coming to them, either to make the initial suggestion or in hopes of influencing their decision.

Party-connected individuals predominated among those contacting and encouraging potential candidates. Little interest group influence was evident during the instigation period.[41] Also, very few "friends, neighbors, and fellow workers" actively contributed to a candidate's decision to file. Only one unsuccessful Democratic candidate and five Republicans, three of whom were unsuccessful, reported such contacts.

The number of opposition party members contacting potential candidates during the instigation period was surprising. A few Republicans supporting a Democrat in the general election would not be uncommon, particularly if the candidate was a personal acquaintance. Party leaders actively recruiting candidates for the other party, however, is most unusual. Yet, ten Republicans and eleven Democrats engaged in such activity.[42] There are many possible explanations for these cross-party contacts. For example, party activists in one party may encourage candidates in another in cases in which: 1. both of the parties share control of some office and compatible working relationships develop among office-holders which the incumbents do not want disturbed; 2. some leaders, dissatisfied with all of the potential candidates for an office in their party, desire someone to contest for the position that they could support; 3. factional partisans, fearing that their candidates will lose

[41] Admittedly, there may be some who are involved in party activity because of their outside group interests, but those persons classified as "political" either held some party office, had been candidates, or were long enough identified with party activity that their concerns were probably as much those of the party as those of their outside group. Therefore, some attorneys are grouped as political and some were seen as independently speaking for themselves and their profession. Or, if an active police chief was instrumental in recruiting a candidate for sheriff, he was viewed as a member of the law enforcement interest, whereas a former sheriff who was also a former county party chairman was considered political if he was reported as a contact with a potential assessor.

[42] Only persons clearly identified as party-connected were included in this category. Those of opposite party who were more clearly identified with their occupation or other interest group were so classified.

and unwilling to support a candidate of another faction, attempt to provide an alternative choice; or, 4. each party interferes with the other in hopes that weaker candidates will be nominated, making its job in the general election easier. In Howard County the most common pattern was a union of office-holders attempting to protect against disruption of an agreeable working climate by influencing nominations in both parties. Factional considerations and a general search for more appealing candidates also occurred. There was no evidence, however, of organized attempts to intentionally weaken the slate being offered by the opposition party.

Key Influential party involvement is proportionately higher for Republicans than for Democrats (Table 6). Factionalism

TABLE 6

DIRECTION AND SOURCE OF INSTIGATION-STAGE CONTACTS OF
HOWARD COUNTY CANDIDATES FOR ALL OFFICES

Source	Contacts			
	Republicans (N = 13)		Democrats (N = 18)	
	From Others	To Others	From Others	To Others
Party Connected:	24	28	25	46
Key Influentials	(12)	(18)	(5)	(16)
Top Influentials	(6)	(4)	(9)	(8)
Party Groups, Candidates and Committeemen	(6)	(6)	(11)	(22)
Interest Groups and Voter Blocs	6	1	5	12
Opposition Party	11	2	4	6
Friends, Neighbors, Fellow Employees	8	1	2	0
TOTAL	49	32	36	64

within the Democratic party that resulted in a comparative lack of party cohesion would help explain this. It is interesting to note that a larger number of Democrats (12) went outside the party to seek interest group support than Republicans (1). Overall though, both party leaders and candidates attributed little influence to such groups in the primary.

The Democratic candidates in Howard County were more "professional" in their approach to politics and appeared to have a more inclusive attitude in building primary coalitions. The Democrats, for example, had a longer record of political involvement and, as the approaches to the interest groups might suggest, attempted to cultivate every possible source of help in their races. Rather than organized groups, the Republicans relied more on "friends, neighbors, and fellow workers," an indication of their relative amateurism. Only one successful candidate reported such contacts.

Reinforcement

Once an individual has filed for candidacy, a new set of interpersonal relationships develops. Candidates are sought out by some with offers of support or, in a few cases, requests to withdraw from the contest. Candidates, of course, also attempt to enlist support from others whom they believe will help them win nomination.

Five of the winners in the Democratic primary reported that someone had approached them about their candidacies. As might be expected, the two unopposed candidates, i.e., the First District Commissioner and the Clerk of the Circuit Court, indicated that they had received no contacts. The only other winning contestant who did not receive any such reinforcement was an incumbent county commissioner. His principal opponent, a contender supported by a Democratic "out" faction, however, had many callers. The dominant party faction apparently felt such supportive activities in behalf of their man's reelection were unnecessary; a realistic appraisal as it turned out.

All but four candidates, two who lost and two who were unopposed in the Republican primary, reported reinforcement-stage contacts.

With few exceptions, after filing for office, the candidates concentrated their energies on appeals to voters. Apparently, at this stage their relationship to the Influentials was well understood and no longer of concern. As Table 7 shows, the total

TABLE 7

DIRECTION AND SOURCE OF REINFORCEMENT-STAGE CONTACTS
OF HOWARD COUNTY CANDIDATES FOR ALL OFFICES

Source	Contacts			
	Republicans		Democrats	
	(N = 13)		(N = 18)	
	From Others	To Others	From Others	To Others
Party Connected:	14	12	36	31
Key Influentials	(7)	(5)	(4)	(2)
Top Influentials	(0)	(3)	(16)	(10)
Party Groups, Candidates and Committeemen	(7)	(4)	(16)	(19)
Interest Groups and Voter Blocs	8	2	5	2
Opposition Party	2	0	8	4
Friends, Neighbors, and Fellow Employees	6	1	0	1
TOTAL	30	15	49	38

number of Republican contacts was reduced from eighty-one to forty-five after filing, suggesting that the heaviest recruitment activity took place at the instigation stage. There was less of a tendency to interfere once potential Republican aspirants had been persuaded to become candidates. The contenders themselves initiated even fewer contacts with organizational personnel, apparently feeling that the role of party people at this point was to remain neutral. Interest groups, friends, neighbors, and fellow workers still continued to seek out candidates, however.

The pattern of activity in the Democratic party was different. The number of people connected with politics who contacted candidates increased after the candidates filed as factions sought to build coalitions behind their favorites, a practice particularly noticeable among partisans below the first level. There were also a substantial number of reinforcement stage contacts initiated by Democratic candidates toward second and third level party groups. And, interestingly, Republicans continued to be involved in Democratic contests.

The total amount of interaction between candidates and supportive groups for each party is proportionately about the same. There were 187 contacts recorded for the eighteen Democratic candidates and 126 for the thirteen Republican candidates.

Apparently, the party leadership initiates most of the direct recruitment contacts. In the Republican party, this activity was almost entirely confined to the Key Influential group. In the Democratic party, Key Influentials were not as active as the Top Influentials. The average number of contacts for leaders in each party, however, was much greater for Key Influentials than for Top Influentials (Table 8). It should be noted that, for the Democrats, there was considerable activity on the part of some committeemen who were not included in the principal leadership groups. The greater number of lower level per-

TABLE 8

HOWARD COUNTY KEY INFLUENTIALS AND TOP INFLUENTIALS
COMPARED ACCORDING TO WITHIN-PARTY INFLUENCE
CONTACTS MADE WITH CANDIDATES

Party Leaders	Contacts			
	Key Influentials		Top Influentials	
	N	$\overline{X}$	N	$\overline{X}$
Republican (N = 29)	42	3.23	13	.81
Democratic (N = 30)	37	3.70	53	1.76

sonnel involved in reinforcement activity again is a function of the division of the Democratic party into three militant factions. Factional support was evident for many candidates.

The data secured from the candidates does not directly address the question of whether Key Influential leadership contacts were instigated by group design or whether they resulted from independent personal initiatives. Some clues were provided by the leaders in explaining their role in candidate selection, however. For the minority Republican party, the pattern is clear. All Key Influentials reported attending from one to four meetings during the filing period to discuss nominations. All offices were considered at these meetings and for most agreement was reached on the individuals the group would actively solicit to run and support for nomination. Contacts with prospective candidates were initiated as a result of these conferences. The leaders agreed that four candidates were recruited in this manner. A fifth office was discussed and a decision made to tacitly support a candidate who had filed on his own initiative. No action was taken on three offices, one of which was independently filed for at a later date. Decisions involving several offices at higher levels, and thus not of immediate concern to this study, were also made. None of the Republican candidacies involved incumbents. Some of the prospects contacted refused to run—specifically, four such cases occurred, and one group member claimed that he was responsible for another man withdrawing from the race for Assessor.

The leaders in the dominant, but deeply split, Democratic party reported holding no meetings specifically concerned with nominations at any point. To be sure, there were meetings of the various factions, but these were called to discuss control of the organization, not nominations. Apparently, there were enough potential candidates that organized recruitment was considered unnecessary. The party also had several incumbents seeking renomination and, while there is no agreement that incumbents are entitled to another term, they hold a campaign edge that makes serious primary opposition difficult. Democratic leaders were influential in the selection process, although they initiated few contacts with potential nominees. The response of leaders to feelers from prospective candidates had much to do with who ran.

Republican leaders de-emphasized the impact of their involvement on the nominating process. None of the leaders perceived themselves as having broad influence. Most would refer to one, two, or perhaps three offices in which they had taken a particular interest, or for which they had been assigned to discuss a race with a prospective candidate. Generally, they were more confident about their influence at the instigation stage than about their contribution to a nominee's victory. The Democratic Key Influential leadership group was even more reticent in evaluating their influence. They reported little direct involvement at instigation and even less during the reinforcement stage. And, although an attempt was made to identify "indirect" influence, in the sense that one leader might deputize someone else to make a contact, only one such incident occurred.

In summary, the foregoing reports of contacts and meetings are indicative of substantial Key Influential party leadership involvement in the Republican party at the instigation stage. The Democratic party with its less cohesive leadership structure evidenced more active lower level participation. *In toto,* many recruitment contacts were made, initiated by both the candidates and others. This pattern was particularly pronounced among successful candidates. Substantial cross-party involvement, especially that initiated by the Republican leaders, also occurred. The Democrats depended more on interest groups for non-party support, the Republicans on personal contacts. In general, there was little interest group involvement in the nominating process, however.

It is more difficult to identify those instrumental in the success of the primary candidates. Many factors—incumbency, political experience, activity within the party, general group membership—contribute to a winning nomination fight, only a few of which are discussed here. This report concentrates on identifying persons and groups represented in the recruitment process and omits assessments of a candidate's previous record or his attractiveness to voters. Nonetheless, some conclusions can be inferred. The findings of this study, in concert with others, call for caution in imputing extensive power over nominations to the formal party organizational personnel. This statement is particularly applicable at the reinforcement stage. In complementary studies of party organizations, Eldersveld found little evidence in Detroit, for example, to support the contention that an "elite" co-opted lower level party personnel, such as precinct leaders, to fortify and perpetuate their control.[43] Leege, in a study of Indiana primaries to select delegates to state conventions, found that a number of factors severely limited the control which entrenched county leaders, both formal and informal, could exercise in recruiting delegates. Once delegates were "elected," both county party officials and candidates for office felt that the chairman was subservient to the preferences of the majority of his delegations, rather than the reverse.[44] The control of these leaders over decisions of a delegation apparently is weak.

However, a clearer indication of the role of Howard County leaders is obtained from an analysis of nomination contests in which the party leadership took an active part.[45] Candidates supported by the Republican Key Influential leaders won in twenty-five such cases and lost in five. Three of the losing candidates were strongly opposed by the party leadership group. Candidates strongly favored by the Key Democratic leadership won in seventeen instances and lost in eight. While impressive, this showing did not equal that of the Republicans, suggesting a reduced effectiveness accompanied the factionalism and lower cohesion evident among Democratic leaders. Finally, most candidates of both parties, winners and losers, thought that the party leadership was active behind the scenes; successful candidates believed themselves to have received leadership support, the losers agreed, feeling that they themselves were not in official favor.[46]

In only one of the six contests in which a Democratic Key Influential was active in the Republican primary did he back a winner. The Republican Key Influentials did better in the

---

[43] Eldersveld, *op. cit.,* p. 126.

[44] David Calhoun Leege, "The Place of the Party Nominating Convention in a Representative Democracy: A Study of Power in the Indiana Democratic Party's State Nominating Conventions, 1956–62," (Indiana University, Unpublished Ph.D. Dissertation, 1965).

[45] The leaders were asked to indicate the candidates they particularly favored or opposed. The question was phrased in this manner to: 1. identify leaders whose attachments were strong enough to have prompted extra effort by a leader in behalf of a candidate; 2. to avoid the necessity of asking the leader how he voted in each case; and, 3. to permit him to express himself for a candidate of the other party. No doubt each leader interviewed made a choice by his vote in each contest.

[46] Only one of twenty-seven county chairmen interviewed reported favoring as many as two major candidates who did not win.

Democratic primary contests in which they took part, supporting three winners and three losers. One other Republican leader unsuccessfully opposed a successful Democratic nominee. It would appear that leader influence across party lines is not as effective at the reinforcement stage as it may have been at the instigation stage. There were only four primary winners of the total thirteen races in which a cross-party interest was indicated.

From the leader interviews, an index of acquaintanceship was constructed for each candidate. All Republican and most Democratic winners appeared to be better acquainted with their respective first level leaders than were the losers. A wide variety of contacts helps a candidate to win office. Apparently, it is equally important to know the "right" people. Successful candidates were better acquainted with a larger number of leaders; they also more accurately perceived who the more important people were. Table 9 supports this interpretation. The candi-

TABLE 9

IDENTIFICATION OF HOWARD COUNTY KEY INFLUENTIALS BY
SUCCESSFUL AND UNSUCCESSFUL CANDIDATES, 1962[47]

Average Score for All Candidates	Candidates		
	Successful	Unsuccessful	(N)
Republicans	41%	19%	(13)
Democrats	41%	25%	(18)
N	14	17	

dates were asked to identify party influentials. From these reports, percentage scores were computed for each candidate according to the number of Key Influential leaders he was able to identify. The successful candidates in both parties were able

[47] On the Republican ticket there were no unsuccessful candidates for judge or prosecutor and no candidates for one commissioner post and for county clerk.

to name a greater percentage of Key Influentials than were the unsuccessful candidates.[48]

Conclusion

This chapter has examined at close range the process of selecting candidates for county office. The emphasis has been on the role of the party leadership as a recruitment vehicle. The findings reported here must be considered as primarily the result of a single case study; as such they cannot justifiably be extended beyond the case. Still, despite small numbers, the cumulative pieces of evidence point to the existence of small informal leadership groups in Howard County and in comparable Indiana counties.

Through reputational models, the more common research focus on formal party positions can be fruitfully expanded to encompass informal, yet potentially equally powerful, influence structures. Informal groups of individuals apparently work closely with the formal organizations.[49] The most visible marriage of the formal and informal party influence structures occurred in this study through the office of county chairman. Because of his importance, at least in Indiana, the incumbent party official at this level is included as a member of most informal party decision-making groups. The chief concern of these less visible groups was with party affairs—candidates for office and the operation of the local organization. Broader policy questions were seldom considered. The full impact of the activities

[48] A Democratic candidate could name as many as ten Democratic Key Influentials. If he named only three, he was given a score of 30%. Average percentage scores were not significantly altered when figures for incumbents were removed or when different combinations of offices were compared.

[49] If anything, political recruitment activities probably over-estimate the number of people actively involved in party decision-making. Nomination decisions call forth *comparatively* large numbers of people, each with an interest in who will run for a particular office. In Howard County, for example, one hundred and thirty-eight different people participated directly in selecting Democratic candidates and ninety-nine participated in Republican recruitment. Most participants, however, confined their activity to one or two candidates. Only the leadership groups were generally active, suggestive of their overall influence on party affairs.

of the informal groups identified in this study upon community political affairs is not clear. These groups did constitute a significant phenomenon in the local party organizations analyzed. Their influence within the party organization, and the community, in other localities warrants continued research, possibly along the conceptual lines of this study.

In a postscript to his Oregon study, Seligman concluded that recruitment agencies serve as the principal vehicles for candidate entry into politics.[50] There is a pressing need for comparative analyses of such recruitment groups, the roles they play, and their interrelationships with other groups and individuals within the party framework. Such research might refine the presently crude notions of the dynamics of the nomination process.

[50] Seligman, *op. cit.*, p. 86.

NINE

The Middlemen of Politics

Dwaine Marvick

University of California, Los Angeles

IN MODERN THEORY about political systems, two human components receive most of the attention—central figures in the decision-making processes of public life and ordinary figures in the
opinion-forming processes of private life. Political leaders occupy the public stage; politicized citizens are an occasionally
attentive audience. What tend to be neglected are the interstitial
components—the cadre: those who man the machinery of government and the apparatuses of politics.

As attention shifts from the central actors to the rest of
the cast, it is the roles and not the actors themselves that count.
Bit players are substitutable; what matters is the instrumental
character of the tasks they perform. In turn, these roles are
located in organizational structures and institutional processes,
inside government, in the political arena, and in other contexts that articulate political interests. Supporting roles are not
peopled, however; commentary ranges ambiguously from how
supporting roles *ought to be* performed to how they *must have
been* performed, judging from results. What is largely missing
is behavioral evidence of how the middlemen of politics do
function, why they do so, and with what consequences.[1]

---

[1] A number of relevant codifications have been made, which point
up the argument here made, that research has concentrated on the
top and the bottom of the political order. See Wendell Bell, Richard
J. Hill and Charles Wright, *Public Leadership* (San Francisco:
Chandler Publishing Co., 1961); Herbert Hyman, *Political Socializa-*

What relevance to the comparative study of political elites
has a discussion about middlemen in politics? An answer requires three distinctions: (a) elite structures are organized to
wield effective power; publics hold only a formal claim to
power, perhaps translatable into effective power by the symbolic
contrivance of a genuinely competitive election, or by linkage
to an elite structure;[2] (b) inter-elite analysis is necessary because an *ad hoc* representation of components from various elite
structures will usually be found in the political arena whenever
a significant public issue (i.e., one which substantially affects
the public) is nearing a decision point;[3] (c) intra-elite analysis
is needed because those in top elite positions differ functionally
(in ways that need to be clarified) from those in lower strata of
the same elite structure. Top elites depend upon, often derive
from, and not infrequently are coerced by those who may be
called middlemen, or cadres. Top elite recruitment and training
are typically handled by cadres;[4] top elite deliberation is rou-

---

tion: A Study in the Psychology of Political Behavior (New York:
The Free Press of Glencoe, 1959); Robert Lane, *Political Life* (New
York: The Free Press of Glencoe, 1959); and Lester Milbrath,
Political Participation (Chicago: Rand McNally and Co., 1965).

[2] The distinction between "effective" and "formal" power follows
Harold D. Lasswell and Abraham Kaplan, *Power and Society* (New
Haven: Yale University Press, 1950), especially pp. 200–205. On
the significance of competitive elections as devices vesting effective
power in the public, see Joseph A. Schumpeter, *Capitalism, Socialism
and Democracy* (New York: Harper, 1947), Chapters 21–23; Robert
A. Dahl, *A Preface to Democratic Theory* (Chicago: University of
Chicago Press, 1956); and Morris Janowitz and Dwaine Marvick,
Competitive Pressure and Democratic Consent (Chicago: Quadrangle
Books, 1964).

[3] A recent survey of elite research is Harold Lasswell's "Agenda for
the Study of Political Elites," in Dwaine Marvick, ed., *Political
Decision Makers* (New York: The Free Press of Glencoe, 1961). In
discussing elite systems in industrialized democratic politics, he
points to the need for analyses of elite alignment at pre-outcome
stages of decision-making processes (p. 279). See also Suzanne
Keller, *Beyond the Ruling Class: Strategic Elites in Modern Society*
(New York: Random House, 1963).

[4] Zbigniew Brzezinski and Samuel P. Huntington, in "Cincinnatus
and the Appartchik," *World Politics,* 16 (October, 1963), pp. 52–78,
make an extended comparison of Soviet and American political
leaders as typical products of contrasting grooming processes. Tu-
torial relationships are explicated usefully by Anthony H. M. Kirk-
Greene, in "Bureaucratic Cadres in a Traditional Milieu," in James
S. Coleman, ed., *Education and Political Development* (Princeton:

tinely shaped by cadres;[5] top elite survival and success are commonly dependent upon cadres.[6] Yet research into these intra-elite relationships has been long neglected. Perhaps because they concern the internal dynamics of particular elite structures, their study may seem less urgent than the analysis of inter-elite maneuvering and struggle, on the one hand, or the study of links between particular elites and the masses, on the other hand.

In any event, these objectives should be high on any agenda for the comparative study of political elites: (a) to think through the set of functional interdependencies and historical trends in leader-cadre relationships; (b) to glean the knowledge available in published work and existing empirical

---

Princeton University Press, 1965). Morris Janowitz, *The Professional Soldier* (New York: The Free Press of Glencoe, 1960), contains a systematic analysis of what grooming the next generation of a functional elite involves. Technical and managerial elites—including diplomatic, military and other civil bureaucratic elites—acquire their skills and knowledge in specialized learning situations and over long time spans. It is not surprising that a political elite should be measurably easier to replace than functional elites; see Lewis J. Edinger, "Post-Totalitarian Leadership: Elites in the German Federal Republic," *American Political Science Review*, 54 (March, 1960), pp. 58–82.

[5] Studies of modern bureaucracy have long emphasized the notion of a decision-making process which produces an organizational product. For recent case studies involving the interaction of political and functional elites which are explicitly concerned with processes of "social choice" from which a commitment results without a "decision" being made, see Charles E. Lindblom, *The Intelligence of Democracy: Decision Making Through Mutual Adjustment* (New York: Macmillan Co., 1965); and Edward Banfield, *Political Influence* (New York: The Free Press of Glencoe, 1961). A somewhat different discussion of relationships within complex decision-making processes is found in Robert Dahl's *Who Governs?* (New Haven: Yale University Press, 1961). The *1984*-like implications of competent cadres wherever needed are explored by Michael Young, *The Rise of the Meritocracy* (Baltimore: Penguin Books, 1960).

[6] Examples which point up the significance of cadre groups—the state bureaucracy, the military, the secret police, and the party cadre—are frequent in studies of community power and in comparative politics. See especially John Wilson Lewis, "Party Cadres in Communist China" in James S. Coleman, *op. cit.;* Myron Weiner, *Politics of Scarcity: Public Pressure and Political Response in India* (Chicago: University of Chicago Press, 1963); and Robert Agger, Daniel Goldrich, and Bert E. Swanson, *The Rulers and the Ruled: Political Power and Impotence in American Communities* (New York: John Wiley and Sons, 1964).

studies; (c) to learn what kinds of people do what tasks, develop what attitudes, and acquire what skills while working in the political infra-structure; and (d) to understand more of what the political arena looks like to those in the middle sectors.[7]

Inter-Elite Analysis

The contemporary history of a modern nation furnishes a rich and varied kaleidoscope of events and personalities, issues and stategies. Political scientists, for the most part, describe and analyze that unfolding history in conventional language, avoiding charges of jargon wherever possible. Why then has there been so much renewed interest in "elite" studies?

Two answers seem relevant. To many, institutional analysis would have been preferred. It takes time, however, to describe the working of the decision-making institutions and mechanisms which give distinctive form to a country's political arena. As a temporary expedient, phrases like "political elites," "alien elites," "bureaucratic elites" or equivalents are pressed into use.[8] The impulse to use functional terms may thus largely be a simple desire to communicate with someone not well-schooled in the country's legal and institutional maze, but who can be brought to an appreciation of some political development if make-shift terms are employed. A survey of academic research shows little sustained or deliberate use of functional models. Although "elite" has considerable vogue, most who use the concept are not consciously seeking to test or reformulate functional theory. Nor is it clear that they should be doing so.

A different set of considerations is involved, however, when serious efforts are made to execute comparative studies of

[7] The contextural determinants of leadership have long been studied in small group research, but there are formidable difficulties in applying those findings to political arenas. See Sidney Verba, *Small Groups and Political Behavior* (Princeton: Princeton University Press, 1961); and Amitai Etzioni, *Complex Organizations* (New York: Holt, Rinehart and Winston, 1961). A suggestive study is Terrance K. Hopkins, *The Exercise of Influence in Small Groups* (Totowa: Bedminster Press, 1964).

[8] An illustration is a collection of six useful articles on African elites, all of which use the term as a convenience in a manner quite different from the lead article by S. Nadel, "African Elites," *International Social Science Bulletin*, No. 3 (1956), pp. 413–424.

political systems.[9] Institutional analysis is set aside deliberately, on grounds that too close a concentration on institutional arrangements and practices will inhibit and even distort efforts to understand the larger political scene. The political and governmental elites are assumed to be sufficiently competent to operate the institutional machinery on which they spent their apprenticeships; if not, it seems probable that the institutional arrangements will be changed, not the elites. Especially in a rapidly changing society, the formal arrangements of government varies from one regime to another. More stability is often discernible by functional than by conventional analysis.[10] Note Lasswell's comment in 1952:

> The scope of comparative politics is to demonstrate the equivalency of diverse patterns as well as the occurrence of identical patterns. . . . The contextural approach directs attention to the support groups active in political situations, and to the values, expectations, and sources of information on the basis of which evaluations are made. Very often the significant result will be to show how a given political pattern is kept the 'same' throughout a given period by varying constellations of support elements; how the values that enter into the calculation of these elements manage to compensate for shifts in the role of any value; and how the expectations that remain steady depend upon compensating sources of information.[11]

In recent studies of the patterns of change in emergent societies, attention is more systematically directed to the im-

[9] The deliberate use of functional categories for ordering evidence and formulating conclusions was given strong impetus in 1960 with the publication of Gabriel Almond and James S. Coleman, eds., *The Politics of the Developing Areas* (Princeton: Princeton University Press, 1960). Since then perhaps the most influential contribution has been Gabriel Almond and Sidney Verba, *The Civic Culture* (Boston: Little, Brown and Co., 1963), which demonstrated the possibilities of quantitative macro-political analysis in functional terms.

[10] For a case study consideration of functional continuity, see Leslie H. Palmier, *Social Status and Power in Java* (New York: Humanities Press, Inc., 1960).

[11] "Comments on the Seminar Report on Comparative Politics," *American Political Science Review*, 47 (September, 1953), pp. 661–663.

pact of technology, urbanization, mass communications media and bureaucratic organization on the social stratification system: that is, on the distribution of valued conditions and scarce resources. Every society has a complex set of mechanisms and processes by which the system consciously seeks to maintain and/or change itself in the face of inescapable historical pressures. The problems of inter-elite analysis arise because, actually and potentially, a variety of power structures in a society can move to invoke some significant machinery for social control.

Lasswell's formulation of "elite" theory recognized this functional relativity.[12] The term "elite" has been used to refer to those who have the most of what there is to get that is widely valued in some profession (e.g., the legal elits),[13] institutional context (e.g., the fashion elite),[14] population segment (e.g., the Negro elite),[15] organized process (e.g., the labor elite),[16]

[12] Lasswell and Kaplan, *op. cit., passim.* An earlier statement was Harold Lasswell, *Politics: Who Gets What, When, How* (New York: McGraw-Hill Co., 1936).

[13] See especially Heinz Eulau and John D. Sprague, *Lawyers in Politics: A Study in Professional Convergence* (Indianapolis: Bobbs-Merrill Co., 1964). The professional group, with its control over standards of performance, training and advancement, has special relevance to the argument of this paper, which sees the crux of the party cadre issue as being the extent to which cadres acquire the hallmarks and preoccupations of "professionalized" people. See William J. Goode, "Community Within a Community: The Professions," *American Sociological Review,* 22 (April, 1957), p. 194–200.

[14] See Elihu Katz and Paul Lazarsfeld, *Personal Influence* (Glencoe, Ill.: The Free Press, 1955), for systematic comparison of marketing leaders, fashion leaders, movie leaders and public affairs leaders among the female population of an Illinois city. Critiques of "Power Structure" studies often stress the presence of more than one elite structure in a community or other institutionalized context: Lawrence J. R. Herson, "In the Footsteps of Community Power," *American Political Science Review,* 55 (December, 1961), pp. 817–830; or Norton Long, "The Local Community as an Ecology of Games," *American Journal of Sociology,* 64 (November, 1958), pp. 251–261. See Nelson W. Polsby, *Community Power and Political Theory* (New Haven: Yale University Press, 1964) for an extended discussion.

[15] See Dwaine Marvick, "The Political Socialization of the American Negro" in Roberta Sigel, ed., *Political Socialization: Its Role in the Political Process* (Philadelphia: The Annals of The American Academy of Political and Social Science, September, 1965), pp. 112–127; also E. Franklin Frazer, *Black Bourgeoisie* (Glencoe, Ill.: The Free Press, 1957); and James Q. Wilson, *Negro Politics: The Search for Leadership* (New York: The Free Press of Glencoe, 1961).

[16] See Seymour M. Lipset, Martin Trow, and James S. Coleman, *Union Democracy* (Glencoe, Ill.: The Free Press, 1956).

or among a functionally-similar set of people (e.g., the intellectual elite).[17] The first crucial point is that different elites do not normally function in the same organizational or institutional matrix, although they are sometimes represented in a common political arena. The second crucial point is that much significant machinery for social control can be invoked over limited domains and on a decentralized basis. This is clear in advanced, pluralist societies; it is more easily overlooked in traditional and transitional systems.

Some corollaries should be noted. Different elite structures in the same society do not necessarily develop the same skills, expectations, desires or attitudes. They are not necessarily animated by similar motives, nor gratified equally by their status achievement, nor called upon to play elite roles a similar portion of the time.

Any elite is perhaps most usefully defined as a status structure—specifically, all those in a society, functional organization, community, or population segment who are conspicuously or notoriously understood to be organized to wield effective power, where power means making decisions to control the allocation of valued conditions and scarce resources.

An elite, thus functionally identified, need not be a social group whose members think alike, have a common sub-culture, or interact harmoniously. Probably, however, elite members are aware that the general public attributes to them distinctive status as insiders—people with presumably effective voices in group decision-making processes.[18]

Functionally, elites are internally differentiated. One can distinguish at least between the larger group, or "cadre," who are typically specialized to implement the specific ends of their organization, and the smaller group of top leaders, or "nu-

[17] See especially E. A. Shils, "Toward a Modern Intellectual Community," in James S. Coleman, *op. cit.* Two examples are Carl E. Schorski, "Politics and the Psyche in *fin de siècle* Vienna," *American Historical Review*, 66 (July, 1961), pp. 930–946; and Y. C. Wang, "Intellectuals and Society in China, 1860–1949," *Comparative Studies in Society and History*, 3 (July, 1961), pp. 395–426.

[18] Much empirical research in recent years has focused on the power structures of local communities. See Morris Janowitz, ed., *Community Political Systems* (New York: The Free Press of Glencoe, 1961), for a representative collection of systematic contributions. The points here emphasized have been obscured because the controversy over research techniques has given them a polemical significance. See Nelson Polsby, *op. cit.*, for a convenient point of ingress.

cleus."[19] These top leaders are expected to consider both the internal and external problems of survival and/or development for their organization, community, group, or polity. "They are oriented toward the broadest social issues, including innovation, self scrutiny, and inter-relations with other elites."[20] On them also rest the necessities of choosing strategies to meet those issues, bolstering morale in their organization, and of screening candidates for elite status.[21]

These then are some of the questions that should be raised in any systematic and comparative study of elites: (1) Who are the members of a nation's functional elites at a given time juncture? (2) What are the chief differences in social origins and career patterns between members of the nucleus and cadre? (3) For the cadre, how professionalized is its outlook, how specialized is its training, how standardized is its indoctrination, how effective is its performance? (4) For the elite nucleus, how well is it performing the crucial functions which will determine the growth or decline of its group as a whole? (5) For the polity, what pattern of involvement by different elite structures is probable on a given issue, or at a given level of governance, or in a particular institutional context, or on a certain structured occasion? (6) For the political participants (elite and cadre alike), concerned with a pending occasion, what potential complications have become remote and what are the operative restrictions on maneuvering?

To identify functional elites empirically and to relativize the term pragmatically are research procedures that do not unduly complicate analysis. Rather, they are indispensable procedures that reflect the disjunctive realities of any complex society. Historical forces are seen as eroding and undermining old patterns of access to the valued conditions of life, and even changing what things are valued.[22] On the other hand, conscious, if groping, efforts to invoke new patterns of access are

[19] Morris Janowitz, "Social Stratification and the Comparative Analysis of Elites," *Explorations in Entrepreneurial History,* 8 (Winter Supplement, 1956), pp. 6–11.

[20] *Ibid.,* p. 9.

[21] See Philip Selznick, *Leadership in Administration* (New York: Harper & Row, 1957); also Harold Lasswell, *Power and Personality* (New York: Viking Press, 1948), especially Chapters 8 and 9, on leadership principles.

[22] See Robert C. Angell, "Social Values of Soviet and American Elites: Content Analysis of Elite Media," *Journal of Conflict Resolution,* 8 (December, 1964), pp. 330–385. Also David McClelland, *The Achieving Society* (Princeton: D. Van Nostrand Co., 1961).

made by the top members of various groups and communities within a social system as well as by political leaders.[23]

It follows from these conceptual distinctions that the operative elite structures in the political arena will vary. To anticipate the political arena's composition—whether the arena is defined by level, process, or issue—is the only way to clarify what is happening. The key problems become: *what* mechanisms of control over access to *which* valued conditions have priority with *which* strata of *what* elite structures?

In any case, the functional approach is meaningful only if the system goals affected by the pending decision in the political arena can be specified, the effects measured, and the repercussions on each elite evaluated in terms of survival and/or development criteria. There has to be a substantively meaningful problem confronting those in the political arena before an analysis of the *arena's* elite composition is efficient.

This approach starts with a broad area of public policy, and examines relevant elite behavior pragmatically in a succession of institutionalized political arenas. For the analysis of public policy formulation and control, Almond's typology is convenient: (a) the political elite, which includes party leaders, elected officials and some high appointees, (b) the bureaucratic elite, including that specialized portion whose policy domain gives it a special interest, familiarity, and continuing contact with related policy problems, (c) the interest elites, including both the spokesmen and the bureaucratic staff of voluntary private associations concerned with the pending decision, (d) the communications elites, including not only the mass media personnel but the notables in every community who repeat, edit and evaluate news about relevant political developments.[24]

Intra-Elite Analysis

A cadre is an elite stratum, typically larger than the elite nucleus, specifically confined to those who are expected to perform instrumental roles in furthering the organization's goals.

[23] See Lucian Pye, *Politics, Personality, and Nation Building: Burma's Search for Identity* (New Haven: Yale University Press, 1962), for an analysis of these complexities in a transitional period for a whole society.

[24] Gabriel Almond, *The American People and Foreign Policy* (New York: Frederick A. Praeger, 1950), pp. 139–140.

The term "cadre" is further limited to those who provide the skeleton staff of an organization, capable of recruiting, training, and organizing additional members. In addition to jobs tailored to the organization's specific work, the instrumental roles include managerial, liaison, staging, coordinating, planning, research, and similar tasks, experience and skill in which are transferrable from one context to another.

The activity patterns which result from cadre efforts do not necessarily have efficient functional consequences. Every elite structure is organized to surmount practical difficulties of access, timing, finances, publicity, housekeeping, and so forth. Emergencies arise, an external threat is posed, a top figure decides to innovate. It is necessary to expect persistent (and sometimes demoralizing) problems of incompetence, apathy, disjunctiveness, instability, and disloyalty, especially in the ranks of voluntary cadres. At the same time, training, indoctrination and improvisation are among the familiar methods by which organized activities are mounted, sustained and improved upon, even though the available cadre were initially considered inadequate to the task.[25]

Originally the term cadre was a military concept, signifying the skeleton organization of a base or fighting unit competent to train recruits and create new units.[26] This notion of a small permanent core of trained personnel who could provide the basis for rapid expansion, should war or other need arise, fitted Lenin's specifications for an army of professional revolutionaries. The term was taken over, and explicitly used to designate the trained, disciplined, dedicated party agent manning a post in the apparatus. In Communist parlance, the "elite party" consists of "leading cadres" and "activists" or ordinary cadres; the "mass party" is made up of simple members of the proletariat and a variable number of "opportunists."

[25] The most extensive and satisfactory treatment of these complexities is Samuel J. Eldersveld's *Political Parties: A Behavioral Analysis* (Chicago: Rand McNally and Co., 1964). See also Phillip Abrams and Alan Little, "The Young Activists in British Politics," *British Journal of Sociology*, 16 (December, 1965), pp. 315–333.

[26] See Morris Janowitz, *Sociology and the Military Establishment* (New York: Russell Sage Foundation, 1959), for a careful survey of the problems. Also P. E. Razzell, "Social Origins of Officers in the Indian and British Home Army," *British Journal of Sociology*, 14 (September, 1963), pp. 248–260, for an interesting empirical inquiry.

Selznick has described in detail what the communists seek to accomplish by changing simple adherents into deployable personnel.[27]

The work of two other scholars has special relevance. One of the manifold results of Lasswell's famous definition, that elites are those who have the most of what there is to get, was to produce a number of empirical studies of cadres. Lasswell held that within any profession, organization, community, or group, it was possible to identify the elite, and go on to analyze the screening process by which individuals acquired and retained elite status. In doing research along these lines, typically one looks for the organizational matrix or pattern which gives form to the elite group. Having specified the rudiments of hierarchical or harmonic order plus a "work flow" sequence, these studies tended to focus on "those who did most of what there was to do"—which means they tended to include many cadres, only some of whom would qualify as top elite figures.[28]

Duverger, in his widely read *Political Parties* (1953), introduced a quite different usage for the phrase "cadre party." While a mass party is one that takes great pains to train and deploy its members who are expected to pay dues and from whose number a new elite is being fashioned, in Duverger's formulation a "cadre party" strictly speaking has no members. Ordinary voters may think of themselves as supporters or adherents of such a party, but in no genuine sense do they make any serious commitment. Those who become activists simply are a grouping of notables who make the necessary preparations for elections, and who keep in touch with the candidates and,

---

[27] Philip Selznick, *The Organizational Weapon* (Glencoe, Ill.: The Free Press, 1952). In *The Dynamics of Communism in Eastern Europe* (Princeton: Princeton University Press, 1961), Richard V. Burks demonstrates the continued importance of ethnic minority status and urban-rural sensitivities in the recruitment to party ranks. While specialized training, permanent status, and prolonged indoctrination are often held to be the ingredients which produce "deployable personnel," these findings suggest that the motives of even dedicated cadres may have little to do with communist doctrine. See also Gabriel Almond, *The Appeals of Communism* (Princeton: Princeton University Press, 1954).

[28] See, for example, Robert M. Marsh, *The Mandarins: The Circulation of Elites in China, 1600–1900* (New York: The Free Press of Glencoe, 1961); a critical appraisal of elite career-pattern studies is Ralph Ross, "Elites and the Methodology of Politics," *Public Opinion Quarterly*, 16 (Spring, 1952), pp. 27–32.

later, the incumbent parliamentarians. Others may support such a "cadre grouping" if they desire; whether they can also become welcome members of a "cadre circle" in such a party is a separate and difficult question.

To summarize, both the terms "elite" and "cadre" have historical associations that make them normatively suspect and cognitively confusing. Must every polity have a "political aristocracy"? The term elite, although those using it often strive to give it functional meaning, often tends to imply that assumption. Must every serious political movement create a disciplined, dedicated, quasi-secret organizational weapon? The term cadre often creates that implication, although those using it typically mean to designate only the available middlemen, leaving it to be empirically established how competent and disciplined they are or need to be for the task at hand. Add to this two special points of confusion: following Lasswell's definition of "elite," a body of research reporting on personnel many of whom were only cadres has tended to build up; following Duverger's usage, the phrase "cadre party" has been pre-empted for bourgeois elite parties.

Max Weber saw that bureaucratization of public life—governmental and political—was favorable to democratization, since making it possible to "live off" government or politics opened careers to previously excluded groups.[29] One danger was that those whose vocation was in government or politics would not be animated by the disinterested motives said to be the stimulus of "notables" devoted voluntarily to public affairs, whose livelihood was not immediately at stake when public decisions had to be taken. Another danger concerned the effects on one's frame of reference which might result from the continuous involvement in public decision-making, made necessary by one's vocation. Weber distinguished between those who live off and those who live for politics; a corresponding distinction is needed between those who are continuously politicized and those only sporadically or segmentally involved in public affairs.

Discussing the difference between revolutionary and established parties, Norton Long has pointed up the segmental commitment of a typical "established-party" politician:[30]

[29] Hans Gerth and C. W. Mills, eds., *From Max Weber: Essays in Sociology* (New York: Oxford University Press, 1946), pp. 224–228.
[30] Norton Long, *The Polity* (Chicago: Rand McNally and Co., 1962), pp. 8–9.

". . . For him politics is perhaps a profession, but in addition he is not without other opportunities for securing a livelihood. Retirement from public office is not an irreparable disaster. He may hope with some reason to move a notch or two higher in the social scale and retire amid the upper classes. A powerful position in state office is not his ultimate dream. His attitude is fundamentally civilian."

V. O. Key, in much of his work, argued that a large part of the explanation of how democratic regimes functioned is to be found in the motives, values, rules, expectations, and circumstances of the "political influentials." He proposed a simple "elitist" theory—that the values and motives of the political activists constitute a distinct subculture: "Processes of indoctrination internalize such norms among those who are born to or climb to positions of power and leadership; they serve as standards of action, which are reinforced by a social discipline among the political activists."[31] What must be the modal norms minimally followed by "the ruling classes of a democratic order" and what variations and lapses can be tolerated: these are among the points he urges as research questions.

The term "middlemen of politics" refers to the occupants of a wide range of varied positions in a going political system. There are persistent motives and purposes engendered and rekindled in a modern pluralist society which cause perhaps every twentieth person to enter politics actively, work at it, accept its terms and sometimes wish to rise in it.[32] Moreover, there are both recurrent and emergent manpower needs in the institutional processes ancillary to popular control of government; these manpower needs prompt those in politics to recruit

[31] V. O. Key, *Public Opinion and American Democracy* (New York: Alfred A. Knopf, 1962), p. 537.

[32] See the cross-national studies of politicization, as disclosed by sample surveys of electoral opinion: Gabriel Almond and Sidney Verba, *op. cit.;* Angus Campbell and Henry Valen, "Party Identification in Norway and the United States," *Public Opinion Quarterly,* 25 (Winter, 1961), pp. 505–525; and Philip Converse and Georges Dupeux, "Politicization of the Electorate in France and the United States," *Public Opinion Quarterly,* 26 (Spring, 1962), pp. 1–26. A useful collection is Paul Tillett, ed., *The Political Vocation* (New York: Basic Books, 1965).

others, offer them appropriate rewards and gratifications, and help some to rise politically.[33]

But relatively little sustained work has been done in studying the intermediate strata in the politics. This is so despite intellectual genuflections which acknowledge the importance of "the middlemen of politics." The cadre, the militants, the active campaign workers, the delegates to conventions: it is often observed that these people do most of what has to be done to sustain a country's basic political processes. Students of political phenomena, however, have little evidence and largely untested concepts for studying the middlemen of politics, in this or any other country.[34]

There is little available that permits us to specify the moti-

---

[33] See Sidney Verba, "Organizational Membership and Democratic Consensus," *Journal of Politics,* 27 (August, 1965), pp. 467–497; and, also, Robert O. Byrd, "Characteristics of Candidates for Election in a Country Approaching Independence: The Case of Uganda," *Midwest Journal of Political Science,* 7 (February, 1963), pp. 1–27; and Heinz Eulau and David Koff, "Occupational Mobility and Political Career," *Western Political Quarterly,* 15 (September, 1962), pp. 507–521.

[34] Systematic work on legislators, their backgrounds and perspectives as well as their work and style as political figures is farther advanced. See John C. Wahlke, Heinz Eulau, William Buchanan and Leroy Ferguson, *Legislative System* (New York: John Wiley and Sons, 1962) for a comprehensive report on four state legislatures. Other relevant studies are James David Barber, *The Lawmakers: Recruitment and Adaption to Legislative Life* (New Haven: Yale University Press, 1964); Donald R. Matthews, *The Social Background of Political Decision-Makers* (Garden City, N.Y.: Doubleday and Company, Inc., 1954); and *U.S. Senators and Their World* (Chapel Hill: University of North Carolina Press, 1960); and a symposium on organizational problems by Ralph Huitt ("Democratic Party Leadership in the Senate," pp. 333–344), Nicholas Masters ("Committee Assignments in the House of Representatives," pp. 345–357), and Charles O. Jones ("Representation in Congress: The Case of the House Agriculture Committee, pp. 358–367), in the *American Political Science Review,* 55 (June, 1961). For England, see Austin Ranney, *Pathways to Parliament: Candidate Selection in Britain* (Madison: University of Wisconsin Press, 1965); and Samuel E. Finer, H. B. Berrington and D. J. Bartholomew, *Backbench Opinion in the House of Commons, 1955–59* (Long Island City: Pergamon Press, 1961). Consult also the special issue of the *International Social Science Journal,* 13 (1961) on "The Parliamentary Profession," pp. 513–649, with articles on France, Israel, Italy, Britain, the United States and the U.S.S.R.

vational considerations of the politically active,[35] to demonstrate how their outlook and affiliations shape decision-making processes or compare with the top and bottom of a political order,[36] or to differentiate among the skills and attitudes affected by advancement through intermediate levels of political life.[37]

Characteristically, however, there is little predictability about political advancement. Both the frequency and the range of opportunities vary capriciously; at any political moment a diversity of people are found working at overlapping and interconnected tasks. A number of convenient and plausible assumptions about political life turn out to be doubtful. It is not really even plausible that, in politics, everyone entering at the bottom wants to get to the top—or even, for that matter, to the upper levels of the political apparatus. It is not often true that the manpower needed for the episodically-used machinery of election campaigns is secured by systematic recruitment and training of personnel. Nor does the manpower need typically lead to an increase in material rewards—patronage, favors, or fees— to ensure what is needed; if it did, it is not clear the appeal

[35] See the useful survey, now somewhat dated, by Wendell Bell, *et al., Public Leadership, op. cit.*

[36] Important exceptions are Samuel J. Eldersveld, *op. cit.;* Herbert McClosky, Paul J. Hoffman, and Rosemary O'Hara, "Issue Conflict and Consensus Among Party Leaders and Followers," *American Political Science Review*, 54 (June, 1960), pp. 406–427; and Daniel Katz and Samuel J. Eldersveld, "The Impact of Local Party Activity upon the Electorate," *Public Opinion Quarterly*, 25 (Spring, 1961), pp. 1–24. Also of interest for their conceptual innovations are Morris Rosenberg's "Self Esteem and Concern with Public Affairs," *Public Opinion Quarterly*, 25 (Summer, 1962), pp. 1–24; Robert Agger, Marshall Goldstein, and Stanley Pearl, "Political Cynicism: Measurement and Meaning," *Journal of Politics*, 13 (August, 1961), pp. 477– 506; and Richard Rose, "The Political Ideas of British Party Activists," *American Political Science Review*, 56 (June, 1962), pp. 360– 371.

[37] See Harold D. Lasswell, "The Selective Effect of Personality on Political Participation," in Richard Cristie and Marie Jahoda, eds., *Studies in the Scope and Method of the 'The Authoritarian Personality'* (Glencoe, Ill.: The Free Press, 1954); and the old but suggestive article by J. P. Roche and S. Sachs, "The Bureaucrat and the Enthusiast: An Exploration of the Leadership of Social Movements," *Western Political Quarterly*, 8 (June, 1955), pp. 248–261. The absence of longitudinal studies of political middlemen is probably the most serious gap. See Morris Janowitz, "The Systematic Analysis of Political Biography," *World Politics*, 6 (April, 1954), pp. 405–420.

would be enough. It is not commonly true, either, that political careers regularly follow a simple ladder from less exacting, less significant or poorly paid posts to more demanding, more important and well paid jobs.[38]

Studies of inter-elite struggle and accommodation have reached a stage where a paradigm of the analytical problem is possible. The important research problems in intra-elite (i.e., elite-cadre) analysis have not been developed with the same clarity.

Historically, political democracy has depended in part on what Max Weber saw as the bureaucratization of public life. Only when positions in politics as well as in government were sufficiently well paid to provide vocations for poor men were those without independent incomes going to be active participants in the political arena; unless a man born with poor "life chances" could live off politics, he would have to forego a full-time career, therein leaving the field to others. The argument needs some modifications, to be sure; it is not at all clear that people want to be represented by "one of their own" nor is it certain he will champion their cause more effectively. A democracy's top political elite might well be composed of men who live for politics but not off it. A crucial question is whether a democracy's political cadres can be largely unpaid volunteers. In what follows, findings from two studies of American party cadres are used to highlight some distinctive features of their outlook and relations. One is a study of active campaign workers, Democrats and Republicans, in three southern California assembly districts in 1956; the other is a study of Democratic national convention delegates from the ten biggest northern states in 1960.

Studying Self-Recruited Cadres

Special difficulties arise in develcping a strategy for studying the involvement, activity and outlook of American party

---

[38] See "The Legislative Career," by Heinz Eulau, in Wahlke, *et al.*, *op. cit.*, pp. 69–134, for a consideration of these points; also Avery Leiserson, *Parties and Politics* (New York: Alfred A. Knopf, 1958), especially Chapter 6; and Dean Mann, "The Selection of Federal Political Executives," *American Political Science Review*, 58 (March, 1964), pp. 81–99.

cadres. Since a systematic, empirically-based literature about the motivations and perspectives of party middlemen has been largely unavailable, political scientists have perhaps tended to describe those who carry the burdens of party work either too cynically—harking back to the days of ward heelers, party hacks, and "honest graft"—or too idealistically—invoking optimistic, egalitarian and liberal prescriptions of what ought to animate those who seek to run the machinery. In either case, there is a tendency to describe their motives and performances in merely plausible ways; too often, contradictory analyses seem equally warranted from the evidence available.

Pragmatically, investigations were oriented towards rank-and-file personnel: in one study, people who voluntarily gave their time and effort to do precinct work during an election campaign; in the other study, people who voluntarily journeyed at considerable expense (as representatives of their state or local party groups, they were very seldom travelling on party expense accounts) to Los Angeles for a national nominating convention.

By extrapolating from studies of opinion formation and voting behavior, one could infer that party cadres were largely to be understood as unusually interested citizens. The casual partisanship shown by the alert "opinion leader" had somehow been heightened; for relatively incidental reasons, he had accepted a campaign worker's or a convention delegate's post.

The difficulty was that this approach assumed the existence of a continuum. In examining behavior patterns and motivational structures, the passive, barely interested voter was known to differ from the highly interested, partisan voter. All the more so, one might expect the organizationally involved, active party cadreman to respond, with the same impulses intensified.

However interested and partisan the voter might be, it was clear that the party cadreman's behavior and orientation to politics might make a great deal of difference. His experience hardly seemed incidental and unimportant. The party worker had joined an organization; the voter had not. This suggested that the worker experienced new sources of gratification and felt new demands for loyalty which were not present for the voter. It suggested that the cadreman was engaged in activity which focused his attention on how to influence the electorate; the voter, on the other hand, could be seen as more single-mindedly intent upon the choices he personally must make on election day. Could one assume that these were minor considerations?

Alternatively, because the party worker's attention was directed to the problems of choosing a presidential nominee or winning election-day support for his side, perhaps he could be largely understood as belonging to the category of politician-officials, although less prominent than those normally thought of under this heading. While it is true that many political leaders started their careers as party cadre, it does not necessarily follow that all party cadre are seeking positions of political power or governmental leadership. Organized party work may provide rewards and satisfactions which positions of leadership can not. It seemed doubtful, then, that one could adequately view party cadres as having the same motivations as top leaders although with lesser intensity, or the same qualities, although less well developed.

The party cadres in the Los Angeles study were asked a battery of questions concerning why they were active as campaign volunteers and also why they thought their fellow workers were active. Table 1 sets forth the basic results for the composite sample, about which a word must be said. In the Los Angeles area, party organization tends to proliferate within state assembly districts and become attenuated between districts. In designing the study, it was decided to secure similar components of Democrats and Republicans actively working in localities of sure, doubtful, and lost party advantage. Three contrasting assembly districts were chosen accordingly; when field work was completed, roughly two-thirds of all the campaign workers known to be active had been interviewed, and approximately one-third of the cadre in each party sample had made their campaign efforts in each kind of locality—sure, doubtful, and lost.[39]

It will be noted that the most frequently cited motives for the self's participation in campaign work are the three which may be associated with "moral" impulsions, i.e., loyalty to issues, party or community. Second as a motivational set are the four connected with social gratifications: the excitement of sociability of the campaign, including perhaps personal friendship for the candidate. Third, and least acceptable as a group of ex-

[39] See Dwaine Marvick and C. R. Nixon, "Recruitment Contrast in Rival Campaign Groups," in Dwaine Marvick, ed., *Political Decision Makers: Recruitment and Performance, op. cit.,* for an extended description of the study design and sampling procedures used.

TABLE 1

IMPORTANCE OF DIFFERENT MOTIVATIONAL AIMS IN EXPLAINING
OWN AND FELLOW WORKER'S CAMPAIGN PARTICIPATION

Question	Self*	Fellow Worker**
1. Concern with public issues	77	69
2. Strong party loyalty	68	69
3. Sense of community obligation	54	49
4. Politics a part of way of life	43	31
5. Fun and excitement of campaign	33	33
6. Social contacts and friends	32	37
7. Personal friendship for candidate	19	16
8. Furthering political ambition	11	9
9. Being near influential people	7	14
10. Making business contacts	5	4

* Per cent saying "very important"
** Number of cases: 299

planations for participation, are the three connected with personal political or economic ambition—those referring to the specific goals of enhancing one's political or economic well being. It may be, as Weber argued, that political democracy is partly sustained by permitting people to "live off" politics. At the level of party cadre in Southern California, there appear to be severe qualifications on this practice, so far as its approval goes.

More interesting, perhaps, is the fact that there is no significant tendency for active campaigners to attribute a different order of motivations to their fellow workers. The "moral" impulses are considered to be as strong for one's colleagues as for oneself; the "sociability" goals neither stronger nor weaker, and there is no discernible inclination to consider others more in search of personal advantage through politics than oneself.

Thus the table suggests that this sample of party cadre is willing to acknowledge a variety of motives for doing the work they do—even personal "climbing" tendencies are not entirely excluded, and "non-moral" sociability goals rank high for a substantial number, as do the similar "acceptable" rationalizations.

Moreover, Table 1 shows no tendency to make invidious comparisons between the other and the self, nor any desire to minimize the importance of public-spirited goals as the motives of one's fellow workers as for oneself. Both these findings might be seen as suggesting the presence among each party's cadre group of rather effective "mutual identification" or group solidarity bonds.

Because of the sampling method, it is possible to distinguish the "core" from the "fringe" workers in each cadre group. Starting with those who held recognized positions in the formal party structure, each person interviewed was asked to name key figures or steady workers in the campaign organization of his area. Anyone so named by two respondents was eligible and was interviewed if possible. Understandably, many persons were named more often than the minimum for inclusion; this gave us a "reputational score" for each worker. Secondly, when each person was interviewed, a battery of questions was asked about "how much voice" he had in party organizational decisions. Putting this "self-rating" together with the "reputational score" provides a double-barreled basis for identifying the "core cadre."

Returning to the questions about why one works as an active campaign worker, by combining responses on similar items, three more general indexes were obtained: one on "public purpose emphasis" (combining scores on Q. 1, 3, 4): one on "private benefit emphasis" (combining scores on Q. 8, 9, 10): and one on "conviviality emphasis" (combining scores on Q. 5, 6). Using these indexes, a summary is facilitated of how different segments in our sample responded (Table 2).

One-third de-emphasized their fellow worker's involvement out of "public purposes," and among each party's core cadre there is very slightly more skepticism. Somewhat smaller proportions (about one in four) were inclined to de-emphasize these reasons in analyzing their own motives.

One-fourth stressed private benefit as an important motivation for fellow-workers; one-fifth stressed the same set of factors

TABLE 2

	De-emphasized Public Purpose as Motive for		Stressed Private Benefits as Motive for		Stressed Conviviality as Motive for	
	Self*	Fellows*	Self**	Fellows**	Self**	Fellows**
Composite Sample	25	36	19	24	45	49
Democrats	27	35	16	21	41	48
Republicans	23	38	22	27	51	50
Democrats:						
Core Cadre	30	37	20	18	44	45
Fringe Cadre	23	34	12	24	38	54
Republican:						
Core Cadre	24	43	28	24	48	40
Fringe Cadre	22	34	16	30	54	60

* Per cent scoring Low on Index
** Per cent scoring High on Index

for explaining the self. No marked party differences appear, and there is only a very slight tendency for the core cadre in each party to be more willing to emphasize their own interest in private benefit (and an equally slight hint that fringe cadres are more wont to attribute private benefit motives to their fellows than to self). Each party's core cadres give similar ratings to their own and their fellow cadres' motives; each party's fringe group sees (nearly twice as often) private-benefit motives animating others as self.

One-half stressed conviviality as a motivation for both self and fellows. The Democratic fringe group is noticeably less inclined than others are to admit much interest in conviviality as a motive for its own participation. On the other hand, the

Republican fringe group compared with the Republican core
cadre places greater emphasis on conviviality as an important
motive both for self and others.

If these findings were to be replicated in other research on
political cadres, they would support the inference that the
core among political workers attribute more public-spirited
motives to their co-workers than to themselves and fewer striv-
ings for either private benefits or convivial gratifications from
party work. On the other hand, the fringe workers tend to make
comparisons between themselves and their colleagues much less
flattering or trusting for the latter. A tentative conclusion might
be that the core cadres of both parties have a stronger sense of
positive identification and solidarity with their organizations
than do the fringe, whose attitudes are more as one would suppose those of the general public to be, in estimating the motives
of people who become active party workers.

Differences in perspective were found among the respective
party cadres on other points also. Midway through each inter-
view, each party worker was given a list of campaign strategies:

"Thinking of the voters your group is trying to reach, would
you feel each of these ideas was good strategy or poor
strategy?

(1) Point out how different issues affect the voter's pocket-
book instead of how issues affect the whole society
and economy.

(2) Lash out at the opposition's record and program instead of calmly presenting your own side's records
and plans.

(3) Place emphasis on the personality of the candidate
rather than on his stand on public issues.

(4) When the other side makes a smear attack, level
fresh charges against them instead of making a rea-
soned explanation of the data.

(5) Stir up strong emotions, hates and fears instead of
presenting a careful discussion of complex problems
facing the country."

In Table 3 the proportions in various segments of the
sample who felt that each proposed strategy would be "poor
strategy" in their locality are given. By combining responses to
these questions, a more general index was constructed, measur-

TABLE 3

PARTY CADRE PERSPECTIVES ON CAMPAIGN STRATEGIES

	Full Sample	Democrats	Republicans	Democrats		Republicans	
				Core Cadre	Fringe Cadre	Core Cadre	Fringe Cadre
	(299)	(169)	(130)	(89)	(80)	(59)	(71)
Would Consider it Poor Strategy in a Campaign to Stress:							
Pocketbook Interest	23	13	36	11	16	38	35
Opponent's Bad Record	43	30	59	28	31	67	52
Personality Appeal	51	52	48	51	52	51	45
Countercharges to Smear	61	50	75	49	53	79	71
Hates, Fears and Emotions	71	62	81	64	61	81	81
Manipulative Strategies							
Seen as Efficacious:	33	49	14	54	43	12	16
Seen as Posing Moral Difficulties:	44	40	48	40	40	37	58
Seen as Posing Practical Difficulties:	70	70	69	81	59	82	58
Objected to *Only* on Practicality Grounds:	25	22	29	20	23	37	23
Comments Reveal Some Contempt for Voters:	39	44	34	43	45	33	35

ing "efficacy of manipulative strategies." Moreover, a very large proportion of the interviews contained explanatory remarks contributed by the party worker to explain his strategy notions. Three separate codings were made of these open-ended responses to "How is that?" probes after each strategy question had been put; 94 per cent agreement on coding decisions was achieved, as each coder was asked to score interviews which contained evidence of (a) unequal difficulties over manipulative strategy use, (b) practical difficulties foreseen over use of such strategies; and (c) attitudes revealing contempt for the voters. Coders were provided with illustrative indicators on each count; where their ratings differered, they "talked out" the reasons why.

The table above shows two noteworthy variations. First there is a greater tendency for Democrats than Republicans to rate manipulative strategies positively. Second, there is a much greater disposition for the core of each party cadre to emphasize the impracticality of using such strategies, compared with each party's fringe group. The tendency is also observable for the Republican fringe to stress the moral difficulties posed by use of manipulative strategies, more so than any other group.

Apparently skepticism about the practicality of manipulative strategies increases in both parties as one moves into more central positions in the cadre, while vulnerability to moral arguments is felt most on the fringe of the Republican party apparatus.

As for the party difference in evaluating manipulative strategies, this may be traceable to factors producing a deeper cynicism among one party's adherents than the other's. Or it may be due to more transitory attitudes, arising from the political fortunes of 1956. Differences are slight between party cadres in the spontaneous emission of remarks showing contempt for the voters. Again, more Republican core cadre than any other group objected to manipulative strategies *only* on the grounds of impracticality. The great successes of the Republican party nationally and in California from 1952 through 1956 may have produced a transient cynicism and over-estimation of the efficacy of manipulative strategies among Democratic party workers. The evidence of Table 3 can be taken to show either party's cadre ready or willing to use manipulative strategies. In any case, the more interesting finding is replicated in each party. The view that manipulative strategies are impractical, so much more strongly manifest among the core cadre than among the fringe in each party, again supports the inference of a greater similarity in outlook between the fringe cadre and the ordinary public. In this case, the fringes show smaller disposition to evaluate campaign strategies in terms of the party organization's interests (i.e., in terms of practicality) and more of a tendency to judge them right or wrong in moral and non-instrumental terms.

So far, the motivations of rival party cadres and their manner of appraising manipulative campaign strategies have been examined. Cadres, apart from the personality springs that animate them and apart from any scruples they have about what is permissible in politics, are supposed to be resilient, versatile, and poised. Table 4 presents data about their attitudes and actual experience in various campaign roles, which bear upon this final question.

The first part of the table shows how much confidence Democratic and Republican cadres feel in performing extra-mural party work, one might say. Each of the activities aims at influencing voters by personal contact, mainly in face-to-face relationships: making speeches, raising money, attending rallies, canvassing door to door. While in both parties the fringe cadres feel more confident in performing the two relatively prosaic tasks than in raising money or making speeches, the core cadres of both parties feel more confident than their respective fringe groups, in performing all four functions—nearly twice as confident, overall.

On the other hand, while core cadres feel more confident than the fringe in performing extra-mural functions, in 1956 they actually performed chiefly intra-mural tasks during the campaign (direction, coordination, planning, and managing party efforts), while the fringe workers were the main agents of extra-mural contacts.

Contrasting with this actual allocation of tasks is the finding that the core cadres in both parties evaluate the campaign work done by the fringe more positively than do the fringe personnel themselves. This core group judgment is from the vantage point of higher positions in the party apparatus (more are engaged in liaison work between various campaign units): it also derives from longer periods of active party service. Again the findings emphasize the similarity of the core cadres in both parties in focusing on the total organizational effort of party work, while the fringe cadres in each party tend to view this effort from a perspective more like that of the general public where the mass communications media are accepted as the most attention-getting foci of the campaign drama.

TABLE 4

CAMPAIGN ROLES, CADRE SELF CONFIDENCE, AND CADRE EXPERIENCE

	Full Sample	Democrats	Republicans	Democrats		Republicans	
				Core Cadre	Fringe Cadre	Core Cadre	Fringe Cadre
	(299)	(169)	(130)	(89)	(80)	(59)	(71)
Feel Considerable Self Confidence as:							
Campaign Speechmaker	58	57	58	77	45	76	46
Party Fundraiser	51	52	49	57	46	58	41
Political Rally Organizer	78	77	82	91	59	92	72
Doorstep Canvasser	71	68	76	76	57	89	63
Campaign Worker in General (Index based on above four specific tasks)	44	42	47	54	30	63	34
Feel Personal Contact Campaign Methods Are More Effective than Mass Media:	33	36	28	43	29	37	19

TABLE 4 (*Continued*)

Campaign Role:						
Did Only Intra-mural Tasks	22	27	16	42	11	27	7
Did Mostly Intra-mural Tasks	13	10	17	15	5	20	14
Did Mostly Extra-mural Tasks	27	24	32	19	30	27	36
Did Only Extra-mural Tasks	38	39	35	24	54	26	43
	100	100	100	100	100	100	100
Party Function:						
Liaison Work	18	16	20	24	8	30	10
Club Functionary	36	37	35	40	35	27	43
Club Member	46	47	45	36	57	43	47
	100	100	100	100	100	100	100
Years of Party Experience:						
Ten or more years	36	39	33	47	30	45	23
Four to nine years	36	29	45	29	29	41	48
Under four years	28	32	22	24	41	14	29
	100	100	100	100	100	100	100

The second study to be analyzed briefly here was conducted in the summer of 1960. A one-page printed mail questionnaire was sent to all delegates and alternates of the ten biggest Northern states to be represented at the Democratic National Convention in Los Angeles. These states cast 612 of the 1,520 convention votes allocated that year. Put another way, 81 per cent of the 761 votes needed to win a presidential nomination could be garnered from these ten states.

A total of 1024 delegates composed these ten groups, some delegates being entitled to cast only fractional votes. Overall, nearly half returned the questionnaire. Not surprisingly, however, returns from some states were especially disappointing. Only a fourth of the delegates from New York, Pennsylvania, and Illinois replied, while slightly more than half of those from the other states did so.

A composite sample was constructed to cross tabulate the data on other grounds. In it, each state is represented by its official quota of delegate strength. Findings that link, say, a background variable to an attitude about campaign tactics are *not* attributable, therefore, to any over-weighting of one state's delegates or under-weighting of another state's party spokesman which might otherwise have resulted because of the differential response rates to our questionnaire.

Apart from questions about personal political and social background and preferences for a presidential nominee, the central battery was designed to secure four responses on each of ten public policy issues from each respondent. First, he was asked whether, on each policy matter, he personally would prefer to see the federal government do more, the same, or less. Second, he was asked whether he felt that, as a campaign issue, the policy question should be stressed, mentioned, or ignored. Third, he was asked what he felt were the views of "the man who leads your delegation" about how much federal action was needed on each policy front—more, the same, or less than now. Fourth, he was asked what his leader would probably favor as a campaign strategy: stress, mention, or ignore each policy issue.[40]

[40] See the forthcoming report, *Convention Participants, 1952–1964,* based on this 1960 study and a 1964 sequel to it, as well as on earlier studies of delegation chairmen in 1952 and 1956. For an article based on those earlier materials, see Dwaine Marvick and Samuel J. Eldersveld, "National Convention Leadership: 1952 and 1956," *Western Political Quarterly,* 14 (March, 1961), pp. 176–194.

Given these data, it is possible to explore some of the tensions in a delegate's mind, especially as it involves his delegation leader. The tension might result from what the delegate feels are differences in substantive political preferences (e.g., the delegate wants more government action to support farm prices but he feels that his leader is satisfied with the existing program) or the tension may result from a difference about what strategy to adopt on a given issue in the coming campaign (e.g., the delegate would like to stress but feels his leader will probably favor ignoring the need for stronger farm supports). Two other tension points are relevant: the delegate's own adjustment of his views to what seems good strategy; his perception of his leader's difficulties in reconciling strategies and personal policy views.

First, consider the levels of support for more government action on ten policy issues (Table 5). At least 7 out of every 8 backed economic growth stimulation, medical care for the aged, federal funds for education, and defense missile expansion. On five other issues, substantial support existed although there was more room for controversy—on fostering free elections abroad, supporting farm prices, extending welfare services, desegregating residential housing, and giving foreign economic aid. On the final question—regulating television—a strong minority wanted more government action.

If we examine the leader's supposed views on these same ten questions, it is apparent that, on most issues, the delegation leaders are seen as more vigorously in favor of government action than the norm for the delegation. As delegation spokesmen, they are doing more than reflecting group preferences. They are giving leadership, especially on issues which have majority support but not extraordinary majority support among rank-and-file convention participants.

Next consider the overall pattern of disparities between delegate strategies and leader's supposed strategies. On every issue, greater willingness to use it as a campaign theme is attributed to the leaders than is acknowledged by the delegates as their own strategic advice. This is especially true on the more controversial issues. For example, on desegregating housing, not quite a majority of delegates favored stressing the issue in the coming campaign. Two-thirds of them thought their delegation leader would favor stressing it.

How does a delegate reconcile his substantive policy preferences with his "political" judgment of what makes effective

campaign strategy? On every issue except farm prices, the average delegate's impulse was to "play down" the issue. On the
overwhelmingly backed measures—those which Kennedy and
other presidential aspirants had already made issues during
the pre-convention months—only a modest de-emphasis was
called for. On the less firmly established issues, however, these
cadremen and women from the ten biggest Northern states
were substantially less willing to stress publicly what they personally preferred as government policy.

This could reflect a realistic awareness that public opinion
on some issue is not ready. It could also denote a self-critical
awareness on the party cadreman's part that he holds "advanced political views" which need curbing. In the former, grave
doubt would presumably be expressed should any political
leader seek to take an aggressive campaign line; if the latter,
cadres might be enthusiastic about a political leader willing to
champion decisively a policy heretofore considered too advanced.

Political cadres are not generally expected to be policy
innovators; that is a function of the top elite. But party cadres
may often have or claim to have a realistic middleman's point
of view from which to criticize the political sagacity of a leader's
innovations. On the other hand, many cadres may well feel
close identification with their political leader, able to appreciate
his difficulties in shaping effective strategy without abandoning
substantive convictions. In this respect, resolving the personal
question of reconciling strategy with convictions is presumably
not something which only happens when delegates receive mail
questionnaires. If being active in politics fairly regularly prompts
a party cadreman to "try his hand" at working out a campaign
strategy, this mental exercise, though it may be timid at first,
is probably going to engender a greater sympathy for—and insight into—the problems confronting top elite leadership than
otherwise would exist.

What then is the leader seen as doing, to reconcile his
views to fit strategic considerations? On eight of the ten issues,
he is seen compromising his views only half as much as the
delegates compromise their own. Only on two issues, where the
leaders were seen as holding very advanced preferences, were
they seen as playing down their personal views somewhat more
than the delegates collectively did their own.

It would appear that the Democratic convention cadres attribute policy views and strategic judgments to their delegation

TABLE 5

PUBLIC POLICY—THE PRIVATE VIEWS AND CAMPAIGN
STRATEGIES WHICH CONVENTION DELEGATES ATTRIBUTE TO
THEMSELVES AND TO THEIR DELEGATION LEADER

	Delegate's Own View*	Leader's Supposed View*	Disparity (DV – LV)	Delegate's Own Strategy**	Leader's Supposed Strategy**	Disparity (DS – LS)
Stimulate economic growth:	96	94	+8	90	95	–5
Give old age medical help:	93	93	0	87	91	–4
Provide funds for education:	87	90	–5	80	87	–7
Develop defense missiles:	86	93	–7	80	90	–10
Foster free elections abroad:	67	72	–5	36	55	–19
Keep up farm prices:	66	75	–9	72	77	–5
Increase welfare services:	63	82	–19	53	70	–17
Desegregate housing:	63	73	–10	47	66	–19
Give foreign economic aid:	54	67	–13	51	61	–10
Regulate television:	44	40	+4	16	26	–10

* Per cent who want the federal government to do "more"
** Per cent who feel that, as a campaign issue, the policy should be "stressed"
Based on a total sample of 476 cases

leaders which are more crystallized, more advanced, and less
subject to political expediency than those same middlemen of
American politics report about themselves. This almost Burkean
image of key convention elite figures is a far cry from the journalistic or "popular" view of the politician. Perhaps it is unfamiliar and strange because so little systematic work has been
done about how the world of politics looks to the middlemen.

The art of politics is learned by example as well as practice. To the party middleman, his *encadrement* may make him
more sensitive to opinion trends, more aware of his relatively
crystallized policy views, more disposed to manipulate and mobilize his fellow citizens, and more consciously willing to set
aside his own views on public questions to be politically effective.
At the same time, his *models* of what constitute effective political leadership are real models, whom he sees and talks with,
works for and becomes knowledgeable about. The average voter's
models are usually either the gross stereotypes of political car-
toonists or the glamorized public faces of the eminent men; seldom does the voter have a personally-known example of a
significant politician to use as a mental benchmark for judging
other politicians. One consequence of an active party middleman's organizational participation is probably the invaluable
corrective to stereotypes and images which comes from face-to-
face contact with other cadre *and* with political leaders, perhaps
even at moments when they are not "performing."

Strictly speaking, we do not have a single sample of a
Democratic convention cadre, although for the purposes here involved this is not important. Actually we have thrown together
ten different samples, not equally fulfilled, one from each of ten
big states. Table 6 is provided as an empirical check on whether
the basic patterns just discussed hold up state-by-state. As the
reader will see, with minor exceptions they do.

Conclusion

The argument of this paper can be stated in six points:

(1) The comparative study of elites, because it deliberately
sets aside legal-institutional analysis, must seek to clarify the
dynamics of political power by methods and evidence which
will disclose the *equivalencies* in power configurations.

(2) A two-component model of a political order, which
classifies people as either elite or mass-public, even with prag-

TABLE 6

TENSION RATIOS DERIVED FROM DELEGATE VIEWS AND
STRATEGIES AND HIS LEADER'S SUPPOSED VIEWS AND
STRATEGIES
—by states—

	Public Policy Support (State-Sample)	Policy View Contrast (LV–DV)	Strategy Contrast (LS–DS)	Delegate's Own Problem (DS–DV)	Leader's Supposed Problem (LS–LV)
MICHIGAN	+4.3	+14.2	+15.9	−12.8	−10.9
MINNESOTA	+3.8	+10.4	+11.5	−15.6	−14.4
NEW JERSEY	+0.2	+ 2.8	+ 9.7	− 8.7	− 1.4
CALIFORNIA	0	+ 0.7	+10.0	− 9.8	− 2.5
MISSOURI	−0.4	− 8.3	− 4.8	−10.2	− 6.7
OHIO	−0.3	− 0.2	+ 7.1	−13.5	− 6.3
NEW YORK	−0.8	+ 5.1	+12.3	− 8.6	− 1.4
MASSACHUSETTS	−0.4	+ 7.6	+16.1	− 6.8	+ 2.2
ILLINOIS	−3.6	+14.9	+25.6	−17.9	− 7.2
PENNSYLVANIA	−6.4	+10.4	+ 6.8	− 6.3	− 9.9

E.g.: Read as follows: Michigan delegates see their leader as averaging 14.2 percentage points more than delegates themselves when it comes to personal desire for more federal action on ten policy questions.

matic embellishments, creates some possibly unjustified expectations about how elites are linked to the publics of a society.

(3) Democracies are seen as power systems in which the
publics are capable of raising their representatives to power, but
incapable of controlling them; only elite structures are organized to wield effective power.

(4) Political cadres are seen as the lower strata of the
political elite, just as there is stratification in each of the various
elite structures relevant to public policy formulation and control.
Problems of intra-elite and inter-elite analysis require separate
treatment.

(5) Not everyone thought to be part of the party cadre—
especially during the heat of a political campaign—shares the
outlook of what V. O. Key has called the subculture of a political elite. Some of those who are active campaign workers have
views, values, expectations, and experience records that place
them not far removed from ordinary citizens. On the other hand,
it is not clear, either, that the top leaders of a local party organization are performing any of the "elite nucleus" functions
earlier discussed. Even among convention cadres, as seen, the
1960 Democratic delegates were rather timid and unsure of
their own strategic judgments—and seemingly happy at the
thought that a forceful leader would act in a manner stylistically
quite different from their own.

(6) If party cadres are not clearly and properly a part of
the political elite structure, or subculture, should the study of
elites continue to use a two-component model. As an alternative,
when elites, cadres, and publics are distinguished at the outset
as different, certain kinds of simplification are avoided and
certain research problems are brought directly into focus, as the
use of findings from two party cadre studies has sought to illustrate.

TEN

Organizational Theory and the Study of State and Local Parties[*]

Lee F. Anderson

Northwestern University

I

THE STUDENT of state and local parties who elects to view and study parties as organizations has no single body of well-developed theory at his disposal. "Organizational theory," March comments, "is a collection of incongruous elements."[1] This paper is an effort to explore the possible relevance of some of these elements.

There are two broad traditions in the history of organizational theory to which we might turn for assistance in our efforts to understand parties as organizations. In one tradition are theories focusing on the rational orientation and instrumental character of organizations; in the other are theories stressing the characteristics organizations share with other social systems.

The first of these traditions provides the student with what

[*] This is a revised version of a paper delivered at the National Center of Education in Politics Teachers' Seminar on State and Local Parties, September, 1963. I am grateful to the participants in this Seminar and to my collegues at Northwestern University for comments on this paper.
[1] James G. March, "Some Recent Substantive and Methodological Developments in the Theory of Organizational Decision-Making," in Austin Ranney, ed., *Essays in the Behavioral Study of Politics* (Urbana: University of Illinois Press, 1962), p. 192.

Gouldner calls a "rational" model and what Etzioni terms a "goal" model of organizational analysis. This model is characterized by an instrumental conception of organizations. An organization is viewed as "a rationally conceived means to the realization of expressly announced goals. Its structures are understood as tools deliberately established for the efficient realization of these group purposes."[2]

The second tradition points in a somewhat different direction and furnishes the student with what is termed a "system" or "natural system" model of analysis.

The natural-system model regards the organization as a "natural whole", or system. The realization of the goals of the system as a whole is but one of several important needs to which the organization is oriented. Its component structures are seen as emergent institutions, which can be understood only in relation to the diverse needs of the total system. The organization, according to this model, strives to survive and maintain its equilibrium, and this striving may persist even after its explicitly held goals have been successfully attained. This strain toward survival may even on occasion lead to the neglect or distortion of the organization's goals.[3]

Etzioni characterizes the model in a similar way.

The starting point for this approach is not the goal itself but a *working model of a social unit which is capable of achieving a goal.* Unlike a goal, or a set of goal activities, it is a model of a multifunctional unit. It is assumed a priori that some means have to be devoted to such non-goal functions as service and custodial activities, including means employed for the maintenance of the unit itself. From the viewpoint of the systems model, such activities are functional and increase the organizational effectiveness.[4]

[2] Alvin Gouldner, "Organizational Analysis," in Robert Merton, *et al.*, eds., *Sociology Today* (New York: Basic Books, 1959), p. 404.
[3] *Ibid.*, p. 405.
[4] Amitai Etzioni, "Two Approaches to Organizational Analysis," *Administrative Science Quarterly*, 5 (September, 1960), p. 261.

The student of party organizations need not choose one of these models to the exclusion of the other. Each has its characteristic strengths and weaknesses. A good deal of the extant parties literature appears to be informed by the spirit even though it may not be consciously grounded in the rational or goal model of organizational analysis. It is valuable in many important respects because of this orientation, but the analysis may also be limited because of it.

The goal model, Etzioni observes, often leads to examinations of organizations in terms of criteria of effectiveness or social utility which are derived from the researcher's assumptions about the organization's goals or purposes. The result is that the findings are often stereotyped as well as determined by the model's assumptions. "Many of these studies show (a) that the organization does not realize its goals effectively, and/or (b) that the organization has different goals from those it claims to have."[5] Such conclusions are recognizable as the type reached in some of the parties literature. A demonstration of either proposition may be valuable in its own right, but the conclusions are rather predictable from the start.

Another weakness in the goal or rational model of analysis is that the stress on the instrumental character of organizational activities often leads to a view of organizations as unifunctional units. It seems both more accurate and fruitful to explicitly view "all social units, including organizations . . . [as] multifunctional units. Therefore, while devoting part of their means directly to goal activities, social units have to devote another part to other functions. . . ."[6]

To the extent that we find the concept of organization helpful in understanding American parties, the natural system model of analysis appears to hold out the most, although not the only, promise. At least it is the implications of this model with which this chapter is concerned.

Inherent in the system model is a functional orientation to organizational analysis. It is possible to adopt a functional approach without necessarily being committed to structural-functional theory and hence also to particular positions in the methodological disputes embroiling anthropology and sociology.[7]

[5] *Ibid.*, p. 258.

[6] *Ibid.*, p. 259.

[7] In a recent essay on explanation in political science, Robert Dahl observes that explanation does not require peculiar functional

Viewing party organizations as natural systems and approaching their analysis from a functional perspective generates two broad types of research concerns.

1. Analysis focusing upon the functions which party organizations perform in the larger political and social systems of which they are a part.

2. Analysis focusing upon the structure and realization of functional values characteristic of parties as social organizations.

II

From the standpoint of political science, this first type of analysis stems from the traditional interest in establishing the broader social import of particular institutional arrangements. From the point of view of theory, it proceeds out of Merton's formulation of the "central orientation of functionalism" as the "practice of interpreting data by establishing their consequences for the larger structure in which they are implicated . . .";[8] or as Parsons puts it, a "functional reference of all particular conditions and processes to the state of the total system as a going concern."[9]

Of course, for the student of parties such an interest is not new. "Functions of" is a major topic in the parties literature. Most scholars would probably agree that, taken as a whole, these discussions are not entirely satisfactory. Two criticisms seem particularly relevant here. The notion of function is used in a variety of different ways with the result that conceptually distinct phenomena are grouped under the common term. Moreover, there appears to be a marked tendency in some of the literature to over-generalize in the imputation of functions to the parties. Certain functions are specified, and the reader is

theories, but that functional theory is useful as a supplier of a check-list of variables. Robert Dahl, "Explanation in Political Science," in Daniel Lerner, ed., *Cause and Effect* (New York: Basic Books, 1966).

[8] Robert Merton, *Social Theory and Social Structure* (rev. ed.; Glencoe: The Free Press, 1957), pp. 46–47.

[9] Talcott Parsons, *Essays in Sociological Theory: Pure and Applied* (Glencoe: The Free Press, 1949), p. 21.

left with the impression that all party organizations perform these functions to the same degree. With exception, relatively little attention is devoted to exploring possible variations in functions party organizations might be performing.

An adequate functional description would seem to require a typology of functions which party organizations *may* perform, and a systematic application of this in a comparative analysis of several organizations in an effort to isolate the similarities and differences among the organizations. Unfortunately, neither functional theory generally nor organizational theory specifically can furnish ready-made typologies which adequately meet the needs of the researcher. However, the literature does provide some kinds of assistance.

The conceptual diversity which characterizes the use of the concept of function in the extant parties literature indicates a need for not one but several typologies of functions. The theory literature suggests a possible continuum of typologies distinguishable by the level of their conceptual abstractness. At the lowest conceptual level would be a typology in which function denotes a set of empirically concrete processes, operations, or activities. At the next level of abstraction would be a typology where function is used to signify some generally recognized use or utility or a normally expected effect of an action or organizational arrangement. At a somewhat higher level would be a typology of functions in which the concept is used to designate a set of consequences that particular types of organizations have for the system to which they belong or their consequences for some specified part of that system. At the highest conceptual level would be a typology of functions in which the concept is used to signify a set of contributions which a party organization makes—or is capable of making—toward the adaptation and integration of the political system of which it is one component part.

What are the concepts and indicators which might be included in such typologies? At the first and perhaps second level, functional or organizational theory as such cannot be particularly helpful. What appears to be required here is a checklist or catalog of empirically concrete activities in which party organizations might engage. Formulated in the form of scales, these could then be used to determine the extent to which particular organizations do in fact, or at least are perceived by their members to, engage in the various activities. Harder and Ungs' study of county chairmen in five midwestern states shows what can be done in this area.[10] By using mail questionnaire data, they mapped similarities and differences in the county chairmen's perceptions of their organizations' activities in four areas: candidate recruitment, raising and allocating money, getting out the vote, and campaigning.

In the construction of typologies at the third and fourth level, some of the current functional theories may prove useful. Aberle, Cohen, Davis, Levy, and Sutton set forth a list of nine factors which, they argue, define the functional prerequisites of a society.[11] Briefly listed these are: provision for adequate relationship to the environment, role differentiation and assignment, communication, shared cognitive orientation, a shared and articulated set of goals, the normative regulation of means, the control of affective expression, socialization and the effective regulation of disruptive forms of behavior. This listing may prove suggestive to the student of party organizations in the systematic identification of major variations in the functional outputs of parties conceived as organizations.

On a somewhat different conceptual order is Parsons' typology of basic functional problems confronting social systems: 1. adaptation to the environment; 2. mobilization of resources to meet system goals; 3. integration of the members; and 4. maintenance of the value and normative system and tension-management.[12] Mitchell suggests that the political system makes at least four major contributions to the solution of these problems on the level of society. These include: 1. the authoritative specification of system goals; 2. the authoritative mobilization of resources to implement goals; 3. the integration of the system; and 4. the allocation of values and costs.[13] The functions of party organizations could be analyzed in terms of the contribution they make to these four functions of the more inclusive political system.

Almond and Coleman's discussion of the four input func-

[10] Marvin Harder and Thomas Ungs, "Notes Toward a Functional Analysis of Local Party Organization" (Paper Delivered at the Midwest Conference of Political Scientists, Chicago, May, 1963).

[11] D. F. Aberle, *et al.*, "The Functional Prerequisites of a Society," *Ethics*, 60 (January, 1950), pp. 100–111.

[12] Talcott Parsons, *The Social System* (New York: The Free Press of Glencoe, 1951).

[13] William C. Mitchell, *The American Polity* (New York: The Free Press of Glencoe, 1962), p. 7.

tions of political systems should also be noted here. They conceptualize these functions as: 1. political socialization and recruitment; 2. interest articulation; 3. interest aggregation; and 4. political communication.[14]

These are a few of the possible analytic schemes that might prove helpful in constructing categories by which to assess the functional outputs of party organizations. While one need not be confined to any single formulation, the Almond and Coleman scheme might hold the most promise, at least initially. Its level of conceptualization approximates that found in much of the literature, and the categories incorporate long-standing interests of students of American parties. This scheme would focus attention upon the degree and the manner in which party organizations function as mechanisms in the processes of recruitment and socialization (particularly office-holder socialization), interest articulation, interest aggregation, and political communication.

Specifying empirical indicators of conceptually abstract functions and devising operational measures of these indicators for a comparative analysis of state and local organizations is difficult at best. Two approaches might be tried, one inductive and the other deductive. The first entails imputing conceptually abstract functions to party organizations on the basis of inferences from data describing the concrete activities in which the organizations are engaged. The second approach involves the imputation of functions on the basis of deductions from generalizations about policy difference produced by different types of party systems. For example, differences in the policy outputs of state political systems with competitive and non-competitive parties suggest possible differences in the functional contributions party organizations are making to the respective systems, particularly with respect to the articulation and aggregation of interests.

III

The second type of analysis included in a functional approach to the study of political parties as organizations which in turn are viewed as natural systems focuses our attention on the management of the internal functional problems of the system. As suggested above, one of the merits of a natural system model of organizational analysis is the emphasis placed on the fact

---

[14] Gabriel Almond and James S. Coleman, eds., *The Politics of Developing Areas* (Princeton: Princeton University Press, 1960).

that organizations are not merely instruments for the achievement of external goals but also social systems with their own functional needs, the satisfaction of which may consume a large proportion of the organizations' resources.

A functionally oriented analysis of internal party organization focuses the researcher's attention on two system states: survival and effectiveness or viability. Since both of these are preferred states for most organizational actors most of the time and often the preference of the observer of an organization as well, it is convenient to refer to these two system states as survival and effectiveness values. Variations among or within units over time in the realization of survival and effectiveness values thus constitutes, as it were, the "end variables" of functionally oriented modes of organizational analysis. Following this orientation, it is thus easy to specify the formal output dimensions of such analysis. These may be briefly summarized as:

1. Statements specifying the primary dimensions of the values of survival and effectiveness.

2. Statements specifying major dimensions in terms of which survival and effectiveness realizing processes or mechanisms can vary; and statements specifying relationships believed to exist between variations in these functional processes and in the realization of survival and effectiveness values.

3. Statements specifying major dimensions in terms of which the role structure of party units can vary; and statements specifying the relationships believed to exist between variations in role structure and variations in (a) functional processes and (b) the realization of survival and effectiveness values.

Statements Specifying the Component Dimensions of Survival and Effectiveness Values

In the imagery of functional theory, the system states summarized by the concepts of survival and effectiveness are pictured as states in which "vital" needs have been satisfied or problems solved. Statements specifying the component dimensions of the values of survival and effectiveness can be considered designations of the "functional needs or requirements" of organizational systems. "A well-developed organizational theory," Etzioni has observed, "will include statements on the functional requirements which various organizational types have to meet."[15] Ideally these statements will be of two types: statements setting forth survival needs of the organizational type and statements setting forth effectiveness needs. Presumably these two sets of statements will refer to the same phenomena but will differ in their specification of critical parameters.

"Survival statements" will be propositions characterizing the specific requirements of parties as an organizational type which, if met, allow the organization to survive. Linked together a set of such statements would provide a survival model of party organization. "In such a model each relationship specified is a prerequisite for the functioning of the system, i.e., a necessary condition; remove any one of them and the system ceases to operate."[16] The validation of such a model and perhaps even its construction might require analysis of simulated organizations. But since the history of American parties provides samples of "dead" as well as "living" organizations, field applications are possible.

While the value of survival is problematic for party organizations in some situations at some times, in most situations effectiveness is the more problematic value. Certainly students of state and local party units are generally more interested in variations in effectiveness than in differences between "dead" and "living" units.

Statements of effectiveness needs are propositions which specify the requirements, which, if not met, preclude the attainment of some specified or implied level of organizational viability or effectiveness. A system of such statements provides what Etzioni calls an "effectiveness model." In contrast to the survival model, an effectiveness model would specify those "patterns of interrelations among the elements of the system which would make it most effective in the service of a given goal." Etzioni summarizes the differences between these models:

> The difference between the two models is considerable. Sets of functional alternatives which are equally satisfactory from the viewpoint of the first model have a different value

[15] Amitai Etzioni, *Modern Organizations* (Englewood Cliffs, N.J.: Prentice-Hall, 1964), p. 18.
[16] "Two Approaches to Organizational Analysis," *op. cit.*, p. 271.

from the viewpoint of the second. The survival model gives
a yes or no answer to the question: Is a specific relationship
functional? The effectiveness model tells us that although
several functional alternatives satisfy a requirement (or a
'need') some are more effective in doing so than others.
There are first, second, third, and nth choices. Only rarely
are two patterns full alternatives in this sense; only rarely
do they have the same effectiveness value.[17]

The literature of organizational theory is rich in efforts to
conceptualize the phenomena to which statements of survival
and effectiveness needs should refer. While similar in many respects, these efforts differ somewhat in both their level of conceptualization and in their elaborateness. One of the least
elaborate and more abstract is Bredemeier and Stephenson's description of the functional requirements of social systems including organizations as a problem of adaptation and integration.

> The *integration* of a group refers to the extent to which the
> group members get from one another the attitudes, serv-
> ices, and goods they have learned to need. The *adaptation*
> of a group refers to the extent to which the group as a
> whole gets from other groups the attitudes, services and
> goods its members have learned to need . . .[18]

Parsons' typology of system problems will be familiar to
most readers. These have been briefly summarized by Scott:

> An "active system" is composed of a number of units
> (which are observable role behaviors in a social system);
> this action system is confronted with a series of basic
> problems which must be solved if it is to continue to
> operate as a system. These are: (1) *adaptive problems*, the
> adaption of behavior to the physical and social environ-
> ment of the system and the manipulation of objects, includ-
> ing persons, so as to make for more favorable relations;
> (2) *gratificatory problems*, activity connected with the at-
> tainment and enjoyment of the goals of the system; (3) *in-*

---

[17] *A Comparative Analysis of Complex Organizations, op. cit.*, p. 78.
[18] Henry C. Bredemeier and Richard M. Stephenson, *The Analysis of Social Systems* (New York: Holt, Rinehart and Winston, 1962), p. 42.

tegrative problems, activity directed to the "adjustment" of the relations of systems' members to each other; and (4) *pattern-maintenance problems*, activity directed toward the maintenance of the identity of the system as a system, renewal and reaffirmation of its own values and existence.[19]

Perrow provides another formulation. He lists four "tasks" which every organization must accomplish if it is to maintain itself: 1. secure inputs in the form of capital sufficient to establish itself, operate, and expand as the need arises; 2. secure acceptance in the form of basic legitimation of activity; 3. marshal the necessary skills; and 4. co-ordinate the activities of its members and the relations of the organization with other organizations and with clients or consumers.[20]

Kaufman, in an effort to develop a theory of organization around the concept of functional requirement, develops a scheme setting forth five processes deemed necessary for the maintenance and survival of any organization.[21]

1. Mechanisms or processes of boundary demarcation; i.e., creation of criteria by which members may be distinguished from non-members.

2. Mechanisms for the replenishment of material and the replacement of personnel.

3. Mechanisms by which to elicit effort from individual members of the organization.

4. Mechanisms for the coordination of individual activities.

5. Mechanisms for the distribution of material, information, and perhaps personnel throughout the organization.

One of the most extended formulations is provided by Parsons' attempt to relate his social systems theory specifically to

[19] Frances Gillespie Scott, "Action Theory and Research in Social Organization," *American Journal of Sociology*, 64 (January, 1959), pp. 386–387.
[20] Charles Perrow, "The Analysis of Goals in Complex Organizations," *American Sociological Review*, 6 (December, 1961), pp. 854–866.
[21] Herbert Kaufman, "Why Organizations Behave as They Do: An Outline of a Theory," in *Administrative Theory* (Austin: University of Texas, 1961).

the study of organizations.[22] He identifies four types of requirements.

1. Mechanisms for the utilization of fluid resources, particularly personnel and capital.
2. Goal-attainment mechanisms, which are formulated in
   terms of three central decision-making processes:
   a. Policy decisions which refer to decisions about the
      means to be employed in the attainment of organiza-
      tional purposes;
   b. Allocative decisions which refer to decisions about the
      internal utilization of resources available to the organi-
      zation, including the allocation of fluid resources in
      accord with these responsibilities;
   c. Integrative decisions which refer to decisions about the
      maintenance of integration within the organization
      through facilitating cooperation and the management of
      motivational problems arising within the organization.
3. Mechanisms for the integration of the organization with
   other organizations and other collectives in the total social
   system.
4. Mechanisms for the generation and allocation of power
   within the organization.

Caplow has developed a set of categories, which he terms
criteria for measuring organizational effectiveness, which share
a number of similarities with the formulations discussed above.[23]
Caplow describes "the fundamental organizational problem" as
one of maintaining and increasing four system states:

1. Stability (maintenance of status differences)
2. Integration (maintenance of interaction)
3. Voluntarism (maintenance of valences)
4. Achievement (maintenance of activities)

The Caplow formulation is particularly promising to students of

[22] Talcott Parsons, "Suggestions for a Sociological Approach to the
Theory of Organizations," *Administrative Science Quarterly*, 1
(June and September, 1956), pp. 63–85, 225–239.
[23] Theodore Caplow, *Principles of Organization* (New York: Harcourt, Brace & World, 1964), pp. 119–168.

party organization, since he is able to elaborate on it at length and demonstrate the uses of the criteria in empirical studies.

Statement Specifying the Major Dimensions of Variation in Functional Processes and Statements Relating Variations in Functional Process to Variations in the Realization of Survival and Effectiveness Values

The second component of a functionally oriented theory of party organization consists of statements which, on the one hand, specify variations in mechanisms of need gratification or processes of problem solution and, on the other, their links to variations of the component dimensions of survival and effectiveness.

The literature suggests some possibilities for general typologies of mechanisms which would permit us to connect party specific variables to basic social science theory. The concept of organizational equilibrium conceives the satisfaction of functional needs as a process of exchange among members of the organization and between the organization and its environment. In this case, a typology of functional alternatives might be constructed in terms of the basic social mechanisms involved in the exchange relationship. Bredemeier and Stephenson have outlined an exchange theory of social systems which specifies four mechanisms of exchange.[24]

1. Mutual cathexis which is characteristic of primary group relations and is based on love, esteem, respect, or comparable emotions.

2. Duty or obligation which is characteristic of relations in formal organizations and is based on recognized status obligations.

3. Bargaining which is based on presence of a mutually recognized set of "procurement" and "disposal" needs which can be traded.

4. Power which is based on the exercise of sanctions not directly dependent on the cooperation or needs of others.

[24] Bredemeier and Stephenson, *op. cit.*, pp. 48–50.

Those familiar with Etzioni's work will recognize the parallel between this and his classification of organizational power as normative, calculative and coercive. This suggests an alternative conceptualization of the processes by which organizations meet functional needs as a process in the exercise of organizational power. Mechanism may then be classified in terms of the type of power each involves.

Such typologies are of only limited interest in themselves. They acquire value if proven useful in the development of propositions linking variations in functional process to the realization of survival and effectiveness values. An example taken from one of the Rossi and Cutright studies of local party organization suggests the type of thing that can be done. The organizations were found to employ both mutual cathexis and bargaining (or alternatively to exercise both normative and calculative power) in eliciting effort from precinct leaders.[25] However, Rossi and Cutright's analysis of voting patterns indicates that bargaining was the more effective of the two mechanisms from the standpoint of the party as a vote-getter. Eldersveld's study is rich in other examples.[26] For instance, he found that district chairmen tended to be inefficient in task performance, a fact attributable in part to the top leader's absence of sanction power over subordinates.

Statements Specifying Major Dimensions of Variation in Role Structure and Statements Relating Variations on these Dimensions to Variations in Functional Processes and to Variations in Value Realization

A third component of a functionally oriented theory of party organization consists of statements which specify the major dimensions of variation in organizational role structure and statements which link these dimensions to functional processes and the realization of survival and effectiveness values. Needless to say, the "structure"-"process" distinction is contextual. A phe-

---

[25] Peter H. Rossi and Phillips Cutright, "Grass Roots Politicians and the Vote," *American Sociological Review*, 23 (April, 1958), pp. 171–179.

[26] Samuel J. Eldersveld, *Political Parties: A Behavioral Analysis* (Chicago: Rand McNally and Company, 1964), p. 346.

nomenon that is seen as a characteristic of role structure from one perspective will be viewed as a process from another. Thus it is the function of a statement in the context of a particular inquiry that determines whether role structure or functional processes is being considered.

Obviously the need is for one or more models of organizational types which could be used in characterizing party units. Unfortunately, the student of political parties faces at least two obstacles in any effort to develop organizational characterizations of state and local parties. One is the wide variation among these organizations on a number of structural dimensions.[27] The other is the absence of any typologies which permit either a simple or exhaustive characterization of parties as organizations. There are two forms which such a classificatory scheme might assume. It might provide for the typing of "whole" organizations; or second, it might provide for the typing of organizations on a set of independent, structurally defined dimensions.

In respect to the first of these possibilities, there is no shortage of classificatory schemes in the literature of organizations. Parsons differentiates four types of organizations on the basis of their principal contribution to more inclusive social systems.[28] Blau and Scott develop a typology based on the criterion of "who benefits" from an organization's activities.[29] Etzioni provides a classificatory scheme based on distinctions in compliance structure.[30] Typologies such as these are useful in locating party organizations relative to other types, but they are of limited value when it comes to analyzing differences among party organizations.

In respect to the second possibility, the student of parties has a number of efforts available to specify dimensions by which to discriminate among groups and organizations.[31] These are

[27] This is well documented in the Eldersveld study. *Ibid.,* pp. 410 ff.

[28] Talcott Parsons, "Pattern Variables Revisited," *American Sociological Review,* 25 (August, 1960), pp. 481–482.

[29] Peter Blau and Richard Scott, *Formal Organizations: A Comparative Approach* (San Francisco: Chandler Publishing Company, 1962).

[30] *A Comparative Analysis of Complex Organizations, op. cit.*

[31] For example see Hanan Selvin and Warren Hagstrom, "The Empirical Classification of Formal Groups," *American Sociological Review,* 28 (June, 1963), pp. 399–411; John K. Hemphill and Charles M. Westie, "The Measurement of Group Dimensions," *Journal*

normally prefaced, however, by an admission of the exploratory
character of the classificatory scheme. Selvin and Hagstrom, in
a recent effort to categorize formal groups, note that "theories
of group structure are still in a primitive state of development,
as indicated by the lack of agreement among various lists of
group properties and by their failure to indicate which properties are conceptually, experimentally, or statistically independent."[32] Likewise, Hemphill observes that while "psychologists
concerned with individual characteristics have made much
progress in the development of terms and concepts that are useful for precise analysis of individual differences . . . unfortunately no comparable precision has been attained by the social
scientist in specifying the characteristics by which differences
among groups are to be described."[33]

If this characterization of the state of the literature is accurate, then it appears that any contribution organizational
theory may make to the analysis of parties as organizational
types must be somewhat piecemeal and selective. One such possibility is that it will be of assistance in conceptually refining
and, hopefully, operationalizing some of the structural variables
traditionally used to describe state and local parties. The remaining pages discuss some of the organization literature relating
to a few of these variables. The reference to the literature is
highly selective, and the list of variables far from complete.[34]

Autonomy

It has long been noted that all organizations are open systems interdependently related to their environments. Organiza-

---

of Psychology, 29 (April, 1950), pp. 325–341; Raymond B. Cottell,
"Types of Group Characteristics," in Harold Guetzkow, ed., *Groups,
Leadership and Men* (Pittsburgh: Carnegie Press, 1951); and
John K. Hemphill, *Group Dimensions: A Manual for Their Measure-
ment* (Columbus: Bureau of Business Research, Ohio State Univer-
sity, 1956).

[32] Selvin and Hagstrom, *op. cit.,* p. 402.

[33] Hemphill, *op. cit.,* p. 1.

[34] For an example of a case study in political party research which
makes imaginative use of some of the ideas discussed in these pages,
see Eldersveld, *op. cit.,* particularly, Part III, "The Party as an Organizational System."

tions differ, however, in the degree of their dependence upon other groups and organizations and hence they vary in the extent to which their activities are subject to external influence. This property or characteristic of organizations, which is normally termed autonomy, can be broadly conceived as the degree to which organizations function free of others and thus generally occupy an independent position in society.

Two facets of autonomy interest students of party organization: the independence of particular organizations relative to non-party groups and organizations, and the independence of particular units relative to other units within the over-all party organization. In either case, the task is one of conceptualizing and measuring the extent of a unit's dependence upon external actors.

Hemphill has developed a set of questionnaire items designed to measure autonomy as one of thirteen dimensions of group structure.[35] It might be possible to administer these or comparably constructed items to defined groups within the party organizations; e.g., state central committee members. This would provide an index of the comparative degree to which a unit's members perceived the unit to be independent and self-regulating.

Another possibility, and one that could prove more rewarding, is an operationalization of Gouldner's concept of "functional automony." This is defined as the degree to which an organizational unit is dependent upon external sources for the satisfaction of its needs. "The concept . . . directs attention to the fact that some parts [of an organization] may survive separation from others, that parts vary in their dependence upon one another, and that their interdependence is not necessarily symmetrical."[36]

"Needs" could be cataloged endlessly. What would be helpful is a listing that could be comparatively applied to several organizations. Bredemeier and Stephenson outline three types of group needs that might serve to specify the major categories of such a listing.[37] Organizations need: (1.) certain *attitudes* from others and the expression of these attitudes in certain re-

[35] Hemphill, *op. cit.*

[36] Alvin Gouldner, "Reciprocity and Autonomy in Functional Theory," in Llewellyn Gross, ed., *Symposium on Sociological Theory* (Evanston: Row, Peterson, 1959), p. 449.

[37] Bredemeier and Stephenson, *op. cit.*

sponses; (2.) *services* from others in the forms of certain kinds
and amounts of labor, protection, information, advice, leadership; and (3.) certain *goods* from others.

It may be possible through survey techniques to compare
party organizations in terms of their relative dependence upon
the external environment for the satisfaction of their attitudinal,
service, and material needs. In some respects the assessment of
attitudinal needs appears the most difficult, but here some encouraging efforts have been made in the study of voluntary associations. Simpson and Gulley developed a scale for measuring
the degree of an association's involvement or dependence on the
surrounding community.[38] Using this in a survey study of
several voluntary organizations, they were able to categorize associations as internally or externally oriented depending on the
extent to which their organizational activities depended upon
satisfying the outside community as well as the organization's
own members.

The application of any such scheme to party organizations
would require the construction of a catalog of rather specific
needs comprising each of the three basic categories of needs.
The compiling of such a listing would be a worthy exercise in its
own right. This might be done in two stages: first, the use of
extended, somewhat open-ended interviews with party officials in
which they would talk about the "needs" of their organization;
and second, the analysis of several such schedules in an effort to
identify factors which could serve as a basis for the construction
of scale items to be applied in a comparative analysis of a number of party organizations.

Control

The structure of control, power or influence within organizations and groups is one of the most ancient of interests. Control can be conceptualized in a great number of ways. Perhaps
it can best be seen as the regulations which an organization imposes upon the behavior of individuals while functioning as
members of the organization. This usage appears to approximate

---

[38] Richard Simpson and William Gulley, "Goals, Environmental
Pressures and Organizational Characteristics," *American Sociological Review*, 27 (June, 1962), pp. 344–351.

rather closely those prevailing in the parties literature, e.g., the notion of control implicit in the concept of party cohesion in legislative voting studies.

Students of organizational behavior have focused upon a number of aspects of organizational control. Three of these appear to be particularly relevant to students of party organizations: the degree or volume of an organization's control, the distribution of control within organizations, and the sources or bases of organizational control.

Party organizations apparently vary in the scope or amount of control which membership implies for the participants. They also differ in the way this control is distributed among the various roles comprising the organization. The question here is whether the literature on organizations can provide the means by which these two dimensions of a party's control structure can be investigated more precisely than is normally the case.

Tannenbaum has developed a descriptive model of these two elements which he terms a "control graph."[39] The graph consists of a horizontal axis on which the various hierarchical levels or other component elements of an organization are plotted, and a vertical axis for plotting the amount of control which an organization's members perceive as being exercised by the different levels or parts: that is, how much effect each level is perceived as having in determining the organization's policies and action. The distribution of control within the organization is thus shown by the shape or slope of the curve, and the total amount or volume of control exercised by all components of the organization as the area under the curve.

These two dimensions may vary independently of one another. "Organizations . . . might have the same general distribution of control while the total amount of control exercised within them differs sharply. On the other hand, organizations, though equal in the amount of control exercised within them, might differ markedly in the way it is distributed."[40]

Various heights and slopes of the curve can be generated, but four prototypic models may be envisaged. 1. An oligarchic hierarchical model in which the amount of control rises with hierarchical ascent. 2. A democratic model in which the curve

[39] Arnold Tannenbaum, "Control and Effectiveness in a Voluntary Organization," *American Journal of Sociology*, 67 (July, 1961), pp. 33–46.
[40] *Ibid.*

declines with hierarchical ascent. 3. An anarchical model in which a zero curve intersects the vertical axis at a low point, indicating relatively little control by any component or level in the organization. 4. A polyarchical model in which a zero curve intersects the vertical axis at a high point, indicating a high level of control by all levels or components of the organization.

The control graph has been applied with apparent success in survey studies of several types of organizations including labor unions, voluntary associations and business firms.[41] Variations in the two dimensions of control were found to associate with other variables, including rate of participation in, loyalty to, and effectiveness of the organization.

The idea of the control graph is applicable to studies of party organizations. It suffers from the difficulties inherent in the use of questionnaire data and the weaknesses of attributional techniques, but it does offer one feasible means of comparatively examining the pattern of control in several organizations.

The source or bases of control is a third aspect of control structures receiving considerable attention in the literature on organizations. Pfiffner and Sherwood among others suggest that two sets of factors affecting an organization's assignment of power to various roles can be usefully distinguished.[42] One set is structural, the other functional.

Three structural factors appear to be particularly important. One is the scope of formal authority embodied in particular roles. A second is the norms and values of organizational members who are subject to official authority. As the work of Gouldner, Blau, Bendix, Gross and others indicate, the norms and values of subordinates affect the extent and kind of control available to their organizational superiors. A third structural factor is the ability of particular role occupants to invoke sanctions in support of their directives. This, as a basis of organizational control, has been systematically explored in a number of organi-

---

[41] See *Ibid.;* Arnold Tannenbaum, "Control Structure and Union Functions," *American Journal of Sociology,* 61 (May, 1956), pp. 536–545; Arnold Tannenbaum and Basil Georgopoulus, "The Distribution of Control in Formal Organizations," *Social Forces,* 36 (October, 1957), pp. 44–50; and Arnold Tannenbaum and Robert Kahn, "Organizational Control Structure: A General Descriptive Technique as Applied to Four Local Unions," *Human Relations,* 10 (May, 1957), pp. 127–140.

[42] John M. Pfiffner and Frank Sherwood, *Administrative Organization* (Englewood Cliffs, N.J.: Prentice-Hall, 1960), pp. 335–338.

zations. Argyris, for example, has studied the organization of a bank and found that very few rewards or penalties were at the disposal of the organizations officials.[43] Pfiffner and Sherwood reach a similar conclusion about organizations in general, observing that "it seems fairly clear from the vast amount of human relations research . . . that neither the 'big stick' nor the 'lollipop' is the best long-run means of exerting influence. Indeed there are enough constraints on the use of sanction-based power in most organizations as to make this a somewhat lesser grant of capacity from the hierarchy than would first appear."[44]

A number of researchers have focused on functional, in contrast to structural, factors as bases of control or influence within organizations. "This perception of function-based power is quite different from structure-based power. Here the fundamental element is the work performed rather than the status position occupied."[45]

In this view, every participant in an organization is seen as possessing some power, but the amount varies with the importance which particular activities are perceived to have for the maintenance and operation of the system. Dublin suggests that the crucial question to ask in an analysis of function-based power is, "How much of a difference the operation of a function makes to a given state of the system?" Equally important is a determination of the number of individuals who perform a function. Dublin advances the hypothesis that "for any given level of functional importance in a system, the power residing in a functional agent . . . is inversely proportional to the number of other . . . agents capable of performing the function."[46]

Perrow develops a similar theory of the functional basis of organizational control. As noted above, he singles out four critical problems or task areas in the maintenance of an organization. At any given time, one of these task areas is likely to be perceived as being more pressing than the others. This, Perrow argues, is a "presumptive basis for control or domination by the

---

[43] C. Argyris, *Organization of a Bank* (New Haven: Labor and Management Center, Yale University, 1954).

[44] Pfiffner and Sherwood, *op. cit.*, p. 335.

[45] *Ibid.*, p. 336.

[46] *Ibid.*, p. 337.

group equipped to meet the problem involved."[47] Since the relative importance of different task areas varies over time, so does the relative power of different groups within an organization.

All of this suggests several questions to be asked in the analysis of the bases of control in party organizations. What structural factors are affecting the control structure of a particular organization? What formal authority is distributed to what roles? What are the norms and values held by organizational members which facilitate or inhibit the exercise of this formal authority? What sanctions are available to which roles? How frequently and with what success are these employed? What are the functional bases of control? What is the most pressing current functional problem and who is capable of contributing most to its solution? Are the functional and structural bases of control congruent or divergent?

Consensus

Consensus or an equivalent is another concept frequently used in describing party organizations. It is argued, for example, that the normal party is an organization with little internal consensus. Broadly conceived, consensus refers to the degree of congruence in the cultural orientations of various individuals and groups comprising an organization.[48]

Several aspects of consensus are relevant to the study of party organizations. One of these is the object of consensus, or what Etzioni terms "consensus-spheres." As he points out, the literature does not offer any single list of spheres appropriate to the study of consensus in all organizations. Listings vary with the problem at hand. Of relevance to students of party organizations is a list employed in a recent study of labor unions.[49] Three spheres or objects of agreement and disagreement among the union members and between members and leadership are specified and investigated: the objectives or goals of the locals, the problems perceived to be blocking their realization, and the resources available to the union for overcoming these obstacles.

---

[47] Perrow, *op. cit.*, p. 856.

[48] *A Comparative Analysis of Complex Organizations, op. cit.*, p. 128.

[49] Glen Miller, Robert Miller and Fredrick Zeller, *The Practice of Local Union Leadership* (Columbus: Labor, Education and Research Service, State University of Ohio).

Etzioni provides a more extended listing which discriminates consensus with respect to: 1. general values, that is, societal or communal values not peculiar to the organization under study; 2. the means available to the organization for achieving goals; 3. the organization's goals; 4. participation in the organization; 5. performance obligations, that is, who is to carry out what duties; and 6. cognitive perspectives, that is, frames of reference and agreed-upon canons for empirical testing.[50]

A second aspect of consensus is the level of agreement in particular consensus spheres. What portion, in short, of an organization is in mutual agreement? A third facet is the distribution of consensus among the various roles comprising the organization, e.g., consensus between higher and lower participants, or in the case of party organization, between different components, e.g., county chairman, state central committee members, legislative leaders, etc.

Involvement

While there is a growing body of literature on political involvement we still know relatively little about the structure of involvement of participants in party organizations. There are several facets of interest.

First, there is the amount of involvement particular roles entail. The amount of time demanded by the roles would provide a rough index to this. Second, there is type of involvement. Here the student of party organization can avail himself of a number of potentially relevant typologies. Miller, Miller, and Zeller have investigated the satisfaction union members derive from their membership.[51] They distinguish two types of satisfactions which serve as a basis for differentiating types of involvement: satisfaction that originates from within the organization itself and satisfaction that originates from the organization's external accomplishments. As applied to party organizations, this classification scheme would have the advantage of paralleling the Survey Research Center's party identification studies which show differ-

---

[50] *A Comparative Analysis of Complex Organizations, op. cit.*, pp. 129–130.
[51] Miller, Miller, and Zeller, *op. cit.*

ences in identification with the party as a social unit and as a program.[52]

Another potentially useful scheme is suggested by Etzioni's differentiation of three modes of organizational involvement.[53] These are alienative involvement characterized as a negative orientation to participation in the organization; calculative involvement characterized as a positive orientation of low intensity and based on a calculation of the benefits of membership; and moral involvement characterized by a positive orientation of high intensity and based either on internalization of the norms and authority of the organization or a sensitivity to pressures from its members.

Formalization

Organizations are frequently said to be blends of formal and informal social systems, and comparisons are made among them in terms of the relative importance of the formalized relationships. Thus party organizations are said to be highly informal compared to business firms or a governmental agency.

The meaning of informal is not always clear in either organizational theory or the literature on American parties. For present purposes a useful distinction can be made between two related but still distinct usages. First, informal may refer to patterns of interaction which are not prescribed by an organization's formal, normally written, charter or rules of procedure. Second, informal may refer to unstructured interactions occurring in the absence of either formally established procedures or traditions and unwritten rules. Using the first meaning of informal, a researcher may find that the bulk of an organization's interactions takes place outside of "formal channels." A quite different picture of the system might emerge if the second usage is employed. As so much of organization analysis has demonstrated, unwritten or non-formal but nevertheless clearly prescribed norms particularly among sub-groups within the

[52] A. Campbell, G. Gurin, and W. Miller, *The Voter Decides* (Evanston: Row, Peterson, 1954), p. 145.
[53] *A Comparative Analysis of Complex Organizations, op. cit.*, pp. 9–12.

organization can be as constraining as the organization's formally prescribed procedures.

Several discussions of the formal-informal dimension are available to students of party organization. Pfiffner and Gore have developed a seven-point continuum of organizational formalization which they call the Organization Maturity Continuum.[54] This is outlined on Chart 1. It would be useful to try to locate various party organizations at different points on this continuum.

An operationally more advanced effort in the direction of measuring formalization is represented by a scheme developed by Hall to identify and measure differences in the bureaucratization of different parts of complex organizations.[55] Hall's procedures provide measures on six dimensions of organizational structure: 1. hierarchy of authority; 2. division of labor based on functional specialization; 3. systems of rules covering rights and duties of role incumbents; 4. systems of precedence for dealing with work situations; 5. impersonality of interpersonal relations; 6. selection for employment and promotion based upon technical competence.

Goals

The concept of goal is one of the most universal, but also one of the most troublesome, notions in organizational analysis. It has received little systematic attention in the parties literature. The inadequacy of dealing only with the parties' public goals is acknowledged, but an entirely satisfactory alternative is not suggested. A common solution is to impute to a party a single goal such as getting and keeping power. This tells us something about the organization, but not very much. What help the literature on organizations can be in the matter of studying party goals is problematic.

A number of studies suggest that an analysis of an organization's goals is vital to fully understanding its structure and operation. Lipset, Trow and Coleman, for instance, hypothesize

[54] Pfiffner and Sherwood, *op. cit.*, p. 212.

[55] Richard Hall, "Intraorganization Structural Variation: Application of the Bureaucratic Model," *Administrative Science Quarterly*, 7 (December, 1962), pp. 395–408.

CHART 1
ORGANIZATION MATURITY CONTINUUM

1	2	3	4	5	6	7
Individuals interacting in same situation but no permanent pattern apparent.	Individuals interacting in same situation with pattern. Pattern breaks if new conditions arise.	Primary groups appear, such as family or isolated work teams.	Hierarchy first appears.	Hierarchy is given formal sanction.	Formally constituted hierarchy.	Formally constituted hierarchy.
	Leadership not apparent but someone makes decisions occasionally.	Indigenous leaders appear, such as family head or leader of work group.	Recognized leaders more or less formally selected appear.	Pattern of leadership is deliberately established.	Pattern of leadership is supplemented by duties statements for each post.	Formally constituted pattern of leadership, with clear channels of communication and authority.
	Individuals not a conscious group, but show in-group pattern.	Deliberate leadership.	Clusters of groups develop within the hierarchy. (Clique Structure.)	Groups in the organization are formally delineated, but not highly "rationalized."	Groups in the organization are formally established and their relationships are stated. May be written organization charts.	Groups in the organization are carefully established on basis of specific criteria such as stage in production process. Organizational charts.
		Group may not be conscious of leadership, depending upon point of evolution of group—but conscious of group or clique membership.	Division of labor around a total production goal may be introduced, but simple independent processes.	Total production process is introduced where succeeding groups are dependent upon work of preceding groups.	Production is broken down into specific jobs and responsibilities of each person are carefully defined. Job descriptions of general nature.	High degree of "rationalization," job duties through such techniques as administrative analyses, time and motion study.
		Single level group.		Articles of incorporation or legislative act containing name, purpose, etc., formally constituted organization in community.		
				Formal basis for membership in group is specified.	Charter is supplemented by manuals or books of rules and regulations.	Comprehensive manuals of detailed formal powers.

CHART 1 (*Continued*)

Organization has legal relationships with other groups in community, thus formal status.

Detailed specifications for membership are set down as criteria for selection.

Organization so integrated into social and economic structure that it is subject to some pressure to coordinate its goals with other organizations.

Introduction of staff personnel who act in the name of constituted leaders.

Charters of legislative acts.

Comprehensive testing program based upon careful job analyses used.

Organization subject to formal control by state, or top of hierarchy if governmental organization, because its product is essential to the over-all socio-economic system.

Organization control appears in the form of official authorization of organizational charts, job descriptions, standard practice manuals.

Written objectives and goals resulting from and revised by staff planning agency.

NOTES:—1. Direct evolution of each factor through these stages is not implied. Only illustrative of different types of informality or formality.

2. Formalization of any organization at one time probably will not fall into any one group at one time.

SOURCE: This chart was prepared by John M. Pfiffner and William J. Gore. The idea was in turn suggested by the seven categories of organization set forth in Carlton S. Coon, *A Reader in General Anthropology* (Holt, 1948).

401

that the most centralized organizations will be those with the most narrowly defined instrumental goals, and the broader the range of goals, the more likely the members are to perceive some measure of control over policies.[56] However, there have been comparatively few studies of the goal structure of organizations,[57] and March indicates that there is little current satisfaction with most traditional treatments of the goal concept.[58]

The literature suggests a few generalizations of possible value. One is the need to distinguish different types of organizational goals. Perrow differentiates three: public or stated goals; operational goals, which refer roughly to the immediate ends-in-view of the operating personnel; and social system goals, which refer to the contributions of an organization in the functioning of the social system of which it is a part.[59] A second point emphasized in current literature is that organizations seldom have only one goal. To the contrary, goal structures will likely be pluralistic and the different goals will not be necessarily consistent.[60] A third point concerns not only the necessity, but also the difficulty of analyzing an organization's operational goals.

The literature suggests that there is no way to establish what these are except through a detailed examination of the organization's operations. Perrow suggests an analysis of operating decisions over time.[61] Etzioni observes that goals can be determined "by an examination of organizational processes such as the flow of work . . . attributes of its structure . . . priorities in the allocation of means . . . or the assignment of personnel."[62] March's theory of goals has similar methodological implications. He suggests that goals can be conceived as "the consequence of a continuous bargaining-learning process" composed of three analytically distinguishable sub-processes: bargaining among potential members of the organization, organizational procedures for establishing and elaborating objectives, and processes of change through learning. He argues that such

---

[56] S. M. Lipset, M. A. Trow, and J. S. Coleman, *Union Democracy* (Glencoe: The Free Press, 1956).

[57] Perrow, *op. cit.*

[58] March, *op. cit.*

[59] Perrow, *op. cit.*

[60] *Modern Organizations, op. cit.*, pp. 5–19.

[61] Perrow, *op. cit.*

[62] *A Comparative Analysis of Complex Organizations, op. cit.*, p. 72.

a theory enables the researcher to "tentatively explain some of the conspicuous features of organizational goals as . . . observe[d] . . . in operating organizations. In particular . . . [it is possible to] predict the rather crude internal rationalization of goals, the wide-spread use of non-operational goals, the shifts of objectives over time, and the sequential attention to goals within organizations."[63]

IV

This chapter has presented a broad outline of some of the possibilities and problems of using organizational theory in the study of state and local political parties. It has been suggested that state and local party units be viewed as natural systems and examined, on the one hand, in terms of variations in the contributions made to the functioning of the larger systems of which they are a part and, on the other, in terms of characteristics of functional processes and the structures affecting the realization of survival and effectiveness values. The presentation has suggested that, in such an analysis, variations in survival and effectiveness values are the "end variables" which the researcher seeks to ultimately understand or explain. Obviously the concepts of survival and effectiveness require component analysis, and this chapter briefly summarizes some of the organizational theory literature helpful in such analysis. The predictors of variations in organizational survival and effectiveness are assumed in this scheme of analysis to be two types of variables: variations in the processes through which functional needs are met and variations in the role structure of the action system. A well-developed theory of party organization within the framework outlined here will consist of a system of propositions asserting relationships among variations in the realization of survival and effectiveness values, variations in functional processes, and variations in characteristics of role structure. The chapter has attempted to identify some of the literature in organizational theory which may prove valuable in specifying significant dimensions of variation in functional process and role structure and in developing empirical indicators of such variations.

[63] March, *op. cit.*, pp. 195–196.

Index

405

Isotonic polity, 77*n*
Issue-less parties, 2
Italy, presidiary system, 97
  PSI study, 116-134

Kansas, county chairman study, 21
Key Influentials, 330, 333-335

Labor force, and competition, 224
Labour party, candidate selection, 148-153
  constituency agentry, 24
  indirect type, 61
  organization, 112-113
Law, and political parties, 10-12
Law of disparity, 19
Leadership, 17
  decision-making process, 341
  Democratic/Republican, 19
  followers and, 19
  honesty in, 136
  orientation, 62
  stability and turnover, 13
Leadership groups, 322
Left/Right, distinction, 162
Legislative bodies, party structures
  within, 15
Legislative recruitment, 312-313
Legislature, defined, 73
Lobbying, 110
Local party, organization theory, 375-402
Localism, in Britain, 155
Low Income groups, 229

Majority party, campaign activities,
  294-297
  candidate recruitment, 294-295
  fund raising, 297-298
  organization, 293-294
Manipulation strategies, 364
Mass behavior patterns, 311
Mass parties, 47, 161
  and cadre party, 351
  collective action, 111
  organization, 134

Mechanisms, organizational, 385
Members, party, 16-25
  orientation, 58, 63
Membership input, 58
Membership patterns, 17
Merit orientation, polities and, 74
Michigan, lobbies study, 25
  party staffing study, 24
Militia party, 47, 161
Minority party, campaign activities,
  294-297
  candidate recruitment, 294-295
  fund raising, 297-298
  organization, 293-294
MIRACODE system, 165-173, 178-183
Mobilization system, 29
Mobilized mobile system, 70, 75
Montonic polity, 77*n*
Movement regimes, 25, 79, 80
Multiparty system, 46
Municipal elections, 265

National elections, 30-31
National party delegates, 21
Negro, party competition, 234
Negro Revolution, 15
New Jersey, county study, 21
New York, antipoverty funds, 15
New York (state), Republicans in, 12
Newark, antipoverty funds, 15
Nominations, assistance in, 327
  factors in, 326-329, 335
  forces affecting, 314
  national level, U.S./G.B., 141
  by office holders, 64
  open/closed, 146
  renomination, 311
  seeking, reason for, 326
  by types, 65-69
Nominator structures, classification, 62-66
Non-competitive party system, 52, 53
Non-coalition parliament dominant party,
  76
Non-farm occupation, and competition,
  221
Non-party polity, 81
Non-party system, 52

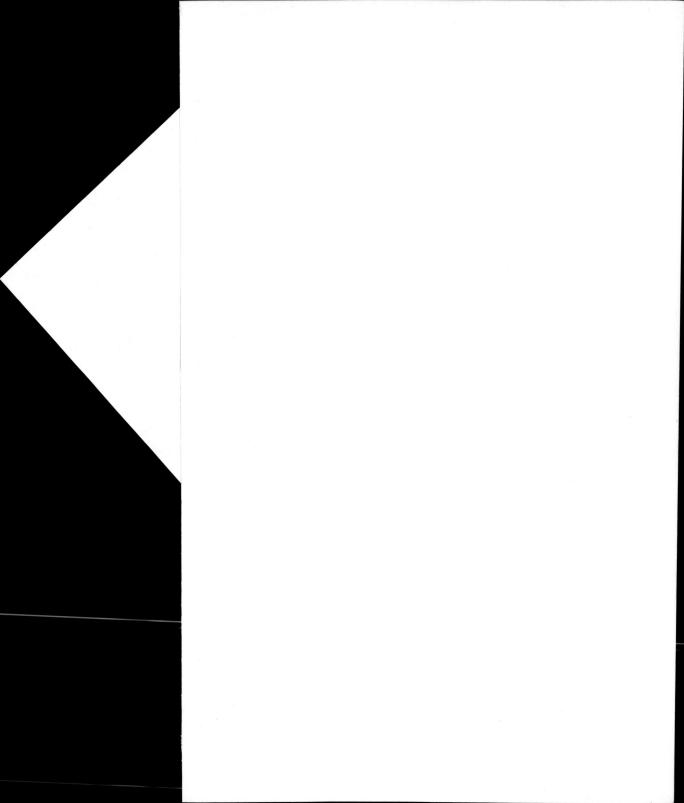

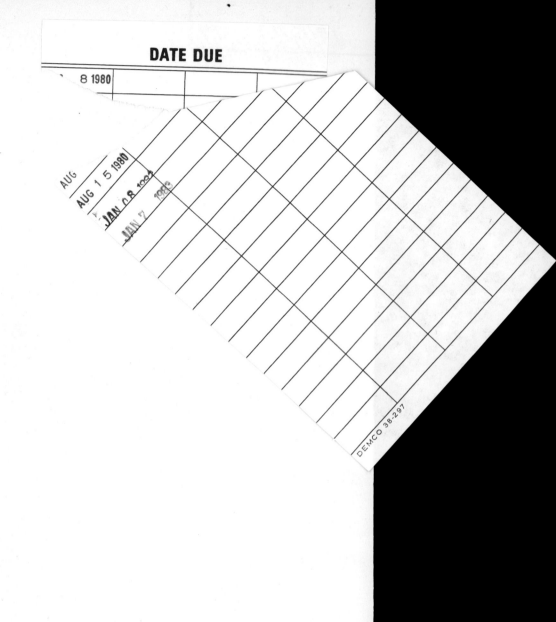